⫞ **W9-ADP-585**

The Editors

HENRY LOUIS GATES, Jr. is the Alphonse Fletcher University Professor and Director of the Hutchins Center for African and African American Research at Harvard University. Emmy Award–winning filmmaker, literary scholar, journalist, cultural critic, and institution builder, Professor Gates has authored or coauthored twenty-one books and created sixteen documentary films, including *Wonders of the African World, African American Lives, Faces of America, Black in Latin America, The African Americans, Many Rivers to Cross, Finding Your Roots,* and *Black America since MLK: And Still I Rise.* His articles and reviews have appeared in, among others, the *New Yorker,* the *New York Times,* and *Time.* The recipient of fifty-five honorary degrees, Professor Gates was a member of the first class awarded "genius grants" by the MacArthur Foundation in 1981, and in 1998 he became the first African American scholar to be awarded the National Humanities Medal.

KEVIN M. BURKE is the Director of Research at the Hutchins Center for African and African American Research at Harvard University. A native of the Hudson River Valley, he also serves as President of the Downing Film Center in Newburgh, New York. Dr. Burke graduated from Harvard College in 1998 and from Harvard Law School in 2003; he received his master's degree in History and Ph.D. in the History of American Civilization from Harvard in 2004 and 2006, respectively. He is research director on the PBS series *Finding Your Roots* and coauthor with Professor Gates of the companion book to the PBS film, *Black America since MLK: And Still I Rise.*

NORTON CRITICAL EDITIONS
AMERICAN REALISM & REFORM

For a complete list of Norton Critical Editions, visit
wwnorton.com/nortoncriticals

A NORTON CRITICAL EDITION

Solomon Northup

TWELVE YEARS A SLAVE

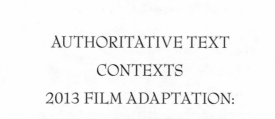

AUTHORITATIVE TEXT

CONTEXTS

2013 FILM ADAPTATION:

CRITICISM, REVIEWS, INTERVIEW

Edited by

HENRY LOUIS GATES, JR.
HARVARD UNIVERSITY

and

KEVIN M. BURKE
HARVARD UNIVERSITY

W · W · NORTON & COMPANY · *New York* · *London*

W. W. Norton & Company has been independent since its founding in 1923, when William Warder Norton and Mary D. Herter Norton first published lectures delivered at the People's Institute, the adult education division of New York City's Cooper Union. The firm soon expanded its program beyond the Institute, publishing books by celebrated academics from America and abroad. By midcentury, the two major pillars of Norton's publishing program—trade books and college texts—were firmly established. In the 1950s, the Norton family transferred control of the company to its employees, and today—with a staff of four hundred and a comparable number of trade, college, and professional titles published each year—W. W. Norton & Company stands as the largest and oldest publishing house owned wholly by its employees.

Copyright © 2017 by W. W. Norton & Company, Inc.

All rights reserved
Printed in the United States of America
First Edition

Library of Congress Cataloging-in-Publication Data

Names: Northup, Solomon, 1808–1863?, author. | Gates, Henry Louis, Jr.,
    editor. | Burke, Kevin M., editor.
Title: Twelve years a slave : authoritative text : contexts, film adaptation :
    criticism, reviews, interviews / Solomon Northup ; edited by Henry
    Louis Gates, Jr., Harvard University ; Kevin Burke, Harvard University.
Description: First edition. | New York : W.W. Norton & Company, [2016] |
    Series: A Norton critical edition | Includes bibliographical references.
Identifiers: LCCN 2016021467 | ISBN 9780393264241 (pbk.)
Subjects: LCSH: Northup, Solomon, 1808–1863? | Slaves—United States—
    Biography. | Slaves' writings, American. | African Americans—
    Biography. | Plantation life—Louisiana—History—19th century. |
    Slavery—Louisiana—History—19th century. | Twelve years a slave
    (Motion picture) | Northup, Solomon, 1808–1863?—Film and video
    adaptations. | Slaves' writings, American—History and criticism.
Classification: LCC E444 .N87 2016 | DDC 306.3/62092—dc23
LC record available at https://lccn.loc.gov/2016021467

ISBN: 978-0-393-26424-1 (pbk.)

W. W. Norton & Company, Inc., 500 Fifth Avenue, New York, NY 10110
wwnorton.com

W. W. Norton & Company Ltd., 15 Carlisle Street, London W1D 3BS

1 2 3 4 5 6 7 8 9 0

Contents

"Its Truth Far Stranger Than Fiction": The Norton Critical Edition of *Twelve Years a Slave*

We are called to study the life and legacy of Solomon Northup more than a century and a half after the abolition of slavery because of the twelve years of suffering Northup endured as a free man kidnapped into slavery, and because of the continuing resonance of the powerful memoir he authored just months after he was returned to freedom and to his family in New York. Published in 1853, *Twelve Years a Slave* not only was a literary sensation that sold 17,000 copies in its first four months in print; it inspired other writers such as Harriet Beecher Stowe, who had published her phenomenally best-selling novel, *Uncle Tom's Cabin*, the year before. Northup's slave narrative represented his effort to bear witness to the horrors he had experienced personally, through the keen senses and deep intelligence of a black man whose identity as a free citizen of New York, like his garments, had been stripped from him by a slave trader hell-bent on profit. In doing so, Northup helped to advance the wider struggle to liberate four million men, women, and children trapped in bondage behind him. By giving them voice through sketches of those he had toiled beside—and under—in the sugar and cotton fields of Louisiana, Northup delivered to the reading public one of the most authentic records of American slavery in print, so that readers might never lose sight of the human costs of an economic system that, over centuries, had enabled the colonization and rise of new worlds created by European explorers, conquistadors, and immigrants on the western side of the Atlantic.

With the publication of this Norton Critical Edition of *Twelve Years a Slave*, we hope future generations will be able to experience Solomon Northup's work from the perspective of its author, in his own words, and, following his text, through the perspectives of his contemporaries and journalists, scholars, and critics coming to it over time, including, most recently, the black British filmmaker Steve McQueen, whose 2013 film adaptation earned the Academy Award for Best Picture and set a new standard for depicting enslavement as it was seen, heard, and felt by those who rarely had been counted as more than mere numbers on a slave schedule. Text and film alike make it impossible to be numb to the lives sacrificed but masked through those numbers—their years on earth, their struggles and their fears, all that was taken away, and all that they transcended.

At its core, *Twelve Years a Slave* is an astonishing story of resiliency and courage, the gripping tale of one free—and then suddenly enslaved—black man's journey that represents both the worst and the best of America at a time when the union holding the fragile country together remained not only imperfect but imperiled under a Constitution which, by letter or interpretation, protected the ownership and sale, the capture and abuse of human beings based on the color of their skin, even as it professed, in sacred language, its commitment to "securing the blessings of liberty to ourselves and our Posterity." For these reasons and more, *Twelve Years a Slave* is among the most significant of the one hundred or so slave narratives published before the Civil War, unique in its vantage point and trajectory, and a key source for anyone seeking to understand how the arc of American history was, to paraphrase abolitionist and freedom fighter alike, bent toward justice by real people who were enslaved, suffered, gained their freedom, and spoke out.

The most famous of all ex-slave memoirists, Frederick Douglass, in his review of Northup's book in *Frederick Douglass' Paper* (Aug. 5, 1853), declared upon reading it:

> What an episode in the life of a man, who from his birth had breathed the free air of the Empire State, and known no master save the God who made him.
>
> It is a strange history, its truth far stranger than fiction. Think of it! For thirty years *a man*, with all a man's hopes, fears and aspirations—with a wife and children to call him by the endearing names of husband and father—with a home, humble it may be, but still a *home*, beneath the shelter of whose roof none had a right to molest or make him afraid—then for twelve years a *thing*, a chattel personal, classed with mules and horses, and treated with less consideration than they, torn from his home and family and the free labor by which he earned their bread and driven to unremitting, unrequited toil in a cotton field, under a burning Southern sun, by the lash of an inhuman master. Oh! It is horrible. It chills the blood to think that such things are.

And yet, as Northup made so vividly clear, such things were and such things remained as long as the institution of slavery itself endured and remained legal under the federal laws of the land.

Recovering the Body

Another "truth far stranger than fiction," borrowing from Douglass's review, is that Solomon Northup the man, having survived slavery and authored his autobiography, vanished from the paper trail sometime after President Abraham Lincoln issued the Emancipation Proclamation at the midpoint of the Civil War. We still do not know—and may never know—what happened to him. And the list of questions we are left with is as long as answers are short. Where did he go after the last person who remembered seeing him alive said he had visited the Reverend John L. Smith, a Methodist minister and fellow Underground Railroad conductor, in Vermont? How did Northup die? What were his final thoughts, spiritual or otherwise, on his life as a black man who had experienced three different kinds of freedom: the first when he was born free in upstate New York in 1807; the second, just after the New Year in 1853, when he was liberated from Edwin Epps's Louisiana plantation; and the third when the freedom of his people became a central military aim of the bloody conflict engulfing the nation in 1863? And whatever happened to his body, the flesh and bones that had been his vessel for experiencing all these things, and more, including marriage, fatherhood, and playing the music he loved?

As strange, just as Northup's physical remains stayed lost, to many over the years it appeared that *Twelve Years a Slave* had vanished both from bookshelves and from memory. To a certain extent, this was true. Northup's memoir, having sold so well in the 1850s, went out of print around the turn of the last century and remained out of print until 1968, when Sue Eakin and Joseph Logsdon issued a new edition through Louisiana State University Press. To put this gap in time in perspective, there was no edition of *Twelve Years a Slave* in print for the entirety of the Reverend Dr. Martin Luther King, Jr.'s life (1929–1968), or, put another way, for a period nearly five times as long as Northup spent in bondage.

Those lost decades prompted us to want to investigate, critically, the genealogy of Northup's text, from its first publication in 1853 to 150 years later, when the brilliant black British auteur Steve McQueen released his Oscar-winning film adaption (for which Professor Gates served as a consultant). If we could not solve the mystery of Northup's physical disappearance after 1863, we hoped we could at least determine how and when his seminal slave narrative had been invoked, interpreted, and deployed as part of the larger black freedom struggle that has continued from his lifetime to ours.

What we learned in the course of our research, to our amazement, was that Northup's text had never truly been forgotten—that, even when scholars, writers, and bibliographers could not easily

access the book because it was out of print, and even when, as a
result perhaps, they misspelled his name (as Northrup or Northrop,
for example), they still managed to carry his story forward, sometimes through material discussions of his life or work, at other times
just by including him as a passing reference, within a footnote, or
among a catalogue of first-person formerly enslaved writers. And,
when the opportunity to rescue his text did present itself, they also
bought up rare copies, a fact we learned from watching Dr. Khalil G.
Muhammad give C-SPAN television a tour of the Schomburg Center
for Research in Black Culture in Harlem, which owns a first edition
of *Twelve Years a Slave*, thanks to the indomitable bibliophile and
African Americanist Arthur Schomburg, who had the foresight to
purchase it a century ago at a price he could afford on his clerk's
wages at the Bankers Trust Company.

As we pressed on in our search for the hidden trail of secondary
sources, we came to realize that Solomon Northup's story, however
well or cursorily known, had been picked up, and passed along, by
some of the most influential creative writers and scholars of the
last hundred years: the literary scholar Vernon Loggins at the end
of the Harlem Renaissance; the historian Herbert Aptheker, the
black poet and critic Sterling A. Brown, and the esteemed African
American professor at Brooklyn College Marion Wilson Starling
in the 1930s and 1940s; and the preeminent African American historian Benjamin Quarles in the mid-twentieth century.

The more traces we discovered, the more committed we became to
establishing *Twelve Years a Slave*'s genealogy in order to give teachers
and students a chance to make their own connections and to investigate for themselves the lineage that extended from Northup's contemporaries to their intellectual heirs in the present, and especially
to those in between during the out-of-print period. This middle group,
who toiled in the libraries and archives during the nadir of the Jim
Crow era, were especially dear to us, because their record of striving
for clues and remembrances proved that writers, and especially black
writers, managed to bring their history forward even when they could
not "see the bodies" they wished to critique and honor.

In constructing the genealogy of selected secondary sources that
appears chronologically in this book (there are some fifty-five sources
in all), along with the annotated original text of *Twelve Years a
Slave*, we believe we have established that Solomon Northup never
disappeared entirely from public memory, that he remained relevant, rather, both as a witness to slavery to those for whom the Civil
War was a close if increasingly distant event (such as the historian
Albert Bushnell Hart, W. E. B. Du Bois's professor at Harvard),
and as a commentator on an economic system that destroyed individual lives and generations of families, black and white. Eakin and

Logsdon's 1968 edition, published soon after the rise of the Black Power and Black Arts movements, also coincided with the arrival of the first "affirmative action generation" at historically white colleges and universities, where black students, demanding changes to the predominantly Eurocentric curriculum they encountered when they arrived, engaged works like Northup's with close readings as never before. It was also at these schools where a new generation of historians of slavery, notably John W. Blassingame at Yale, treated texts like Northup's in a serious scholarly manner, authenticating their testimony as valid sources of historical data.

Bearing Witness

As important as organizing a genealogy of sources across time, our aim in editing this Norton Critical Edition of *Twelve Years a Slave* was to gather in one place the wide array of contemporary sources that spoke to the urgency of Northup's writing in his own time, especially to the events surrounding his rescue, his abolitionist activities, the publication of his book, and its reception in the North and South, including the botched prosecution of his kidnappers after the book led to their capture by jarring the memory of a witness. Not only are these contemporary accounts fascinating to read for their various voices and styles; they help to situate Northup in the mid-nineteenth century as a real person whose illegal suffering shocked the conscience and captured the imagination, whose book was a thrilling best-seller, and whose attempt to seek justice played out in a court system downstream from the U.S. Supreme Court, which, in the 1857 *Dred Scott* case, denied blacks the rights and duties of U.S. citizenship.

After Northup's return to freedom in 1853, following twelve years of captivity, the first major reporting on his case appeared in the *New York Times* on January 20 of that year, under the headline "The Kidnapping Case. Narrative of the Seizure and Recovery of Solomon Northrup—Interesting Disclosures." The misspelling of his name (a correction was not issued until 2014) added insult to a far more grievous injury: after all he had been through, beginning with the denial of his identity as a free man in the shadows of the U.S. Capitol, Northup was not allowed to testify against his jailer, James H. Birch (or "Burch," in Northup's memoir), in Washington, D.C., in January 1853, simply because he was black. Even when he was permitted to give testimony against his kidnappers, Alexander Merrill and Joseph Russell, in state court in New York in July 1854, the case was ultimately dropped by the prosecution, following an appeal included in this volume. No one observing these events at the time captured the exasperation and injustice better than the pioneering historian and abolitionist, the black Bostonian William Cooper Nell, who, in *The Liberator* on August 28, 1857, wrote:

> How stands it with Solomon Northup, a colored citizen of the Empire State, as certified by His Excellency, Washington Hunt? He was kidnapped and carried into slavery, and held for twelve years, but finally found his way back to his family. 'He brought suit some time ago against his kidnappers, whom he knew, and who certainly would have fared hard under an investigation; but since the Dred Scott decision, he has been obliged to abandon all hope of bringing them to justice, because he cannot sue in the United States courts. This is democratic *equal* justice and equal rights.'

Through witnesses like Nell, Solomon Northup comes to life in the contemporary accounts we curated for this volume to show how diverse the perspectives about him and his book were at the time: black and white, northern and southern, journalistic and legal, polished and crude, sober and propagandistic. Each bears witness to the fact that Northup was a man and not just a figment of a white editor's imagination. Tracing his steps after his rescue allows it to become clear that Northup was directing his activities as best he could within a society compromised by slavery and a legal system that supported it. If he could not have his day in court, he could testify against slavery and its agents in the court of public opinion by authoring a memoir that would be a complete rendering of the facts from his point of view. That made *Twelve Years a Slave* more than an autobiography; it was a black male freed slave's roadmap for identifying and indicting his white captors, a development that transpired, astonishingly, when a reader of Northup's book recognized the two men who had kidnapped him as Alexander Merrill and Joseph Russell. Even if they eventually eluded prosecution, they could not outrun the reach of Northup's text or the judgments of his readers.

A Survivor's Statement: The Personal Northup

There is, in *Twelve Years a Slave,* the historical Northup, the man who, in layering his story with detail, made clear he was no literary archetype like Mrs. Stowe's Uncle Tom, but a free black citizen whose best years had been taken from him to feed the southern slave economy. Through our annotations of his book, to explain words, moments, and passages that might escape easy understanding, we hope it becomes increasingly clear to the reader just how grounded Northup's story was in the truths and meanings of the time he inhabited. There was also the personal Northup, the husband and father who returned to his family after a long captivity tantamount to that of a modern-day prisoner of war.

We must not lose sight of this Northup. Thinking of him, one has to wonder, given the fact that Northup started working on his book so soon after his homecoming, whether, in addition to trying to attract some income after losing twelve years of prime earning potential, he was striving to put down what had happened to him before he forgot any of the details so that his family, and not just the reading public, would know the personal trauma he had suffered while he was away. After all, Northup had been married to Anne Hampton since 1828 (not 1829, as stated in Northup's memoir), and they had had three children before his kidnapping (Elizabeth, Margaret, and Alonzo), children who had to grow up largely in his absence. Unforgettably, in the last scene of the film adaptation of *Twelve Years a Slave*, Northup is seen returning home to them and hugging them without words.

But words surely were needed—words that must have been extremely difficult to convey in one or even a few sittings "around the fire." Thus, we are left to imagine if Northup, besides testifying in his own way against the slave system, needed space to work his memories out with an editor, the attorney David Wilson, who could help him document his thoughts and experiences so that his family, for whom there must have been no easy words, could understand where he was when they were living their lives without him. The nation would come to understand, too.

In a way, we can frame the resulting book, at least in part, as Northup's survivor's statement, beyond whatever instrumental value it had as an income stream and as a political document that could be used in service of the abolitionist movement. It also was a warning to other unsuspecting free black citizens of the North that kidnapping was terrifyingly real and that it could happen to them and their families, too, if they were not vigilant. After all, Northup had learned firsthand that the law could not be relied upon to save a free black man from such a terrible trauma and fate. Nor could the law be relied upon to offer him justice if ever he was rescued. But perhaps the words of a survivor could.

"Let them know the HEART of the poor slave"

In his way, Northup, with the writing of *Twelve Years a Slave*, anticipated Walt Whitman's line in *Leaves of Grass*, first published two years later:

I am the man, I suffered, I was there.

Northup wanted his readers to know what a true rendering of slavery was, apart from the fiction consuming the country at the time through Mrs. Stowe's page-turner, which Abraham Lincoln would one day credit as playing a key part in precipitating the Civil War. As Northup wrote of his nonfictional approach in *Twelve Years a Slave:*

> There may be humane masters, as there certainly are inhuman ones—there may be slaves well-clothed, well-fed, and happy, as there surely are those half-clad, half-starved and miserable. . . . Men may write fictions portraying lowly life as it is, or as it is not—may expatiate with owlish gravity upon the bliss of ignorance—discourse flippantly from arm chairs of the pleasures of slave life; but let them toil with him in the field—sleep with him in the cabin—feed with him on husks; let them behold him scourged, hunted, trampled on, and they will come back with another story in their mouths. Let them know the *heart* of the poor slave—learn his secret thoughts—thoughts he dare not utter in the hearing of the white man; let them sit by him in the silent watches of the night—converse with him in trustful confidence, of "life, liberty, and the pursuit of happiness," and they will find that ninety-nine out of every hundred are intelligent enough to understand their situation, and to cherish in their bosoms the love of freedom, as passionately as themselves.*

Throughout the text, Northup uses numerous internal mechanisms to establish the authenticity of his testimony. It had to be obvious on its face that his book could have been written only by one man—*this* man—who had experienced decades of freedom before he served twelve years as a slave. For instance, Northup's early background of working odd jobs as a free man in the North, including carpentry, developed in him a curiosity and appreciation for ingenuity and industry that we glean in his detailed explanations to the reader of how the slave economy functioned in practice, including the finer points of sugar caning. There was no way Northup's editor, David Wilson, a local attorney in upstate New York, could have known such things. For its keen observations about the workings of slave life and labor alone, *Twelve Years a Slave* warrants close study.

But the text also commands our attention because, unlike the many slave narratives in print that follow a trajectory up from slavery *to* freedom, Northup's is the only one that follows a person down from freedom to bondage and back to freedom again, revealing along the way the levels of violence inflicted on the black body, especially enslaved women, from the perspective of one for whom this and the other evils of slavery were as shocking and brutalizing to

---

* This passage was cited by John Blassingame in his influential article "Using the Testimony of Ex-Slaves: Approaches and Problems," which appeared in the *Journal of Southern History* 41.4 (Nov. 1975). Here Northup seems to be making a direct reference to Harriet Beecher Stowe's antislavery novel *Uncle Tom's Cabin,* which is subtitled "Life Among the Lowly."

encounter as they were for other free, mostly white northerners to read. Through Northup's unique entanglement in the slave system as an outsider and insider at the same time, we, his readers, come as close as possible to knowing the system at the heart of American capitalism and its brutal effects on all parties, from the most physically vulnerable slaves to the most powerful and brutal slave owners.

Frederick Douglass picked up on Northup's dedication to authenticity right away, writing in his review of the book: "The Narrative of Solomon Northup, recently issued from the press of Derby & Miller of Auburn, is a plain unvarnished history. . . . There was no need of invoking the aid of the imagination to adorn this tale of horrors. The hero needed only to tell 'what he did know, and testify of what he had seen.'"

In a country where black men faced obstacles to testifying against white men, Northup seized the opportunity of authoring his memoir to do just that—authentically testifying against his oppressors in order to take justice into his own hands and to warn or save others from the same fate. In doing so, Northup placed his book, as a physical object of the printing press and bookseller, into the hands of others who, upon reading it, might change their beliefs about slavery or increase their efforts to unmask those who continued to profit from its crimes, including kidnapping, in the lead-up to the Civil War.

From Slave to Screen

The 2013 film adaptation of *Twelve Years a Slave* by Steve McQueen was a watershed moment in the history of cinema that honored the author's emphasis on "plain unvarnished" truth. In translating text to screen, McQueen worked on every sense of the viewer, especially through sound, and, crucially, he brought the book's character of the female slave Patsey fully into view in an unforgettable, haunting, Oscar-winning performance by Lupita Nyong'o. Indeed, it is fair to say that her performance has opened new lines of inquiry and interpretation for scholars who study the complex, often fraught intersections of race and gender under slavery. At the same time, McQueen's film keeps track of the psychological costs to Edwin Epps, the slave master who abuses Patsey's body with a lustful obsession that threatens to destroy both Epps and his family. These characters, woven into Northup's original text, are fully revealed through McQueen's lens, and the resulting effect is at times almost overwhelming.

Reviewing McQueen's masterpiece for the *New York Times* on October 17, 2013, critic Manohla Dargis wrote: "*12 Years a Slave* isn't the first movie about slavery in the United States—but it may be the one that finally makes it impossible for American cinema to

continue to sell the ugly lies it's been hawking for more than a
century. . . . It's at once a familiar, utterly strange and deeply
American story in which the period trappings long beloved by
Hollywood—the paternalistic gentry with their pretty plantations,
their genteel manners and all the fiddle-dee-dee rest—are the backdrop for an outrage."

Dargis wasn't the only film reviewer who reacted to Northup's story
in surprisingly parallel ways to those who read the book 150 years
before. There was, in both the original text and McQueen's film
adaptation, a fierce commitment to authenticity that made it feel as if
one were experiencing slavery, for real, for the first time, never to be
forgotten. For this reason, we felt strongly that the film deserved serious study within the same volume as the book itself. This Norton
Critical Edition delivers on that conviction, connecting reviews and
critical essays about the film, along with an interview with McQueen,
to the longer arc of writings about Northup and his book.

No amount of book sales could ever compensate Northup and his
family for all that was taken from them during his twelve years of
bondage. Nor could commercial success and notoriety make up for
the fact that he was captured in the shadows of the U.S. Capitol in
1841, and in 1853 kept from testifying there against the slave trader
who had denied him his freedom and sold him for gain at a time
when black lives did not matter. That said, Northup made *his* life
matter by surviving his unimaginable ordeal and by writing it down.
We, the editors of this volume, by placing the text alongside contemporary and secondary readings, hope to ensure the fullest possible engagement by students and teachers alike. While we have taken
the liberty of correcting—and, when doing so, notating—spelling
errors that were especially distracting to the eye in Northup's memoir,
we have kept the editing light in the surrounding commentary out
of a desire to place readers today as close as possible to the sources
as they would have appeared to contemporary readers. For example,
in the newspaper reports tracking the Northup story in the after-
math of his rescue, we have left misspellings and other mistakes
untouched.

We are thrilled that our editors at W. W. Norton have recognized
the importance of *Twelve Years a Slave* and are supporting it in such
a robust way. In doing so as part of its preeminent Critical Editions
series, Norton is enhancing the teaching of literature and history in
our schools, colleges, and universities at a time when so many are
starved to learn more about the history of slavery and race in America,
a "truth," to quote Douglass again, that was and remains "far stranger than fiction." We may never know what happened to Solomon
Northup after he disappeared during the Civil War, but, thankfully,
this edition will help to keep his voice from ever being lost again.

Acknowledgments

We, the editors of this Norton Critical Edition of *Twelve Years a Slave*, wish to thank the following individuals for their timely, and indispensable, support at various stages of publication:

- Steve McQueen—for sitting down for a three-part interview with Professor Gates for TheRoot.com in December 2013, following the release of his astonishing film adaptation of Solomon Northup's *Twelve Years a Slave*; and for giving Norton his blessing to use a production photo from the film as the cover image of this book.
- Jeremy Kleiner—for helping to bridge the worlds of the book and film as one of the Oscar-winning producers of *12 Years a Slave* and as copresident of Plan B Productions.
- David Fiske—for examining the contents of the book and supporting materials based on his unique vantage point as Northup's most dedicated living biographer.
- Carra Glatt—for transcribing especially hard-to-read contemporary sources and for providing invaluable support in researching the annotations to the original text of *Twelve Years a Slave*.
- Rebeca Hey-Colon—for helping to track down dozens of contemporary and secondary sources contained in this book.
- Bryan Sinche—for reviewing the manuscript and offering vital insights as an expert on the publication history of American slave narratives.

We also are deeply grateful to our partners at W. W. Norton & Company, especially Carol Bemis, Thea Goodrich, and Rachel Goodman, who kept us on track and provided sage advice and critical assistance from start to finish. Vital as well are our cherished colleagues at the Hutchins Center for African and African American Research at Harvard University, especially Sheldon Cheek, Karen Dalton, Amy Gosdanian, Steven Niven, and Abby Wolf.

In addition, Professor Gates writes: On a personal note, I would like to thank Dr. Marial Iglesias Utset; Jeremy Kleiner at Plan B and Steve McQueen for according me the pleasure of being the historical advisor for *12 Years a Slave*; Bennett Ashley, my literary lawyer; Paul Lucas, my literary agent; my colleagues John Stauffer, Donald Yacovone, and William L. Andrews; and the late John W. Blassingame, Sr. for introducing me to Solomon Northup's slave narrative when I was a student at Yale University. I dedicate this book to Eleanor Margaret Gates-Hatley.

Dr. Burke writes: A native of Newburgh, New York, I owe a debt of thanks to my Brooklyn family for tolerating the binders of materials that spent months as company in our house: my loving wife, Anna Barranca-Burke, Carol Barranca, Joseph Barranca, and Gasper Barranca. My fascination with the Civil War era is rooted in childhood, when my older brother, Dr. Christopher Burke, and I first watched the television miniseries *The Blue and the Gray* (1982) and begged our parents, Brian and Sharon, to take us to Gettysburg. This is for them, too, and for Daniel T. Wakeman, my great-great-grandfather on my maternal grandmother Blanche Williams Kolassa's line. Wakeman enlisted as a private in Company C of the 56th New York Infantry Regiment out of New Paltz in 1861 and served in the Union Army for the duration of the Civil War until being mustered out in Charleston, South Carolina, in 1865. Subsequently, Wakeman settled in Newburgh to raise his children with his wife, my great-great-grandmother Rosanna Girven, an immigrant from northern Ireland. Though the Wakemans are buried with other family members in Woodlawn Cemetery, little more than a mile from where I grew up, I did not discover them until 2015.

The Text of
TWELVE YEARS A SLAVE

SOLOMON IN HIS PLANTATION SUIT.

Solomon Northup

Courtesy of the UNC–CH Library, The University of North Carolina at Chapel Hill.

TO

HARRIET BEECHER STOWE:

WHOSE NAME,

THROUGHOUT THE WORLD, IS IDENTIFIED WITH THE

GREAT REFORM:

THIS NARRATIVE, AFFORDING ANOTHER

Key to Uncle Tom's Cabin,

IS RESPECTFULLY DEDICATED

"Such dupes are men to custom, and so prone
To reverence what is ancient, and can plead
A course of long observance for its use,
That even servitude, the worst of ills,
Because delivered down from sire to son,
Is kept and guarded as a sacred thing.
But is it fit, or can it bear the shock
Of rational discussion, that a man
Compounded and made up, like other men,
Of elements tumultuous, in whom lust
And folly in as ample measure meet,
As in the bosom of the slave he rules,
Should be a despot absolute, and boast
Himself the only freeman of his land?"
                                    Cowper.[†]

---

† From *The Task* (1785) by William Cowper.

Contents

5

CHAPTER IV.

CHAPTER V.

CHAPTER VI.

CHAPTER VII.

CHAPTER VIII.

CHAPTER IX.

CHAPTER X.

CHAPTER XI.

CHAPTER XII.

CHAPTER XIII.

CHAPTER XIV.

CHAPTER XV.

CHAPTER XVI.

CHAPTER XVII.

---

* The transcriber changed "Chalenged" to "Challenged".
** The text is not always consistent in its use of the possessive form, e.g., "Epps'" versus "Epps's".

CHAPTER XVIII.

CHAPTER XIX.

CHAPTER XX.

---

*   The transcriber changed "Coversation" to "Conversation".

CHAPTER XXI.

CHAPTER XXII.

LIST OF ILLUSTRATIONS.

Editor's Preface.

When the editor commenced the preparation of the following narrative, he did not suppose it would reach the size of this volume. In order, however, to present all the facts which have been communicated to him, it has seemed necessary to extend it to its present length.

Many of the statements contained in the following pages are corroborated by abundant evidence—others rest entirely upon Solomon's assertion. That he has adhered strictly to the truth, the editor, at least, who has had an opportunity of detecting any contradiction or discrepancy in his statements, is well satisfied. He has invariably repeated the same story without deviating in the slightest particular, and has also carefully perused the manuscript, dictating an alteration wherever the most trivial inaccuracy has appeared.

It was Solomon's fortune, during his captivity, to be owned by several masters. The treatment he received while at the "Pine Woods" shows that among slaveholders there are men of humanity as well as of cruelty. Some of them are spoken of with emotions of gratitude— others in a spirit of bitterness. It is believed that the following account of his experience on Bayou Bœuf presents a correct picture of Slavery, in all its lights and shadows, as it now exists in that locality. Unbiased, as he conceives, by any prepossessions or prejudices, the only object of the editor has been to give a faithful history of Solomon Northup's life, as he received it from his lips.

In the accomplishment of that object, he trusts he has succeeded, notwithstanding the numerous faults of style and of expression[*] it may be found to contain.

DAVID WILSON.

WHITEHALL, N.Y., May, 1853.

---

[*] The transcriber changed "expresssion" to "expression".

Twelve Years a Slave

Chapter I.

INTRODUCTORY—ANCESTRY—THE NORTHUP FAMILY—BIRTH AND
PARENTAGE—MINTUS NORTHUP—MARRIAGE WITH ANNE
HAMPTON—GOOD RESOLUTIONS—CHAMPLAIN CANAL—RAFTING
EXCURSION TO CANADA—FARMING—THE VIOLIN—COOKING—
REMOVAL TO SARATOGA—PARKER AND PERRY—SLAVES AND
SLAVERY—THE CHILDREN—THE BEGINNING OF SORROW.

Having been born a freeman, and for more than thirty years enjoyed
the blessings of liberty in a free State[1]—and having at the end of
that time been kidnapped and sold into Slavery, where I remained,
until happily rescued in the month of January, 1853, after a bondage of twelve years—it has been suggested that an account of my life
and fortunes would not be uninteresting to the public.

Since my return to liberty, I have not failed to perceive the increasing interest throughout the Northern States, in regard to the subject of Slavery. Works of fiction, professing to portray its features in
their more pleasing as well as more repugnant aspects, have been
circulated to an extent unprecedented, and, as I understand, have
created a fruitful topic of comment and discussion.[2]

I can speak of Slavery only so far as it came under my own
observation—only so far as I have known and experienced it in my
own person. My object is, to give a candid and truthful statement of
facts: to repeat the story of my life, without exaggeration, leaving it
for others to determine, whether even the pages of fiction present a
picture of more cruel wrong or a severer bondage.

As far back as I have been able to ascertain, my ancestors on
the paternal side were slaves in Rhode Island. They belonged to a
family by the name of Northup, one of whom, removing to the State

---

1. At the time of Northup's capture in 1841 the United States was evenly divided into
thirteen free and thirteen slave states.
2. In 1852, the white abolitionist Harriet Beecher Stowe, to whom *Twelve Years a Slave* is
dedicated, published *Uncle Tom's Cabin,* a sentimental novel intended to illustrate the
horrors of slavery. It was the best-selling novel of the nineteenth century and increased
support for abolition in the North. A number of southern writers responded with "anti-
Tom" literature depicting slavery as a benevolent institution.

of New-York, settled at Hoosic, in Rensselaer county. He brought with him Mintus Northup, my father. On the death of this gentleman, which must have occurred some fifty years ago, my father became free, having been emancipated by a direction in his will.

Henry B. Northup, Esq., of Sandy Hill, a distinguished counselor at law, and the man to whom, under Providence, I am indebted for my present liberty, and my return to the society of my wife and children, is a relative of the family in which my forefathers were thus held to service, and from which they took the name I bear. To this fact may be attributed the persevering interest he has taken in my behalf.

Sometime after my father's liberation, he removed to the town of Minerva, Essex county N. Y., where I was born, in the month of July, 1808. How long he remained in the latter place I have not the means of definitely ascertaining. From thence he removed to Granville, Washington county, near a place known as Slyborough, where, for some years, he labored on the farm of Clark Northup, also a relative of his old master; from thence he removed to the Alden farm, at Moss Street, a short distance north of the village of Sandy Hill; and from thence to the farm now owned by Russel Pratt, situated on the road leading from Fort Edward to Argyle, where he continued to reside until his death, which took place on the 22d day of November, 1829. He left a widow and two children—myself, and Joseph, an elder brother. The latter is still living in the county of Oswego, near the city of that name; my mother died during the period of my captivity.

Though born a slave, and laboring under the disadvantages to which my unfortunate race is subjected, my father was a man respected for his industry and integrity, as many now living, who well remember him, are ready to testify. His whole life was passed in the peaceful pursuits of agriculture, never seeking employment in those more menial positions, which seem to be especially allotted to the children of Africa. Besides giving us an education surpassing that ordinarily bestowed upon children in our condition, he acquired, by his diligence and economy, a sufficient property qualification to entitle him to the right of suffrage.[3] He was accustomed to speak to us of his early life; and although at all times cherishing the warmest emotions of kindness, and even of affection towards the family, in whose house he had been a bondsman, he nevertheless comprehended the system of Slavery, and dwelt with sorrow on the degradation of his race. He endeavored to imbue our minds with sentiments of morality, and to teach us to place our trust and confidence in Him who regards

---

3. New York, in its 1821 Constitution, eliminated its $250 property requirement for white male voters, but retained it for blacks. The new Constitution was ratified and took effect in 1822. Mintus Northup, who died in 1829, would have been one of a small number of black New Yorkers with enough property to be eligible to vote in the state.

the humblest as well as the highest of his creatures. How often since that time has the recollection of his paternal counsels occurred to me, while lying in a slave hut in the distant and sickly regions of Louisiana, smarting with the undeserved wounds which an inhuman master had inflicted, and longing only for the grave which had covered him, to shield me also from the lash of the oppressor. In the church-yard at Sandy Hill, an humble stone marks the spot where he reposes, after having worthily performed the duties appertaining to the lowly sphere wherein God had appointed him to walk.

Up to this period I had been principally engaged with my father in the labors of the farm. The leisure hours allowed me were generally either employed over my books, or playing on the violin—an amuse-ment which was the ruling passion of my youth. It has also been the source of consolation since, affording pleasure to the simple beings with whom my lot was cast, and beguiling my own thoughts, for many hours, from the painful contemplation of my fate.

On Christmas day, 1829,[4] I was married to Anne Hampton, a col-ored girl then living in the vicinity of our residence. The ceremony was performed at Fort Edward, by Timothy Eddy, Esq., a magistrate of that town, and still a prominent citizen of the place. She had resided a long time at Sandy Hill, with Mr. Baird, proprietor of the Eagle Tavern, and also in the family of Rev. Alexander Proudfit, of Salem. This gentleman for many years had presided over the Pres-byterian society at the latter place, and was widely distinguished for his learning and piety. Anne still holds in grateful remembrance the exceeding kindness and the excellent counsels of that good man. She is not able to determine the exact line of her descent, but the blood of three races mingles in her veins. It is difficult to tell whether the red,[5] white, or black predominates. The union of them all, how-ever, in her origin, has given her a singular but pleasing expression, such as is rarely to be seen. Though somewhat resembling, yet she cannot properly be styled a quadroon,[6] a class to which, I have omit-ted to mention, my mother belonged.

I had just now passed the period of my minority, having reached the age of twenty-one years in the month of July previous. Deprived of the advice and assistance of my father, with a wife dependent upon me for support, I resolved to enter upon a life of industry; and notwithstanding the obstacle of color, and the consciousness of my

---

4. In a sworn deposition, Anne Hampton Northup said Solomon Northup and she had been married on December 25, 1828. Others, including Timothy Eddy and Josiah Hand, confirmed this, leading Northup's biographers, Fiske et al., to conclude that Northup or his editor, David Wilson, erred in dating the marriage to 1829, a mistake picked up in contemporary news coverage of *Twelve Years a Slave*. For the statements of Anne Northup, Timothy Eddy, and Josiah Hand, please see Appendix B of *Twelve Years a Slave* (pp. 185–88 of this volume).
5. Native American.
6. Person of one-quarter African descent.

lowly state, indulged in pleasant dreams of a good time coming, when the possession of some humble habitation, with a few surrounding acres, should reward my labors, and bring me the means of happiness and comfort.

From the time of my marriage to this day the love I have borne my wife has been sincere and unabated; and only those who have felt the glowing tenderness a father cherishes for his offspring, can appreciate my affection for the beloved children which have since been born to us. This much I deem appropriate and necessary to say, in order that those who read these pages, may comprehend the poignancy of those sufferings I have been doomed to bear.

Immediately upon our marriage we commenced house-keeping, in the old yellow building then standing at the southern extremity of Fort Edward village, and which has since been transformed into a modern mansion, and lately occupied by Captain Lathrop. It is known as the Fort House. In this building the courts were sometime held after the organization of the county. It was also occupied by Burgoyne in 1777,[7] being situated near the old Fort on the left bank of the Hudson.

During the winter I was employed with others repairing the Champlain Canal,[8] on that section over which William Van Nortwick was superintendent. David McEachron had the immediate charge of the men in whose company I labored. By the time the canal opened in the spring, I was enabled, from the savings of my wages, to purchase a pair of horses, and other things necessarily required in the business of navigation.

Having hired several efficient hands to assist me, I entered into contracts for the transportation of large rafts of timber from Lake Champlain to Troy. Dyer Beckwith and a Mr. Bartemy, of Whitehall, accompanied me on several trips. During the season I became perfectly familiar with the art and mysteries of rafting—a knowledge which afterwards enabled me to render profitable service to a worthy master, and to astonish the simple-witted lumbermen on the banks of the Bayou Bœuf.

In one of my voyages down Lake Champlain, I was induced to make a visit to Canada. Repairing to Montreal, I visited the cathedral and other places of interest in that city, from whence I continued my excursion to Kingston and other towns, obtaining a knowledge of localities, which was also of service to me afterwards, as will appear towards the close of this narrative.

Having completed my contracts on the canal satisfactorily to myself and to my employer, and not wishing to remain idle, now

7. John Burgoyne (1722–1792), British general during the Revolutionary War.
8. Canal connecting the base of Lake Champlain (which forms the northern part of the Vermont/New York border) to the Hudson River.

that the navigation of the canal was again suspended, I entered into another contract with Medad Gunn, to cut a large quantity of wood. In this business I was engaged during the winter of 1831–32.

With the return of spring, Anne and myself conceived the project of taking a farm in the neighborhood. I had been accustomed from earliest youth to agricultural labors, and it was an occupation congenial to my tastes. I accordingly entered into arrangements for a part of the old Alden farm, on which my father formerly resided. With one cow, one swine, a yoke of fine oxen I had lately purchased of Lewis Brown, in Hartford, and other personal property and effects, we proceeded to our new home in Kingsbury. That year I planted twenty-five acres of corn, sowed large fields of oats, and commenced farming upon as large a scale as my utmost means would permit. Anne was diligent about the house affairs, while I toiled laboriously in the field.

On this place we continued to reside until 1834. In the winter season I had numerous calls to play on the violin. Wherever the young people assembled to dance, I was almost invariably there. Throughout the surrounding villages my fiddle was notorious. Anne, also, during her long residence at the Eagle Tavern, had become somewhat famous as a cook. During court weeks, and on public occasions, she was employed at high wages in the kitchen at Sherrill's Coffee House.

We always returned home from the performance of these services with money in our pockets; so that, with fiddling, cooking, and farming, we soon found ourselves in the possession of abundance, and, in fact, leading a happy and prosperous life. Well, indeed, would it have been for us had we remained on the farm at Kingsbury; but the time came when the next step was to be taken towards the cruel destiny that awaited me.

In March, 1834, we removed to Saratoga Springs.[9] We occupied a house belonging to Daniel O'Brien, on the north side of Washington street. At that time Isaac Taylor kept a large boarding house, known as Washington Hall, at the north end of Broadway. He employed me to drive a hack,[1] in which capacity I worked for him two years. After this time I was generally employed through the visiting season, as also was Anne, in the United States Hotel, and other public houses of the place. In winter seasons I relied upon my violin, though during the construction of the Troy and Saratoga railroad, I performed many hard days' labor upon it.

I was in the habit, at Saratoga, of purchasing articles necessary for my family at the stores of Mr. Cephas Parker and Mr. William Perry, gentlemen towards whom, for many acts of kindness, I

9. Move of about twenty-five miles.
1. Hackney coach, or horse-drawn carriage kept for hire.

entertained feelings of strong regard. It was for this reason that, twelve years afterwards, I caused to be directed to them the letter, which is hereinafter inserted, and which was the means, in the hands of Mr. Northup, of my fortunate deliverance.

While living at the United States Hotel, I frequently met with slaves, who had accompanied their masters from the South. They were always well dressed and well provided for, leading apparently an easy life, with but few of its ordinary troubles to perplex them. Many times they entered into conversation with me on the subject of Slavery. Almost uniformly I found they cherished a secret desire for liberty. Some of them expressed the most ardent anxiety to escape, and consulted me on the best method of effecting it. The fear of punishment, however, which they knew was certain to attend their re-capture and return, in all cases proved sufficient to deter them from the experiment. Having all my life breathed the free air of the North, and conscious that I possessed the same feelings and affections that find a place in the white man's breast; conscious, moreover, of an intelligence equal to that of some men, at least, with a fairer skin, I was too ignorant, perhaps too independent, to conceive how any one could be content to live in the abject condition of a slave. I could not comprehend the justice of that law, or that religion, which upholds or recognizes the principle of Slavery; and never once, I am proud to say, did I fail to counsel any one who came to me, to watch his opportunity, and strike for freedom.

I continued to reside at Saratoga until the spring of 1841. The flattering anticipations which, seven years before, had seduced us from the quiet farm-house, on the east side of the Hudson, had not been realized. Though always in comfortable circumstances, we had not prospered. The society and associations at that world-renowned watering place,[2] were not calculated to preserve the simple habits of industry and economy to which I had been accustomed, but, on the contrary, to substitute others in their stead, tending to shiftlessness and extravagance.

At this time we were the parents of three children—Elizabeth, Margaret, and Alonzo. Elizabeth, the eldest, was in her tenth year; Margaret was two years younger, and little Alonzo had just passed his fifth birth-day. They filled our house with gladness. Their young voices were music in our ears. Many an airy castle did their mother and myself build for the little innocents. When not at labor I was always walking with them, clad in their best attire, through the streets and groves of Saratoga. Their presence was my delight; and I clasped

2. Resort or spa area near a body of water; Saratoga Springs was considered a fashionable vacation spot during the period.

them to my bosom with as warm and tender love as if their clouded skins had been as white as snow.

Thus far the history of my life presents nothing whatever unusual—nothing but the common hopes, and loves, and labors of an obscure colored man, making his humble progress in the world. But now I had reached a turning point in my existence—reached the threshold of unutterable wrong, and sorrow, and despair. Now had I approached within the shadow of the cloud, into the thick darkness whereof I was soon to disappear, thenceforward to be hidden from the eyes of all my kindred, and shut out from the sweet light of liberty, for many a weary year.

Chapter II.

THE TWO STRANGERS—THE CIRCUS COMPANY—DEPARTURE FROM
SARATOGA—VENTRILOQUISM AND LEGERDEMAIN—JOURNEY TO
NEW-YORK—FREE PAPERS—BROWN AND HAMILTON—THE HASTE TO
REACH THE CIRCUS—ARRIVAL IN WASHINGTON—FUNERAL OF
HARRISON—THE SUDDEN SICKNESS—THE TORMENT OF THIRST—THE
RECEDING LIGHT—INSENSIBILITY—CHAINS AND DARKNESS.

One morning, towards the latter part of the month of March, 1841, having at that time no particular business to engage my attention, I was walking about the village of Saratoga Springs, thinking to myself where I might obtain some present employment, until the busy season should arrive. Anne, as was her usual custom, had gone over to Sandy Hill, a distance of some twenty miles, to take charge of the culinary department at Sherrill's Coffee House, during the session of the court. Elizabeth, I think, had accompanied her. Margaret and Alonzo were with their aunt at Saratoga.

On the corner of Congress street and Broadway, near the tavern, then, and for aught I know to the contrary, still kept by Mr. Moon, I was met by two gentlemen of respectable appearance, both of whom were entirely unknown to me. I have the impression that they were introduced to me by some one of my acquaintances, but who, I have in vain endeavored to recall, with the remark that I was an expert player on the violin.

At any rate, they immediately entered into conversation on that subject, making numerous inquiries touching my proficiency in that respect. My responses being to all appearances satisfactory, they proposed to engage my services for a short period, stating, at the same time, I was just such a person as their business required. Their names, as they afterwards gave them to me, were Merrill Brown and Abram Hamilton, though whether these were their true appellations,

I have strong reasons to doubt. The former was a man apparently forty years of age, somewhat short and thick-set, with a countenance indicating shrewdness and intelligence. He wore a black frock coat and black hat, and said he resided either at Rochester or at Syracuse. The latter was a young man of fair complexion and light eyes, and, I should judge, had not passed the age of twenty-five. He was tall and slender, dressed in a snuff-colored coat, with glossy hat, and vest of elegant pattern. His whole apparel was in the extreme of fashion. His appearance was somewhat effeminate, but prepossessing, and there was about him an easy air, that showed he had mingled with the world. They were connected, as they informed me, with a circus company, then in the city of Washington; that they were on their way thither to rejoin it, having left it for a short time to make an excursion northward, for the purpose of seeing the country, and were paying their expenses by an occasional exhibition. They also remarked that they had found much difficulty in procuring music for their entertainments, and that if I would accompany them as far as New-York, they would give me one dollar for each day's services, and three dollars in addition for every night I played at their performances, besides sufficient to pay the expenses of my return from New-York to Saratoga.

I at once accepted the tempting offer, both for the reward it promised, and from a desire to visit the metropolis. They were anxious to leave immediately. Thinking my absence would be brief, I did not deem it necessary to write to Anne whither I had gone; in fact supposing that my return, perhaps, would be as soon as hers. So taking a change of linen and my violin, I was ready to depart. The carriage was brought round—a covered one, drawn by a pair of noble bays, altogether forming an elegant establishment. Their baggage, consisting of three large trunks, was fastened on the rack, and mounting to the driver's seat, while they took their places in the rear, I drove away from Saratoga on the road to Albany, elated with my new position, and happy as I had ever been, on any day in all my life.

We passed through Ballston, and striking the ridge road, as it is called, if my memory correctly serves me, followed it direct to Albany. We reached that city before dark, and stopped at a hotel southward from the Museum.

This night I had an opportunity of witnessing one of their performances—the only one, during the whole period I was with them. Hamilton was stationed at the door; I formed the orchestra, while Brown provided the entertainment. It consisted in throwing balls, dancing on the rope, frying pancakes in a hat, causing invisible pigs to squeal, and other like feats of ventriloquism and legerdemain.[3]

3. Trickery or sleight-of-hand.

The audience was extraordinarily sparse, and not of the selectest character at that, and Hamilton's report of the proceeds presented but a "beggarly account of empty boxes."

Early next morning we renewed our journey. The burden of their conversation now was the expression of an anxiety to reach the circus without delay. They hurried forward, without again stopping to exhibit, and in due course of time, we reached New-York, taking lodgings at a house on the west side of the city, in a street running from Broadway to the river. I supposed my journey was at an end, and expected in a day or two at least, to return to my friends and family at Saratoga. Brown and Hamilton, however, began to importune me to continue with them to Washington. They alleged that immediately on their arrival, now that the summer season was approaching, the circus would set out for the north. They promised me a situation and high wages if I would accompany them. Largely did they expatiate on the advantages that would result to me, and such were the flattering representations they made, that I finally concluded to accept the offer.

The next morning they suggested that, inasmuch as we were about entering a slave State, it would be well, before leaving New-York, to procure free papers. The idea struck me as a prudent one, though I think it would scarcely have occurred to me, had they not proposed it. We proceeded at once to what I understood to be the Custom House. They made oath to certain facts showing I was a free man. A paper was drawn up and handed us, with the direction to take it to the clerk's office. We did so, and the clerk having added something to it, for which he was paid six shillings, we returned again to the Custom House. Some further formalities were gone through with before it was completed, when, paying the officer two dollars, I placed the papers in my pocket, and started with my two friends to our hotel. I thought at the time, I must confess, that the papers were scarcely worth the cost of obtaining them—the apprehension of danger to my personal safety never having suggested itself to me in the remotest manner. The clerk, to whom we were directed, I remember, made a memorandum in a large book, which, I presume, is in the office yet. A reference to the entries during the latter part of March, or first of April, 1841, I have no doubt will satisfy the incredulous, at least so far as this particular transaction is concerned.

With the evidence of freedom in my possession, the next day after our arrival in New-York, we crossed the ferry to Jersey City, and took the road to Philadelphia. Here we remained one night, continuing our journey towards Baltimore early in the morning. In due time, we arrived in the latter city, and stopped at a hotel near the railroad depot, either kept by a Mr. Rathbone, or known as the Rathbone House. All the way from New-York, their anxiety to reach the circus seemed to grow more and more intense. We left the carriage at Baltimore, and entering the cars,[4] proceeded to Washington, at which place we arrived just at nightfall, the evening previous to the funeral of General Harrison,[5] and stopped at Gadsby's Hotel, on Pennsylvania Avenue.

After supper they called me to their apartments, and paid me forty-three dollars, a sum greater than my wages amounted to, which act of generosity was in consequence, they said, of their not having exhibited as often as they had given me to anticipate, during our trip from Saratoga. They moreover informed me that it had been the intention of the circus company to leave Washington the next morning, but that on account of the funeral, they had concluded to remain another day. They were then, as they had been from the time of our first meeting, extremely kind. No opportunity was omitted of addressing me in the language of approbation; while, on the other hand, I was certainly much prepossessed in their favor. I gave them my confidence without reserve, and would freely have trusted them to almost any extent. Their constant conversation and manner towards me—their foresight in suggesting the idea of free papers, and a hundred other little acts, unnecessary to be repeated—all indicated that they were friends indeed, sincerely solicitous for my welfare. I know not but they were. I know not but they were innocent of the great wickedness of which I now believe them guilty. Whether they were accessory to my misfortunes—subtle and inhuman monsters in the shape of men—designedly luring me away from home and family, and liberty, for the sake of gold—those who read these pages will have the same means of determining as myself. If they were innocent, my sudden disappearance must have been unaccountable indeed; but revolving in my mind all the attending circumstances, I never yet could indulge, towards them, so charitable a supposition.

After receiving the money from them, of which they appeared to have an abundance, they advised me not to go into the streets that night, inasmuch as I was unacquainted with the customs of the city. Promising to remember their advice, I left them together, and soon after was shown by a colored servant to a sleeping room in the back part of the hotel, on the ground floor. I laid down to rest, thinking of home and wife, and children, and the long distance that stretched between us, until I fell asleep. But no good angel of pity came to my bedside, bidding me to fly—no voice of mercy forewarned me in my dreams of the trials that were just at hand.

4. I.e., railroad cars.
5. William Henry Harrison (1773–1841), the ninth President of the United States. Harrison died of pneumonia on April 4, 1841, just thirty-two days into his presidency. His funeral took place on April 7.

The next day there was a great pageant in Washington. The roar of cannon and the tolling of bells filled the air, while many houses were shrouded with crape,[6] and the streets were black with people. As the day advanced, the procession made its appearance, coming slowly through the Avenue, carriage after carriage, in long succession, while thousands upon thousands followed on foot—all moving to the sound of melancholy music. They were bearing the dead body of Harrison to the grave.

From early in the morning, I was constantly in the company of Hamilton and Brown. They were the only persons I knew in Washington. We stood together as the funeral pomp passed by. I remember distinctly how the window glass would break and rattle to the ground, after each report of the cannon they were firing in the burial ground. We went to the Capitol, and walked a long time about the grounds. In the afternoon, they strolled towards the President's House, all the time keeping me near to them, and pointing out various places of interest. As yet, I had seen nothing of the circus. In fact, I had thought of it but little, if at all, amidst the excitement of the day.

My friends, several times during the afternoon, entered drinking saloons, and called for liquor. They were by no means in the habit, however, so far as I knew them, of indulging to excess. On these occasions, after serving themselves, they would pour out a glass and hand it to me. I did not become intoxicated, as may be inferred from what subsequently occurred. Towards evening, and soon after partaking of one of these potations, I began to experience most unpleasant sensations. I felt extremely ill. My head commenced aching—a dull, heavy pain, inexpressibly disagreeable. At the supper table, I was without appetite; the sight and flavor of food was nauseous. About dark the same servant conducted me to the room I had occupied the previous night. Brown and Hamilton advised me to retire, commiserating me kindly, and expressing hopes that I would be better in the morning. Divesting myself of coat and boots merely, I threw myself upon the bed. It was impossible to sleep. The pain in my head continued to increase, until it became almost unbearable. In a short time I became thirsty. My lips were parched. I could think of nothing but water—of lakes and flowing rivers, of brooks where I had stooped to drink, and of the dripping bucket, rising with its cool and overflowing nectar, from the bottom of the well. Towards midnight, as near as I could judge, I arose, unable longer to bear such intensity of thirst. I was a stranger in the house, and knew nothing of its apartments. There was no one up, as I could observe. Groping about at random, I knew not where, I found

6. Crepe: black fabric associated with mourning.

the way at last to a kitchen in the basement. Two or three colored servants were moving through it, one of whom, a woman, gave me two glasses of water. It afforded momentary relief, but by the time I had reached my room again, the same burning desire of drink, the same tormenting thirst, had again returned. It was even more torturing than before, as was also the wild pain in my head, if such a thing could be. I was in sore distress—in most excruciating agony! I seemed to stand on the brink of madness! The memory of that night of horrible suffering will follow me to the grave.

In the course of an hour or more after my return from the kitchen, I was conscious of some one entering my room. There seemed to be several—a mingling of various voices,—but how many, or who they were, I cannot tell. Whether Brown and Hamilton were among them, is a mere matter of conjecture. I only remember, with any degree of distinctness, that I was told it was necessary to go to a physician and procure medicine, and that pulling on my boots, without coat or hat, I followed them through a long passage-way, or alley, into the open street. It ran out at right angles from Pennsylvania Avenue. On the opposite side there was a light burning in a window. My impression is there were then three persons with me, but it is altogether indefinite and vague, and like the memory of a painful dream. Going towards the light, which I imagined proceeded from a physician's office, and which seemed to recede as I advanced, is the last glimmering recollection I can now recall. From that moment I was insensible. How long I remained in that condition—whether only that night, or many days and nights—I do not know; but when consciousness returned, I found myself alone, in utter darkness, and in chains.

The pain in my head had subsided in a measure, but I was very faint and weak. I was sitting upon a low bench, made of rough boards, and without coat or hat. I was hand-cuffed. Around my ankles also were a pair of heavy fetters. One end of a chain was fastened to a large ring in the floor, the other to the fetters on my ankles. I tried in vain to stand upon my feet. Waking from such a painful trance, it was some time before I could collect my thoughts. Where was I? What was the meaning of these chains? Where were Brown and Hamilton? What had I done to deserve imprisonment in such a dungeon? I could not comprehend. There was a blank of some indefinite period, preceding my awakening in that lonely place, the events of which the utmost stretch of memory was unable to recall. I listened intently for some sign or sound of life, but nothing broke the oppressive silence, save the clinking of my chains, whenever I chanced to move. I spoke aloud, but the sound of my voice startled me. I felt of my pockets, so far as the fetters would allow—far enough, indeed, to ascertain that I had not only been robbed of liberty, but that my money and free papers were also gone! Then did the idea begin to

break upon my mind, at first dim and confused, that I had been kidnapped. But that I thought was incredible. There must have been
some misapprehension—some unfortunate mistake. It could not
be that a free citizen of New-York, who had wronged no man, nor
violated any law, should be dealt with thus inhumanly. The more I
contemplated my situation, however, the more I became confirmed
in my suspicions. It was a desolate thought, indeed. I felt there was
no trust or mercy in unfeeling man; and commending myself to the
God of the oppressed, bowed my head upon my fettered hands, and
wept most bitterly.

Chapter III.

PAINFUL MEDITATIONS—JAMES H. BURCH—WILLIAMS' SLAVE PEN IN
WASHINGTON—THE LACKEY, RADBURN—ASSERT MY FREEDOM—THE
ANGER OF THE TRADER—THE PADDLE AND CAT-O'-NINE-TAILS—THE
WHIPPING—NEW ACQUAINTANCES—RAY, WILLIAMS, AND RANDALL—
ARRIVAL OF LITTLE EMILY AND HER MOTHER IN THE PEN—MATERNAL
SORROWS—THE STORY OF ELIZA.

Some three hours elapsed, during which time I remained seated on
the low bench, absorbed in painful meditations. At length I heard the
crowing of a cock, and soon a distant rumbling sound, as of carriages
hurrying through the streets, came to my ears, and I knew that it was
day. No ray of light, however, penetrated my prison. Finally, I heard
footsteps immediately overhead, as of some one walking to and fro. It
occurred to me then that I must be in an underground apartment,
and the damp, mouldy odors of the place confirmed the supposition.
The noise above continued for at least an hour, when, at last, I heard
footsteps approaching from without. A key rattled in the lock—a
strong door swung back upon its hinges, admitting a flood of light,
and two men entered and stood before me. One of them was a large,
powerful man, forty years of age, perhaps, with dark, chestnut-colored
hair, slightly interspersed with gray. His face was full, his complexion
flush, his features grossly coarse, expressive of nothing but cruelty
and cunning. He was about five feet ten inches high, of full habit,[7]
and, without prejudice, I must be allowed to say, was a man whose
whole appearance was sinister and repugnant. His name was James H.
Burch, as I learned afterwards—a well-known slave-dealer in Washington; and then, or lately, connected in business, as a partner, with
Theophilus Freeman, of New-Orleans. The person who accompanied him was a simple lackey, named Ebenezer Radburn, who acted

7. Overweight.

merely in the capacity of turnkey. Both of these men still live in
Washington, or did, at the time of my return through that city from
slavery in January last.

The light admitted through the open door enabled me to observe
the room in which I was confined. It was about twelve feet square—
the walls of solid masonry. The floor was of heavy plank. There was
one small window, crossed with great iron bars, with an outside
shutter, securely fastened.

An iron-bound door led into an adjoining cell, or vault, wholly destitute of windows, or any means of admitting light. The furniture of
the room in which I was, consisted of the wooden bench on which I
sat, an old-fashioned, dirty box stove, and besides these, in either cell,
there was neither bed, nor blanket, nor any other thing whatever.
The door, through which Burch and Radburn entered, led through
a small passage, up a flight of steps into a yard, surrounded by a brick
wall ten or twelve feet high, immediately in rear of a building of the
same width as itself. The yard extended rearward from the house
about thirty feet. In one part of the wall there was a strongly ironed
door, opening into a narrow, covered passage, leading along one side
of the house into the street. The doom of the colored man, upon
whom the door leading out of that narrow passage closed, was
sealed. The top of the wall supported one end of a roof, which
ascended inwards, forming a kind of open shed. Underneath the roof
there was a crazy loft all round, where slaves, if so disposed, might
sleep at night, or in inclement weather seek shelter from the storm.
It was like a farmer's barnyard in most respects, save it was so constructed that the outside world could never see the human cattle that
were herded there.

The building to which the yard was attached, was two stories
high, fronting on one of the public streets of Washington. Its outside presented only the appearance of a quiet private residence. A
stranger looking at it, would never have dreamed of its execrable
uses. Strange as it may seem, within plain sight of this same house,
looking down from its commanding height upon it, was the Capitol.
The voices of patriotic representatives boasting of freedom and equality, and the rattling of the poor slave's chains, almost commingled.
A slave pen within the very shadow of the Capitol!

Such is a correct description as it was in 1841, of Williams' slave
pen in Washington, in one of the cellars of which I found myself so
unaccountably confined.

"Well, my boy, how do you feel now?" said Burch, as he entered
through the open door. I replied that I was sick, and inquired the
cause of my imprisonment. He answered that I was his slave—that
he had bought me, and that he was about to send me to New-Orleans.

I asserted, aloud and boldly, that I was a free man—a resident of Saratoga, where I had a wife and children, who were also free, and that my name was Northup. I complained bitterly of the strange treatment I had received, and threatened, upon my liberation, to have satisfaction for the wrong. He denied that I was free, and with an emphatic oath, declared that I came from Georgia. Again and again I asserted I was no man's slave, and insisted upon his taking off my chains at once. He endeavored to hush me, as if he feared my voice would be overheard. But I would not be silent, and denounced the authors of my imprisonment, whoever they might be, as unmitigated villains. Finding he could not quiet me, he flew into a towering passion. With blasphemous oaths, he called me a black liar, a runaway from Georgia, and every other profane and vulgar epithet that the most indecent fancy could conceive.

During this time Radburn was standing silently by. His business was, to oversee this human, or rather inhuman stable, receiving slaves, feeding and whipping them, at the rate of two shillings a head per day. Turning to him, Burch ordered the paddle and cat-o'-ninetails to be brought in. He disappeared, and in a few moments returned with these instruments of torture. The paddle, as it is termed in slave-beating parlance, or at least the one with which I first became acquainted, and of which I now speak, was a piece of hardwood board, eighteen or twenty inches long, moulded to the shape of an old-fashioned pudding stick, or ordinary oar. The flattened portion, which was about the size in circumference of two open hands, was bored with a small auger in numerous places. The cat was a large rope of many strands—the strands unraveled, and a knot tied at the extremity of each.

As soon as these formidable whips appeared, I was seized by both of them, and roughly divested of my clothing. My feet, as has been stated, were fastened to the floor. Drawing me over the bench, face downwards, Radburn placed his heavy foot upon the fetters, between my wrists, holding them painfully to the floor. With the paddle, Burch commenced beating me. Blow after blow was inflicted upon my naked body. When his unrelenting arm grew tired, he stopped and asked if I still insisted I was a free man. I did insist upon it, and then the blows were renewed, faster and more energetically, if possible, than before. When again tired, he would repeat the same question, and receiving the same answer, continue his cruel labor. All this time, the incarnate devil was uttering most fiendish oaths. At length the paddle broke, leaving the useless handle in his hand. Still I would not yield. All his brutal blows could not force from my lips the foul lie that I was a slave. Casting madly on the floor the handle of the broken paddle, he seized the rope. This was far more painful than the other. I struggled with all my power, but it was in vain. I

SCENE IN THE SLAVE PEN AT WASHINGTON.

Courtesy of the UNC–CH Library, The University of North Carolina at Chapel Hill.

prayed for mercy, but my prayer was only answered with imprecations and with stripes. I thought I must die beneath the lashes of
the accursed brute. Even now the flesh crawls upon my bones, as I
recall the scene. I was all on fire. My sufferings I can compare to
nothing else than the burning agonies of hell!

At last I became silent to his repeated questions. I would make
no reply. In fact, I was becoming almost unable to speak. Still he
plied the lash without stint upon my poor body, until it seemed that
the lacerated flesh was stripped from my bones at every stroke. A
man with a particle of mercy in his soul would not have beaten
even a dog so cruelly. At length Radburn said that it was useless to
whip me any more—that I would be sore enough. Thereupon, Burch
desisted, saying, with an admonitory shake of his fist in my face,
and hissing the words through his firm-set teeth, that if ever I dared
to utter again that I was entitled to my freedom, that I had been
kidnapped, or any thing whatever of the kind, the castigation I had
just received was nothing in comparison with what would follow.
He swore that he would either conquer or kill me. With these con-
solatory words, the fetters were taken from my wrists, my feet still
remaining fastened to the ring; the shutter of the little barred window, which had been opened, was again closed, and going out,
locking the great door behind them, I was left in darkness as before.

In an hour, perhaps two, my heart leaped to my throat, as the key
rattled in the door again. I, who had been so lonely, and who had
longed so ardently to see some one, I cared not who, now shuddered
at the thought of man's approach. A human face was fearful to me,
especially a white one. Radburn entered, bringing with him, on a
tin plate, a piece of shriveled fried pork, a slice of bread and a cup
of water. He asked me how I felt, and remarked that I had received
a pretty severe flogging. He remonstrated with me against the propriety of asserting my freedom. In rather a patronizing and confi-
dential manner, he gave it to me as his advice, that the less I said on
that subject the better it would be for me. The man evidently endeavored to appear kind—whether touched at the sight of my sad condition, or with the view of silencing, on my part, any further expression
of my rights, it is not necessary now to conjecture. He unlocked the
fetters from my ankles, opened the shutters of the little window,
and departed, leaving me again alone.

By this time I had become stiff and sore; my body was covered
with blisters, and it was with great pain and difficulty that I could
move. From the window I could observe nothing but the roof resting
on the adjacent wall. At night I laid down upon the damp, hard floor,
without any pillow or covering whatever. Punctually, twice a day,
Radburn came in, with his pork, and bread, and water. I had but
little appetite, though I was tormented with continual thirst. My

wounds would not permit me to remain but a few minutes in any one position; so, sitting, or standing, or moving slowly round, I passed the days and nights. I was heart sick and discouraged. Thoughts of my family, of my wife and children, continually occupied my mind. When sleep overpowered me I dreamed of them—dreamed I was again in Saratoga—that I could see their faces, and hear their voices calling me. Awakening from the pleasant phantasms of sleep to the bitter realities around me, I could but groan and weep. Still my spirit was not broken. I indulged the anticipation of escape, and that speedily. It was impossible, I reasoned, that men could be so unjust as to detain me as a slave, when the truth of my case was known. Burch, ascertaining I was no runaway from Georgia, would certainly let me go. Though suspicions of Brown and Hamilton were not unfrequent, I could not reconcile myself to the idea that they were instrumental to my imprisonment. Surely they would seek me out—they would deliver me from thraldom. Alas! I had not then learned the measure of "man's inhumanity to man,"[8] nor to what limitless extent of wickedness he will go for the love of gain.

In the course of several days the outer door was thrown open, allowing me the liberty of the yard. There I found three slaves—one of them a lad of ten years, the others young men of about twenty and twenty-five. I was not long in forming an acquaintance, and learning their names and the particulars of their history.

The eldest was a colored man named Clemens Ray. He had lived in Washington; had driven a hack, and worked in a livery stable there for a long time. He was very intelligent, and fully comprehended his situation. The thought of going south overwhelmed him with grief. Burch had purchased him a few days before, and had placed him there until such time as he was ready to send him to the New-Orleans market. From him I learned for the first time that I was in William's Slave Pen, a place I had never heard of previously. He described to me the uses for which it was designed. I repeated to him the particulars of my unhappy story, but he could only give me the consolation of his sympathy. He also advised me to be silent henceforth on the subject of my freedom; for, knowing the character of Burch, he assured me that it would only be attended with renewed whipping. The next eldest was named John Williams. He was raised in Virginia, not far from Washington. Burch had taken him in payment of a debt, and he constantly entertained the hope that his master would redeem him—a hope that was subsequently realized. The lad was a sprightly child, that answered to the name of Randall. Most of the time he was playing about the yard, but

8. From the closing lines of Robert Burns's 1784 poem "Man Was Made to Mourn": "man's inhumanity to man / makes countless thousands mourn."

occasionally would cry, calling for his mother, and wondering when she would come. His mother's absence seemed to be the great and only grief in his little heart. He was too young to realize his condition, and when the memory of his mother was not in his mind, he amused us with his pleasant pranks.

At night, Ray, Williams, and the boy, slept in the loft of the shed, while I was locked in the cell. Finally we were each provided with blankets, such as are used upon horses—the only bedding I was allowed to have for twelve years afterwards. Ray and Williams asked me many questions about New-York—how colored people were treated there; how they could have homes and families of their own, with none to disturb and oppress them; and Ray, especially, sighed continually for freedom. Such conversations, however, were not in the hearing of Burch, or the keeper Radburn. Aspirations such as these would have brought down the lash upon our backs.

It is necessary in this narrative, in order to present a full and truthful statement of all the principal events in the history of my life, and to portray the institution of Slavery as I have seen and known it, to speak of well-known places, and of many persons who are yet living. I am, and always was, an entire stranger in Washington and its vicinity—aside from Burch and Radburn, knowing no man there, except as I have heard of them through my enslaved companions. What I am about to say, if false, can be easily contradicted.

I remained in Williams' slave pen about two weeks. The night previous to my departure a woman was brought in, weeping bitterly, and leading by the hand a little child. They were Randall's mother and half-sister. On meeting them he was overjoyed, clinging to her dress, kissing the child, and exhibiting every demonstration of delight. The mother also clasped him in her arms, embraced him tenderly, and gazed at him fondly through her tears, calling him by many an endearing name.

Emily, the child, was seven or eight years old, of light complexion, and with a face of admirable beauty. Her hair fell in curls around her neck, while the style and richness of her dress, and the neatness of her whole appearance indicated she had been brought up in the midst of wealth. She was a sweet child indeed. The woman also was arrayed in silk, with rings upon her fingers, and golden ornaments suspended from her ears. Her air and manners, the correctness and propriety of her language—all showed, evidently, that she had sometime stood above the common level of a slave. She seemed to be amazed at finding herself in such a place as that. It was plainly a sudden and unexpected turn of fortune that had brought her there. Filling the air with her complainings, she was hustled, with the children and myself, into the cell. Language can convey but an inadequate impression of the lamentations to which she gave

incessant utterance. Throwing herself upon the floor, and encir-
cling the children in her arms, she poured forth such touching words
as only maternal love and kindness can suggest. They nestled
closely to her, as if *there* only was there any safety or protection. At
last they slept, their heads resting upon her lap. While they slum-
bered, she smoothed the hair back from their little foreheads, and
talked to them all night long. She called them her darlings—her
sweet babes—poor innocent things, that knew not the misery they
were destined to endure. Soon they would have no mother to comfort them—they would be taken from her. What would become of
them? Oh! she could not live away from her little Emmy and her
dear boy. They had always been good children, and had such loving
ways. It would break her heart, God knew, she said, if they were taken
from her; and yet she knew they meant to sell them, and, may be,
they would be separated, and could never see each other any more. It
was enough to melt a heart of stone to listen to the pitiful expressions
of that desolate and distracted mother. Her name was Eliza; and this
was the story of her life, as she afterwards related it:

She was the slave of Elisha Berry, a rich man, living in the neighborhood of Washington. She was born, I think she said, on his
plantation. Years before, he had fallen into dissipated habits, and
quarreled with his wife. In fact, soon after the birth of Randall,
they separated. Leaving his wife and daughter in the house they
had always occupied, he erected a new one near by, on the estate.
Into this house he brought Eliza; and, on condition of her living
with him, she and her children were to be emancipated. She resided
with him there nine years, with servants to attend upon her, and
provided with every comfort and luxury of life. Emily was his child!
Finally, her young mistress, who had always remained with her
mother at the homestead, married a Mr. Jacob Brooks. At length,
for some cause, (as I gathered from her relation,) beyond Berry's
control, a division of his property was made. She and her children
fell to the share of Mr. Brooks. During the nine years she had lived
with Berry, in consequence of the position she was compelled to
occupy, she and Emily had become the object of Mrs. Berry and
her daughter's hatred and dislike. Berry himself she represented as
a man of naturally a kind heart, who always promised her that she
should have her freedom, and who, she had no doubt, would grant
it to her then, if it were only in his power. As soon as they thus came
into the possession and control of the daughter, it became very manifest they would not live long together. The sight of Eliza seemed to
be odious to Mrs. Brooks; neither could she bear to look upon the
child, half-sister, and beautiful as she was!

The day she was led into the pen, Brooks had brought her from the
estate into the city, under pretence that the time had come when

her free papers were to be executed, in fulfillment of her master's promise. Elated at the prospect of immediate liberty, she decked herself and little Emmy in their best apparel, and accompanied him with a joyful heart. On their arrival in the city, instead of being baptized into the family of freemen, she was delivered to the trader Burch. The paper that was executed was a bill of sale. The hope of years was blasted in a moment. From the height* of most exulting happiness to the utmost depths of wretchedness, she had that day descended. No wonder that she wept, and filled the pen with wailings and expressions of heart-rending woe.

Eliza is now dead. Far up the Red River, where it pours its waters sluggishly through the unhealthy low lands of Louisiana, she rests in the grave at last—the only resting place of the poor slave! How all her fears were realized—how she mourned day and night, and never would be comforted—how, as she predicted, her heart did indeed break, with the burden of maternal sorrow, will be seen as the narrative proceeds.

Chapter IV.

ELIZA'S SORROWS—PREPARATION TO EMBARK—DRIVEN THROUGH
THE STREETS OF WASHINGTON—HAIL, COLUMBIA—THE TOMB OF
WASHINGTON—CLEM RAY—THE BREAKFAST ON THE STEAMER—THE
HAPPY BIRDS—AQUIA CREEK—FREDERICKSBURGH—ARRIVAL IN
RICHMOND—GOODIN AND HIS SLAVE PEN—ROBERT, OF
CINCINNATI—DAVID AND HIS WIFE—MARY AND LETHE—CLEM'S
RETURN—HIS SUBSEQUENT ESCAPE TO CANADA—THE BRIG
ORLEANS—JAMES H. BURCH.

At intervals during the first night of Eliza's incarceration in the pen, she complained bitterly of Jacob Brooks, her young mistress' husband. She declared that had she been aware of the deception he intended to practice upon her, he never would have brought her there alive. They had chosen the opportunity of getting her away when Master Berry was absent from the plantation. He had always been kind to her. She wished that she could see him; but she knew that even he was unable now to rescue her. Then would she commence weeping again—kissing the sleeping children—talking first to one, then to the other, as they lay in their unconscious slumbers, with their heads upon her lap. So wore the long night away; and when the morning dawned, and night had come again, still she kept mourning on, and would not be consoled.

* The transcriber changed "hight" to "height".

About midnight following, the cell door opened, and Burch and
Radburn entered, with lanterns in their hands. Burch, with an oath,
ordered us to roll up our blankets without delay, and get ready to go
on board the boat. He swore we would be left unless we hurried fast.
He aroused the children from their slumbers with a rough shake,
and said they were d—d sleepy, it appeared. Going out into the yard,
he called Clem Ray, ordering him to leave the loft and come into the
cell, and bring his blanket with him. When Clem appeared, he placed
us side by side, and fastened us together with hand-cuffs—my left
hand to his right. John Williams had been taken out a day or two
before, his master having redeemed him, greatly to his delight. Clem
and I were ordered to march, Eliza and the children following. We
were conducted into the yard, from thence into the covered passage,
and up a flight of steps through a side door into the upper room,
where I had heard the walking to and fro. Its furniture was a stove, a
few old chairs, and a long table, covered with papers. It was a white-
washed room, without any carpet on the floor, and seemed a sort of
office. By one of the windows, I remember, hung a rusty sword,
which attracted my attention. Burch's trunk was there. In obedience
to his orders, I took hold of one of its handles with my unfettered
hand, while he taking hold of the other, we proceeded out of the
front door into the street in the same order as we had left the cell.

It was a dark night. All was quiet. I could see lights, or the reflection of them, over towards Pennsylvania Avenue, but there was no
one, not even a straggler, to be seen. I was almost resolved to attempt
to break away. Had I not been hand-cuffed the attempt would certainly have been made, whatever consequence might have followed.
Radburn was in the rear, carrying a large stick, and hurrying up the
children as fast as the little ones could walk. So we passed, hand-
cuffed and in silence, through the streets of Washington—through
the Capital of a nation, whose theory of government, we are told,
rests on the foundation of man's inalienable right to life, liberty, and
the pursuit of happiness! Hail! Columbia,[9] happy land, indeed!

Reaching the steamboat, we were quickly hustled into the hold,
among barrels and boxes of freight. A colored servant brought a
light, the bell rung, and soon the vessel started down the Potomac,
carrying us we knew not where. The bell tolled as we passed the tomb
of Washington! Burch, no doubt, with uncovered head, bowed rev-
erently before the sacred ashes of the man who devoted his illustri-
ous life to the liberty of his country.

None of us slept that night but Randall and little Emmy. For the
first time Clem Ray was wholly overcome. To him the idea of going
south was terrible in the extreme. He was leaving the friends and

9. Traditional name for the United States, after Christopher Columbus.

associations of his youth—every thing that was dear and precious to his heart—in all probability never to return. He and Eliza mingled their tears together, bemoaning their cruel fate. For my own part, difficult as it was, I endeavored to keep up my spirits. I resolved in my mind a hundred plans of escape, and fully determined to make the attempt the first desperate chance that offered. I had by this time become satisfied, however, that my true policy was to say nothing further on the subject of my having been born a freeman. It would but expose me to maltreatment, and diminish the chances of liberation.

After sunrise in the morning we were called up on deck to breakfast. Burch took our hand-cuffs off, and we sat down to table. He asked Eliza if she would take a dram. She declined, thanking him politely. During the meal we were all silent—not a word passed between us. A mulatto[1] woman who served at table seemed to take an interest in our behalf—told us to cheer up, and not to be so cast down. Breakfast over, the hand-cuffs were restored, and Burch ordered us out on the stern deck. We sat down together on some boxes, still saying nothing in Burch's presence. Occasionally a passenger would walk out to where we were, look at us for a while, then silently return.

It was a very pleasant morning. The fields along the river were covered with verdure, far in advance of what I had been accustomed to see at that season of the year. The sun shone out warmly; the birds were singing in the trees. The happy birds—I envied them. I wished for wings like them, that I might cleave the air to where my birdlings waited vainly for their father's coming, in the cooler region of the North.

In the forenoon the steamer reached Aquia Creek.[2] There the passengers took stages—Burch and his five slaves occupying one exclusively. He laughed with the children, and at one stopping place went so far as to purchase them a piece of gingerbread. He told me to hold up my head and look smart. That I might, perhaps, get a good master if I behaved myself. I made him no reply. His face was hateful to me, and I could not bear to look upon it. I sat in the corner, cherishing in my heart the hope, not yet extinct, of some day meeting the tyrant on the soil of my native State.

At Fredericksburgh we were transferred from the stage coach to a car, and before dark arrived in Richmond, the chief city of Virginia. At this city we were taken from the cars, and driven through the street to a slave pen, between the railroad depot and the river, kept by

1. Mixed-race.
2. Creek that meets the Potomac River at Aquia Landing. Steamers stopped there to transfer passengers to the Richmond, Fredericksburg, and Potomac train line that terminated at the landing.

a Mr. Goodin. This pen is similar to Williams' in Washington, except it is somewhat larger; and besides, there were two small houses standing at opposite corners within the yard. These houses are usually* found within slave yards, being used as rooms for the examination of human chattels by purchasers before concluding a bargain. Unsoundness in a slave, as well as in a horse, detracts materially from his value. If no warranty is given, a close examination is a matter of particular importance to the negro jockey.

We were met at the door of Goodin's yard by that gentleman himself—a short, fat man, with a round, plump face, black hair and whiskers, and a complexion almost as dark as some of his own negroes. He had a hard, stern look, and was perhaps about fifty years of age. Burch and he met with great cordiality. They were evidently old friends. Shaking each other warmly by the hand, Burch remarked he had brought some company, inquired at what time the brig would leave, and was answered that it would probably leave the next day at such an hour. Goodin then turned to me, took hold of my arm, turned me partly round, looked at me sharply with the air of one who considered himself a good judge of property, and as if estimating in his own mind about how much I was worth.

"Well, boy, where did you come from?"

Forgetting myself, for a moment, I answered, "From New-York."

"New-York! H—l! what have you been doing up there?" was his astonished interrogatory.

Observing Burch at this moment looking at me with an angry expression that conveyed a meaning it was not difficult to understand, I immediately said, "O, I have only been up that way a piece," in a manner intended to imply that although I might have been as far as New-York, yet I wished it distinctly understood that I did not belong to that free State, nor to any other.

Goodin then turned to Clem, and then to Eliza and the children, examining them severally, and asking various questions. He was pleased with Emily, as was every one who saw the child's sweet countenance. She was not as tidy as when I first beheld her; her hair was now somewhat disheveled; but through its unkempt and soft profusion there still beamed a little face of most surpassing loveliness. "Altogether we were a fair lot—a devilish good lot," he said, enforcing that opinion with more than one emphatic adjective not found in the Christian vocabulary. Thereupon we passed into the yard. Quite a number of slaves, as many as thirty I should say, were moving about, or sitting on benches under the shed. They were all cleanly dressed—the men with hats, the women with handkerchiefs tied about their heads.

---

* The transcriber changed "susually" to "usually".

Burch and Goodin, after separating from us, walked up the steps at the back part of the main building, and sat down upon the door sill. They entered into conversation, but the subject of it I could not hear. Presently Burch came down into the yard, unfettered me, and led me into one of the small houses.

"You told that man you came from New-York," said he.

I replied, "I told him I had been up as far as New-York, to be sure, but did not tell him I belonged there, nor that I was a freeman. I meant no harm at all, Master Burch. I would not have said it had I thought."

He looked at me a moment as if he was ready to devour me, then turning round went out. In a few minutes he returned. "If ever I hear you say a word about New-York, or about your freedom, I will be the death of you—I will kill you; you may rely on that," he ejaculated fiercely.

I doubt not he understood then better than I did, the danger and the penalty of selling a free man into slavery. He felt the necessity of closing my mouth against the crime he knew he was committing. Of course, my life would not have weighed a feather, in any emergency requiring such a sacrifice. Undoubtedly, he meant precisely what he said.

Under the shed on one side of the yard, there was constructed a rough table, while overhead were sleeping lofts—the same as in the pen at Washington. After partaking at this table of our supper of pork and bread, I was hand-cuffed to a large yellow[3] man, quite stout and fleshy, with a countenance expressive of the utmost melancholy. He was a man of intelligence and information. Chained together, it was not long before we became acquainted with each other's history. His name was Robert. Like myself, he had been born free, and had a wife and two children in Cincinnati. He said he had come south with two men, who had hired him in the city of his residence. Without free papers, he had been seized at Fredericksburgh, placed in confinement, and beaten until he had learned, as I had, the necessity and the policy of silence. He had been in Goodin's pen about three weeks. To this man I became much attached. We could sympathize with, and understand each other. It was with tears and a heavy heart, not many days subsequently, that I saw him die, and looked for the last time upon his lifeless form!

Robert and myself, with Clem, Eliza and her children, slept that night upon our blankets, in one of the small houses in the yard. There were four others, all from the same plantation, who had been sold, and were now on their way south, who also occupied it with us. David and his wife, Caroline, both mulattoes, were exceedingly

3. Contemporary term for a light-skinned black person of mixed ancestry.

affected. They dreaded the thought of being put into the cane and cotton fields; but their greatest source of anxiety was the apprehension of being separated. Mary, a tall, lithe girl, of a most jetty black, was listless and apparently indifferent. Like many of the class, she scarcely knew there was such a word as freedom. Brought up in the ignorance of a brute, she possessed but little more than a brute's intelligence. She was one of those, and there are very many, who fear nothing but their master's lash, and know no further duty than to obey his voice. The other was Lethe. She was of an entirely different character. She had long, straight hair, and bore more the appearance of an Indian than a negro woman. She had sharp and spiteful eyes, and continually gave utterance to the language of hatred and revenge. Her husband had been sold. She knew not where she was. An exchange of masters, she was sure, could not be for the worse. She cared not whither they might carry her. Pointing to the scars upon her face, the desperate creature wished that she might see the day when she could wipe them off in some man's blood!

While we were thus learning the history of each other's wretchedness, Eliza was seated in a corner by herself, singing hymns and praying for her children. Wearied from the loss of so much sleep, I could no longer bear up against the advances of that "sweet restorer,"[4] and laying down by the side of Robert, on the floor, soon forgot my troubles, and slept until the dawn of day.

In the morning, having swept the yard, and washed ourselves, under Goodin's superintendence, we were ordered to roll up our blankets, and make ready for the continuance of our journey. Clem Ray was informed that he would go no further, Burch, for some cause, having concluded to carry him back to Washington. He was much rejoiced. Shaking hands, we parted in the slave pen at Richmond, and I have not seen him since. But, much to my surprise, since my return, I learned that he had escaped from bondage, and on his way to the free soil of Canada, lodged one night at the house of my brother-in-law in Saratoga, informing my family of the place and the condition in which he left me.

In the afternoon we were drawn up, two abreast, Robert and myself in advance, and in this order, driven by Burch and Goodin from the yard, through the streets of Richmond to the brig Orleans. She was a vessel of respectable size, full rigged, and freighted principally with tobacco. We were all on board by five o'clock. Burch brought us each a tin cup and a spoon. There were forty of us in the brig, being all, except Clem, that were in the pen.

4. From "Night Thoughts," by the English poet Edward Young (1683–1765): "Tired nature's sweet restorer, balmy sleep!"

With a small pocket knife that had not been taken from me, I began cutting the initials of my name upon the tin cup. The others immediately flocked round me, requesting me to mark theirs in a similar manner. In time, I gratified them all, of which they did not appear to be forgetful.

We were all stowed away in the hold at night, and the hatch barred down. We laid on boxes, or where-ever there was room enough to stretch our blankets on the floor.

Burch accompanied us no farther than Richmond, returning from that point to the capital with Clem. Not until the lapse of almost twelve years, to wit, in January last, in the Washington police office, did I set my eyes upon his face again.

James H. Burch was a slave-trader—buying men, women and children at low prices, and selling them at an advance. He was a speculator in human flesh—a disreputable calling—and so considered at the South. For the present he disappears from the scenes recorded in this narrative, but he will appear again before its close, not in the character of a man-whipping tyrant, but as an arrested, cringing criminal in a court of law, that failed to do him justice.

Chapter V.

ARRIVAL AT NORFOLK—FREDERICK AND MARIA—ARTHUR, THE FREEMAN—APPOINTED STEWARD—JIM, CUFFEE, AND JENNY—THE STORM—BAHAMA BANKS—THE CALM—THE CONSPIRACY—THE LONG BOAT—THE SMALL-POX—DEATH OF ROBERT—MANNING, THE SAILOR—THE MEETING IN THE FORECASTLE—THE LETTER—ARRIVAL AT NEW-ORLEANS—ARTHUR'S RESCUE—THEOPHILUS FREEMAN, THE CONSIGNEE—PLATT—FIRST NIGHT IN THE NEW-ORLEANS SLAVE PEN.

After we were all on board, the brig Orleans proceeded down James River. Passing into Chesapeake Bay, we arrived next day opposite the city of Norfolk. While lying at anchor, a lighter[5] approached us from the town, bringing four more slaves. Frederick, a boy of eighteen, had been born a slave, as also had Henry, who was some years older. They had both been house servants in the city. Maria was a rather genteel looking colored girl, with a faultless form, but ignorant and extremely vain. The idea of going to New-Orleans was pleasing to her. She entertained an extravagantly high opinion of her own attractions. Assuming a haughty mien, she declared to her companions, that immediately on our arrival in New-Orleans, she had no

5. Type of barge for carrying freight.

doubt, some wealthy single gentleman of good taste would purchase her at once!

But the most prominent of the four, was a man named Arthur. As the lighter approached, he struggled stoutly with his keepers. It was with main force that he was dragged aboard the brig. He protested, in a loud voice, against the treatment he was receiving, and demanded to be released. His face was swollen, and covered with wounds and bruises, and, indeed, one side of it was a complete raw sore. He was forced, with all haste, down the hatchway into the hold. I caught an outline of his story as he was borne struggling along, of which he afterwards gave me a more full relation, and it was as follows: He had long resided in the city of Norfolk, and was a free man. He had a family living there, and was a mason by trade. Having been unusually detained, he was returning late one night to his house in the suburbs of the city, when he was attacked by a gang of persons in an unfrequented street. He fought until his strength failed him. Overpowered at last, he was gagged and bound with ropes, and beaten, until he became insensible. For several days they secreted him in the slave pen at Norfolk—a very common establishment, it appears, in the cities of the South. The night before, he had been taken out and put on board the lighter, which, pushing out from shore, had awaited our arrival. For some time he continued his protestations, and was altogether irreconcilable. At length, however, he became silent. He sank into a gloomy and thoughtful mood, and appeared to be counseling with himself. There was in the man's determined face, something that suggested the thought of desperation.

After leaving Norfolk the hand-cuffs were taken off, and during the day we were allowed to remain on deck. The captain selected Robert as his waiter, and I was appointed to superintend the cooking department, and the distribution of food and water. I had three assistants, Jim, Cuffee and Jenny. Jenny's business was to prepare the coffee, which consisted of corn meal scorched in a kettle, boiled and sweetened with molasses. Jim and Cuffee baked the hoe-cake and boiled the bacon.

Standing by a table, formed of a wide board resting on the heads of the barrels, I cut and handed to each a slice of meat and a "dodger" of the bread, and from Jenny's kettle also dipped out for each a cup of the coffee. The use of plates was dispensed with, and their sable fingers took the place of knives and forks. Jim and Cuffee were very demure and attentive to business, somewhat inflated with their situation as second cooks, and without doubt feeling that there was a great responsibility resting on them. I was called steward—a name given me by the captain.

The slaves were fed twice a day, at ten and five o'clock—always receiving the same kind and quantity of fare, and in the same manner as above described. At night we were driven into the hold, and securely fastened down.

Scarcely were we out of sight of land before we were overtaken by a violent storm. The brig rolled and plunged until we feared she would go down. Some were sea-sick, others on their knees praying, while some were fast holding to each other, paralyzed with fear. The sea-sickness rendered the place of our confinement loathsome and disgusting. It would have been a happy thing for most of us—it would have saved the agony of many hundred lashes, and miserable deaths at last—had the compassionate sea snatched us that day from the clutches of remorseless men. The thought of Randall and little Emmy sinking down among the monsters of the deep, is a more pleasant contemplation than to think of them as they are now, perhaps, dragging out lives of unrequited toil.

When in sight of the Bahama Banks, at a place called Old Point Compass, or the Hole in the Wall, we were becalmed three days. There was scarcely a breath of air. The waters of the gulf presented a singularly white appearance, like lime water.

In the order of events, I come now to the relation of an occurrence, which I never call to mind but with sensations of regret. I thank God, who has since permitted me to escape from the thralldom of slavery, that through his merciful interposition I was prevented from imbruing my hands in the blood of his creatures. Let not those who have never been placed in like circumstances, judge me harshly. Until they have been chained and beaten—until they find themselves in the situation I was, borne away from home and family towards a land of bondage—let them refrain from saying what they would not do for liberty. How far I should have been justified in the sight of God and man, it is unnecessary now to speculate upon. It is enough to say that I am able to congratulate myself upon the harmless termination of an affair which threatened, for a time, to be attended with serious results.

Towards evening, on the first day of the calm, Arthur and myself were in the bow of the vessel, seated on the windlass. We were conversing together of the probable destiny that awaited us, and mourning together over our misfortunes. Arthur said, and I agreed with him, that death was far less terrible than the living prospect that was before us. For a long time we talked of our children, our past lives, and of the probabilities of escape. Obtaining possession of the brig was suggested by one of us. We discussed the possibility of our being able, in such an event, to make our way to the harbor of New-York. I knew little of the compass; but the idea of risking the experiment was eagerly entertained. The chances, for and against us, in an encounter with the crew, was canvassed. Who could be relied upon, and who could not, the proper time and manner of the attack, were all talked over and over again. From the moment the plot suggested itself I began to hope. I revolved it constantly in my mind. As difficulty after difficulty arose, some ready conceit was at hand, demonstrating how it could be overcome. While others slept, Arthur and I were maturing our plans. At length, with much caution, Robert was gradually made acquainted with our intentions. He approved of them at once, and entered into the conspiracy with a zealous spirit. There was not another slave we dared to trust. Brought up in fear and ignorance as they are, it can scarcely be conceived how servilely they will cringe before a white man's look. It was not safe to deposit so bold a secret with any of them, and finally we three resolved to take upon ourselves alone the fearful responsibility of the attempt.

At night, as has been said, we were driven into the hold, and the hatch barred down. How to reach the deck was the first difficulty that presented itself. On the bow of the brig, however, I had observed the small boat lying bottom upwards. It occurred to me that by secreting ourselves underneath it, we would not be missed from the crowd, as they were hurried down into the hold at night. I was selected to make the experiment, in order to satisfy ourselves of its feasibility. The next evening, accordingly, after supper, watching my opportunity, I hastily concealed myself beneath it. Lying close upon the deck, I could see what was going on around me, while wholly unperceived myself. In the morning, as they came up, I slipped from my hiding place without being observed. The result was entirely satisfactory.

The captain and mate slept in the cabin of the former. From Robert, who had frequent occasion, in his capacity of waiter, to make observations in that quarter, we ascertained the exact position of their respective berths. He further informed us that there were always two pistols and a cutlass lying on the table. The crew's cook slept in the cook galley on deck, a sort of vehicle on wheels, that could be moved about as convenience required, while the sailors, numbering only six, either slept in the forecastle, or in hammocks swung among the rigging.

Finally our arrangements were all completed. Arthur and I were to steal silently to the captain's cabin, seize the pistols and cutlass, and as quickly as possible despatch him and the mate. Robert, with a club, was to stand by the door leading from the deck down into the cabin, and, in case of necessity, beat back the sailors, until we could hurry to his assistance. We were to proceed then as circumstances might require. Should the attack be so sudden and successful as to prevent resistance, the hatch was to remain barred down; otherwise the slaves were to be called up, and in the crowd, and hurry, and confusion of the time, we resolved to regain our liberty or lose our lives. I was then to assume the unaccustomed place of pilot, and, steering northward, we trusted that some lucky wind might bear us to the soil of freedom.

The mate's name was Biddee, the captain's I cannot now recall, though I rarely ever forget a name once heard. The captain was a small, genteel man, erect and prompt, with a proud bearing, and looked the personification of courage. If he is still living, and these pages should chance to meet his eye, he will learn a fact connected with the voyage of the brig, from Richmond to New-Orleans, in 1841, not entered on his log-book.

We were all prepared, and impatiently waiting an opportunity of putting our designs into execution, when they were frustrated by a sad and unforeseen event. Robert was taken ill. It was soon announced that he had the small-pox. He continued to grow worse, and four days previous to our arrival in New-Orleans he died. One of the sailors sewed him in his blanket, with a large stone from the ballast at his feet, and then laying him on a hatchway, and elevating it with tackles above the railing, the inanimate body of poor Robert was consigned to the white waters of the gulf.

We were all panic-stricken by the appearance of the small-pox. The captain ordered lime[6] to be scattered through the hold, and other prudent precautions to be taken. The death of Robert, however, and the presence of the malady, oppressed me sadly, and I gazed out over the great waste of waters with a spirit that was indeed disconsolate.

An evening or two after Robert's burial, I was leaning on the hatch-way near the forecastle, full of desponding thoughts, when a sailor in a kind voice asked me why I was so down-hearted. The tone and manner of the man assured me, and I answered, because I was a freeman, and had been kidnapped. He remarked that it was enough to make any one down-hearted, and continued to interrogate me until he learned the particulars of my whole history. He was evidently much interested in my behalf, and, in the blunt speech of a sailor, swore he would aid me all he could, if it "split his timbers." I requested him to furnish me pen, ink and paper, in order that I might write to some of my friends. He promised to obtain them—but how I could use them undiscovered was a difficulty. If I could only get into the forecastle while his watch was off, and the other sailors asleep, the thing could be accomplished. The small boat instantly occurred to me. He thought we were not far from the Balize, at the mouth of the Mississippi, and it was necessary that the letter be written soon, or the opportunity would be lost. Accordingly, by

6. Powder sometimes used as a disinfectant.

arrangement, I managed the next night to secret myself again under the long-boat.[7] His watch was off at twelve. I saw him pass into the forecastle, and in about an hour followed him. He was nodding over a table, half asleep, on which a sickly light was flickering, and on which also was a pen and sheet of paper. As I entered he aroused, beckoned me to a seat beside him, and pointed to the paper. I directed the letter to Henry B. Northup, of Sandy Hill—stating that I had been kidnapped, was then on board the brig Orleans, bound for New-Orleans; that it was then impossible for me to conjecture my ultimate destination, and requesting he would take measures to rescue me. The letter was sealed and directed, and Manning, having read it, promised to deposit it in the New-Orleans post-office. I hastened back to my place under the long-boat, and in the morning, as the slaves came up and were walking round, crept out unnoticed and mingled with them.

My good friend, whose name was John Manning, was an Englishman by birth, and a noble-hearted, generous sailor as ever walked a deck. He had lived in Boston—was a tall, well-built man, about twenty-four years old, with a face somewhat pock-marked, but full of benevolent expression.

Nothing to vary the monotony of our daily life occurred, until we reached New-Orleans. On coming to the levee, and before the vessel was made fast, I saw Manning leap on shore and hurry away into the city. As he started off he looked back over his shoulder significantly, giving me to understand the object of his errand. Presently he returned, and passing close by me, hunched me with his elbow, with a peculiar wink, as much as to say, "it is all right."

The letter, as I have since learned, reached Sandy Hill. Mr. Northup visited Albany and laid it before Governor Seward,[8] but inasmuch as it gave no definite information as to my probable locality, it was not, at that time, deemed advisable to institute measures for my liberation. It was concluded to delay, trusting that a knowledge of where I was might eventually be obtained.

A happy and touching scene was witnessed immediately upon our reaching the levee. Just as Manning left the brig, on his way to the post-office, two men came up and called aloud for Arthur. The latter, as he recognized them, was almost crazy with delight. He could hardly be restrained from leaping over the brig's side; and when they met soon after, he grasped them by the hand, and clung to them a long, long time. They were men from Norfolk, who had come on

---

7. Large ships carried smaller boats that could be used for repair, rescue, and other purposes requiring the transfer of a small number of people or freight. Longboats like the one that Northup hides under would typically hold eight to ten oarsmen.
8. William Henry Seward (1801–1872), then Governor of New York and later United States Secretary of State.

to New-Orleans to rescue him. His kidnappers, they informed him, had been arrested, and were then confined in the Norfolk prison. They conversed a few moments with the captain, and then departed with the rejoicing Arthur.

But in all the crowd that thronged the wharf, there was no one who knew or cared for me. Not one. No familiar voice greeted my ears, nor was there a single face that I had ever seen. Soon Arthur would rejoin his family, and have the satisfaction of seeing his wrongs avenged: my family, alas, should I ever see them more? There was a feeling of utter desolation in my heart, filling it with a despairing and regretful sense, that I had not gone down with Robert to the bottom of the sea.

Very soon traders and consignees came on board. One, a tall, thin-faced man, with light complexion and a little bent, made his appearance, with a paper in his hand. Burch's gang, consisting of myself, Eliza and her children, Harry, Lethe, and some others, who had joined us at Richmond, were consigned to him. This gentleman was Mr. Theophilus Freeman. Reading from his paper, he called, "Platt." No one answered. The name was called again and again, but still there was no reply. Then Lethe was called, then Eliza, then Harry, until the list was finished, each one stepping forward as his or her name was called.

"Captain, where's Platt?" demanded Theophilus Freeman.

The captain was unable to inform him, no one being on board answering to that name.

"Who shipped *that* nigger?" he again inquired of the captain, pointing to me.

"Burch," replied the captain.

"Your name is Platt—you answer my description. Why don't you come forward?" he demanded of me, in an angry tone.

I informed him that was not my name; that I had never been called by it, but that I had no objection to it as I knew of.

"Well, I will learn you your name," said he; "and so you won't forget it either, by ——," he added.

Mr. Theophilus Freeman, by the way, was not a whit behind his partner, Burch, in the matter of blasphemy. On the vessel I had gone by the name of "Steward," and this was the first time I had ever been designated as Platt—the name forwarded by Burch to his consignee. From the vessel I observed the chain-gang at work on the levee. We passed near them as we were driven to Freeman's slave pen. This pen is very similar to Goodin's in Richmond, except the yard was enclosed by plank, standing upright, with ends sharpened, instead of brick walls.

Including us, there were now at least fifty in this pen. Depositing our blankets in one of the small buildings in the yard, and having

been called up and fed, we were allowed to saunter about the enclo-
sure until night, when we wrapped our blankets round us and laid
down under the shed, or in the loft, or in the open yard, just as each
one preferred.

It was but a short time I closed my eyes that night. Thought was
busy in my brain. Could it be possible that I was thousands of miles
from home—that I had been driven through the streets like a dumb
beast—that I had been chained and beaten without mercy—that I
was even then herded with a drove of slaves, a slave myself? Were
the events of the last few weeks realities indeed?—or was I passing
only through the dismal phases of a long, protracted dream? It was
no illusion. My cup of sorrow was full to overflowing. Then I lifted up
my hands to God, and in the still watches of the night, surrounded
by the sleeping forms of my companions, begged for mercy on the
poor, forsaken captive. To the Almighty Father of us all—the freeman and the slave—I poured forth the supplications of a broken
spirit, imploring strength from on high to bear up against the burden of my troubles, until the morning light aroused the slumberers,
ushering in another day of bondage.

Chapter VI.

FREEMAN'S INDUSTRY—CLEANLINESS AND CLOTHES—EXERCISING IN
THE SHOW ROOM—THE DANCE—BOB, THE FIDDLER—ARRIVAL OF
CUSTOMERS—SLAVES EXAMINED—THE OLD GENTLEMAN OF
NEW-ORLEANS—SALE OF DAVID, CAROLINE AND LETHE—PARTING OF
RANDALL AND ELIZA—SMALL-POX—THE HOSPITAL—RECOVERY AND
RETURN TO FREEMAN'S SLAVE PEN—THE PURCHASER OF ELIZA,
HARRY, AND PLATT—ELIZA'S AGONY ON PARTING FROM LITTLE EMILY.

The very amiable, pious-hearted Mr. Theophilus Freeman, partner
or consignee of James H. Burch, and keeper of the slave pen in
New-Orleans, was out among his animals early in the morning. With
an occasional kick of the older men and women, and many a sharp
crack of the whip about the ears of the younger slaves, it was not
long before they were all astir, and wide awake. Mr. Theophilus
Freeman bustled about in a very industrious manner, getting his
property ready for the sales-room, intending, no doubt, to do that
day a rousing business.

In the first place we were required to wash thoroughly, and those
with beards, to shave. We were then furnished with a new suit each,
cheap, but clean. The men had hat, coat, shirt, pants and shoes; the
women frocks of calico, and handkerchiefs to bind about their
heads. We were now conducted into a large room in the front part

of the building to which the yard was attached, in order to be properly trained, before the admission of customers. The men were arranged on one side of the room, the women on the other. The tallest was placed at the head of the row, then the next tallest, and so on in the order of their respective heights. Emily was at the foot of the line of women. Freeman charged us to remember our places; exhorted us to appear smart and lively,—sometimes threatening, and again, holding out various inducements. During the day he exercised us in the art of "looking smart," and of moving to our places with exact precision.

After being fed, in the afternoon, we were again paraded and made to dance. Bob, a colored boy, who had some time belonged to Freeman, played on the violin. Standing near him, I made bold to inquire if he could play the "Virginia Reel." He answered he could not, and asked me if I could play. Replying in the affirmative, he handed me the violin. I struck up a tune, and finished it. Freeman ordered me to continue playing, and seemed well pleased, telling Bob that I far excelled him—a remark that seemed to grieve my musical companion very much.

Next day many customers called to examine Freeman's "new lot." The latter gentleman was very loquacious, dwelling at much length upon our several good points and qualities. He would make us hold up our heads, walk briskly back and forth, while customers would feel of our hands and arms and bodies, turn us about, ask us what we could do, make us open our mouths and show our teeth, precisely as a jockey examines a horse which he is about to barter for or purchase. Sometimes a man or woman was taken back to the small house in the yard, stripped, and inspected more minutely. Scars upon a slave's back were considered evidence of a rebellious or unruly spirit, and hurt his sale.

One old gentleman, who said he wanted a coachman, appeared to take a fancy to me. From his conversation with Burch, I learned he was a resident in the city. I very much desired that he would buy me, because I conceived it would not be difficult to make my escape from New-Orleans on some northern vessel. Freeman asked him fifteen hundred dollars for me. The old gentleman insisted it was too much, as times were very hard. Freeman, however, declared that I was sound and healthy, of a good constitution, and intelligent. He made it a point to enlarge upon my musical attainments. The old gentleman argued quite adroitly that there was nothing extraordinary about the nigger, and finally, to my regret, went out, saying he would call again. During the day, however, a number of sales were made. David and Caroline were purchased together by a Natchez planter. They left us, grinning broadly, and in the most happy state of mind, caused by the fact of their not being separated. Lethe was sold to a planter of Baton Rouge, her eyes flashing with anger as she was led away.

The same man also purchased Randall. The little fellow was made to jump, and run across the floor, and perform many other feats, exhibiting his activity and condition. All the time the trade was going on, Eliza was crying aloud, and wringing her hands. She besought the man not to buy him, unless he also bought herself and Emily. She promised, in that case, to be the most faithful slave that ever lived. The man answered that he could not afford it, and then Eliza burst into a paroxysm of grief, weeping plaintively. Freeman turned round to her, savagely, with his whip in his uplifted hand, ordering her to stop her noise, or he would flog her. He would not have such work—such snivelling; and unless she ceased that minute, he would take her to the yard and give her a hundred lashes. Yes, he would take the nonsense out of her pretty quick—if he didn't, might he be d—d. Eliza shrunk before him, and tried to wipe away her tears, but it was all in vain. She wanted to be with her children, she said, the little time she had to live. All the frowns and threats of Freeman, could not wholly silence the afflicted mother. She kept on begging and beseeching them, most piteously, not to separate the three. Over and over again she told them how she loved her boy. A great many times she repeated her former promises—how very faithful and obedient she would be; how hard she would labor day and night, to the last moment of her life, if he would only buy them all together. But it was of no avail; the man could not afford it. The bargain was agreed upon, and Randall must go alone. Then Eliza ran to him; embraced him passionately; kissed him again and again; told him to remember her—all the while her tears falling in the boy's face like rain.

Freeman damned her, calling her a blubbering, bawling wench, and ordered her to go to her place, and behave herself, and be somebody. He swore he wouldn't stand such stuff but a little longer. He would soon give her something to cry about, if she was not mighty careful, and *that* she might depend upon.

The planter from Baton Rouge, with his new purchases, was ready to depart.

"Don't cry, mama. I will be a good boy. Don't cry," said Randall, looking back, as they passed out of the door.

What has become of the lad, God knows. It was a mournful scene indeed. I would have cried myself if I had dared.

That night, nearly all who came in on the brig Orleans, were taken ill. They complained of violent pain in the head and back. Little Emily—a thing unusual with her—cried constantly. In the morning a physician was called in, but was unable to determine the nature of our complaint. While examining me, and asking questions touching my symptoms, I gave it as my opinion that it was an attack of small-pox—mentioning the fact of Robert's death as the reason of my belief. It might be so indeed, he thought, and he would send for the head physician of the hospital. Shortly, the head physician came—a small, light-haired man, whom they called Dr. Carr. He pronounced it small-pox, whereupon there was much alarm throughout the yard. Soon after Dr. Carr left, Eliza, Emmy, Harry and myself were put into a hack and driven to the hospital—a large white marble building, standing on the outskirts of the city. Harry and I were placed in a room in one of the upper stories. I became very sick. For three days I was entirely blind. While lying in this state one day, Bob came in, saying to Dr. Carr that Freeman had sent him over to inquire how we were getting on. Tell him, said the doctor, that Platt is very bad, but that if he survives until nine o'clock, he may recover.

I expected to die. Though there was little in the prospect before me worth living for, the near approach of death appalled me. I thought I could have been resigned to yield up my life in the bosom of my family, but to expire in the midst of strangers, under such circumstances, was a bitter reflection.

There were a great number in the hospital, of both sexes, and of all ages. In the rear of the building coffins were manufactured. When one died, the bell tolled—a signal to the undertaker to come and bear away the body to the potter's field.[9] Many times, each day and night, the tolling bell sent forth its melancholy voice, announcing another death. But my time had not yet come. The crisis having passed, I began to revive, and at the end of two weeks and two days, returned with Harry to the pen, bearing upon my face the effects of the malady, which to this day continues to disfigure it. Eliza and Emily were also brought back next day in a hack, and again were we paraded in the sales-room, for the inspection and examination of purchasers. I still indulged the hope that the old gentleman in search of a coachman would call again, as he had promised, and purchase me. In that event I felt an abiding confidence that I would soon regain my liberty. Customer after customer entered, but the old gentleman never made his appearance.

At length, one day, while we were in the yard, Freeman came out and ordered us to our places, in the great room. A gentleman was waiting for us as we entered, and inasmuch as he will be often mentioned in the progress of this narrative, a description of his personal appearance, and my estimation of his character, at first sight, may not be out of place.

He was a man above the ordinary height, somewhat bent and stooping forward. He was a good-looking man, and appeared to have

9. Public burial place for unclaimed bodies and those whose families could not afford a private plot.

reached about the middle age of life. There was nothing repulsive in his presence; but on the other hand, there was something cheerful and attractive in his face, and in his tone of voice. The finer elements were all kindly mingled in his breast, as any one could see. He moved about among us, asking many questions, as to what we could do, and what labor we had been accustomed to; if we thought we would like to live with him, and would be good boys if he would buy us, and other interrogatories of like character.

After some further inspection, and conversation touching prices, he finally offered Freeman one thousand dollars for me, nine hundred for Harry, and seven hundred for Eliza. Whether the smallpox had depreciated our value, or from what cause Freeman had concluded to fall five hundred dollars from the price I was before held at, I cannot say. At any rate, after a little shrewd reflection, he announced his acceptance of the offer.

As soon as Eliza heard it, she was in an agony again. By this time she had become haggard and hollow-eyed with sickness and with sorrow. It would be a relief if I could consistently pass over in silence the scene that now ensued. It recalls memories more mournful and affecting than any language can portray. I have seen mothers kissing for the last time the faces of their dead offspring; I have seen them looking down into the grave, as the earth fell with a dull sound upon their coffins, hiding them from their eyes forever; but never have I seen such an exhibition of intense, unmeasured, and unbounded grief, as when Eliza was parted from her child. She broke from her place in the line of women, and rushing down where Emily was standing, caught her in her arms. The child, sensible of some impending danger, instinctively fastened her hands around her mother's neck, and nestled her little head upon her bosom. Freeman sternly ordered her to be quiet, but she did not heed him. He caught her by the arm and pulled her rudely, but she only clung the closer to the child. Then, with a volley of great oaths, he struck her such a heartless blow, that she staggered backward, and was like to fall. Oh! how piteously then did she beseech and beg and pray that they might not be separated. Why could they not be purchased together? Why not let her have one of her dear children? "Mercy, mercy, master!" she cried, falling on her knees. "Please, master, buy Emily. I can never work any if she is taken from me: I will die."

Freeman interfered again, but, disregarding him, she still plead most earnestly, telling how Randall had been taken from her— how she never would see him again, and now it was too bad—oh, God! it was too bad, too cruel, to take her away from Emily—her pride—her only darling, that could not live, it was so young, without its mother!

Finally, after much more of supplication, the purchaser of Eliza stepped forward, evidently affected, and said to Freeman he would buy Emily, and asked him what her price was.

"What is her *price*? *Buy* her?" was the responsive interrogatory of Theophilus Freeman. And instantly answering his own inquiry, he added, "I won't sell her. She's not for sale."*

The man remarked he was not in need of one so young—that it would be of no profit to him, but since the mother was so fond of her, rather than see them separated, he would pay a reasonable price. But to this humane proposal Freeman was entirely deaf. He would not sell her then on any account whatever. There were heaps and piles of money to be made of her, he said, when she was a few years older. There were men enough in New-Orleans who would give five thousand dollars for such an extra, handsome, fancy piece as Emily would be, rather than not get her. No, no, he would not sell her then. She was a beauty—a picture—a doll—one of the regular bloods—none of your thick-lipped, bullet-headed, cotton-picking niggers—if she was might he be d—d.

When Eliza heard Freeman's determination not to part with Emily, she became absolutely frantic.

"I will *not* go without her. They shall *not* take her from me," she fairly shrieked, her shrieks commingling with the loud and angry voice of Freeman, commanding her to be silent.

Meantime Harry and myself had been to the yard and returned with our blankets, and were at the front door ready to leave. Our purchaser stood near us, gazing at Eliza with an expression indicative of regret at having bought her at the expense of so much sorrow. We waited some time, when, finally, Freeman, out of patience, tore Emily from her mother by main force, the two clinging to each other with all their might.

"Don't leave me, mama—don't leave me," screamed the child, as its mother was pushed harshly forward; "Don't leave me—come back, mama," she still cried, stretching forth her little arms imploringly. But she cried in vain. Out of the door and into the street we were quickly hurried. Still we could hear her calling to her mother, "Come back—don't leave me—come back, mama," until her infant voice grew faint and still more faint, and gradually died away, as distance intervened, and finally was wholly lost.

Eliza never after saw or heard of Emily or Randall. Day nor night, however, were they ever absent from her memory. In the cotton field, in the cabin, always and everywhere, she was talking of them—often *to* them, as if they were actually present. Only when absorbed

* The transcriber added the close quotation marks after "sale."

SEPERATION OF ELIZA AND HER LAST CHILD.

Courtesy of the UNC–CH Library, The University of North Carolina at Chapel Hill.

in that illusion, or asleep, did she ever have a moment's comfort afterwards.

She was no common slave, as has been said. To a large share of natural intelligence which she possessed, was added a general knowledge and information on most subjects. She had enjoyed opportunities such as are afforded to very few of her oppressed class. She had been lifted up into the regions of a higher life. Freedom—freedom for herself and for her offspring, for many years had been her cloud by day, her pillar of fire by night. In her pilgrimage through the wilderness of bondage, with eyes fixed upon that hope-inspiring beacon, she had at length ascended to "the top of Pisgah," and beheld "the land of promise."[1] In an unexpected moment she was utterly overwhelmed with disappointment and despair. The glorious vision of liberty faded from her sight as they led her away into captivity. Now "she weepeth sore in the night, and tears are on her cheeks: all her friends have dealt treacherously with her: they have become her enemies."[2]

Chapter VII.

THE STEAMBOAT RODOLPH—DEPARTURE FROM NEW-ORLEANS—
WILLIAM FORD—ARRIVAL AT ALEXANDRIA, ON RED RIVER—
RESOLUTIONS—THE GREAT PINE WOODS—WILD CATTLE—MARTIN'S
SUMMER RESIDENCE—THE TEXAS ROAD—ARRIVAL AT MASTER
FORD'S—ROSE—MISTRESS FORD—SALLY, AND HER
CHILDREN—JOHN, THE COOK—WALTER, SAM, AND ANTONY—THE
MILLS ON INDIAN CREEK—SABBATH DAYS—SAM'S CONVERSION—THE
PROFIT OF KINDNESS—RAFTING—ADAM TAYDEM, THE LITTLE WHITE
MAN—CASCALLA AND HIS TRIBE—THE INDIAN BALL—JOHN M.
TIBEATS—THE STORM APPROACHING.

On leaving the New-Orleans slave pen, Harry and I followed our new master through the streets, while Eliza, crying and turning back, was forced along by Freeman and his minions, until we found ourselves on board the steamboat Rodolph, then lying at the levee. In the course of half an hour we were moving briskly up the Mississippi, bound for some point on Red River. There were quite a number of slaves on board beside ourselves, just purchased in the New-Orleans market. I remember a Mr. Kelsow, who was said to be a well known and extensive planter, had in charge a gang of women.

1. God permits Moses to see the Promised Land from the peak of Mount Pisgah just before he dies (Deuteronomy 34.1–4).
2. From Lamentations 1.2.

Our master's name was William Ford. He resided then in the "Great Pine Woods," in the parish[3] of Avoyelles, situated on the right bank of Red River, in the heart of Louisiana. He is now a Baptist preacher. Throughout the whole parish of Avoyelles, and especially along both shores of Bayou Bœuf, where he is more intimately known, he is accounted by his fellow-citizens as a worthy minister of God. In many northern minds, perhaps, the idea of a man holding his brother man in servitude, and the traffic in human flesh, may seem altogether incompatible with their conceptions of a moral or religious life. From descriptions of such men as Burch and Freeman, and others hereinafter mentioned, they are led to despise and execrate the whole class of slaveholders, indiscriminately. But I was sometime his slave, and had an opportunity of learning well his character and disposition, and it is but simple justice to him when I say, in my opinion, there never was a more kind, noble, candid, Christian man than William Ford. The influences and associations that had always surrounded him, blinded him to the inherent wrong at the bottom of the system of Slavery. He never doubted the moral right of one man holding another in subjection. Looking through the same medium with his fathers before him, he saw things in the same light. Brought up under other circumstances and other influences, his notions would undoubtedly have been different. Nevertheless, he was a model master, walking uprightly, according to the light of his understanding, and fortunate was the slave who came to his possession. Were all men such as he, Slavery would be deprived of more than half its bitterness.

We were two days and three nights on board the steamboat Rodolph, during which time nothing of particular interest occurred. I was now known as Platt, the name given me by Burch, and by which I was designated through the whole period of my servitude. Eliza was sold by the name of "Dradey." She was so distinguished in the conveyance to Ford, now on record in the recorder's office in New-Orleans.

On our passage I was constantly reflecting on my situation, and consulting with myself on the best course to pursue in order to effect my ultimate escape. Sometimes, not only then, but afterwards, I was almost on the point of disclosing fully to Ford the facts of my history. I am inclined now to the opinion it would have resulted in my benefit. This course was often considered, but through fear of its miscarriage, never put into execution, until eventually my transfer and his pecuniary embarrassments rendered it evidently unsafe. Afterwards, under other masters, unlike William Ford, I knew well enough the slightest knowledge of my real character would consign

---

3. Louisiana equivalent of counties in other states.

me at once to the remoter depths of Slavery. I was too costly a chattel to be lost, and was well aware that I would be taken farther on,
into some by-place, over the Texan border, perhaps, and sold; that I
would be disposed of as the thief disposes of his stolen horse, if my
right to freedom was even whispered. So I resolved to lock the
secret closely in my heart—never to utter one word or syllable as to
who or what I was—trusting in Providence and my own shrewdness
for deliverance.

At length we left the steamboat Rodolph at a place called Alexandria, several hundred miles from New-Orleans. It is a small town
on the southern shore of Red River. Having remained there over
night, we entered the morning train of cars, and were soon at Bayou
Lamourie, a still smaller place, distant eighteen miles from Alexandria. At that time it was the termination of the railroad. Ford's plantation was situated on the Texas road, twelve miles from Lamourie, in
the Great Pine Woods. This distance, it was announced to us, must
be traveled on foot, there being public conveyances no farther.
Accordingly we all set out in the company of Ford. It was an exces-
sively hot day. Harry, Eliza, and myself were yet weak, and the
bottoms of our feet were very tender from the effects of the small-
pox. We proceeded slowly, Ford telling us to take our time and sit
down and rest whenever we desired—a privilege that was taken
advantage of quite frequently. After leaving Lamourie and crossing
two plantations, one belonging to Mr. Carnell, the other to a
Mr. Flint, we reached the Pine Woods, a wilderness that stretches
to the Sabine River.

The whole country about Red River is low and marshy. The Pine
Woods, as they are called, is comparatively upland, with frequent
small intervals, however, running through them. This upland is
covered with numerous trees—the white oak, the chincopin,
resembling chestnut, but principally the yellow pine. They are of
great size, running up sixty feet, and perfectly straight. The woods
were full of cattle, very shy and wild, dashing away in herds, with
a loud snuff, at our approach. Some of them were marked or
branded, the rest appeared to be in their wild and untamed state.
They are much smaller than northern breeds, and the peculiarity
about them that most attracted my attention was their horns. They
stand out from the sides of the head precisely straight, like two
iron spikes.

At noon we reached a cleared piece of ground containing three or
four acres. Upon it was a small, unpainted, wooden house, a corn-
crib, or, as we would say, a barn, and a log kitchen, standing about a
rod from the house. It was the summer residence of Mr. Martin.
Rich planters, having large establishments on Bayou Bœuf, are
accustomed to spend the warmer season in these woods. Here they

find clear water and delightful shades. In fact, these retreats are to the planters of that section of the country what Newport[4] and Saratoga are to the wealthier inhabitants of northern cities.

We were sent around into the kitchen, and supplied with sweet potatoes, corn-bread, and bacon, while Master Ford dined with Martin in the house. There were several slaves about the premises. Martin came out and took a look at us, asking Ford the price of each, if we were green hands, and so forth, and making inquiries in relation to the slave market generally.

After a long rest we set forth again, following the Texas road, which had the appearance of being very rarely traveled. For five miles we passed through continuous woods without observing a single habitation. At length, just as the sun was sinking in the west, we entered another opening, containing some twelve or fifteen acres.

In this opening stood a house much larger than Mr. Martin's. It was two stories high, with a piazza[5] in front. In the rear of it was also a log kitchen, poultry house, corncribs, and several negro cabins. Near the house was a peach orchard, and gardens of orange and pomegranate trees. The space was entirely surrounded by woods, and covered with a carpet of rich, rank verdure. It was a quiet, lonely, pleasant place—literally a green spot in the wilderness. It was the residence of my master, William Ford.

As we approached, a yellow girl—her name was Rose—was standing on the piazza. Going to the door, she called her mistress, who presently came running out to meet her lord. She kissed him, and laughingly demanded if he had bought "those niggers." Ford said he had, and told us to go round to Sally's cabin and rest ourselves. Turning the corner of the house, we discovered Sally washing—her two baby children near her, rolling on the grass. They jumped up and toddled towards us, looked at us a moment like a brace of rabbits, then ran back to their mother as if afraid of us.

Sally conducted us into the cabin, told us to lay down our bundles and be seated, for she was sure that we were tired. Just then John, the cook, a boy some sixteen years of age, and blacker than any crow, came running in, looked steadily in our faces, then turning round, without saying as much as "how d'ye do," ran back to the kitchen, laughing loudly, as if our coming was a great joke indeed.

Much wearied with our walk, as soon as it was dark, Harry and I wrapped our blankets round us, and laid down upon the cabin floor. My thoughts, as usual, wandered back to my wife and children. The consciousness of my real situation; the hopelessness of any effort to

4. City in Rhode Island known for its grand mansions, which served as summer homes for some of the wealthiest American families.
5. Large covered porch.

escape through the wide forests of Avoyelles, pressed heavily upon me, yet my heart was at home in Saratoga.

I was awakened early in the morning by the voice of Master Ford, calling Rose. She hastened into the house to dress the children, Sally to the field to milk the cows, while John was busy in the kitchen preparing breakfast. In the meantime Harry and I were strolling about the yard, looking at our new quarters. Just after breakfast a colored man, driving three yoke of oxen, attached to a wagon load of lumber, drove into the opening. He was a slave of Ford's, named Walton, the husband of Rose. By the way, Rose was a native of Washington, and had been brought from thence five years before. She had never seen Eliza, but she had heard of Berry, and they knew the same streets, and the same people, either personally, or by reputation. They became fast friends immediately, and talked a great deal together of old times, and of friends they had left behind.

Ford was at that time a wealthy man. Besides his seat in the Pine Woods, he owned a large lumbering establishment on Indian Creek, four miles distant, and also, in his wife's right, an extensive plantation and many slaves on Bayou Bœuf.

Walton had come with his load of lumber from the mills on Indian Creek. Ford directed us to return with him, saying he would follow us as soon as possible. Before leaving, Mistress Ford called me into the store-room, and handed me, as it is there termed, a tin bucket of molasses for Harry and myself.

Eliza was still ringing her hands and deploring the loss of her children. Ford tried as much as possible to console her—told her she need not work very hard; that she might remain with Rose, and assist the madam in the house affairs.

Riding with Walton in the wagon, Harry and I became quite well acquainted with him long before reaching Indian Creek. He was a "born thrall" of Ford's, and spoke kindly and affectionately of him, as a child would speak of his own father. In answer to his inquiries from whence I came, I told him from Washington. Of that city, he had heard much from his wife, Rose, and all the way plied me with many extravagant and absurd questions.

On reaching the mills at Indian Creek, we found two more of Ford's slaves, Sam and Antony. Sam, also, was a Washingtonian, having been brought out in the same gang with Rose. He had worked on a farm near Georgetown. Antony was a blacksmith, from Kentucky, who had been in his present master's service about ten years. Sam knew Burch, and when informed that he was the trader who had sent me on from Washington, it was remarkable how well we agreed upon the subject of his superlative rascality. He had forwarded Sam, also.

On Ford's arrival at the mill, we were employed in piling lumber, and chopping logs, which occupation we continued during the remainder of the summer.

We usually spent our Sabbaths at the opening, on which days our master would gather all his slaves about him, and read and expound the Scriptures. He sought to inculcate in our minds feelings of kindness towards each other, of dependence upon God—setting forth the rewards promised unto those who lead an upright and prayerful life. Seated in the doorway of his house, surrounded by his man-servants and his maid-servants, who looked* earnestly into the good man's face, he spoke of the loving kindness of the Creator, and of the life that is to come. Often did the voice of prayer ascend from his lips to heaven, the only sound that broke the solitude of the place.

In the course of the summer Sam became deeply convicted, his mind dwelling intensely on the subject of religion. His mistress gave him a Bible, which he carried with him to his work. Whatever leisure time was allowed him, he spent in perusing it, though it was only with great difficulty that he could master any part of it. I often read to him, a favor which he well repaid me by many expressions of gratitude. Sam's piety was frequently observed by white men who came to the mill, and the remark it most generally provoked was, that a man like Ford, who allowed his slaves to have Bibles, was "not fit to own a nigger."

He, however, lost nothing by his kindness. It is a fact I have more than once observed, that those who treated their slaves most leniently, were rewarded by the greatest amount of labor. I know it from my own experience. It was a source of pleasure to surprise Master Ford with a greater day's work than was required, while, under subsequent masters, there was no prompter to extra effort but the overseer's lash.

It was the desire of Ford's approving voice that suggested to me an idea that resulted to his profit. The lumber we were manufacturing was contracted to be delivered at Lamourie. It had hitherto been transported by land, and was an important item of expense. Indian Creek, upon which the mills were situated, was a narrow but deep stream emptying into Bayou Bœuf. In some places it was not more than twelve feet wide, and much obstructed with trunks of trees. Bayou Bœuf was connected with Bayou Lamourie. I ascertained the distance from the mills to the point on the latter bayou, where our lumber was to be delivered, was but a few miles less by land than by water. Provided the creek could be made navigable for rafts, it occurred to me that the expense of transportation would be materially diminished.

* The transcriber changed "looded" to "looked".

Adam Taydem, a little white man, who had been a soldier in Florida, and had strolled into that distant region, was foreman and superintendent of the mills. He scouted[6] the idea; but Ford, when I laid it before him, received it favorably, and permitted me to try the experiment.

Having removed the obstructions, I made up a narrow raft, consisting of twelve cribs. At this business I think I was quite skillful, not having forgotten my experience years before on the Champlain canal. I labored hard, being extremely anxious to succeed, both from a desire to please my master, and to show Adam Taydem that my scheme was not such a visionary one as he incessantly pronounced it. One hand could manage three cribs. I took charge of the forward three, and commenced poling down the creek. In due time we entered the first bayou, and finally reached our destination in a shorter period of time than I had anticipated.

The arrival of the raft at Lamourie created a sensation, while Mr. Ford loaded me with commendations. On all sides I heard Ford's Platt pronounced the "smartest nigger in the Pine Woods"—in fact I was the Fulton of Indian Creek.[7] I was not insensible to the praise bestowed upon me, and enjoyed, especially, my triumph over Taydem, whose half-malicious ridicule had stung my pride. From this time the entire control of bringing the lumber to Lamourie was placed in my hands until the contract was fulfilled.

Indian Creek, in its whole length, flows through a magnificent forest. There dwells on its shore a tribe of Indians, a remnant of the Chickasaws or Chickopees,[8] if I remember rightly. They live in simple huts, ten or twelve feet square, constructed of pine poles and covered with bark. They subsist principally on the flesh of the deer, the coon, and opossum, all of which are plenty in these woods. Sometimes they exchange venison for a little corn and whisky with the planters on the bayous. Their usual dress is buckskin breeches and calico hunting shirts of fantastic colors, buttoned from belt to chin. They wear brass rings on their wrists, and in their ears and noses. The dress of the squaws is very similar. They are fond of dogs and horses—owning many of the latter, of a small, tough breed—and are skillful riders. Their bridles, girths and saddles were made of raw skins of animals; their stirrups of a certain kind of wood. Mounted astride their ponies, men and women, I have seen them dash out into the woods at the utmost of their speed, following narrow winding paths, and dodging trees, in a manner that eclipsed the most miraculous feats of civilized equestrianism. Circling away

6. Scoffed at; dismissed.
7. Robert Fulton (1767–1815), credited with developing the first commercially viable steamboat.
8. The former is correct.

in various directions, the forest echoing and re-echoing with their whoops, they would presently return at the same dashing, headlong speed with which they started. Their village was on Indian Creek, known as Indian Castle, but their range extended to the Sabine River. Occasionally a tribe from Texas would come over on a visit, and then there was indeed a carnival in the "Great Pine Woods." Chief of the tribe was Cascalla; second in rank, John Baltese, his son-in-law; with both of whom, as with many others of the tribe, I became acquainted during my frequent voyages down the creek with rafts. Sam and myself would often visit them when the day's task was done. They were obedient to the chief; the word of Cascalla was their law. They were a rude but harmless people, and enjoyed their wild mode of life. They had little fancy for the open country, the cleared lands on the shores of the bayous, but preferred to hide themselves within the shadows of the forest. They worshiped the Great Spirit, loved whisky, and were happy.

On one occasion I was present at a dance, when a roving herd from Texas had encamped in their village. The entire carcass of a deer was roasting before a large fire, which threw its light a long distance among the trees under which they were assembled. When they had formed in a ring, men and squaws alternately, a sort of Indian fiddle set up an indescribable tune. It was a continuous, melancholy kind of wavy sound, with the slightest possible variation. At the first note, if indeed there was more than one note in the whole tune, they circled around, trotting after each other, and giving utterance to a guttural, sing-song noise, equally as nondescript as the music of the fiddle. At the end of the third circuit, they would stop suddenly, whoop as if their lungs would crack, then break from the ring, forming in couples, man and squaw, each jumping backwards as far as possible from the other, then forwards—which graceful feat having been twice or thrice accomplished, they would form in a ring, and go trotting round again. The best dancer appeared to be considered the one who could whoop the loudest, jump the farthest, and utter the most excruciating noise. At intervals, one or more would leave the dancing circle, and going to the fire, cut from the roasting carcass a slice of venison.

In a hole, shaped like a mortar, cut in the trunk of a fallen tree, they pounded corn with a wooden pestle, and of the meal made cake. Alternately they danced and ate. Thus were the visitors from Texas entertained by the dusky sons and daughters of the Chicopees, and such is a description, as I saw it, of an Indian ball in the Pine Woods of Avoyelles.

In the autumn, I left the mills, and was employed at the opening. One day the mistress was urging Ford to procure a loom, in order that Sally might commence weaving cloth for the winter garments of the slaves. He could not imagine where one was to be found, when I suggested that the easiest way to get one would be to make it, informing him at the same time, that I was a sort of "Jack at all trades," and would attempt it, with his permission. It was granted very readily, and I was allowed to go to a neighboring planter's to inspect one before commencing the undertaking. At length it was finished and pronounced by Sally to be perfect. She could easily weave her task of fourteen yards, milk the cows, and have leisure time besides each day. It worked so well, I was continued in the employment of making looms, which were taken down to the plantation on the bayou.

At this time one John M. Tibeats,[9] a carpenter,* came to the opening to do some work on master's house. I was directed to quit the looms and assist him. For two weeks I was in his company, planning and matching boards for ceiling, a plastered room being a rare thing in the parish of Avoyelles.

John M. Tibeats was the opposite of Ford in all respects. He was a small, crabbed, quick-tempered, spiteful man. He had no fixed residence that I ever heard of, but passed from one plantation to another, wherever he could find employment. He was without standing in the community, not esteemed by white men, nor even respected by slaves. He was ignorant, withal, and of a revengeful disposition. He left the parish long before I did, and I know not whether he is at present alive or dead. Certain it is, it was a most unlucky day for me that brought us together. During my residence with Master Ford I had seen only the bright side of slavery. His was no heavy hand crushing us to the earth. *He* pointed upwards, and with benign and cheering words addressed us as his fellow-mortals, accountable, like himself, to the Maker of us all. I think of him with affection, and had my family been with me, could have borne his gentle servitude, without murmuring, all my days. But clouds were gathering in the horizon—forerunners of a pitiless storm that was soon to break over me. I was doomed to endure such bitter trials as the poor slave only knows, and to lead no more the comparatively happy life which I had led in the "Great Pine Woods."

9. Or Tibaut, according to historical records.
* The transcriber changed "capenter" to "carpenter".

Chapter VIII.

William Ford unfortunately became embarrassed in his pecuniary
affairs. A heavy judgment was rendered against him in consequence
of his having become security for his brother, Franklin Ford, residing on Red River, above Alexandria, and who had failed to meet his
liabilities.[1] He was also indebted to John M. Tibeats to a considerable amount in consideration of his services in building the mills
on Indian Creek, and also a weaving-house, corn-mill and other
erections on the plantation at Bayou Bœuf, not yet completed. It
was therefore necessary, in order to meet these demands, to dispose
of eighteen slaves, myself among the number. Seventeen of them,
including Sam and Harry, were purchased by Peter Compton, a
planter also residing on Red River.

I was sold to Tibeats, in consequence, undoubtedly, of my slight
skill as a carpenter. This was in the winter of 1842. The deed of
myself from Freeman to Ford, as I ascertained from the public records in New-Orleans on my return, was dated June 23d, 1841. At the
time of my sale to Tibeats, the price agreed to be given for me being
more than the debt, Ford took a chattel mortgage of four hundred
dollars. I am indebted for my life, as will hereafter be seen, to that
mortgage.[2]

I bade farewell to my good friends at the opening, and departed
with my new master Tibeats. We went down to the plantation on
Bayou Bœuf, distant twenty-seven miles from the Pine Woods, to
complete the unfinished contract. Bayou Bœuf is a sluggish, winding stream—one of those stagnant bodies of water common in that
region, setting back from Red River. It stretches from a point not
far from Alexandria, in a south-easterly direction, and following its
tortuous course, is more than fifty miles in length. Large cotton

1. Franklin Ford had borrowed money to open a private girls' boarding school in Min-
den, Louisiana. When he defaulted, his brother, as his guarantor, was also liable for
the debt.
2. Until Tibeats paid the full $400 with interest, Ford would still be part owner of Northup.

and sugar plantations line each shore, extending back to the borders of interminable swamps. It is alive with alligators,* rendering it unsafe for swine, or unthinking slave children to stroll along its banks. Upon a bend in this bayou, a short distance from Cheneyville, was situated the plantation of Madam Ford—her brother, Peter Tanner, a great landholder, living on the opposite side.

On my arrival at Bayou Bœuf, I had the pleasure of meeting Eliza, whom I had not seen for several months. She had not pleased Mrs. Ford, being more occupied in brooding over her sorrows than in attending to her business, and had, in consequence, been sent down to work in the field on the plantation. She had grown feeble and emaciated, and was still mourning for her children. She asked me if I had forgotten them, and a great many times inquired if I still remembered how handsome little Emily was—how much Randall loved her—and wondered if they were living still, and where the darlings could then be. She had sunk beneath the weight of an excessive grief. Her drooping form and hollow cheeks too plainly indicated that she had well nigh reached the end of her weary road.

Ford's overseer on this plantation, and who had the exclusive charge of it, was a Mr. Chapin, a kindly-disposed man, and a native of Pennsylvania. In common with others, he held Tibeats in light estimation, which fact, in connection with the four hundred dollar mortgage, was fortunate for me.

I was now compelled to labor very hard. From earliest dawn until late at night, I was not allowed to be a moment idle. Notwithstanding which, Tibeats was never satisfied. He was continually cursing and complaining. He never spoke to me a kind word. I was his faithful slave, and earned him large wages every day, and yet I went to my cabin nightly, loaded with abuse and stinging epithets.

We had completed the corn mill, the kitchen, and so forth, and were at work upon the weaving-house, when I was guilty of an act, in that State punishable with death. It was my first fight with Tibeats. The weaving-house we were erecting stood in the orchard a few rods from the residence of Chapin, or the "great house," as it was called. One night, having worked until it was too dark to see, I was ordered by Tibeats to rise very early in the morning, procure a keg of nails from Chapin, and commence putting on the clapboards. I retired to the cabin extremely tired, and having cooked a supper of bacon and corn cake, and conversed a while with Eliza, who occupied the same cabin, as also did Lawson and his wife Mary, and a slave named Bristol, laid down upon the ground floor, little dreaming of the sufferings that awaited me on the morrow. Before daylight I was on the piazza of the "great house," awaiting the appearance of

---

* The transcriber changed "aligators" to "alligators".

overseer Chapin. To have aroused him from his slumbers and stated my errand, would have been an unpardonable boldness. At length he came out. Taking off my hat, I informed him Master Tibeats had directed me to call upon him for a keg of nails. Going into the store-room, he rolled it out, at the same time saying, if Tibeats preferred a different size, he would endeavor to furnish them, but that I might use those until further directed. Then mounting his horse, which stood saddled and bridled at the door, he rode away into the field, whither the slaves had preceded him, while I took the keg on my shoulder, and proceeding to the weaving-house, broke in the head, and commenced nailing on the clapboards.

As the day began to open, Tibeats came out of the house to where I was, hard at work. He seemed to be that morning even more morose and disagreeable than usual. He was my master, entitled by law to my flesh and blood, and to exercise over me such tyrannical control as his mean nature prompted; but there was no law that could prevent my looking upon him with intense contempt. I despised both his disposition and his intellect. I had just come round to the keg for a further supply of nails, as he reached the weaving-house.

"I thought I told you to commence putting on weather-boards this morning," he remarked.

"Yes, master, and I am about it," I replied.

"Where?" he demanded.

"On the other side," was my answer.

He walked round to the other side, examined my work for a while, muttering to himself in a fault-finding tone.

"Didn't I tell you last night to get a keg of nails of Chapin?" he broke forth again.

"Yes, master, and so I did; and overseer said he would get another size for you, if you wanted them, when he came back from the field."

Tibeats walked to the keg, looked a moment at the contents, then kicked it violently. Coming towards me in a great passion, he exclaimed,

"G—d d—n you! I thought you *knowed* something."

I made answer: "I tried to do as you told me, master. I didn't mean anything wrong. Overseer said—" But he interrupted me with such a flood of curses that I was unable to finish the sentence. At length he ran towards the house, and going to the piazza, took down one of the overseer's whips. The whip had a short wooden stock, braided over with leather, and was loaded at the butt. The lash was three feet long, or thereabouts, and made of raw-hide strands.

At first I was somewhat frightened, and my impulse was to run. There was no one about except Rachel, the cook, and Chapin's wife, and neither of them were to be seen. The rest were in the field. I knew he intended to whip me, and it was the first time any one had attempted it since my arrival at Avoyelles. I felt, moreover, that I had been faithful—that I was guilty of no wrong whatever, and deserved commendation rather than punishment. My fear changed to anger, and before he reached me I had made up my mind fully not to be whipped, let the result be life or death.

Winding the lash around his hand, and taking hold of the small end of the stock, he walked up to me, and with a malignant look, ordered me to strip.

"Master Tibeats" said I, looking him boldly in the face, "I will *not*." I was about to say something further in justification, but with concentrated vengeance, he sprang upon me, seizing me by the throat with one hand, raising the whip with the other, in the act of striking. Before the blow descended, however, I had caught him by the collar of the coat, and drawn him closely to me. Reaching down, I seized him by the ankle, and pushing him back with the other hand, he fell over on the ground. Putting one arm around his leg, and holding it to my breast, so that his head and shoulders only touched the ground, I placed my foot upon his neck. He was completely in my power. My blood was up. It seemed to course through my veins like fire. In the frenzy of my madness I snatched the whip from his hand. He struggled with all his power; swore that I should not live to see another day; and that he would tear out my heart. But his struggles and his threats were alike in vain. I cannot tell how many times I struck him. Blow after blow fell fast and heavy upon his wriggling form. At length he screamed—cried murder—and at last the blasphemous tyrant called on God for mercy. But he who had never shown mercy did not receive it. The stiff stock of the whip warped round his cringing body until my right arm ached.

Until this time I had been too busy to look about me. Desisting for a moment, I saw Mrs. Chapin looking from the window, and Rachel standing in the kitchen door. Their attitudes expressed the utmost excitement and alarm. His screams had been heard in the field. Chapin was coming as fast as he could ride. I struck him a blow or two more, then pushed him from me with such a well-directed kick that he went rolling over on the ground.

Rising to his feet, and brushing the dirt from his hair, he stood looking at me, pale with rage. We gazed at each other in silence. Not a word was uttered until Chapin galloped up to us.

"What is the matter?" he cried out.

"Master Tibeats wants to whip me for using the nails you gave me," I replied.

"What is the matter with the nails?" he inquired, turning to Tibeats.

Tibeats answered to the effect that they were too large, paying little heed, however, to Chapin's question, but still keeping his snakish eyes fastened maliciously on me.

"I am overseer here," Chapin began. "I told Platt to take them and use them, and if they were not of the proper size I would get others on returning from the field. It is not his fault. Besides, I shall furnish such nails as I please. I hope you will understand *that*, Mr. Tibeats."

Tibeats made no reply, but, grinding his teeth and shaking his fist, swore he would have satisfaction, and that it was not half over yet. Thereupon he walked away, followed by the overseer, and entered the house, the latter talking to him all the while in a suppressed tone, and with earnest gestures.

I remained where I was, doubting whether it was better to fly or abide the result, whatever it might be. Presently Tibeats came out of the house, and, saddling his horse, the only property he possessed besides myself, departed on the road to Cheneyville.*

When he was gone, Chapin came out, visibly excited, telling me not to stir, not to attempt to leave the plantation on any account whatever. He then went to the kitchen, and calling Rachel out, conversed with her some time. Coming back, he again charged me with great earnestness not to run, saying my master was a rascal; that he had left on no good errand, and that there might be trouble before night. But at all events, he insisted upon it, I must not stir.

As I stood there, feelings of unutterable agony overwhelmed me. I was conscious that I had subjected myself to unimaginable punishment. The reaction that followed my extreme ebullition of anger produced the most painful sensations of regret. An unfriended, helpless slave—what could I *do*, what could I *say*, to justify, in the remotest manner, the heinous act I had committed, of resenting a *white* man's contumely and abuse. I tried to pray—I tried to beseech my Heavenly Father to sustain me in my sore extremity, but emotion choked my utterance, and I could only bow my head upon my hands and weep. For at least an hour I remained in this situation, finding relief only in tears, when, looking up, I beheld Tibeats, accompanied by two horsemen, coming down the bayou. They rode into the yard, jumped from their horses, and approached me with large whips, one of them also carrying a coil of rope.

"Cross your hands," commanded Tibeats, with the addition of such a shuddering expression of blasphemy as is not decorous to repeat.

"You need not bind me, Master Tibeats, I am ready to go with you anywhere," said I.

* The transcriber changed "Chenyville" to "Cheneyville".

One of his companions then stepped forward, swearing if I made the least resistance he would break my head—he would tear me limb from limb—he would cut my black throat—and giving wide scope to other similar expressions. Perceiving any importunity altogether vain, I crossed my hands, submitting humbly to whatever disposition they might please to make of me. Thereupon Tibeats tied my wrists, drawing the rope around them with his utmost strength. Then he bound my ankles in the same manner. In the meantime the other two had slipped a cord within my elbows, running it across my back, and tying it firmly. It was utterly impossible to move hand or foot. With a remaining piece of rope Tibeats made an awkward noose, and placed it about my neck.

"Now, then," inquired one of Tibeats' companions, "where shall we hang the nigger?"

One proposed such a limb, extending from the body of a peach tree, near the spot where we were standing. His comrade objected to it, alleging it would break, and proposed another. Finally they fixed upon the latter.

During this conversation, and all the time they were binding me, I uttered not a word. Overseer Chapin, during the progress of the scene, was walking hastily back and forth on the piazza. Rachel was crying by the kitchen door, and Mrs. Chapin was still looking from the window. Hope died within my heart. Surely my time had come. I should never behold the light of another day—never behold the faces of my children—the sweet anticipation I had cherished with such fondness. I should that hour struggle through the fearful agonies of death! None would mourn for me—none revenge me. Soon my form would be mouldering in that distant soil, or, perhaps, be cast to the slimy reptiles that filled the stagnant waters of the bayou! Tears flowed down my cheeks, but they only afforded a subject of insulting comment for my executioners.

At length, as they were dragging me towards the tree, Chapin, who had momentarily disappeared from the piazza, came out of the house and walked towards us. He had a pistol in each hand, and as near as I can now recall to mind, spoke in a firm, determined manner, as follows:

"Gentlemen, I have a few words to say. You had better listen to them. Whoever moves that slave another foot from where he stands is a dead man. In the first place, he does not deserve this treatment. It is a shame to murder him in this manner. I never knew a more faithful boy than Platt. You, Tibeats, are in the fault yourself. You are pretty much of a scoundrel, and I know it, and you richly deserve the flogging you have received. In the next place, I have been overseer on this plantation seven years, and, in the absence of William Ford, am master here. My duty is to protect his interests, and that

CHAPIN RESCUES SOLOMON FROM HANGING.

Courtesy of the UNC–CH Library, The University of North Carolina at Chapel Hill.

duty I shall perform. You are not responsible—you are a worthless fellow. Ford holds a mortgage on Platt of four hundred dollars. If you hang him he loses his debt. Until that is canceled you have no right to take his life. You have no right to take it any way. There is a law for the slave as well as for the white man. You are no better than a murderer.

"As for you," addressing Cook and Ramsay, a couple of overseers from neighboring plantations, "as for you—begone! If you have any regard for your own safety, I say, begone."

Cook and Ramsay, without a further word, mounted their horses and rode away. Tibeats, in a few minutes, evidently in fear, and overawed by the decided tone of Chapin, sneaked off like a coward, as he was, and mounting his horse, followed his companions.

I remained standing where I was, still bound, with the rope around my neck. As soon as they were gone, Chapin called Rachel, ordering her to run to the field, and tell Lawson to hurry to the house without delay, and bring the brown mule with him, an animal much prized for its unusual fleetness. Presently the boy appeared.

"Lawson," said Chapin, "you must go to the Pine Woods. Tell your master Ford to come here at once—that he must not delay a single moment. Tell him they are trying to murder Platt. Now hurry, boy. Be at the Pine Woods by noon if you kill the mule."

Chapin stepped into the house and wrote a pass. When he returned, Lawson was at the door, mounted on his mule. Receiving the pass, he plied the whip right smartly to the beast, dashed out of the yard, and turning up the bayou on a hard gallop, in less time than it has taken me to describe the scene, was out of sight.

Chapter IX.

THE HOT SUN—YET BOUND—THE CORDS SINK INTO MY FLESH—
CHAPIN'S UNEASINESS—SPECULATION—RACHEL, AND HER CUP OF
WATER—SUFFERING INCREASES—THE HAPPINESS OF SLAVERY—
ARRIVAL OF FORD—HE CUTS THE CORDS WHICH BIND ME, AND TAKES
THE ROPE FROM MY NECK—MISERY—THE GATHERING OF THE SLAVES
IN ELIZA'S CABIN—THEIR KINDNESS—RACHEL REPEATS THE
OCCURRENCES OF THE DAY—LAWSON ENTERTAINS HIS COMPANIONS
WITH AN ACCOUNT OF HIS RIDE—CHAPIN'S APPREHENSIONS OF
TIBEATS—HIRED TO PETER TANNER—PETER EXPOUNDS THE
SCRIPTURES—DESCRIPTION OF THE STOCKS.

As the sun approached the meridian that day it became insufferably warm. Its hot rays scorched the ground. The earth almost blistered the foot that stood upon it. I was without coat or hat, standing bare-headed, exposed to its burning blaze. Great drops of perspiration rolled down my face, drenching the scanty apparel wherewith I was clothed. Over the fence, a very little way off, the peach trees cast their cool, delicious shadows on the grass. I would gladly have given a long year of service to have been enabled to exchange the heated oven, as it were, wherein I stood, for a seat beneath their branches. But I was yet bound, the rope still dangling from my neck, and standing in the same tracks where Tibeats and his comrades left me. I could not move an inch, so firmly had I been bound. To have been enabled to lean against the weaving house would have been a luxury indeed. But it was far beyond my reach, though distant less than twenty feet. I wanted to lie down, but knew I could not rise again. The ground was so parched and boiling hot I was aware it would but add to the discomfort of my situation. If I could have only moved my position, however slightly, it would have been relief unspeakable. But the hot rays of a southern sun, beating all the long summer day on my bare head, produced not half the suffering I experienced from my aching limbs. My wrists and ankles, and the cords of my legs and arms began to swell, burying the rope that bound them into the swollen flesh.

All day Chapin walked back and forth upon the stoop, but not once approached me. He appeared to be in a state of great uneasiness, looking first towards me, and then up the road, as if expecting some arrival every moment. He did not go to the field, as was his custom. It was evident from his manner that he supposed Tibeats would return with more and better armed assistance, perhaps, to renew the quarrel, and it was equally evident he had prepared his mind to defend my life at whatever hazard. Why he did not relieve me—why he suffered me to remain in agony the whole weary day, I never knew. It was not for want of sympathy, I am certain. Perhaps he wished Ford to see the rope about my neck, and the brutal manner in which I had been bound; perhaps his interference with another's property in which he had no legal interest might have been a trespass, which would have subjected him to the penalty of the law. Why Tibeats was all day absent was another mystery I never could divine. He knew well enough that Chapin would not harm him unless he persisted in his design against me. Lawson told me afterwards, that, as he passed the plantation of John David Cheney, he saw the three, and that they turned and looked after him as he flew by. I think his supposition was, that Lawson had been sent out by Overseer Chapin to arouse the neighboring planters, and to call on them to come to his assistance. He, therefore, undoubtedly, acted on the principle, that "discretion is the better part of valor," and kept away.

But whatever motive may have governed the cowardly and malignant tyrant, it is of no importance. There I still stood in the noon-tide sun, groaning with pain. From long before daylight I had not eaten a morsel. I was growing faint from pain, and thirst, and hunger. Once only, in the very hottest portion of the day, Rachel, half fearful she was acting contrary to the overseer's wishes, ventured to me, and held a cup of water to my lips. The humble creature never knew, nor could she comprehend if she had heard them, the blessings I invoked upon her, for that balmy draught. She could only say, "Oh, Platt, how I do pity you," and then hastened back to her labors in the kitchen.

Never did the sun move so slowly through the heavens—never did it shower down such fervent and fiery rays, as it did that day. At least, so it appeared to me. What my meditations were—the innumerable thoughts that thronged through my distracted brain—I will not attempt to give expression to. Suffice it to say, during the whole long day I came not to the conclusion, even once, that the southern slave, fed, clothed, whipped and protected by his master, is happier than the free colored citizen of the North. To that conclusion I have never since arrived. There are many, however, even in the Northern States, benevolent and well-disposed men, who will pronounce my opinion erroneous, and gravely proceed to substantiate the assertion with an argument. Alas! they have never drunk, as I have, from the bitter cup of slavery. Just at sunset my heart leaped with unbounded joy, as Ford came riding into the yard, his horse covered with foam. Chapin met him at the door, and after conversing a short time, he walked directly to me.

"Poor Platt, you are in a bad state," was the only expression that escaped his lips.

"Thank God!" said I, "thank God, Master Ford, that you have come at last."

Drawing a knife from his pocket, he indignantly cut the cord from my wrists, arms, and ankles, and slipped the noose from my neck. I attempted to walk, but staggered like a drunken man, and fell partially to the ground.

Ford returned immediately to the house, leaving me alone again. As he reached the piazza, Tibeats and his two friends rode up. A long dialogue followed. I could hear the sound of their voices, the mild tones of Ford mingling with the angry accents of Tibeats, but was unable to distinguish what was said. Finally the three departed again, apparently not well pleased.

I endeavored to raise the hammer, thinking to show Ford how willing I was to work, by proceeding with my labors on the weaving house, but it fell from my nerveless hand. At dark I crawled into the cabin, and laid down. I was in great misery—all sore and swollen—the slightest movement producing excruciating suffering. Soon the hands came in from the field. Rachel, when she went after Lawson, had told them what had happened. Eliza and Mary broiled me a piece of bacon, but my appetite was gone. Then they scorched some corn meal and made coffee. It was all that I could take. Eliza consoled me and was very kind. It was not long before the cabin was full of slaves. They gathered round me, asking many questions about the difficulty with Tibeats in the morning—and the particulars of all the occurrences of the day. Then Rachel came in, and in her simple language, repeated it over again—dwelling emphatically on the kick that sent Tibeats rolling over on the ground—whereupon there was a general titter throughout the crowd. Then she described how Chapin walked out with his pistols and rescued me, and how Master Ford cut the ropes with his knife, just as if he was mad.

By this time Lawson had returned. He had to regale them with an account of his trip to the Pine Woods—how the brown mule bore him faster than a "streak o'lightnin"—how he astonished everybody as he flew along—how Master Ford started right away—how he said Platt was a good nigger, and they shouldn't kill him, concluding with pretty strong intimations that there was not another human being in the wide world, who could have created such a universal sensation on the road, or performed such a marvelous John Gilpin feat,[3] as he had done that day on the brown mule.

The kind creatures loaded me with the expression of their sympathy—saying, Tibeats was a hard, cruel man, and hoping "Massa Ford" would get me back again. In this manner they passed the time, discussing, chatting, talking over and over again the exciting affair, until suddenly Chapin presented himself at the cabin door and called me.

"Platt," said he, "you will sleep on the floor in the great house to-night; bring your blanket with you."

I arose as quickly as I was able, took my blanket in my hand, and followed him. On the way he informed me that he should not wonder if Tibeats was back again before morning—that he intended to kill me—and that he did not mean he should do it without witnesses. Had he stabbed me to the heart in the presence of a hundred slaves, not one of them, by the laws of Louisiana, could have given evidence against him. I laid down on the floor in the "great house"—the first and the last time such a sumptuous resting place was granted me during my twelve years of bondage—and tried to sleep. Near midnight the dog began to bark. Chapin arose, looked from the window, but could discover nothing. At length the dog was quiet. As he returned to his room, he said,

"I believe, Platt, that scoundrel is skulking about the premises somewhere. If the dog barks again, and I am sleeping, wake me."

---

3. In "The Diverting History of John Gilpin," a popular comic ballad by William Cowper (1731–1800), Gilpin takes a long ride on a runaway horse.

I promised to do so. After the lapse of an hour or more, the dog re-commenced his clamor, running towards the gate, then back again, all the while barking furiously.

Chapin was out of bed without waiting to be called. On this occasion, he stepped forth upon the piazza, and remained standing there a considerable length of time. Nothing, however, was to be seen, and the dog returned to his kennel. We were not disturbed again during the night. The excessive pain that I suffered, and the dread of some impending danger, prevented any rest whatever. Whether or not Tibeats did actually return to the plantation that night, seeking an opportunity to wreak his vengeance upon me, is a secret known only to himself, perhaps. I thought then, however, and have the strong impression still, that he was there. At all events, he had the disposition of an assassin—cowering before a brave man's words, but ready to strike his helpless or unsuspecting victim in the back, as I had reason afterwards to know.

At daylight in the morning, I arose, sore and weary, having rested little. Nevertheless, after partaking breakfast, which Mary and Eliza had prepared for me in the cabin, I proceeded to the weaving house and commenced the labors of another day. It was Chapin's practice, as it is the practice of overseers generally, immediately on arising, to bestride his horse, always saddled and bridled and ready for him—the particular business of some slave—and ride into the field. This morning, on the contrary, he came to the weaving house, asking if I had seen anything of Tibeats yet. Replying in the negative, he remarked there was something not right about the fellow— there was bad blood in him—that I must keep a sharp watch of him, or he would do me wrong some day when I least expected it.

While he was yet speaking, Tibeats rode in, hitched his horse, and entered the house. I had little fear of him while Ford and Chapin were at hand, but they could not be near me always.

Oh! how heavily the weight of slavery pressed upon me then. I must toil day after day, endure abuse and taunts and scoffs, sleep on the hard ground, live on the coarsest fare, and not only this, but live the slave of a blood-seeking wretch, of whom I must stand henceforth in continued fear and dread. Why had I not died in my young years—before God had given me children to love and live for? What unhappiness and suffering and sorrow it would have prevented. I sighed for liberty; but the bondman's chain was round me, and could not be shaken off. I could only gaze wistfully towards the North, and think of the thousands of miles that stretched between me and the soil of freedom, over which a *black* freeman may not pass.

Tibeats, in the course of half an hour, walked over to the weaving-house, looked at me sharply, then returned without saying anything. Most of the forenoon he sat on the piazza, reading a newspaper and conversing with Ford. After dinner, the latter left for the Pine Woods, and it was indeed with regret that I beheld him depart from the plantation.

Once more during the day Tibeats came to me, gave me some order, and returned.

During the week the weaving-house was completed—Tibeats in the meantime making no allusion whatever to the difficulty—when I was informed he had hired me to Peter Tanner, to work under another carpenter by the name of Myers. This announcement was received with gratification, as any place was desirable that would relieve me of his hateful presence.

Peter Tanner, as the reader has already been informed, lived on the opposite shore, and was the brother of Mistress Ford. He is one of the most extensive planters on Bayou Bœuf, and owns a large number of slaves.

Over I went to Tanner's, joyfully enough. He had heard of my late difficulties—in fact, I ascertained the flogging of Tibeats was soon blazoned far and wide. This affair, together with my rafting experiment, had rendered me somewhat notorious. More than once I heard it said that Platt Ford, now Platt Tibeats—a slave's name changes with his change of master—was "a devil of a nigger." But I was destined to make a still further noise, as will presently be seen, throughout the little world of Bayou Bœuf.

Peter Tanner endeavored to impress upon me the idea that he was quite severe, though I could perceive there was a vein of good humor in the old fellow, after all.

"You're the nigger," he said to me on my arrival—"You're the nigger that flogged your master, eh? You're the nigger that kicks, and holds carpenter Tibeats by the leg, and wallops him, are ye? I'd like to see you hold me by the leg—I should. You're a 'portant character—you're a great nigger—very remarkable nigger, ain't ye? I'd lash you—I'd take the tantrums out of ye. Jest take hold of my leg, if you please. None of your pranks here, my boy, remember that. Now go to work, you kickin' rascal," concluded Peter Tanner, unable to suppress a half-comical grin at his own wit and sarcasm.

After listening to this salutation, I was taken charge of by Myers, and labored under his direction for a month, to his and my own satisfaction.

Like William Ford, his brother-in-law, Tanner was in the habit of reading the Bible to his slaves on the Sabbath, but in a somewhat different spirit. He was an impressive commentator on the New Testament. The first Sunday after my coming to the plantation, he called them together, and began to read the twelfth chapter of Luke. When he came to the 47th verse, he looked deliberately around him, and continued—"And that servant which knew his lord's *will*,"—here he paused, looking around more deliberately than before, and again proceeded—"which knew his lord's *will*, and *prepared* not himself"—here was another pause—"*prepared* not himself, neither did *according* to his will, shall be beaten with many *stripes*."

"D'ye hear that?" demanded Peter, emphatically. "*Stripes*," he repeated, slowly and distinctly, taking off his spectacles, preparatory to making a few remarks.

"That nigger that don't take care—that don't obey his lord— that's his master—d'ye see?—that 'ere nigger shall be beaten with many stripes. Now, 'many' signifies a *great* many—forty, a hundred, a hundred and fifty lashes. *That's* Scripter!" and so Peter continued to elucidate the subject for a great length of time, much to the edification of his sable audience.

At the conclusion of the exercises, calling up three of his slaves, Warner, Will and Major, he cried out to me—

"Here, Platt, you held Tibeats by the legs; now I'll see if you can hold these rascals in the same way, till I get back from meetin'."

Thereupon he ordered them to the stocks—a common thing on plantations in the Red River country. The stocks are formed of two planks, the lower one made fast at the ends to two short posts, driven firmly into the ground. At regular distances half circles are cut in the upper edge. The other plank is fastened to one of the posts by a hinge, so that it can be opened or shut down, in the same manner as the blade of a pocket-knife is shut or opened. In the lower edge of the upper plank corresponding half circles are also cut, so that when they close, a row of holes is formed large enough to admit a negro's leg above the ankle, but not large enough to enable him to draw out his foot. The other end of the upper plank, opposite the hinge, is fastened to its post by lock and key. The slave is made to sit upon the ground, when the uppermost plank is elevated, his legs, just above the ankles, placed in the sub-half circles, and shutting it down again, and locking it, he is held secure and fast. Very often the neck instead of the ankle is enclosed. In this manner they are held during the operation of whipping.

Warner, Will and Major, according to Tanner's account of them, were melon-stealing, Sabbath-breaking niggers, and not approving of such wickedness, he felt it his duty to put them in the stocks. Handing me the key, himself, Myers, Mistress Tanner and the children entered the carriage and drove away to church at Cheneyville. When they were gone, the boys begged me to let them out. I felt sorry to see them sitting on the hot ground, and remembered my own sufferings in the sun. Upon their promise to return to the stocks at any moment they were required to do so, I consented to release them. Grateful for the lenity shown them, and in order in some measure to repay it, they could do no less, of course, than pilot me to the melon-patch.

Shortly before Tanner's return, they were in the stocks again. Finally he drove up, and looking at the boys, said, with a chuckle,—

"Aha! ye havn't been strolling about much to-day, any way. I'll teach you what's what. I'll tire ye of eating water-melons on the Lord's day, ye Sabbath-breaking niggers."

Peter Tanner prided himself upon his strict religious observances: he was a deacon in the church.

But I have now reached a point in the progress of my narrative, when it becomes necessary to turn away from these light descriptions, to the more grave and weighty matter of the second battle with Master Tibeats, and the flight through the great Pacoudrie Swamp.

Chapter X.

RETURN TO TIBEATS—IMPOSSIBILITY OF PLEASING HIM—HE ATTACKS ME WITH A HATCHET—THE STRUGGLE OVER THE BROAD AXE—THE TEMPTATION TO MURDER HIM—ESCAPE ACROSS THE PLANTATION—OBSERVATIONS FROM THE FENCE—TIBEATS APPROACHES, FOLLOWED BY THE HOUNDS—THEY TAKE MY TRACK—THEIR LOUD YELLS—THEY ALMOST OVERTAKE ME—I REACH THE WATER—THE HOUNDS CONFUSED—MOCCASIN SNAKES—ALLIGATORS—NIGHT IN THE "GREAT PACOUDRIE SWAMP"—THE SOUNDS OF LIFE—NORTH-WEST COURSE—EMERGE INTO THE PINE WOODS—THE SLAVE AND HIS YOUNG MASTER—ARRIVAL AT FORD'S—FOOD AND REST.

At the end of a month, my services being no longer required at Tanner's I was sent over the bayou again to my master, whom I found engaged in building the cotton press. This was situated at some distance from the great house, in a rather retired place. I commenced working once more in company with Tibeats, being entirely alone with him most part of the time. I remembered the words of Chapin, his precautions, his advice to beware, lest in some unsuspecting moment he might injure me. They were always in my mind, so that I lived in a most uneasy state of apprehension and fear. One eye was on my work, the other on my master. I determined to give him no cause of offence, to work still more diligently, if possible, than I had done, to bear whatever abuse he might heap upon me, save bodily injury, humbly and patiently, hoping thereby to soften in some degree his manner towards me, until the blessed time might come when I should be delivered from his clutches.

The third morning after my return, Chapin left the plantation for Cheneyville, to be absent until night. Tibeats, on that morning, was attacked with one of those periodical fits of spleen and ill-humor to

which he was frequently subject, rendering him still more disagreeable and venomous than usual.

It was about nine o'clock in the forenoon, when I was busily
employed with the jack-plane on one of the sweeps. Tibeats was
standing by the work-bench, fitting a handle into the chisel, with
which he had been engaged previously in cutting the thread of the
screw.

"You are not planing that down enough," said he.

"It is just even with the line," I replied.

"You're a d—d liar," he exclaimed passionately.

"Oh, well, master," I said, mildly, "I will plane it down more if you
say so," at the same time proceeding to do as I supposed he desired.
Before one shaving had been removed, however, he cried out, saying I had now planed it too deep—it was too small—I had spoiled
the sweep entirely. Then followed curses and imprecations. I had
endeavored to do exactly as he directed, but nothing would satisfy
the unreasonable man. In silence and in dread I stood by the sweep,
holding the jack-plane in my hand, not knowing what to do, and not
daring to be idle. His anger grew more and more violent, until,
finally, with an oath, such a bitter, frightful oath as only Tibeats
could utter, he seized a hatchet from the work-bench and darted
towards me, swearing he would cut my head open.

It was a moment of life or death. The sharp, bright blade of the
hatchet glittered in the sun. In another instant it would be buried
in my brain, and yet in that instant—so quick will a man's thoughts
come to him in such a fearful strait—I reasoned with myself. If I
stood still, my doom was certain; if I fled, ten chances to one the
hatchet, flying from his hand with a too-deadly and unerring aim,
would strike me in the back. There was but one course to take.
Springing towards him with all my power, and meeting him full
half-way, before he could bring down the blow, with one hand I
caught his uplifted arm, with the other seized him by the throat. We
stood looking each other in the eyes. In his I could see murder. I felt
as if I had a serpent by the neck, watching the slightest relaxation
of my grip,* to coil itself round my body, crushing and stinging it to
death. I thought to scream aloud, trusting that some ear might catch
the sound—but Chapin was away; the hands were in the field; there
was no living soul in sight or hearing.

The good genius, which thus far through life has saved me from the
hands of violence, at that moment suggested a lucky thought. With
a vigorous and sudden kick, that brought him on one knee, with a
groan, I released my hold upon his throat, snatched the hatchet, and
cast it beyond reach.

* The transcriber changed "gripe" to "grip".

Frantic with rage, maddened beyond control, he seized a white oak stick, five feet long, perhaps, and as large in circumference as his hand could grasp, which was lying on the ground. Again he rushed towards me, and again I met him, seized him about the waist, and being the stronger of the two, bore him to the earth. While in that position I obtained possession of the stick, and rising, cast it from me, also.

He likewise arose and ran for the broad-axe, on the work-bench. Fortunately, there was a heavy plank lying upon its broad blade, in such a manner that he could not extricate it, before I had sprung upon his back. Pressing him down closely and heavily on the plank, so that the axe was held more firmly to its place, I endeavored, but in vain, to break his grasp upon the handle. In that position we remained some minutes.

There have been hours in my unhappy life, many of them, when the contemplation of death as the end of earthly sorrow—of the grave as a resting place for the tired and worn out body—has been pleasant to dwell upon. But such contemplations vanish in the hour of peril. No man, in his full strength, can stand undismayed, in the presence of the "king of terrors."[4] Life is dear to every living thing; the worm that crawls upon the ground will struggle for it. At that moment it was dear to me, enslaved and treated as I was.

Not able to unloose his hand, once more I seized him by the throat, and this time, with a vice-like gripe* that soon relaxed his hold. He became pliant and unstrung. His face, that had been white with passion, was now black from suffocation. Those small serpent eyes that spat such venom, were now full of horror—two great white orbs starting from their sockets!

There was "a lurking devil" in my heart that prompted me to kill the human blood-hound on the spot—to retain the grip on his accursed throat till the breath of life was gone! I dared not murder him, and I dared not let him live. If I killed him, my life must pay the forfeit—if he lived, my life only would satisfy his vengeance. A voice within whispered me to fly. To be a wanderer among the swamps, a fugitive and a vagabond on the face of the earth, was preferable to the life that I was leading.

My resolution was soon formed, and swinging him from the work-bench to the ground, I leaped a fence near by, and hurried across the plantation, passing the slaves at work in the cotton field. At the end of a quarter of a mile I reached the wood-pasture, and it was a short time indeed that I had been running it. Climbing on to a high fence, I could see the cotton press, the great house, and the space between. It was a conspicuous position, from whence the

4. Death, Job 18.14.
* For "grip" (error in original).

whole plantation was in view. I saw Tibeats cross the field towards the house, and enter it—then he came out, carrying his saddle, and presently mounted his horse and galloped away.

I was desolate, but thankful. Thankful that my life was spared,—desolate and discouraged with the prospect before me. What would become of me? Who would befriend me? Whither should I fly?[5] Oh, God! Thou who gavest me life, and implanted in my bosom the love of life—who filled it with emotions such as other men, thy creatures, have, do not forsake me. Have pity on the poor slave—let me not perish. If thou dost not protect me, I am lost—lost! Such supplications, silently and unuttered, ascended from my inmost heart to Heaven. But there was no answering voice—no sweet, low tone, coming down from on high, whispering to my soul, "It is I, be not afraid."[6] I was the forsaken of God, it seemed—the despised and hated of men!

In about three-fourths of an hour several of the slaves shouted and made signs for me to run. Presently, looking up the bayou, I saw Tibeats and two others on horse-back, coming at a fast gait, followed by a troop of dogs. There were as many as eight or ten. Distant as I was, I knew them. They belonged on the adjoining plantation. The dogs used on Bayou Bœuf for hunting slaves are a kind of bloodhound, but a far more savage breed than is found in the Northern States. They will attack a negro, at their master's bidding, and cling to him as the common bull-dog will cling to a four footed animal. Frequently their loud bay is heard in the swamps, and then there is speculation as to what point the runaway will be overhauled—the same as a New-York hunter stops to listen to the hounds coursing along the hillsides, and suggests to his companion that the fox will be taken at such a place. I never knew a slave escaping with his life from Bayou Bœuf. One reason is, they are not allowed to learn the art of swimming, and are incapable of crossing the most inconsiderable stream. In their flight they can go in no direction but a little way without coming to a bayou, when the inevitable alternative is presented, of being drowned or overtaken by the dogs. In youth I had practised in the clear streams that flow through my native district, until I had become an expert swimmer, and felt at home in the watery element.

I stood upon the fence until the dogs had reached the cotton press. In an instant more, their long, savage yells announced they were on my track. Leaping down from my position, I ran towards the swamp. Fear gave me strength, and I exerted it to the utmost. Every few moments I could hear the yelpings of the dogs. They were gaining upon me. Every howl was nearer and nearer. Each moment I expected they would spring upon my back—expected to feel their

5. Possibly a reference to *Macbeth* 2.4, in which Lady MacDuff says these words when she learns of a plot against her family.
6. John 6.20.

long teeth sinking into my flesh. There were so many of them, I knew they would tear me to pieces, that they would worry me, at once, to death. I gasped for breath—gasped forth a half-uttered, choking prayer to the Almighty to save me—to give me strength to reach some wide, deep bayou where I could throw them off the track, or sink into its waters. Presently I reached a thick palmetto bottom. As I fled through them they made a loud rustling noise, not loud enough, however, to drown the voices of the dogs.

Continuing my course due south, as nearly as I can judge, I came at length to water just over shoe. The hounds at that moment could not have been five rods behind me. I could hear them crashing and plunging through the palmettoes, their loud, eager yells making the whole swamp clamorous with the sound. Hope revived a little as I reached the water. If it were only deeper, they might lose* the scent, and thus disconcerted, afford me the opportunity of evading them. Luckily, it grew deeper the farther I proceeded—now over my ankles—now half-way to my knees—now sinking a moment to my waist, and then emerging presently into more shallow places. The dogs had not gained upon me since I struck the water. Evidently they were confused. Now their savage intonations grew more and more distant, assuring me that I was leaving them. Finally I stopped to listen, but the long howl came booming on the air again, telling me I was not yet safe. From bog to bog, where I had stepped, they could still keep upon the track, though impeded by the water. At length, to my great joy, I came to a wide bayou, and plunging in, had soon stemmed its sluggish current to the other side. There, certainly, the dogs would be confounded—the current carrying down the stream all traces of that slight, mysterious scent, which enables the quick-smelling hound to follow in the track of the fugitive.

After crossing this bayou the water became so deep I could not run. I was now in what I afterwards learned was the "Great Pacoudrie Swamp." It was filled with immense trees—the sycamore, the gum, the cotton wood and cypress, and extends, I am informed, to the shore of the Calcasieu river. For thirty or forty miles it is without inhabitants, save wild beasts—the bear, the wild-cat, the tiger, and great slimy reptiles, that are crawling through it everywhere. Long before I reached the bayou, in fact, from the time I struck the water until I emerged from the swamp on my return, these reptiles surrounded me. I saw hundreds of moccasin snakes. Every log and bog—every trunk of a fallen tree, over which I was compelled to step or climb, was alive with them. They crawled away at my approach, but sometimes in my haste, I almost placed my hand or foot upon them. They are poisonous serpents—their bite more fatal than the

---

* The transcriber changed "loose" to "lose".

rattlesnake's. Besides, I had lost one shoe, the sole having come entirely off, leaving the upper only dangling to my ankle.

I saw also many alligators, great and small, lying in the water, or on pieces of floodwood. The noise I made usually startled them, when they moved off and plunged into the deepest places. Sometimes, however, I would come directly upon a monster before observing it. In such cases, I would start back, run a short way round, and in that manner shun them. Straight forward, they will run a short distance rapidly, but do not possess the power of turning. In a crooked race, there is no difficulty in evading them.

About two o'clock in the afternoon, I heard the last of the hounds. Probably they did not cross the bayou. Wet and weary, but relieved from the sense of instant peril, I continued on, more cautious and afraid, however, of the snakes and alligators than I had been in the earlier portion of my flight. Now, before stepping into a muddy pool, I would strike the water with a stick. If the waters moved, I would go around it, if not, would venture through.

At length the sun went down, and gradually night's trailing mantle shrouded the great swamp in darkness. Still I staggered on, fearing every instant I should feel the dreadful sting of the moccasin, or be crushed within the jaws of some disturbed alligator. The dread of them now almost equaled the fear of the pursuing hounds. The moon arose after a time, its mild light creeping through the overspreading branches, loaded with long, pendent moss. I kept traveling forwards until after midnight, hoping all the while that I would soon emerge into some less desolate and dangerous region. But the water grew deeper and the walking more difficult than ever. I perceived it would be impossible to proceed much farther, and knew not, moreover, what hands I might fall into, should I succeed in reaching a human habitation. Not provided with a pass,[7] any white man would be at liberty to arrest me, and place me in prison until such time as my master should "prove property, pay charges, and take me away." I was an estray,[8] and if so unfortunate as to meet a law-abiding citizen of Louisiana, he would deem it his duty to his neighbor, perhaps, to put me forthwith in the pound. Really, it was difficult to determine which I had most reason to fear—dogs, alligators or men!

After midnight, however, I came to a halt. Imagination cannot picture the dreariness of the scene. The swamp was resonant with the quacking of innumerable ducks! Since the foundation of the earth, in all probability, a human footstep had never before so far

7. Document signifying that a slave has his master's permission to leave the plantation grounds.
8. Legal term for a domestic animal found wandering without an owner.

penetrated the recesses of the swamp. It was not silent now—silent
to a degree that rendered it oppressive,—as it was when the sun
was shining in the heavens. My midnight intrusion had awakened
the feathered tribes, which seemed to throng the morass in hundreds of thousands, and their garrulous throats poured forth such
multitudinous sounds—there was such a fluttering of wings—such
sullen plunges in the water all around me—that I was affrighted
and appalled. All the fowls of the air, and all the creeping things of
the earth appeared to have assembled together in that particular
place,[9] for the purpose of filling it with clamor and confusion. Not
by human dwellings—not in crowded cities alone, are the sights
and sounds of life. The wildest places of the earth are full of them.
Even in the heart of that dismal swamp, God had provided a refuge
and a dwelling place for millions of living things.

The moon had now risen above the trees, when I resolved upon a
new project. Thus far I had endeavored to travel as nearly south as
possible. Turning about I proceeded in a north-west direction, my
object being to strike the Pine Woods in the vicinity of Master
Ford's. Once within the shadow of his protection, I felt I would be
comparatively safe.

My clothes were in tatters, my hands, face, and body covered with
scratches, received from the sharp knots of fallen trees, and in
climbing over piles of brush and floodwood. My bare foot was full
of thorns. I was besmeared with muck and mud, and the green
slime that had collected on the surface of the dead water, in which
I had been immersed to the neck many times during the day and
night. Hour after hour, and tiresome indeed had they become, I
continued to plod along on my north-west course. The water began
to grow less deep, and the ground more firm under my feet. At last I
reached the Pacoudrie, the same wide bayou I had swam while "out-
ward bound." I swam it again, and shortly after thought I heard a
cock crow, but the sound was faint, and it might have been a mock-
ery of the ear. The water receded from my advancing footsteps—
now I had left the bogs behind me—now I was on dry land that
gradually ascended to the plain, and I knew I was somewhere in the
"Great Pine Woods."

Just at day-break I came to an opening—a sort of small
plantation—but one I had never seen before. In the edge of the
woods I came upon two men, a slave and his young master, engaged
in catching wild hogs. The white man I knew would demand my
pass, and not able to give him one, would take me into possession. I
was too wearied to run again, and too desperate to be taken, and

9. Reference to Genesis 8.19, part of the story of Noah's ark: "Every beast, every creeping
thing, and every fowl, and whatsoever creepeth upon the earth, after their kinds, went
forth out of the ark."

therefore adopted a ruse that proved entirely successful. Assuming a fierce expression, I walked directly towards him, looking him steadily in the face. As I approached, he moved backwards with an air of alarm. It was plain he was much affrighted—that he looked upon me as some infernal goblin, just arisen from the bowels of the swamp!

"Where does William Ford live?" I demanded, in no gentle tone.

"He lives seven miles from here," was the reply.

"Which is the way to his place?" I again demanded, trying to look more fiercely than ever.

"Do you see those pine trees yonder?" he asked, pointing to two, a mile distant, that rose far above their fellows, like a couple of tall sentinels, overlooking the broad expanse of forest.

"I see them," was the answer.

"At the feet of those pine trees," he continued, "runs the Texas road. Turn to the left, and it will lead you to William Ford's."

Without farther parley, I hastened forward, happy as he was, no doubt, to place the widest possible distance between us. Striking the Texas road, I turned to the left hand, as directed, and soon passed a great fire, where a pile of logs were burning. I went to it, thinking I would dry my clothes; but the gray light of the morning was fast breaking away,—some passing white man might observe me; besides, the heat overpowered me with the desire of sleep: so, lingering no longer, I continued my travels, and finally, about eight o'clock, reached the house of Master Ford.

The slaves were all absent from the quarters, at their work. Stepping on to the piazza, I knocked at the door, which was soon opened by Mistress Ford. My appearance was so changed—I was in such a wobegone and forlorn condition, she did not know me. Inquiring if Master Ford was at home, that good man made his appearance, before the question could be answered. I told him of my flight, and all the particulars connected with it. He listened attentively, and when I had concluded, spoke to me kindly and sympathetically, and taking me to the kitchen, called John, and ordered him to prepare me food. I had tasted nothing since daylight the previous morning.

When John had set the meal before me, the madam came out with a bowl of milk, and many little delicious dainties, such as rarely please the palate of a slave. I was hungry, and I was weary, but neither food nor rest afforded half the pleasure as did the blessed voices speaking kindness and consolation. It was the oil and the wine which the Good Samaritan[1] in the "Great Pine Woods" was ready to pour into the wounded spirit of the slave, who came to him, stripped of his raiment and half-dead.

---

1. Man who helps an injured stranger in a New Testament parable (Luke 10.29–37).

They left me in the cabin, that I might rest. Blessed be sleep! It visiteth all alike, descending as the dews of heaven on the bond and free. Soon it nestled to my bosom, driving away the troubles that oppressed it, and bearing me to that shadowy region, where I saw again the faces, and listened to the voices of my children, who, alas, for aught I knew in my waking hours, had fallen into the arms of that *other* sleep, from which they *never* would arouse.

Chapter XI.

THE MISTRESS' GARDEN—THE CRIMSON AND GOLDEN FRUIT—
ORANGE AND POMEGRANATE TREES—RETURN TO BAYOU BŒUF—
MASTER FORD'S REMARKS ON THE WAY—THE MEETING WITH
TIBEATS—HIS ACCOUNT OF THE CHASE—FORD CENSURES HIS
BRUTALITY—ARRIVAL AT THE PLANTATION—ASTONISHMENT OF THE
SLAVES ON SEEING ME—THE ANTICIPATED FLOGGING—KENTUCKY
JOHN—MR. ELDRET, THE PLANTER—ELDRET'S SAM—TRIP TO THE
"BIG CANE BRAKE"—THE TRADITION OF "SUTTON'S FIELD"—FOREST
TREES—GNATS AND MOSQUITOS—THE ARRIVAL OF BLACK WOMEN
IN THE BIG CANE—LUMBER WOMEN—SUDDEN APPEARANCE OF
TIBEATS—HIS PROVOKING TREATMENT—VISIT TO BAYOU BŒUF—
THE SLAVE PASS—SOUTHERN HOSPITALITY—THE LAST OF ELIZA—
SALE TO EDWIN EPPS.

After a long sleep, sometime in the afternoon I awoke, refreshed, but very sore and stiff. Sally came in and talked with me, while John cooked me some dinner. Sally was in great trouble, as well as myself, one of her children being ill, and she feared it could not survive. Dinner over, after walking about the quarters for a while, visiting Sally's cabin and looking at the sick child, I strolled into the madam's garden. Though it was a season of the year when the voices of the birds are silent, and the trees are stripped of their summer glories in more frigid climes, yet the whole variety of roses were then blooming there, and the long, luxuriant vines creeping over the frames. The crimson and golden fruit hung half hidden amidst the younger and older blossoms of the peach, the orange, the plum, and the pomegranate; for, in that region of almost perpetual warmth, the leaves are falling and the buds bursting into bloom the whole year long.

I indulged the most grateful feelings towards Master and Mistress Ford, and wishing in some manner to repay their kindness, commenced trimming the vines, and afterwards weeding out the grass from among the orange and pomegranate trees. The latter grows eight or ten feet high, and its fruit, though larger, is similar in appearance to the jelly-flower. It has the luscious flavor of the strawberry. Oranges, peaches, plums, and most other fruits are indigenous to the rich, warm soil of Avoyelles; but the apple, the most common of them all in colder latitudes, is rarely to be seen.

Mistress Ford came out presently, saying it was praise-worthy in me, but I was not in a condition to labor, and might rest myself at the quarters until master should go down to Bayou Bœuf, which would not be that day, and it might not be the next. I said to her— to be sure, I felt bad, and was stiff, and that my foot pained me, the stubs and thorns having so torn it, but thought such exercise would not hurt me, and that it was a great pleasure to work for so good a mistress. Thereupon she returned to the great house, and for three days I was diligent in the garden, cleaning the walks, weeding the flower beds, and pulling up the rank grass beneath the jessamine vines, which the gentle and generous hand of my protectress had taught to clamber along the walls.

The fourth morning, having become recruited and refreshed, Master Ford ordered me to make ready to accompany him to the bayou. There was but one saddle horse at the opening, all the others with the mules having been sent down to the plantation. I said I could walk, and bidding Sally and John goodbye, left the opening, trotting along by the horse's side.

That little paradise in the Great Pine Woods was the oasis in the desert, towards which my heart turned lovingly, during many years of bondage. I went forth from it now with regret and sorrow, not so overwhelming, however, as if it had then been given me to know that I should never return to it again.

Master Ford urged me to take his place occasionally on the horse, to rest me; but I said no, I was not tired, and it was better for me to walk than him. He said many kind and cheering things to me on the way, riding slowly, in order that I might keep pace with him. The goodness of God was manifest, he declared, in my miraculous escape from the swamp. As Daniel came forth unharmed from the den of lions, and as Jonah had been preserved in the whale's belly,[2] even so had I been delivered from evil by the Almighty. He interrogated me in regard to the various fears and emotions I had experienced during the day and night, and if I had felt, at any time, a desire to pray. I felt forsaken of the whole world, I answered him, and was praying mentally all the while. At such times, said he, the heart of man turns instinctively towards his Maker. In prosperity, and when there is nothing to injure or make him afraid, he remembers Him not, and is ready to defy Him; but place him in the midst of dangers, cut him off from human aid, let the grave open before him—then it is, in the time of his tribulation, that the scoffer and unbelieving

2. Both Daniel and Jonah are biblical prophets.

man turns to God for help, feeling there is no other hope, or refuge, or safety, save in his protecting arm.

So did that benignant man speak to me of this life and of the life hereafter; of the goodness and power of God, and of the vanity of earthly things, as we journeyed along the solitary road towards Bayou Bœuf.

When within some five miles of the plantation, we discovered a horseman at a distance, galloping towards us. As he came near I saw that it was Tibeats! He looked at me a moment, but did not address me, and turning about, rode along side by side with Ford. I trotted silently at their horses' heels, listening* to their conversation. Ford informed him of my arrival in the Pine Woods three days before, of the sad plight I was in, and of the difficulties and dangers I had encountered.

"Well," exclaimed Tibeats, omitting his usual oaths in the presence of Ford, "I never saw such running before. I'll bet him against a hundred dollars, he'll beat any nigger in Louisiana. I offered John David Cheney twenty-five dollars to catch him, dead or alive, but he outran his dogs in a fair race. Them Cheney dogs ain't much, after all. Dunwoodie's hounds would have had him down before he touched the palmettoes. Somehow the dogs got off the track, and we had to give up the hunt. We rode the horses as far as we could, and then kept on foot till the water was three feet deep. The boys said he was drowned, sure. I allow I wanted a shot at him mightily. Ever since, I have been riding up and down the bayou, but had'nt much hope of catching him—thought he was dead, *sartin*. Oh, he's a cuss to run—that nigger is!"

In this way Tibeats ran on, describing his search in the swamp, the wonderful speed with which I had fled before the hounds, and when he had finished, Master Ford responded by saying, I had always been a willing and faithful boy with him; that he was sorry we had such trouble; that, according to Platt's story, he had been inhumanly treated, and that he, Tibeats, was himself in fault. Using hatchets and broad-axes upon slaves was shameful, and should not be allowed, he remarked. "This is no way of dealing with them, when first brought into the country. It will have a pernicious influence, and set them all running away. The swamps will be full of them. A little kindness would be far more effectual in restraining them, and rendering them obedient, than the use of such deadly weapons. Every planter on the bayou should frown upon such inhumanity. It is for the interest of all to do so. It is evident enough, Mr. Tibeats, that you and Platt cannot live together. You dislike him, and would not hesitate to kill him,

---

* The transcriber changed "listing" to "listening".

and knowing it, he will run from you again through fear of his life. Now, Tibeats, you must sell him, or hire him out,[3] at least. Unless you do so, I shall take measures to get him out of your possession."

In this spirit Ford addressed him the remainder of the distance. I opened not my mouth. On reaching the plantation they entered the great house, while I repaired to Eliza's cabin. The slaves were astonished to find me there, on returning from the field, supposing I was drowned. That night, again, they gathered about the cabin to listen to the story of my adventure. They took it for granted I would be whipped, and that it would be severe, the well-known penalty of running away being five hundred lashes.

"Poor fellow," said Eliza, taking me by the hand, "it would have been better for you if you had drowned. You have a cruel master, and he will kill you yet, I am afraid."

Lawson suggested that it might be, overseer Chapin would be appointed to inflict the punishment, in which case it would not be severe, whereupon Mary, Rachel, Bristol, and others hoped it would be Master Ford, and then it would be no whipping at all. They all pitied me and tried to console me, and were sad in view of the castigation that awaited me, except Kentucky John. There were no bounds to his laughter; he filled the cabin with cachinnations,[4] holding his sides to prevent an explosion, and the cause of his noisy mirth was the idea of my outstripping the hounds. Somehow, he looked at the subject in a comical light. "I *know'd* dey would'nt cotch him, when he run cross de plantation. O, de lor', did'nt Platt pick his feet right up, tho', hey? When dem dogs got whar he was, he was'nt *dar*—haw, haw, haw! O, de lor' a' mity!"—and then Kentucky John relapsed into another of his boisterous fits.

Early the next morning, Tibeats left the plantation. In the course of the forenoon, while sauntering about the gin-house, a tall, good-looking man came to me, and inquired if I was Tibeats' boy, that youthful appellation being applied indiscriminately to slaves even though they may have passed the number of three score years and ten.[5] I took off my hat, and answered that I was.

"How would you like to work for me?" he inquired.

"Oh, I would like to, very much," said I, inspired with a sudden hope of getting away from Tibeats.

"You worked under Myers at Peter Tanner's, didn't you?"

I replied I had, adding some complimentary remarks that Myers had made concerning me.

3. Ford is suggesting that Tibeats subcontract Northup's labor to a third party while retaining technical ownership of him.
4. Wild, excessive laughter.
5. Seventy years, which is the natural span of a human life according to Psalm 90.

"Well, boy," said he, "I have hired you of your master to work for me in the "Big Cane Brake," thirty-eight miles from here, down on Red River."

This man was Mr. Eldret, who lived below Ford's, on the same side of the bayou. I accompanied him to his plantation, and in the morning started with his slave Sam, and a wagon-load of provisions, drawn by four mules, for the Big Cane, Eldret and Myers having preceded us on horseback. This Sam was a native of Charleston, where he had a mother, brother and sisters. He "allowed"—a common word among both black and white—that Tibeats was a mean man, and hoped, as I most earnestly did also, that his master would buy me.

We proceeded down the south shore of the bayou, crossing it at Carey's plantation; from thence to Huff Power, passing which, we came upon the Bayou Rouge road, which runs towards Red River. After passing through Bayou Rouge Swamp, and just at sunset, turning from the highway, we struck off into the "Big Cane Brake." We followed an unbeaten track, scarcely wide enough to admit the wagon. The cane, such as are used for fishing-rods, were as thick as they could stand. A person could not be seen through them the distance of a rod. The paths of wild beasts run through them in various directions—the bear and the American tiger abounding in these brakes, and wherever there is a basin of stagnant water, it is full of alligators.

We kept on our lonely course through the "Big Cane" several miles, when we entered a clearing, known as "Sutton's Field." Many years before, a man by the name of Sutton had penetrated the wilderness of cane to this solitary place. Tradition has it, that he fled thither, a fugitive, not from service, but from justice. Here he lived alone—recluse and hermit of the swamp—with his own hands planting the seed and gathering in the harvest. One day a band of Indians stole upon his solitude, and after a bloody battle, overpowered and massacred him. For miles the country round, in the slaves' quarters, and on the piazzas of "great houses," where white children listen to superstitious tales, the story goes, that that spot, in the heart of the "Big Cane," is a haunted place. For more than a quarter of a century, human voices had rarely, if ever, disturbed the silence of the clearing. Rank and noxious weeds had overspread the once cultivated field—serpents sunned themselves on the doorway of the crumbling cabin. It was indeed a dreary picture of desolation.

Passing "Sutton's Field," we followed a new-cut road two miles farther, which brought us to its termination. We had now reached the wild lands of Mr. Eldret, where he contemplated clearing up an extensive plantation. We went to work next morning with our cane-knives, and cleared a sufficient space to allow the erection of two cabins—one for Myers and Eldret, the other for Sam, myself, and the slaves that were to join us. We were now in the midst of trees of enormous growth, whose wide-spreading branches almost shut out the light of the sun, while the space between the trunks was an impervious mass of cane, with here and there an occasional palmetto.

The bay and the sycamore, the oak and the cypress, reach a growth unparalleled, in those fertile lowlands bordering the Red River. From every tree, moreover, hang long, large masses of moss, presenting to the eye unaccustomed to them, a striking and singular appearance. This moss, in large quantities, is sent north, and there used for manufacturing purposes.

We cut down oaks, split them into rails, and with these erected temporary cabins. We covered the roofs with the broad palmetto leaf, an excellent substitute for shingles, as long as they last.

The greatest annoyance I met with here were small flies, gnats and mosquitoes. They swarmed the air. They penetrated the porches of the ear, the nose, the eyes, the mouth. They sucked themselves beneath the skin. It was impossible to brush or beat them off. It seemed, indeed, as if they would devour us—carry us away piece-meal, in their small tormenting mouths.

A lonelier spot, or one more disagreeable, than the centre of the "Big Cane Brake," it would be difficult to conceive; yet to me it was a paradise, in comparison with any other place in the company of Master Tibeats. I labored hard, and oft-times was weary and fatigued, yet I could lie down at night in peace, and arise in the morning without fear.

In the course of a fortnight, four black girls came down from Eldret's plantation—Charlotte, Fanny, Cresia and Nelly. They were all large and stout. Axes were put into their hands, and they were sent out with Sam and myself to cut trees. They were excellent choppers, the largest oak or sycamore standing but a brief season before their heavy and well-directed blows. At piling logs, they were equal to any man. There are lumberwomen as well as lumbermen in the forests of the South. In fact, in the region of the Bayou Bœuf they perform their share of all the labor required on the plantation. They plough, drag, drive team, clear wild lands, work on the highway, and so forth. Some planters, owning large cotton and sugar plantations, have none other than the labor of slave women. Such a one* is Jim Burns, who lives on the north shore of the bayou, opposite the plantation of John Fogaman.

On our arrival in the brake, Eldret promised me, if I worked well, I might go up to visit my friends at Ford's in four weeks. On Saturday night of the fifth week, I reminded him of his promise, when he told me I had done so well, that I might go. I had set my heart

* The transcriber changed "an one" to "a one".

upon it, and Eldret's announcement thrilled me with pleasure. I was to return in time to commence the labors of the day on Tuesday morning.

While indulging the pleasant anticipation of so soon meeting my old friends again, suddenly the hateful form of Tibeats appeared among us. He inquired how Myers and Platt got along together, and was told, very well, and that Platt was going up to Ford's plantation in the morning on a visit.

"Poh, poh!" sneered Tibeats; "it isn't worth while—the nigger will get unsteady. He can't go."

But Eldret insisted I had worked faithfully—that he had given me his promise, and that, under the circumstances, I ought not to be disappointed. They then, it being about dark, entered one cabin and I the other. I could not give up the idea of going; it was a sore disappointment. Before morning I resolved, if Eldret made no objection, to leave at all hazards. At daylight I was at his door, with my blanket rolled up into a bundle, and hanging on a stick over my shoulder, waiting for a pass. Tibeats came out presently in one of his disagreeable moods, washed his face, and going to a stump near by, sat down upon it, apparently busily thinking with himself. After standing there a long time, impelled by a sudden impulse of impatience, I started off.

"Are you going without a pass?" he cried out to me.

"Yes, master, I thought I would," I answered.

"How do you think you'll get there?" demanded he.

"Don't know," was all the reply I made him.

"You'd be taken and sent to jail, where you ought to be, before you got half-way there," he added, passing into the cabin as he said it. He came out soon with the pass in his hand, and calling me a "d—d nigger that deserved a hundred lashes," threw it on the ground. I picked it up, and hurried away right speedily.

A slave caught off his master's plantation without a pass, may be seized and whipped by any white man whom he meets. The one I now received was dated, and read as follows:

"Platt has permission to go to Ford's plantation, on Bayou Bœuf, and return by Tuesday morning.
                    John M. Tibeats."

This is the usual form. On the way, a great many demanded it, read it, and passed on. Those having the air and appearance of gentlemen, whose dress indicated the possession of wealth, frequently took no notice of me whatever; but a shabby fellow, an unmistakable loafer, never failed to hail me, and to scrutinize and examine me in the most thorough manner. Catching runaways is sometimes a money-making business. If, after advertising, no owner appears, they may be sold to the highest bidder; and certain fees are allowed the finder for his services, at all events, even if reclaimed. "A mean white," therefore,—a name applied to the species loafer—considers it a god-send to meet an unknown negro without a pass.

There are no inns along the highways in that portion of the State where I sojourned. I was wholly destitute of money, neither did I carry any provisions, on my journey from the Big Cane to Bayou Bœuf; nevertheless, with his pass in his hand, a slave need never suffer from hunger or from thirst. It is only necessary to present it to the master or overseer of a plantation, and state his wants, when he will be sent round to the kitchen and provided with food or shelter, as the case may require. The traveler stops at any house and calls for a meal with as much freedom as if it was a public tavern. It is the general custom of the country. Whatever their faults may be, it is certain the inhabitants along Red River, and around the bayous in the interior of Louisiana are not wanting in hospitality.

I arrived at Ford's plantation towards the close of the afternoon, passing the evening in Eliza's cabin, with Lawson, Rachel, and others of my acquaintance. When we left Washington Eliza's form was round and plump. She stood erect, and in her silks and jewels, presented a picture of graceful strength and elegance. Now she was but a thin shadow of her former self. Her face had become ghastly haggard, and the once straight and active form was bowed down, as if bearing the weight of a hundred years. Crouching on her cabin floor, and clad in the coarse garments of a slave, old Elisha Berry would not have recognized the mother of his child. I never saw her afterwards. Having become useless in the cotton-field, she was bartered for a trifle, to some man residing in the vicinity of Peter Compton's. Grief had gnawed remorselessly at her heart, until her strength was gone; and for that, her last master, it is said, lashed and abused her most unmercifully. But he could not whip back the departed vigor of her youth, nor straighten up that bended body to its full height, such as it was when her children were around her, and the light of freedom was shining on her path.

I learned the particulars relative to her departure from this world, from some of Compton's slaves, who had come over Red River to the bayou, to assist young Madam Tanner during the "busy season." She became at length, they said, utterly helpless, for several weeks lying on the ground floor in a dilapidated cabin, dependent upon the mercy of her fellow-thralls for an occasional drop of water, and a morsel of food. Her master did not "knock her on the head," as is sometimes done to put a suffering animal out of misery, but left her unprovided for, and unprotected, to linger through a life of pain and wretchedness to its natural close. When the hands returned from the field one night they found her dead! During the day, the Angel of the

Lord, who moveth invisibly over all the earth, gathering in his harvest of departing souls, had silently entered the cabin of the dying woman, and taken her from thence. She was *free* at last!

Next day, rolling up my blanket, I started on my return to the Big Cane. After traveling five miles, at a place called Huff Power, the ever-present Tibeats met me in the road. He inquired why I was going back so soon, and when informed I was anxious to return by the time I was directed, he said I need go no farther than the next plantation, as he had that day sold me to Edwin Epps. We walked down into the yard, where we met the latter gentleman, who examined me, and asked me the usual questions propounded by purchasers. Having been duly delivered over, I was ordered to the quarters, and at the same time directed to make a hoe and axe handle for myself.

I was now no longer the property of Tibeats—his dog, his brute, dreading his wrath and cruelty day and night; and whoever or whatever my new master might prove to be, I could not, certainly, regret the change. So it was good news when the sale was announced, and with a sigh of relief I sat down for the first time in my new abode.

Tibeats soon after disappeared from that section of the country. Once afterwards, and only once, I caught a glimpse of him. It was many miles from Bayou Bœuf. He was seated in the doorway of a low groggery.[6] I was passing, in a drove of slaves, through St. Mary's parish.

Chapter XII.

PERSONAL APPEARANCE OF EPPS—EPPS, DRUNK AND SOBER—A GLIMPSE OF HIS HISTORY—COTTON GROWING—THE MODE OF PLOUGHING AND PREPARING GROUND—OF PLANTING, OF HOEING, OF PICKING, OF TREATING RAW HANDS—THE DIFFERENCE IN COTTON PICKERS—PATSEY A REMARKABLE ONE—TASKED ACCORDING TO ABILITY—BEAUTY OF A COTTON FIELD—THE SLAVE'S LABORS—FEAR ON APPROACHING THE GIN-HOUSE—WEIGHING—"CHORES"—CABIN LIFE—THE CORN MILL—THE USES OF THE GOURD—FEAR OF OVERSLEEPING—FEAR CONTINUALLY—MODE OF CULTIVATING CORN—SWEET POTATOES—FERTILITY OF THE SOIL—FATTENING HOGS—PRESERVING BACON—RAISING CATTLE—SHOOTING-MATCHES— GARDEN PRODUCTS—FLOWERS AND VERDURE.

Edwin Epps, of whom much will be said during the remainder of this history, is a large, portly, heavy-bodied man with light hair, high cheek bones, and a Roman nose of extraordinary dimensions. He

6. Barroom; "grog" is a type of alcoholic beverage most often associated with sailors.

has blue eyes, a fair complexion, and is, as I should say, full six feet high. He has the sharp, inquisitive expression of a jockey. His manners are repulsive and coarse, and his language gives speedy and unequivocal evidence that he has never enjoyed the advantages of an education. He has the faculty of saying most provoking things, in that respect even excelling old Peter Tanner. At the time I came into his possession, Edwin Epps was fond of the bottle, his "sprees" sometimes extending over the space of two whole weeks. Latterly, however, he had reformed his habits, and when I left him, was as strict a specimen of temperance as could be found on Bayou Bœuf. When "in his cups," Master Epps was a roystering, blustering, noisy fellow, whose chief delight was in dancing with his "niggers," or lashing them about the yard with his long whip, just for the pleasure of hearing them screech and scream, as the great welts were planted on their backs. When sober, he was silent, reserved and cunning, not beating us indiscriminately, as in his drunken moments, but sending the end of his rawhide to some tender spot of a lagging slave, with a sly dexterity peculiar to himself.

He had been a driver and overseer in his younger years, but at this time was in possession of a plantation on Bayou Huff Power, two and a half miles from Holmesville, eighteen from Marksville, and twelve from Cheneyville. It belonged to Joseph B. Roberts, his wife's uncle, and was leased by Epps. His principal business was raising cotton, and inasmuch as some may read this book who have never seen a cotton field, a description of the manner of its culture may not be out of place.

The ground is prepared by throwing up beds or ridges, with the plough—back-furrowing, it is called. Oxen and mules, the latter almost exclusively, are used in ploughing. The women as frequently as the men perform this labor, feeding, currying, and taking care of their teams, and in all respects doing the field and stable work, precisely as do the ploughboys of the North.

The beds, or ridges, are six feet wide, that is, from water furrow to water furrow. A plough drawn by one mule is then run along the top of the ridge or center of the bed, making the drill, into which a girl usually drops the seed, which she carries in a bag hung round her neck. Behind her comes a mule and harrow, covering up the seed, so that two mules, three slaves, a plough and harrow, are employed in planting a row of cotton. This is done in the months of March and April. Corn is planted in February. When there are no cold rains, the cotton usually makes its appearance in a week. In the course of eight or ten days afterwards the first hoeing is commenced. This is performed in part, also, by the aid of the plough and mule. The plough passes as near as possible to the cotton on both sides, throwing the furrow from it. Slaves follow with their hoes, cutting up the grass and cotton, leaving hills two feet and a half apart. This is called scraping cotton. In two weeks more commences the second hoeing. This time the furrow is thrown towards the cotton. Only one stalk, the largest, is now left standing in each hill. In another fortnight it is hoed the third time, throwing the furrow towards the cotton in the same manner as before, and killing all the grass between the rows. About the first of July, when it is a foot high or thereabouts, it is hoed the fourth and last time. Now the whole space between the rows is ploughed, leaving a deep water furrow in the center. During all these hoeings the overseer or driver follows the slaves on horseback with a whip, such as has been described. The fastest hoer takes the lead row. He is usually about a rod in advance of his companions. If one of them passes him, he is whipped. If one falls behind or is a moment idle, he is whipped. In fact, the lash is flying from morning until night, the whole day long. The hoeing season thus continues from April until July, a field having no sooner been finished once, than it is commenced again.

In the latter part of August begins the cotton picking season. At this time each slave is presented with a sack. A strap is fastened to it, which goes over the neck, holding the mouth of the sack breast high, while the bottom reaches nearly to the ground. Each one is also presented with a large basket that will hold about two barrels. This is to put the cotton in when the sack is filled. The baskets are carried to the field and placed at the beginning of the rows.

When a new hand, one unaccustomed to the business, is sent for the first time into the field, he is whipped up smartly, and made for that day to pick as fast as he can possibly. At night it is weighed, so that his capability in cotton picking is known. He must bring in the same weight each night following. If it falls short, it is considered evidence that he has been laggard, and a greater or less number of lashes is the penalty.

An ordinary day's work is two hundred pounds. A slave who is accustomed to picking, is punished, if he or she brings in a less quantity than that. There is a great difference among them as regards this kind of labor. Some of them seem to have a natural knack, or quickness, which enables them to pick with great celerity, and with both hands, while others, with whatever practice or industry, are utterly unable to come up to the ordinary standard. Such hands are taken from the cotton field and employed in other business. Patsey, of whom I shall have more to say, was known as the most remarkable cotton picker on Bayou Bœuf. She picked with both hands and with such surprising rapidity, that five hundred pounds a day was not unusual for her.

Each one is tasked, therefore, according to his picking abilities, none, however, to come short of two hundred weight. I, being unskillful always in that business, would have satisfied my master by bringing in the latter quantity, while on the other hand, Patsey would surely have been beaten if she failed to produce twice as much.

The cotton grows from five to seven feet high, each stalk having a great many branches, shooting out in all directions, and lapping each other above the water furrow.

There are few sights more pleasant to the eye, than a wide cotton field when it is in the bloom. It presents an appearance of purity, like an immaculate expanse of light, new-fallen snow.

Sometimes the slave picks down one side of a row, and back upon the other, but more usually, there is one on either side, gathering all that has blossomed, leaving the unopened bolls for a succeeding picking. When the sack is filled, it is emptied into the basket and trodden down. It is necessary to be extremely careful the first time going through the field, in order not to break the branches off the stalks. The cotton will not bloom upon a broken branch. Epps never failed to inflict the severest chastisement on the unlucky servant who, either carelessly or unavoidably, was guilty in the least degree in this respect.

The hands are required to be in the cotton field as soon as it is light in the morning, and, with the exception of ten or fifteen minutes, which is given them at noon to swallow their allowance of cold bacon, they are not permitted to be a moment idle until it is too dark to see, and when the moon is full, they often times labor till the middle of the night. They do not dare to stop even at dinner time, nor return to the quarters, however late it be, until the order to halt is given by the driver.

The day's work over in the field, the baskets are "toted," or in other words, carried to the gin-house, where the cotton is weighed. No matter how fatigued and weary he may be—no matter how much he longs for sleep and rest—a slave never approaches the gin-house with his basket of cotton but with fear. If it falls short in weight—if he has not performed the full task appointed him, he knows that he must suffer. And if he has exceeded it by ten or twenty pounds, in all probability his master will measure the next day's task accordingly. So, whether he has too little or too much, his approach to the gin-house is always with fear and trembling. Most frequently they have too little, and therefore it is they are not anxious to leave the field. After weighing, follow the whippings; and then the baskets are carried to the cotton house, and their contents stored away like hay, all hands being sent in to tramp it down. If the cotton is not dry, instead of taking it to the gin-house at once, it is laid upon platforms, two feet high, and some three times as wide, covered with boards or plank, with narrow walks running between them.

This done, the labor of the day is not yet ended, by any means. Each one must then attend to his respective chores. One feeds the mules, another the swine—another cuts the wood, and so forth; besides, the packing is all done by candle light. Finally, at a late hour, they reach the quarters, sleepy and overcome with the long day's toil. Then a fire must be kindled in the cabin, the corn ground in the small hand-mill, and supper, and dinner for the next day in the field, prepared. All that is allowed them is corn and bacon, which is given out at the corncrib and smoke-house every Sunday morning. Each one receives, as his weekly allowance, three and a half pounds of bacon, and corn enough to make a peck of meal. That is all—no tea, coffee, sugar, and with the exception of a very scanty sprinkling now and then, no salt. I can say, from a ten years' residence with Master Epps, that no slave of his is ever likely to suffer from the gout, superinduced by excessive high living.[7] Master Epps' hogs were fed on *shelled* corn—it was thrown out to his "niggers" in the ear. The former, he thought, would fatten faster by shelling, and soaking it in the water—the latter, perhaps, if treated in the same manner, might grow too fat to labor. Master Epps was a shrewd calculator, and knew how to manage his own animals, drunk or sober.

The corn mill stands in the yard beneath a shelter. It is like a common coffee mill, the hopper holding about six quarts. There was one privilege which Master Epps granted freely to every slave he had. They might grind their corn nightly, in such small quantities as their daily wants required, or they might grind the whole week's allowance at one time, on Sundays, just as they preferred. A very generous man was Master Epps!

I kept my corn in a small wooden box, the meal in a gourd; and, by the way, the gourd is one of the most convenient and necessary utensils on a plantation. Besides supplying the place of all kinds of crockery in a slave cabin, it is used for carrying water to the fields. Another, also, contains the dinner. It dispenses with the necessity of pails, dippers, basins, and such tin and wooden superfluities altogether.

When the corn is ground, and fire is made, the bacon is taken down from the nail on which it hangs, a slice cut off and thrown upon the coals to broil. The majority of slaves have no knife, much less a fork. They cut their bacon with the axe at the wood-pile. The corn meal is mixed with a little water, placed in the fire, and baked. When it is "done brown," the ashes are scraped off, and being placed upon a chip, which answers for a table, the tenant of the slave hut is ready to sit down upon the ground to supper. By this time it is usually midnight. The same fear of punishment with which they approach the gin-house, possesses them again on lying down to get a snatch of rest. It is the fear of oversleeping in the morning. Such an offence

7. Gout, an inflammation most frequently affecting the big toe, was once believed to be exclusive to the wealthy, whose rich diets made them more susceptible to the disease within certain periods and cultures.

would certainly be attended with not less than twenty lashes. With a prayer that he may be on his feet and wide awake at the first sound of the horn, he sinks to his slumbers nightly.

The softest couches in the world are not to be found in the log mansion of the slave. The one whereon I reclined year after year, was a plank twelve inches wide and ten feet long. My pillow was a stick of wood. The bedding was a coarse blanket, and not a rag or shred beside. Moss might be used, were it not that it directly breeds a swarm of fleas.

The cabin is constructed of logs, without floor or window. The latter is altogether unnecessary, the crevices between the logs admitting sufficient light. In stormy weather the rain drives through them, rendering it comfortless and extremely disagreeable. The rude door hangs on great wooden hinges. In one end is constructed an awkward fire-place.

An hour before day light the horn is blown. Then the slaves arouse, prepare their breakfast, fill a gourd with water, in another deposit their dinner of cold bacon and corn cake, and hurry to the field again. It is an offence invariably followed by a flogging, to be found at the quarters after daybreak. Then the fears and labors of another day begin; and until its close there is no such thing as rest. He fears he will be caught lagging through the day; he fears to approach the gin-house with his basket-load of cotton at night; he fears, when he lies down, that he will oversleep himself in the morning. Such is a true, faithful, unexaggerated picture and description of the slave's daily life, during the time of cotton-picking, on the shores of Bayou Bœuf.

In the month of January, generally, the fourth and last picking is completed. Then commences the harvesting of corn. This is considered a secondary crop, and receives far less attention than the cotton. It is planted, as already mentioned, in February. Corn is grown in that region for the purpose of fattening hogs and feeding slaves; very little, if any, being sent to market. It is the white variety, the ear of great size, and the stalk growing to the height of eight, and often times ten feet. In August the leaves are stripped off, dried in the sun, bound in small bundles, and stored away as provender for the mules and oxen. After this the slaves go through the field, turning down the ear, for the purpose of keeping the rains from penetrating to the grain. It is left in this condition until after cotton-picking is over, whether earlier or later. Then the ears are separated from the stalks, and deposited in the corncrib with the husks on; otherwise, stripped of the husks, the weevil would destroy it. The stalks are left standing in the field.

The Carolina, or sweet potato, is also grown in that region to some extent. They are not fed, however, to hogs or cattle, and are considered but of small importance. They are preserved by placing them upon the surface of the ground, with a slight covering of earth or cornstalks. There is not a cellar on Bayou Bœuf. The ground is so low it would fill with water. Potatoes are worth from two to three "bits," or shillings a barrel; corn, except when there is an unusual scarcity, can be purchased at the same rate.

As soon as the cotton and corn crops are secured, the stalks are pulled up, thrown into piles and burned. The ploughs are started at the same time, throwing up the beds again, preparatory to another planting. The soil, in the parishes of Rapides and Avoyelles, and throughout the whole country, so far as my observation extended, is of exceeding richness and fertility. It is a kind of marl, of a brown or reddish color. It does not require those invigorating composts necessary to more barren lands, and on the same field the same crop is grown for many successive years.

Ploughing, planting, picking cotton, gathering the corn, and pulling and burning stalks, occupies the whole of the four seasons of the year. Drawing and cutting wood, pressing cotton, fattening and killing hogs, are but incidental labors.

In the month of September or October, the hogs are run out of the swamps by dogs, and confined in pens. On a cold morning, generally about New Year's day, they are slaughtered. Each carcass is cut into six parts, and piled one above the other in salt, upon large tables in the smoke-house. In this condition it remains a fortnight, when it is hung up, and a fire built, and continued more than half the time during the remainder of the year. This thorough smoking is necessary to prevent the bacon from becoming infested with worms. In so warm a climate it is difficult to preserve it, and very many times myself and my companions have received our weekly allowance of three pounds and a half, when it was full of these disgusting vermin.

Although the swamps are overrun with cattle, they are never made the source of profit, to any considerable extent. The planter cuts his mark upon the ear, or brands his initials upon the side, and turns them into the swamps, to roam unrestricted within their almost limitless confines. They are the Spanish breed, small and spike-horned. I have known of droves being taken from Bayou Bœuf, but it is of very rare occurrence. The value of the best cows is about five dollars each. Two quarts at one milking, would be considered an unusual large quantity. They furnish little tallow, and that of a soft, inferior quality. Notwithstanding the great number of cows that throng the swamps, the planters are indebted to the North for their cheese and butter, which is purchased in the New-Orleans market. Salted beef is not an article of food either in the great house, or in the cabin.

Master Epps was accustomed to attend shooting matches for the purpose of obtaining what fresh beef he required. These sports occurred weekly at the neighboring village of Holmesville. Fat beeves are driven thither and shot at, a stipulated price being demanded for the privilege. The lucky marksman divides the flesh among his fellows, and in this manner the attending planters are supplied.

The great number of tame and untamed cattle which swarm the woods and swamps of Bayou Bœuf, most probably suggested that appellation to the French, inasmuch as the term, translated, signifies the creek or river of the wild ox.

Garden products, such as cabbages, turnips and the like, are cultivated for the use of the master and his family. They have greens and vegetables at all times and seasons of the year. "The grass withereth and the flower fadeth"[8] before the desolating winds of autumn in the chill northern latitudes, but perpetual verdure overspreads the hot lowlands, and flowers bloom in the heart of winter, in the region of Bayou Bœuf.

There are no meadows appropriated to the cultivation of the grasses. The leaves of the corn supply a sufficiency of food for the laboring cattle, while the rest provide for themselves all the year in the ever-growing pasture.

There are many other peculiarities of climate, habit, custom, and of the manner of living and laboring at the South, but the foregoing, it is supposed, will give the reader an insight and general idea of life on a cotton plantation in Louisiana. The mode of cultivating cane, and the process of sugar manufacturing, will be mentioned in another place.

Chapter XIII.

THE CURIOUS AXE-HELVE—SYMPTOMS OF APPROACHING ILLNESS—
CONTINUE TO DECLINE—THE WHIP INEFFECTUAL—CONFINED TO
THE CABIN—VISIT BY DR. WINES—PARTIAL RECOVERY—FAILURE AT
COTTON PICKING—WHAT MAY BE HEARD ON EPPS' PLANTATION—
LASHES GRADUATED—EPPS IN A WHIPPING MOOD—EPPS IN A
DANCING MOOD—DESCRIPTION OF THE DANCE—LOSS OF REST NO
EXCUSE—EPPS' CHARACTERISTICS—JIM BURNS—REMOVAL FROM
HUFF POWER TO BAYOU BŒUF—DESCRIPTION OF UNCLE ABRAM; OF
WILEY; OF AUNT PHEBE; OF BOB, HENRY, AND EDWARD; OF PATSEY;
WITH A GENEALOGICAL ACCOUNT OF EACH—SOMETHING OF THEIR
PAST HISTORY, AND PECULIAR CHARACTERISTICS—JEALOUSY AND
LUST—PATSEY, THE VICTIM.

On my arrival at Master Epps', in obedience to his order, the first business upon which I entered was the making of an axe-helve. The handles in use there are simply a round, straight stick. I made a

---

8. From Isaiah 40.8: "The grass withereth, the flower fadeth: but the word of our God shall stand forever."

crooked one, shaped like those to which I had been accustomed at
the North. When finished, and presented to Epps, he looked at it with
astonishment, unable to determine exactly what it was. He had
never before seen such a handle, and when I explained its conveniences, he was forcibly struck with the novelty of the idea. He kept
it in the house a long time, and when his friends called, was wont
to exhibit it as a curiosity.

It was now the season of hoeing. I was first sent into the corn-field,
and afterwards set to scraping cotton. In this employment I remained
until hoeing time was nearly passed, when I began to experience
the symptoms of approaching illness. I was attacked with chills,
which were succeeded by a burning fever. I became weak and emaciated, and frequently so dizzy that it caused me to reel and stagger
like a drunken man. Nevertheless, I was compelled to keep up my
row. When in health I found little difficulty in keeping pace with
my fellow-laborers, but now it seemed to be an utter impossibility.
Often I fell behind, when the driver's lash was sure to greet my back,
infusing into my sick and drooping body a little temporary energy. I
continued to decline until at length the whip became entirely ineffectual. The sharpest sting of the rawhide could not arouse me.
Finally, in September, when the busy season of cotton picking was at
hand, I was unable to leave my cabin. Up to this time I had received
no medicine, nor any attention from my master or mistress. The old
cook visited me occasionally, preparing me corn-coffee, and sometimes boiling a bit of bacon, when I had grown too feeble to accomplish it myself.

When it was said that I would die, Master Epps, unwilling to
bear the loss, which the death of an animal worth a thousand dollars would bring upon him, concluded to incur the expense of sending to Holmesville for Dr. Wines. He announced to Epps that it was
the effect of the climate, and there was a probability of his losing
me. He directed me to eat no meat, and to partake of no more food
than was absolutely necessary to sustain life. Several weeks elapsed,
during which time, under the scanty diet to which I was subjected,
I had partially recovered. One morning, long before I was in a
proper condition to labor, Epps appeared at the cabin door, and,
presenting me a sack, ordered me to the cotton field. At this time I
had had no experience whatever in cotton picking. It was an awkward business indeed. While others used both hands, snatching the
cotton and depositing it in the mouth of the sack, with a precision
and dexterity that was incomprehensible to me, I had to seize the
boll with one hand, and deliberately draw out the white, gushing
blossom with the other.

Depositing the cotton in the sack, moreover, was a difficulty that
demanded the exercise of both hands and eyes. I was compelled to

pick it from the ground where it would fall, nearly as often as from the stalk where it had grown. I made havoc also with the branches, loaded with the yet unbroken bolls, the long, cumbersome sack swinging from side to side in a manner not allowable in the cotton field. After a most laborious day I arrived at the gin-house with my load. When the scale determined its weight to be only ninety-five pounds, not half the quantity required of the poorest picker, Epps threatened the severest flogging, but in consideration of my being a "raw hand," concluded to pardon me on that occasion. The following day, and many days succeeding, I returned at night with no better success—I was evidently not designed for that kind of labor. I had not the gift—the dexterous fingers and quick motion of Patsey, who could fly along one side of a row of cotton, stripping it of its unde-filed and fleecy whiteness miraculously fast. Practice and whipping were alike unavailing, and Epps, satisfied of it at last, swore I was a disgrace—that I was not fit to associate with a cotton-picking "nigger"—that I could not pick enough in a day to pay the trouble of weighing it, and that I should go into the cotton field no more. I was now employed in cutting and hauling wood, drawing cotton from the field to the gin-house, and performed whatever other service was required. Suffice to say, I was never permitted to be idle.

It was rarely that a day passed by without one or more whippings. This occurred at the time the cotton was weighed. The delinquent, whose weight had fallen short, was taken out, stripped, made to lie upon the ground, face downwards, when he received a punishment proportioned to his offence. It is the literal, unvarnished truth, that the crack of the lash, and the shrieking of the slaves, can be heard from dark till bed time, on Epps' plantation, any day almost during the entire period of the cotton-picking season.

The number of lashes is graduated according to the nature of the case. Twenty-five are deemed a mere brush, inflicted, for instance, when a dry leaf or piece of boll is found in the cotton, or when a branch is broken in the field; fifty is the ordinary penalty following all delinquencies of the next higher grade; one hundred is called severe: it is the punishment inflicted for the serious offence of standing idle in the field; from one hundred and fifty to two hundred is bestowed upon him who quarrels with his cabin-mates, and five hundred, well laid on, besides the mangling of the dogs, perhaps, is certain to consign the poor, unpitied runaway to weeks of pain and agony.

During the two years Epps remained on the plantation at Bayou Huff Power, he was in the habit, as often as once in a fortnight at least, of coming home intoxicated from Holmesville. The shooting-matches almost invariably concluded with a debauch. At such times he was boisterous and half-crazy. Often he would break the dishes, chairs, and whatever furniture he could lay his hands on.

When satisfied with his amusement in the house, he would seize the whip and walk forth into the yard. Then it behooved the slaves to be watchful and exceeding wary. The first one who came within reach felt the smart of his lash. Sometimes for hours he would keep them running in all directions, dodging around the corners of the cabins. Occasionally he would come upon one unawares, and if he succeeded in inflicting a fair, round blow, it was a feat that much delighted him. The younger children, and the aged, who had become inactive, suffered then. In the midst of the confusion he would slily take his stand behind a cabin, waiting with raised whip, to dash it into the first black face that peeped cautiously around the corner.

At other times he would come home in a less brutal humor. Then there must be a merry-making. Then all must move to the measure of a tune. Then Master Epps must needs regale his melodious ears with the music of a fiddle. Then did he become buoyant, elastic, gaily "tripping the light fantastic toe"[9] around the piazza and all through the house.

Tibeats, at the time of my sale, had informed him I could play on the violin. He had received his information from Ford. Through the importunities of Mistress Epps, her husband had been induced to purchase me one during a visit to New-Orleans. Frequently I was called into the house to play before the family, mistress being passionately fond of music.

All of us would be assembled in the large room of the great house, whenever Epps came home in one of his dancing moods. No matter how worn out and tired we were, there must be a general dance. When properly stationed on the floor, I would strike up a tune.

"Dance, you d—d niggers, dance," Epps would shout.

Then there must be no halting or delay, no slow or languid movements; all must be brisk, and lively, and alert. "Up and down, heel and toe, and away we go,"[1] was the order of the hour. Epps' portly form mingled with those of his dusky slaves, moving rapidly through all the mazes of the dance.

Usually his whip was in his hand, ready to fall about the ears of the presumptuous thrall, who dared to rest a moment, or even stop to catch his breath. When he was himself exhausted, there would be a brief cessation, but it would be very brief. With a slash, and crack, and flourish of the whip, he would shout again, "Dance, niggers, dance," and away they would go once more, pell-mell, while I spurred by an occasional sharp touch of the lash, sat in a corner, extracting from my violin a marvelous quick-stepping tune. The mistress often upbraided him, declaring she would return to her

9. The phrase, meaning to dance nimbly, comes originally from John Milton's "L'Allegro" (1645): "Come and trip it as you go / On the light fantastic toe."
1. A line from a version of the children's dancing game "Hansel and Gretel."

father's house at Cheneyville; nevertheless, there were times she could not restrain a burst of laughter, on witnessing his uproarious pranks. Frequently, we were thus detained until almost morning. Bent with excessive toil—actually suffering for a little refreshing rest, and feeling rather as if we could cast ourselves upon the earth and weep, many a night in the house of Edwin Epps have his unhappy slaves been made to dance and laugh.

Notwithstanding these deprivations in order to gratify the whim of an unreasonable master, we had to be in the field as soon as it was light, and during the day perform the ordinary and accustomed task. Such deprivations could not be urged at the scales in extenuation of any lack of weight, or in the cornfield for not hoeing with the usual rapidity. The whippings were just as severe as if we had gone forth in the morning, strengthened and invigorated by a night's repose. Indeed, after such frantic revels, he was always more sour and savage than before, punishing for slighter causes, and using the whip with increased and more vindictive energy.

Ten years I toiled for that man without reward. Ten years of my incessant labor has contributed to increase the bulk of his possessions. Ten years I was compelled to address him with down-cast eyes and uncovered head—in the attitude and language of a slave. I am indebted to him for nothing, save undeserved abuse and stripes.

Beyond the reach of his inhuman thong, and standing on the soil of the free State where I was born, thanks be to Heaven, I can raise my head once more among men. I can speak of the wrongs I have suffered, and of those who inflicted them, with upraised eyes. But I have no desire to speak of him or any other one otherwise than truthfully. Yet to speak truthfully of Edwin Epps would be to say— he is a man in whose heart the quality of kindness or of justice is not found. A rough, rude energy, united with an uncultivated mind and an avaricious spirit, are his prominent characteristics. He is known as a "nigger breaker," distinguished for his faculty of subduing the spirit of the slave, and priding himself upon his reputation in this respect, as a jockey boasts of his skill in managing a refractory horse. He looked upon a colored man, not as a human being, responsible to his Creator for the small talent entrusted to him, but as a "chattel personal," as mere live property, no better, except in value, than his mule or dog. When the evidence, clear and indisputable, was laid before him that I was a free man, and as much entitled to my liberty as he—when, on the day I left, he was informed that I had a wife and children, as dear to me as his own babes to him, he only raved and swore, denouncing the law that tore me from him, and declaring he would find out the man who had forwarded the letter that disclosed the place of my captivity, if there was any virtue or power in money, and would take his life. He thought of nothing but his loss, and cursed me for having been born free. He could have stood unmoved and seen the tongues of his poor slaves torn out by the roots—he could have seen them burned to ashes over a slow fire, or gnawed to death by dogs, if it only brought him profit. Such a hard, cruel, unjust man is Edwin Epps.

There was but one greater savage on Bayou Bœuf than he. Jim Burns' plantation was cultivated, as already mentioned, exclusively by women. That barbarian kept their backs so sore and raw, that they could not perform the customary labor demanded daily of the slave. He boasted of his cruelty, and through all the country round was accounted a more thorough-going, energetic man than even Epps. A brute himself, Jim Burns had not a particle of mercy for his subject brutes, and like a fool, whipped and scourged away the very strength upon which depended his amount of gain.

Epps remained on Huff Power two years, when, having accumulated a considerable sum of money, he expended it in the purchase of the plantation on the east bank of Bayou Bœuf, where he still continues to reside. He took possession of it in 1845, after the holidays were passed. He carried thither with him nine slaves, all of whom, except myself, and Susan, who has since died, remain there yet. He made no addition to this force, and for eight years the following were my companions in his quarters, viz: Abram, Wiley, Phebe, Bob, Henry, Edward, and Patsey. All these, except Edward, born since, were purchased out of a drove by Epps during the time he was overseer for Archy B. Williams, whose plantation is situated on the shore of Red River, not far from Alexandria.

Abram was tall, standing a full head above any common man. He is sixty years of age, and was born in Tennessee. Twenty years ago, he was purchased by a trader, carried into South Carolina, and sold to James Buford, of Williamsburgh county, in that State. In his youth he was renowned for his great strength, but age and unremitting toil have somewhat shattered his powerful frame and enfeebled his mental faculties.

Wiley is forty-eight. He was born on the estate of William Tassle, and for many years took charge of that gentleman's ferry over the Big Black River, in South Carolina.

Phebe was a slave of Buford, Tassle's neighbor, and having married Wiley, he bought the latter, at her instigation. Buford was a kind master, sheriff of the county, and in those days a man of wealth.

Bob and Henry are Phebe's children, by a former husband, their father having been abandoned to give place to Wiley. That seductive youth had insinuated himself into Phebe's affections, and therefore the faithless spouse had gently kicked her first husband out of her cabin door. Edward had been born to them on Bayou Huff Power.

Patsey is twenty-three—also from Buford's plantation. She is in no wise connected with the others, but glories in the fact that she is the offspring of a "Guinea nigger," brought over to Cuba in a slave ship, and in the course of trade transferred to Buford, who was her mother's owner.[2]

This, as I learned from them, is a genealogical account of my master's slaves. For years they had been together. Often they recalled the memories of other days, and sighed to retrace their steps to the old home in Carolina. Troubles came upon their master Buford, which brought far greater troubles upon them. He became involved in debt, and unable to bear up against his failing fortunes, was compelled to sell these, and others of his slaves. In a chain gang they had been driven from beyond the Mississippi to the plantation of Archy B. Williams. Edwin Epps, who, for a long while had been his driver and overseer, was about establishing himself in business on his own account, at the time of their arrival, and accepted them in payment of his wages.

Old Abram was a kind-hearted being—a sort of patriarch among us, fond of entertaining his younger brethren with grave and serious discourse. He was deeply versed in such philosophy as is taught in the cabin of the slave; but the great absorbing hobby of Uncle Abram was General Jackson,[3] whom his young master in Tennessee had followed to the wars. He loved to wander back, in imagination, to the place where he was born, and to recount the scenes of his youth during those stirring times when the nation was in arms. He had been athletic, and more keen and powerful than the generality of his race, but now his eye had become dim, and his natural force abated. Very often, indeed, while discussing the best method of baking the hoe-cake, or expatiating at large upon the glory of Jackson, he would forget where he left his hat, or his hoe, or his basket; and then would the old man be laughed at, if Epps was absent, and whipped if he was present. So was he perplexed continually, and sighed to think that he was growing aged and going to decay. Philosophy and Jackson and forgetfulness had played the mischief with him, and it was evident that all of them combined were fast bringing down the gray hairs of Uncle Abram to the grave.

Aunt Phebe had been an excellent field hand, but latterly was put into the kitchen, where she remained, except occasionally, in a time

2. By law, the United States prohibited the importation of slaves effective January 1, 1808. Cuba, where the transatlantic slave trade was still legal, became a popular source of foreign-born slaves for American traders looking to circumvent the law. The ending of the international slave trade in the United States also increased the incentive to kidnap free blacks like Northup into slavery.

3. Andrew Jackson (1767–1845), President of the United States from 1829 to 1837. Jackson gained distinction as a general during the War of 1812, leading his troops to victory over a larger British force at the Battle of New Orleans.

of uncommon hurry. She was a sly old creature, and when not in the presence of her mistress or her master, was garrulous in the extreme.

Wiley, on the contrary, was silent. He performed his task without murmur or complaint, seldom indulging in the luxury of speech, except to utter a wish, that he was away from Epps, and back once more in South Carolina.

Bob and Henry had reached the ages of twenty and twenty-three, and were distinguished for nothing extraordinary or unusual, while Edward, a lad of thirteen, not yet able to maintain his row in the corn or the cotton field, was kept in the great house, to wait on the little Eppses.

Patsey was slim and straight. She stood erect as the human form is capable of standing. There was an air of loftiness in her movement, that neither labor, nor weariness, nor punishment could destroy. Truly, Patsey was a splendid animal, and were it not that bondage had enshrouded her intellect in utter and everlasting darkness, would have been chief among ten thousand of her people. She could leap the highest fences, and a fleet hound it was indeed, that could outstrip her in a race. No horse could fling her from his back. She was a skillful teamster.[4] She turned as true a furrow as the best, and at splitting rails there were none who could excel her. When the order to halt was heard at night, she would have her mules at the crib, unharnessed, fed and curried, before uncle Abram had found his hat. Not, however, for all or any of these, was she chiefly famous. Such lightning-like motion was in her fingers as no other fingers ever possessed, and therefore it was, that in cotton picking time, Patsey was queen of the field.

She had a genial and pleasant temper, and was faithful and obedient. Naturally, she was a joyous creature, a laughing, light-hearted girl, rejoicing in the mere sense of existence. Yet Patsey wept oftener, and suffered more, than any of her companions. She had been literally excoriated. Her back bore the scars of a thousand stripes; not because she was backward in her work, nor because she was of an unmindful and rebellious spirit, but because it had fallen to her lot to be the slave of a licentious master and a jealous mistress. She shrank before the lustful eye of the one, and was in danger even of her life at the hands of the other, and between the two, she was indeed accursed. In the great house, for days together, there were high and angry words, poutings and estrangement, whereof she was the innocent cause. Nothing delighted the mistress so much as to see her suffer, and more than once, when Epps had refused to sell her, has she tempted me with bribes to put her secretly to death,

4. In other words, she could handle a team of mules for plowing.

and bury her body in some lonely place in the margin of the swamp. Gladly would Patsey have appeased this unforgiving spirit, if it had been in her power, but not like Joseph, dared she escape from Master Epps, leaving her garment in his hand.[5] Patsey walked under a cloud. If she uttered a word in opposition to her master's will, the lash was resorted to at once, to bring her to subjection; if she was not watchful when about her cabin, or when walking in the yard, a billet of wood, or a broken bottle perhaps, hurled from her mistress' hand, would smite her unexpectedly in the face. The enslaved victim of lust and hate, Patsey had no comfort of her life.

These were my companions and fellow-slaves, with whom I was accustomed to be driven to the field, and with whom it has been my lot to dwell for ten years in the log cabins of Edwin Epps. They, if living, are yet toiling on the banks of Bayou Bœuf, never destined to breathe, as I now do, the blessed air of liberty, nor to shake off the heavy shackles that enthrall them, until they shall lie down forever in the dust.

Chapter XIV.

DESTRUCTION OF THE COTTON CROP IN 1845—DEMAND FOR
LABORERS IN ST. MARY'S PARISH—SENT THITHER IN A DROVE—
THE ORDER OF THE MARCH—THE GRAND COTEAU—HIRED TO
JUDGE TURNER ON BAYOU SALLE—APPOINTED DRIVER IN HIS
SUGAR HOUSE—SUNDAY SERVICES—SLAVE FURNITURE; HOW
OBTAINED—THE PARTY AT YARNEY'S IN CENTREVILLE—GOOD
FORTUNE—THE CAPTAIN OF THE STEAMER—HIS REFUSAL TO
SECRETE ME—RETURN TO BAYOU BŒUF—SIGHT OF TIBEATS—
PATSEY'S SORROWS—TUMULT AND CONTENTION—HUNTING THE
COON AND OPOSSUM—THE CUNNING OF THE LATTER—THE LEAN
CONDITION OF THE SLAVE—DESCRIPTION OF THE FISH TRAP—
THE MURDER OF THE MAN FROM NATCHEZ—EPPS CHALLENGED
BY MARSHALL—THE INFLUENCE OF SLAVERY—THE LOVE
OF FREEDOM.

The first year of Epps' residence on the bayou, 1845, the caterpillars almost totally destroyed the cotton crop throughout that region. There was little to be done, so that the slaves were necessarily idle half the time. However, there came a rumor to Bayou Bœuf that wages were high, and laborers in great demand on the sugar plantations in St. Mary's parish. This parish is situated on the coast of the Gulf of Mexico, about one hundred and forty miles from Avoyelles.

---

5. Joseph, while enslaved in Egypt, resisted the advances of his master's wife (Genesis 39).

The Rio Teche, a considerable stream, flows through St. Mary's to the gulf.

It was determined by the planters, on the receipt of this intelligence, to make up a drove of slaves to be sent down to Tuckapaw in St. Mary's, for the purpose of hiring them out in the cane fields. Accordingly, in the month of September, there were one hundred and forty-seven collected at Holmesville, Abram, Bob and myself among the number. Of these about one-half were women. Epps, Alonson Pierce, Henry Toler, and Addison Roberts, were the white men, selected to accompany, and take charge of the drove. They had a two-horse carriage and two saddle horses for their use. A large wagon, drawn by four horses, and driven by John, a boy belonging to Mr. Roberts, carried the blankets and provisions.

About 2 o'clock in the afternoon, having been fed, preparations were made to depart. The duty assigned me was, to take charge of the blankets and provisions, and see that none were lost by the way. The carriage proceeded in advance, the wagon following; behind this the slaves were arranged, while the two horsemen brought up the rear, and in this order the procession moved out of Holmesville.

That night we reached a Mr. McCrow's plantation, a distance of ten or fifteen miles, when we were ordered to halt. Large fires were built, and each one spreading his blanket on the ground, laid down upon it. The white men lodged in the great house. An hour before day we were aroused by the drivers coming among us, cracking their whips and ordering us to arise. Then the blankets were rolled up, and being severally delivered to me and deposited in the wagon, the procession set forth again.

The following night it rained violently. We were all drenched, our clothes saturated with mud and water. Reaching an open shed, formerly a gin-house, we found beneath it such shelter as it afforded. There was not room for all of us to lay down. There we remained, huddled together, through the night, continuing our march, as usual, in the morning. During the journey we were fed twice a day, boiling our bacon and baking our corn-cake at the fires in the same manner as in our huts. We passed through Lafayetteville, Mountsville, New-Town, to Centreville, where Bob and Uncle Abram were hired. Our number decreased as we advanced—nearly every sugar plantation requiring the services of one or more.

On our route we passed the Grand Coteau or prairie, a vast space of level, monotonous country, without a tree, except an occasional one which had been transplanted near some dilapidated dwelling. It was once thickly populated, and under cultivation, but for some cause had been abandoned. The business of the scattered inhabitants that now dwell upon it is principally raising cattle. Immense herds were feeding upon it as we passed. In the centre of the Grand Coteau one feels as if he were on the ocean, out of sight of land. As far as the eye can see, in all directions, it is but a ruined and deserted waste.

I was hired to Judge Turner, a distinguished man and extensive planter, whose large estate is situated on Bayou Salle, within a few miles of the gulf. Bayou Salle is a small stream flowing into the bay of Atchafalaya. For some days I was employed at Turner's in repairing his sugar house, when a cane knife was put into my hand, and with thirty or forty others, I was sent into the field. I found no such difficulty in learning the art of cutting cane that I had in picking cotton. It came to me naturally and intuitively, and in a short time I was able to keep up with the fastest knife. Before the cutting was over, however, Judge Turner transferred me from the field to the sugar house, to act there in the capacity of driver. From the time of the commencement of sugar making to the close, the grinding and boiling does not cease day or night. The whip was given me with directions to use it upon any one who was caught standing idle. If I failed to obey them to the letter, there was another one for my own back. In addition to this my duty was to call on and off the different gangs at the proper time. I had no regular periods of rest, and could never snatch but a few moments of sleep at a time.

It is the custom in Louisiana, as I presume it is in other slave States, to allow the slave to retain whatever compensation he may obtain for services performed on Sundays. In this way, only, are they able to provide themselves with any luxury or convenience whatever. When a slave, purchased, or kidnapped in the North, is transported to a cabin on Bayou Bœuf he is furnished with neither knife, nor fork, nor dish, nor kettle, nor any other thing in the shape of crockery, or furniture of any nature or description. He is furnished with a blanket before he reaches there, and wrapping that around him, he can either stand up, or lie down upon the ground, or on a board, if his master has no use for it. He is at liberty to find a gourd in which to keep his meal, or he can eat his corn from the cob, just as he pleases. To ask the master for a knife, or skillet, or any small convenience of the kind, would be answered with a kick, or laughed at as a joke. Whatever necessary article of this nature is found in a cabin has been purchased with Sunday money. However injurious to the morals, it is certainly a blessing to the physical condition of the slave, to be permitted to break the Sabbath. Otherwise there would be no way to provide himself with any utensils, which seem to be indispensable to him who is compelled to be his own cook.

On cane plantations in sugar time, there is no distinction as to the days of the week. It is well understood that all hands must labor on the Sabbath, and it is equally well understood that those especially who are hired, as I was to Judge Turner, and others in succeeding years, shall receive remuneration for it. It is usual, also, in the most hurrying time of cotton-picking, to require the same extra service. From this source, slaves generally are afforded an opportunity of earning sufficient to purchase a knife, a kettle, tobacco and so forth. The females, discarding the latter luxury, are apt to expend their little revenue in the purchase of gaudy ribbons, wherewithal to deck their hair in the merry season of the holidays.

I remained in St. Mary's until the first of January, during which time my Sunday money amounted to ten dollars. I met with other good fortune, for which I was indebted to my violin, my constant companion, the source of profit, and soother of my sorrows during years of servitude. There was a grand party of whites assembled at Mr. Yarney's, in Centreville, a hamlet in the vicinity of Turner's plantation. I was employed to play for them, and so well pleased were the merry-makers with my performance, that a contribution was taken for my benefit, which amounted to seventeen dollars.

With this sum in possession, I was looked upon by my fellows as a millionaire. It afforded me great pleasure to look at it—to count it over and over again, day after day. Visions of cabin furniture, of water pails, of pocket knives, new shoes and coats and hats, floated through my fancy, and up through all rose the triumphant contemplation, that I was the wealthiest "nigger" on Bayou Bœuf.

Vessels run up the Rio Teche to Centreville. While there, I was bold enough one day to present myself before the captain of a steamer, and beg permission to hide myself among the freight. I was emboldened to risk the hazard of such a step, from overhearing a conversation, in the course of which I ascertained he was a native of the North. I did not relate to him the particulars of my history, but only expressed an ardent desire to escape from slavery to a free State. He pitied me, but said it would be impossible to avoid the vigilant custom house officers in New-Orleans, and that detection would subject him to punishment, and his vessel to confiscation. My earnest entreaties evidently excited his sympathies, and doubtless he would have yielded to them, could he have done so with any kind of safety. I was compelled to smother the sudden flame that lighted up my bosom with sweet hopes of liberation, and turn my steps once more towards the increasing darkness of despair.

Immediately after this event the drove assembled at Centreville, and several of the owners having arrived and collected the monies due for our services, we were driven back to Bayou Bœuf. It was on our return, while passing through a small village, that I caught sight of Tibeats, seated in the door of a dirty grocery, looking somewhat seedy and out of repair. Passion and poor whisky, I doubt not, have ere this laid him on the shelf.

During our absence, I learned from Aunt Phebe and Patsey, that the latter had been getting deeper and deeper into trouble. The poor girl was truly an object of pity. "Old Hogjaw," the name by which Epps was called, when the slaves were by themselves, had beaten her more severely and frequently than ever. As surely as he came from Holmesville, elated with liquor—and it was often in those days—he would whip her, merely to gratify the mistress; would punish her to an extent almost beyond endurance, for an offence of which he himself was the sole and irresistible cause. In his sober moments he could not always be prevailed upon to indulge his wife's insatiable thirst for vengeance.

To be rid of Patsey—to place her beyond sight or reach, by sale, or death, or in any other manner, of late years, seemed to be the ruling thought and passion of my mistress. Patsey had been a favorite when a child, even in the great house. She had been petted and admired for her uncommon sprightliness and pleasant disposition. She had been fed many a time, so Uncle Abram said, even on biscuit and milk, when the madam, in her younger days, was wont to call her to the piazza, and fondle her as she would a playful Kitten. But a sad change had come over the spirit of the woman. Now, only black and angry fiends ministered in the temple of her heart, until she could look on Patsey but with concentrated venom.

Mistress Epps was not naturally such an evil woman, after all. She was possessed of the devil, jealousy, it is true, but aside from that, there was much in her character to admire. Her father, Mr. Roberts, resided in Cheneyville, an influential and honorable man, and as much respected throughout the parish as any other citizen. She had been well educated at some institution this side the Mississippi; was beautiful, accomplished, and usually good-humored. She was kind to all of us but Patsey—frequently, in the absence of her husband, sending out to us some little dainty from her own table. In other situations—in a different society from that which exists on the shores of Bayou Bœuf, she would have been pronounced an elegant and fascinating woman. An ill wind it was that blew her into the arms of Epps.

He respected and loved his wife as much as a coarse nature like his is capable of loving, but supreme selfishness always overmastered conjugal affection.

> "He loved as well as baser natures can,
> But a mean heart and soul were in that man."[6]

He was ready to gratify any whim—to grant any request she made, provided it did not cost too much. Patsey was equal to any two of his slaves in the cotton field. He could not replace her with

6. From "A Destiny," a poem by English author and reformer Caroline Sheridan Norton (1808–1877).

the same money she would bring. The idea of disposing of her, therefore, could not be entertained. The mistress did not regard her at all in that light. The pride of the haughty woman was aroused; the blood of the fiery southern boiled at the sight of Patsey, and nothing less than trampling out the life of the helpless bondwoman would satisfy her.

Sometimes the current of her wrath turned upon him whom she had just cause to hate. But the storm of angry words would pass over at length, and there would be a season of calm again. At such times Patsey trembled with fear, and cried as if her heart would break, for she knew from painful experience, that if mistress should work herself to the red-hot pitch of rage, Epps would quiet her at last with a promise that Patsey should be flogged—a promise he was sure to keep. Thus did pride, and jealousy, and vengeance war with avarice and brute-passion in the mansion of my master, filling it with daily tumult and contention. Thus, upon the head of Patsey—the simple-minded slave, in whose heart God had implanted the seeds of virtue—the force of all these domestic tempests spent itself at last.

During the summer succeeding my return from St. Mary's parish, I conceived a plan of providing myself with food, which, though simple, succeeded beyond expectation. It has been followed by many others in my condition, up and down the bayou, and of such benefit has it become that I am almost persuaded to look upon myself as a benefactor. That summer the worms got into the bacon. Nothing but ravenous hunger could induce us to swallow it. The weekly allowance of meal scarcely sufficed to satisfy us. It was customary with us, as it is with all in that region, where the allowance is exhausted before Saturday night, or is in such a state as to render it nauseous and disgusting, to hunt in the swamps for coon and opossum. This, however, must be done at night, after the day's work is accomplished. There are planters whose slaves, for months at a time, have no other meat than such as is obtained in this manner. No objections are made to hunting, inasmuch as it dispenses with drafts upon the smoke-house, and because every marauding coon that is killed is so much saved from the standing corn. They are hunted with dogs and clubs, slaves not being allowed the use of fire-arms.

The flesh of the coon is palatable, but verily there is nothing in all butcherdom so delicious as a roasted 'possum. They are a round, rather long-bodied, little animal, of a whitish color, with nose like a pig, and caudal extremity like a rat. They burrow among the roots and in the hollows of the gum tree, and are clumsy and slow of motion. They are deceitful and cunning creatures. On receiving the slightest tap of a stick, they will roll over on the ground and feign death. If the hunter leaves him, in pursuit of another, without first taking particular pains to break his neck, the chances are, on his return, he is not to be found. The little animal has out witted the enemy—has "played 'possum"—and is off. But after a long and hard day's work, the weary slave feels little like going to the swamp for his supper, and half the time prefers throwing himself on the cabin floor without it. It is for the interest of the master that the servant should not suffer in health from starvation, and it is also for his interest that he should not become gross from over-feeding. In the estimation of the owner, a slave is the most serviceable when in rather a lean and lank condition, such a condition as the race-horse is in, when fitted for the course, and in that condition they are generally to be found on the sugar and cotton plantations along Red River.

My cabin was within a few rods of the bayou bank, and necessity being indeed the mother of invention, I resolved upon a mode of obtaining the requisite amount of food, without the trouble of resorting nightly to the woods. This was to construct a fish trap. Having, in my mind, conceived the manner in which it could be done, the next Sunday I set about putting it into practical execution. It may be impossible for me to convey to the reader a full and correct idea of its construction, but the following will serve as a general description:

A frame between two and three feet square is made, and of a greater or less height, according to the depth of water. Boards or slats are nailed on three sides of this frame, not so closely, however, as to prevent the water circulating freely through it. A door is fitted into the fourth side, in such manner that it will slide easily up and down in the grooves cut in the two posts. A movable bottom is then so fitted that it can be raised to the top of the frame without difficulty. In the centre of the movable bottom an auger hole is bored, and into this one end of a handle or round stick is fastened on the under side so loosely that it will turn. The handle ascends from the centre of the movable bottom to the top of the frame, or as much higher as is desirable. Up and down this handle, in a great many places, are gimlet holes, through which small sticks are inserted, extending to opposite sides of the frame. So many of these small sticks are running out from the handle in all directions, that a fish of any considerable dimensions cannot pass through without hitting one of them. The frame is then placed in the water and made stationary.

The trap is "set" by sliding or drawing up the door, and kept in that position by another stick, one end of which rests in a notch on the inner side, the other end in a notch made in the handle, running up from the centre of the movable bottom. The trap is baited by rolling a handful of wet meal and cotton together until it becomes hard, and depositing it in the back part of the frame. A fish swimming through the upraised door towards the bait, necessarily strikes one of the small sticks turning the handle, which displacing the stick supporting the door, the latter falls, securing the fish within the frame. Taking hold of the top of the handle, the movable bottom is then drawn up to the surface of the water, and the fish taken out. There may have been other such traps in use before mine was constructed, but if there were I had never happened to see one. Bayou Bœuf abounds in fish of large size and excellent quality, and after this time I was very rarely in want of one for myself, or for my comrades. Thus a mine was opened—a new resource was developed, hitherto unthought of by the enslaved children of Africa, who toil and hunger along the shores of that sluggish, but prolific stream.

About the time of which I am now writing, an event occurred in our immediate neighborhood, which made a deep impression upon me, and which shows the state of society existing there, and the manner in which affronts are oftentimes avenged. Directly opposite our quarters, on the other side of the bayou, was situated the plantation of Mr. Marshall. He belonged to a family among the most wealthy and aristocratic in the country. A gentleman from the vicinity of Natchez had been negotiating with him for the purchase of the estate. One day a messenger came in great haste to our plantation, saying that a bloody and fearful battle was going on at Marshall's— that blood had been spilled—and unless the combatants were forthwith separated, the result would be disastrous.

On repairing to Marshall's house, a scene presented itself that beggars description. On the floor of one of the rooms lay the ghastly corpse of the man from Natchez, while Marshall, enraged and covered with wounds and blood, was stalking back and forth, "breathing out threatenings and slaughter."[7] A difficulty had arisen in the course of their negotiation, high words ensued, when drawing their weapons, the deadly strife began that ended so unfortunately. Marshall was never placed in confinement. A sort of trial or investigation was had at Marksville, when he was acquitted, and returned to his plantation, rather more respected, as I thought, than ever, from the fact that the blood of a fellow being was on his soul.

Epps interested himself in his behalf, accompanying him to Marksville, and on all occasions loudly justifying him, but his services in this respect did not afterwards deter a kinsman of this same Marshall from seeking his life also. A brawl occurred between them over a gambling-table, which terminated in a deadly feud. Riding up on horseback in front of the house one day, armed with pistols and bowie knife, Marshall challenged him to come forth and make a final settlement of the quarrel, or he would brand him as a coward, and

7. From Acts 9.1: "And Saul, yet breathing out threatening and slaughter against the disciples of the Lord, went unto the high priest."

shoot him like a dog the first opportunity. Not through cowardice, nor from any conscientious scruples, in my opinion, but through the influence of his wife, he was restrained from accepting the challenge of his enemy. A reconciliation, however, was effected afterward, since which time they have been on terms of the closest intimacy.

Such occurrences, which would bring upon the parties concerned in them merited and condign punishment in the Northern States, are frequent on the bayou, and pass without notice, and almost without comment. Every man carries his bowie knife, and when two fall out, they set to work hacking and thrusting at each other, more like savages than civilized and enlightened beings.

The existence of Slavery in its most cruel form among them, has a tendency to brutalize the humane and finer feelings of their nature. Daily witnesses of human suffering—listening to the agonizing screeches of the slave—beholding him writhing beneath the merciless lash—bitten and torn by dogs—dying without attention, and buried without shroud or coffin—it cannot otherwise be expected, than that they should become brutified and reckless of human life. It is true there are many kind-hearted and good men in the parish of Avoyelles—such men as William Ford—who can look with pity upon the sufferings of a slave, just as there are, over all the world, sensitive and sympathetic spirits, who cannot look with indifference upon the sufferings of any creature which the Almighty has endowed with life. It is not the fault of the slaveholder that he is cruel, so much as it is the fault of the system under which he lives. He cannot withstand the influence of habit and associations that surround him. Taught from earliest childhood, by all that he sees and hears, that the rod is for the slave's back, he will not be apt to change his opinions in maturer years.

There may be humane masters, as there certainly are inhuman ones—there may be slaves well-clothed, well-fed, and happy, as there surely are those half-clad, half-starved and miserable; nevertheless, the institution that tolerates such wrong and inhumanity as I have witnessed, is a cruel, unjust, and barbarous one. Men may write fictions portraying lowly life[8] as it is, or as it is not—may expatiate with owlish gravity upon the bliss of ignorance—discourse flippantly from arm chairs of the pleasures of slave life; but let them toil with him in the field—sleep with him in the cabin—feed with him on husks; let them behold him scourged, hunted, trampled on, and they will come back with another story in their mouths. Let them know the *heart* of the poor slave—learn his secret thoughts—thoughts

8. As stated in the note on p. xvi, Northup here seems to be making a direct reference to Stowe's *Uncle Tom's Cabin*, which is subtitled "Life Among the Lowly."

he dare not utter in the hearing of the white man; let them sit by him in the silent watches of the night—converse with him in trustful confidence, of "life, liberty, and the pursuit of happiness," and they will find that ninety-nine out of every hundred are intelligent enough to understand their situation, and to cherish in their bosoms the love of freedom, as passionately as themselves.

Chapter XV.

LABORS ON SUGAR PLANTATIONS—THE MODE OF PLANTING
CANE—OF HOEING CANE—CANE RICKS—CUTTING CANE—
DESCRIPTION OF THE CANE KNIFE—WINROWING—PREPARING FOR
SUCCEEDING CROPS—DESCRIPTION OF HAWKINS' SUGAR MILL ON
BAYOU BŒUF—THE CHRISTMAS HOLIDAYS—THE CARNIVAL SEASON
OF THE CHILDREN OF BONDAGE—THE CHRISTMAS SUPPER—RED,
THE FAVORITE COLOR—THE VIOLIN, AND THE CONSOLATION IT
AFFORDED—THE CHRISTMAS DANCE—LIVELY, THE COQUETTE—
SAM ROBERTS, AND HIS RIVALS—SLAVE SONGS—SOUTHERN LIFE AS
IT IS—THREE DAYS IN THE YEAR—THE SYSTEM OF MARRIAGE—
UNCLE ABRAM'S CONTEMPT OF MATRIMONY.

In consequence of my inability in cotton-picking, Epps was in the habit of hiring me out on sugar plantations during the season of cane-cutting and sugar-making. He received for my services a dollar a day, with the money supplying my place on his cotton plantation. Cutting cane was an employment that suited me, and for three successive years I held the lead row at Hawkins', leading a gang of from fifty to an hundred hands.

In a previous chapter the mode of cultivating cotton is described. This may be the proper place to speak of the manner of cultivating cane.

The ground is prepared in beds, the same as it is prepared for the reception of the cotton seed, except it is ploughed deeper. Drills are made in the same manner. Planting commences in January, and continues until April. It is necessary to plant a sugar field only once in three years. Three crops are taken before the seed or plant is exhausted.

Three gangs are employed in the operation. One draws the cane from the rick, or stack, cutting the top and flags from the stalk, leaving only that part which is sound and healthy. Each joint of the cane has an eye, like the eye of a potato, which sends forth a sprout when buried in the soil. Another gang lays the cane in the drill, placing two stalks side by side in such manner that joints will occur once in four or six inches. The third gang follows with hoes, drawing earth upon the stalks, and covering them to the depth, of three inches.

In four weeks, at the farthest, the sprouts appear above the ground, and from this time forward grow with great rapidity. A sugar field is hoed three times, the same as cotton, save that a greater quantity of earth is drawn to the roots. By the first of August hoeing is usually over. About the middle of September, whatever is required for seed is cut and stacked in ricks, as they are termed. In October it is ready for the mill or sugar-house, and then the general cutting begins. The blade of a cane-knife is fifteen inches long, three inches wide in the middle, and tapering towards the point and handle. The blade is thin, and in order to be at all serviceable must be kept very sharp. Every third hand takes the lead of two others, one of whom is on each side of him. The lead hand, in the first place, with a blow of his knife shears the flags from the stalk. He next cuts off the top down as far as it is green. He must be careful to sever all the green from the ripe part, inasmuch as the juice of the former sours the molasses, and renders it unsalable. Then he severs the stalk at the root, and lays it directly behind him. His right and left hand companions lay their stalks, when cut in the same manner, upon his. To every three hands there is a cart, which follows, and the stalks are thrown into it by the younger slaves, when it is drawn to the sugar-house and ground.

If the planter apprehends a frost, the cane is winrowed. Winrowing is the cutting the stalks at an early period and throwing them lengthwise in the water furrow in such a manner that the tops will cover the butts of the stalks. They will remain in this condition three weeks or a month without souring, and secure from frost. When the proper time arrives, they are taken up, trimmed and carted to the sugar-house.

In the month of January the slaves enter the field again to prepare for another crop. The ground is now strewn with the tops, and flags cut from the past year's cane. On a dry day fire is set to this combustible refuse, which sweeps over the field, leaving it bare and clean, and ready for the hoes. The earth is loosened about the roots of the old stubble, and in process of time another crop springs up from the last year's seed. It is the same the year following; but the third year the seed has exhausted its strength, and the field must be ploughed and planted again. The second year the cane is sweeter and yields more than the first, and the third year more than the second.

During the three seasons I labored on Hawkins' plantation, I was employed a considerable portion of the time in the sugar-house. He is celebrated as the producer of the finest variety of white sugar. The following is a general description of his sugar-house and the process of manufacture:

The mill is an immense brick building, standing on the shore of the bayou. Running out from the building is an open shed, at least an hundred feet in length and forty or fifty feet in width. The boiler in which the steam is generated is situated outside the main building; the machinery and engine rest on a brick pier, fifteen feet above the floor, within the body of the building. The machinery turns two great iron rollers, between two and three feet in diameter and six or eight feet in length. They are elevated above the brick pier, and roll in towards each other. An endless carrier, made of chain and wood, like leathern belts used in small mills, extends from the iron rollers out of the main building and through the entire length of the open shed. The carts in which the cane is brought from the field as fast as it is cut, are unloaded at the sides of the shed. All along the endless carrier are ranged slave children, whose business it is to place the cane upon it, when it is conveyed through the shed into the main building, where it falls between the rollers, is crushed, and drops upon another carrier that conveys it out of the main building in an opposite direction, depositing it in the top of a chimney upon a fire beneath, which consumes it. It is necessary to burn it in this manner, because otherwise it would soon fill the building, and more especially because it would soon sour and engender disease. The juice of the cane falls into a conductor underneath the iron rollers, and is carried into a reservoir. Pipes convey it from thence into five filterers, holding several hogsheads each.[9] These filterers are filled with bone-black, a substance resembling pulverized charcoal. It is made of bones calcinated in close vessels, and is used for the purpose of decolorizing, by filtration, the cane juice before boiling. Through these five filterers it passes in succession, and then runs into a large reservoir underneath the ground floor, from whence it is carried up, by means of a steam pump, into a clarifier made of sheet iron, where it is heated by steam until it boils. From the first clarifier it is carried in pipes to a second and a third, and thence into close iron pans, through which tubes pass, filled with steam. While in a boiling state it flows through three pans in succession, and is then carried in other pipes down to the coolers on the ground floor. Coolers are wooden boxes with sieve bottoms made of the finest wire. As soon as the syrup passes into the coolers, and is met by the air, it grains, and the molasses at once escapes through the sieves into a cistern below. It is then white or loaf sugar of the finest kind—clear, clean, and as white as snow. When cool, it is taken out, packed in hogsheads, and is ready for market. The molasses is then carried from the cistern into the upper story again, and by another process converted into brown sugar.

9. Large barrels whose volume depends on the type of liquid they contain. In terms of fixed measurements, a standard hogshead can hold 63 U.S. gallons of wine or 64.85 U.S. gallons of beer, according to the *Oxford English Dictionary*.

There are larger mills, and those constructed differently from the one thus imperfectly described, but none, perhaps, more celebrated than this anywhere on Bayou Bœuf. Lambert, of New-Orleans, is a partner of Hawkins. He is a man of vast wealth, holding, as I have been told, an interest in over forty different sugar plantations in Louisiana.

The only respite from constant labor the slave has through the whole year, is during the Christmas holidays. Epps allowed us three—others allow four, five and six days, according to the measure of their generosity. It is the only time to which they look forward with any interest or pleasure. They are glad when night comes, not only because it brings them a few hours repose, but because it brings them one day nearer Christmas. It is hailed with equal delight by the old and the young; even Uncle Abram ceases to glorify Andrew Jackson, and Patsey forgets her many sorrows, amid the general hilarity of the holidays. It is the time of feasting, and frolicking, and fiddling—the carnival season[1] with the children of bondage. They are the only days when they are allowed a little restricted liberty, and heartily indeed do they enjoy it.

It is the custom for one planter to give a "Christmas supper," inviting the slaves from neighboring plantations to join his own on the occasion; for instance, one year it is given by Epps, the next by Marshall, the next by Hawkins, and so on. Usually from three to five hundred are assembled, coming together on foot, in carts, on horseback, on mules, riding double and triple, sometimes a boy and girl, at others a girl and two boys, and at others again a boy, a girl and an old woman. Uncle Abram astride a mule, with Aunt Phebe and Patsey behind him, trotting towards a Christmas supper, would be no uncommon sight on Bayou Bœuf.

Then, too, "of all days i' the year,"[2] they array themselves in their best attire. The cotton coat has been washed clean, the stump of a tallow candle has been applied to the shoes, and if so fortunate as to possess a rimless or a crownless hat, it is placed jauntily on the head. They are welcomed with equal cordiality, however, if they come bare-headed and barefooted to the feast. As a general thing, the women wear handkerchiefs tied about their heads, but if chance has thrown in their way a fiery red ribbon, or a cast-off bonnet of their mistress' grandmother, it is sure to be worn on such occasions.

1. Period in the Catholic calendar just before Lent, traditionally a time of celebration, parades, and a relaxation of ordinary social and moral conventions. New Orleans' Mardi Gras festival is one such celebration.
2. From *Hamlet* 5.1. The line is uttered by the gravedigger who reminds Hamlet of his mortality, adding a potential irony to Northup's use of it here.

Red—the deep blood red—is decidedly the favorite color among the enslaved damsels of my acquaintance. If a red ribbon does not encircle the neck, you will be certain to find all the hair of their woolly heads tied up with red strings of one sort or another.

The table is spread in the open air, and loaded with varieties of meat and piles of vegetables. Bacon and corn meal at such times are dispensed with. Sometimes the cooking is performed in the kitchen on the plantation, at others in the shade of wide branching trees. In the latter case, a ditch is dug in the ground, and wood laid in and burned until it is filled with glowing coals, over which chickens, ducks, turkeys, pigs, and not unfrequently the entire body of a wild ox, are roasted. They are furnished also with flour, of which biscuits are made, and often with peach and other preserves, with tarts, and every manner and description of pies, except the mince, that being an article of pastry as yet unknown among them. Only the slave who has lived all the years on his scanty allowance of meal and bacon, can appreciate such suppers. White people in great numbers assemble to witness the gastronomical enjoyments.

They seat themselves at the rustic table—the males on one side, the females on the other. The two between whom there may have been an exchange of tenderness, invariably manage to sit opposite; for the omnipresent Cupid disdains not to hurl his arrows into the simple hearts of slaves. Unalloyed and exulting happiness lights up the dark faces of them all. The ivory teeth, contrasting with their black complexions, exhibit two long, white streaks the whole extent of the table. All round the bountiful board a multitude of eyes roll in ecstacy. Giggling and laughter and the clattering of cutlery and crockery succeed. Cuffee's elbow hunches his neighbor's side, impelled by an involuntary impulse of delight; Nelly shakes her finger at Sambo and laughs,[3] she knows not why, and so the fun and merriment flows on.

When the viands have disappeared, and the hungry maws of the children of toil are satisfied, then, next in the order of amusement, is the Christmas dance. My business on these gala days always was to play on the violin. The African race is a music-loving one, proverbially; and many there were among my fellow-bondsmen whose organs of tune were strikingly developed, and who could thumb the banjo with dexterity; but at the expense of appearing egotistical, I must, nevertheless, declare, that I was considered the Ole Bull of Bayou Bœuf. My master often received letters, sometimes from a distance of ten miles, requesting him to send me to play at a ball or

3. Cuffee and Sambo were derogatory names given to black men. Addressing a slave as "Sambo" or referring to him as "a Sambo" signified that he was foolish and lazy, a common racist stereotype. The term became more popular well after slavery with the 1899 publication of the children's book *Little Black Sambo*, whose exaggerated illustrations of its dark-skinned title character inspired Sambo caricatures, ornaments, and toys well into the twentieth century.

festival of the whites. He received his compensation, and usually I also returned with many picayunes[4] jingling in my pockets—the extra contributions of those to whose delight I had administered. In this manner I became more acquainted than I otherwise would, up and down the bayou. The young men and maidens of Holmesville always knew there was to be a jollification somewhere, whenever Platt Epps was seen passing through the town with his fiddle in his hand. "Where are you going now, Platt?" and "What is coming off tonight, Platt?" would be interrogatories issuing from every door and window, and many a time when there was no special hurry, yielding to pressing importunities, Platt would draw his bow, and sitting astride his mule, perhaps, discourse musically to a crowd of delighted children, gathered around him in the street.

Alas! had it not been for my beloved violin, I scarcely can conceive how I could have endured the long years of bondage. It introduced me to great houses—relieved me of many days' labor in the field—supplied me with conveniences for my cabin—with pipes and tobacco, and extra pairs of shoes, and oftentimes led me away from the presence of a hard master, to witness scenes of jollity and mirth. It was my companion—the friend of my bosom—triumphing loudly when I was joyful, and uttering its soft, melodious consolations when I was sad. Often, at midnight, when sleep had fled affrighted from the cabin, and my soul was disturbed and troubled with the contemplation of my fate, it would sing me a song of peace. On holy Sabbath days, when an hour or two of leisure was allowed, it would accompany me to some quiet place on the bayou bank, and, lifting up its voice, discourse kindly and pleasantly indeed. It heralded my name round the country—made me friends, who, otherwise would not have noticed me—gave me an honored seat at the yearly feasts, and secured the loudest and heartiest welcome of them all at the Christmas dance. The Christmas dance! Oh, ye pleasure-seeking sons and daughters of idleness, who move with measured step, listless and snail-like, through the slow-winding cotillon, if ye wish to look upon the celerity, if not the "poetry of motion"[5]—upon genuine happiness, rampant and unrestrained—go down to Louisiana, and see the slaves dancing in the starlight of a Christmas night.

On that particular Christmas I have now in my mind, a description whereof will serve as a description of the day generally, Miss Lively and Mr. Sam, the first belonging to Stewart, the latter to Roberts,

---

4. Spanish coins used as legal currency in parts of the southern United States until 1857.
5. The *Oxford English Dictionary* traces the use of this phrase to *Morning Thoughts: Or Poëtical Meditations, Moral, Divine and Miscellaneous; Together with Several Other Poems on Various Subjects* (1776), a posthumous collection of the writings of Jonathan Richardson (d. 1745), an English portrait artist and critic. Richardson refers to dancing as "the poetry of motion, and therefore a most agreeable and a rational diversion."

started the ball. It was well known that Sam cherished an ardent passion for Lively, as also did one of Marshall's and another of Carey's boys; for Lively was *lively* indeed, and a heart-breaking coquette withal. It was a victory for Sam Roberts, when, rising from the repast, she gave him her hand for the first "figure" in preference to either of his rivals. They were somewhat crest-fallen, and, shaking their heads angrily, rather intimated they would like to pitch into Mr. Sam and hurt him badly. But not an emotion of wrath ruffled the placid bosom of Samuel, as his legs flew like drum-sticks down the outside and up the middle, by the side of his bewitching partner. The whole company cheered them vociferously, and, excited with the applause, they continued "tearing down" after all the others had become exhausted and halted a moment to recover breath. But Sam's super-human exertions overcame him finally, leaving Lively alone, yet whirling like a top. Thereupon one of Sam's rivals, Pete Marshall, dashed in, and, with might and main, leaped and shuffled and threw himself into every conceivable shape, as if determined to show Miss Lively and all the world that Sam Roberts was of no account.

Pete's affection, however, was greater than his discretion. Such violent exercise took the breath out of him directly, and he dropped like an empty bag. Then was the time for Harry Carey to try his hand; but Lively also soon out-winded him, amidst hurrahs and shouts, fully sustaining her well-earned reputation of being the "fastest gal" on the bayou.

One "set" off, another takes its place, he or she remaining longest on the floor receiving the most uproarious commendation, and so the dancing continues until broad daylight. It does not cease with the sound of the fiddle, but in that case they set up a music peculiar to themselves. This is called "patting," accompanied with one of those unmeaning songs, composed rather for its adaptation to a certain tune or measure, than for the purpose of expressing any distinct idea. The patting is performed by striking the hands on the knees, then striking the hands together, then striking the right shoulder with one hand, the left with the other—all the while keeping time with the feet, and singing, perhaps, this song:[6]

> "Harper's creek and roarin' ribber,
> Thar, my dear, we'll live forebber;
> Den we'll go to de Ingin nation,
> All I want in dis creation,
> Is pretty little wife and big plantation.
>
> *Chorus.* Up dat oak and down dat ribber,
> Two overseers and one little nigger."

6. Northup seems to be the only extant source for this and the following two songs.

Or, if these words are not adapted to the tune called for, it may be that "Old Hog Eye"*is*—a rather solemn and startling specimen of versification, not, however, to be appreciated unless heard at the South. It runneth as follows:

> "Who's been here since I've been gone?
> Pretty little gal wid a josey on.
>
> Hog Eye!
> Old Hog Eye,
> And Hosey too!
>
> Never see de like since I was born,
> Here come a little gal wid a josey on.
>
> Hog Eye!
> Old Hog Eye!
> And Hosey too!"

Or, may be the following, perhaps, equally nonsensical, but full of melody, nevertheless, as it flows from the negro's mouth:

> "Ebo Dick and Jurdan's Jo,
> Them two niggers stole my yo'.
>
> *Chorus.* Hop Jim along,
> Walk Jim along,
> Talk Jim along," &c.
>
> Old black Dan, as black as tar,
> He dam glad he was not dar.
>
> Hop Jim along," &c.

During the remaining holidays succeeding Christmas, they are provided with passes, and permitted to go where they please within a limited distance, or they may remain and labor on the plantation, in which case they are paid for it. It is very rarely, however, that the latter alternative is accepted. They may be seen at these times hurrying in all directions, as happy looking mortals as can be found on the face of the earth. They are different beings from what they are in the field; the temporary relaxation, the brief deliverance from fear, and from the lash, producing an entire metamorphosis in their appearance and demeanor. In visiting, riding, renewing old friendships, or, perchance, reviving some old attachment, or pursuing whatever pleasure may suggest itself, the time is occupied. Such is "southern life as it is,"[7] *three days in the year*, as I found it—the other three hundred and sixty-two being days of weariness, and fear, and suffering, and unremitting labor.

Marriage is frequently contracted during the holidays, if such an institution may be said to exist among them. The only ceremony required before entering into that "holy estate,"[8] is to obtain the consent of the respective owners. It is usually encouraged by the masters of female slaves. Either party can have as many husbands or wives as the owner will permit, and either is at liberty to discard the other at pleasure. The law in relation to divorce, or to bigamy, and so forth, is not applicable to property, of course. If the wife does not belong on the same plantation with the husband, the latter is permitted to visit her on Saturday nights, if the distance is not too far. Uncle Abram's wife lived seven miles from Epps', on Bayou Huff Power. He had permission to visit her once a fortnight, but he was growing old, as has been said, and truth to say, had latterly well nigh forgotten her. Uncle Abram had no time to spare from his meditations on General Jackson—connubial dalliance being well enough for the young and thoughtless, but unbecoming a grave and solemn philosopher like himself.

Chapter XVI.

OVERSEERS—HOW THEY ARE ARMED AND ACCOMPANIED—THE HOMICIDE—HIS EXECUTION AT MARKSVILLE—SLAVE DRIVERS—APPOINTED DRIVER ON REMOVING TO BAYOU BŒUF— PRACTICE MAKES PERFECT—EPPS' ATTEMPT TO CUT PLATT'S THROAT—THE ESCAPE FROM HIM—PROTECTED BY THE MISTRESS— FORBIDS READING AND WRITING—OBTAIN A SHEET OF PAPER AFTER NINE YEARS' EFFORT—THE LETTER—ARMSBY, THE MEAN WHITE— PARTIALLY CONFIDE IN HIM—HIS TREACHERY—EPPS' SUSPICIONS— HOW THEY WERE QUIETED—BURNING THE LETTER—ARMSBY LEAVES THE BAYOU—DISAPPOINTMENT AND DESPAIR.

With the exception of my trip to St. Mary's parish, and my absence during the cane-cutting seasons, I was constantly employed on the plantation of Master Epps. He was considered but a small planter, not having a sufficient number of hands to require the services of an overseer, acting in the latter capacity himself. Not able to increase his force, it was his custom to hire during the hurry of cotton-picking.

7. An ironic reference to Mary Henderson Eastman's *Aunt Phillis's Cabin; or, Southern Life as It Is* (1852), one of the pro-slavery, "anti-Tom" novels published in response to *Uncle Tom's Cabin* (1852).
8. Reference to the language of the marriage service in the 1789 Anglican Book of Common Prayer.

On larger estates, employing fifty or a hundred, or perhaps two hundred hands, an overseer is deemed indispensable. These gentlemen ride into the field on horseback, without an exception, to my knowledge, armed with pistols, bowie knife, whip, and accompanied by several dogs. They follow, equipped in this fashion, in rear of the slaves, keeping a sharp lookout upon them all. The requisite qualifications in an overseer are utter heartlessness, brutality and cruelty. It is his business to produce large crops, and if that is accomplished, no matter what amount of suffering it may have cost. The presence of the dogs are necessary to overhaul a fugitive who may take to his heels, as is sometimes the case, when faint or sick, he is unable to maintain* his row, and unable, also, to endure the whip. The pistols are reserved for any dangerous emergency, there having been instances when such weapons were necessary. Goaded into uncontrollable madness, even the slave will sometimes turn upon his oppressor. The gallows were standing at Marksville last January, upon which one was executed a year ago for killing his overseer. It occurred not many miles from Epps' plantation on Red River. The slave was given his task at splitting rails. In the course of the day the overseer sent him on an errand, which occupied so much time that it was not possible for him to perform the task. The next day he was called to an account, but the loss of time occasioned by the errand was no excuse, and he was ordered to kneel and bare his back for the reception of the lash. They were in the woods alone— beyond the reach of sight or hearing. The boy submitted until maddened at such injustice, and insane with pain, he sprang to his feet, and seizing an axe, literally chopped the overseer in pieces. He made no attempt whatever at concealment, but hastening to his master, related the whole affair, and declared himself ready to expiate the wrong by the sacrifice of his life. He was led to the scaffold, and while the rope was around his neck, maintained an undismayed and fearless bearing, and with his last words justified the act.

Besides the overseer, there are drivers under him, the number being in proportion to the number of hands in the field. The drivers are black, who, in addition to the performance of their equal share of work, are compelled to do the whipping of their several gangs. Whips hang around their necks, and if they fail to use them thoroughly, are whipped themselves. They have a few privileges, however; for example, in cane-cutting the hands are not allowed to sit down long enough to eat their dinners. Carts filled with corn cake, cooked at the kitchen, are driven into the field at noon. The cake is distributed by the drivers, and must be eaten with the least possible delay.

* The transcriber changed "maintin" to "maintain".

When the slave ceases to perspire, as he often does when taxed beyond his strength, he falls to the ground and becomes entirely helpless. It is then the duty of the driver to drag him into the shade of the standing cotton or cane, or of a neighboring tree, where he dashes buckets of water upon him, and uses other means of bringing out perspiration again, when he is ordered to his place, and compelled to continue his labor.

At Huff Power, when I first came to Epps', Tom, one of Roberts' negroes, was driver. He was a burly fellow, and severe in the extreme. After Epps' removal to Bayou Bœuf, that distinguished honor was conferred upon myself. Up to the time of my departure I had to wear a whip about my neck in the field. If Epps was present, I dared not show any lenity, not having the Christian fortitude of a certain well-known Uncle Tom sufficiently to brave his wrath, by refusing to perform the office. In that way, only, I escaped the immediate martyrdom he suffered, and, withal, saved my companions much suffering, as it proved in the end. Epps, I soon found, whether actually in the field or not, had his eyes pretty generally upon us. From the piazza, from behind some adjacent tree, or other concealed point of observation, he was perpetually on the watch. If one of us had been backward or idle through the day, we were apt to be told all about it on returning to the quarters, and as it was a matter of principle with him to reprove every offence of that kind that came within his knowledge, the offender not only was certain of receiving a castigation for his tardiness, but I likewise was punished for permitting it.

If, on the other hand, he had seen me use the lash freely, the man was satisfied. "Practice makes perfect," truly; and during my eight years' experience as a driver, I learned to handle the whip with marvelous dexterity and precision, throwing the lash within a hair's breadth of the back, the ear, the nose, without, however, touching either of them. If Epps was observed at a distance, or we had reason to apprehend he was sneaking somewhere in the vicinity, I would commence plying the lash vigorously, when, according to arrangement, they would squirm and screech as if in agony, although not one of them had in fact been even grazed. Patsey would take occasion, if he made his appearance presently, to mumble in his hearing some complaints that Platt was lashing them the whole time, and Uncle Abram, with an appearance of honesty peculiar to himself, would declare roundly I had just whipped them worse than General Jackson whipped the enemy at New-Orleans. If Epps was not drunk, and in one of his beastly humors, this was, in general, satisfactory. If he was, some one or more of us must suffer, as a matter of course. Sometimes his violence assumed a dangerous form, placing the lives of his human stock in jeopardy.

On one occasion the drunken madman thought to amuse himself by cutting my throat.

He had been absent at Holmesville, in attendance at a shooting-match, and none of us were aware of his return. While hoeing by the side of Patsey, she exclaimed, in a low voice, suddenly, "Platt, d'ye see old Hog-Jaw beckoning me to come to him?"

Glancing sideways, I discovered him in the edge of the field, motioning and grimacing, as was his habit when half-intoxicated. Aware of his lewd intentions, Patsey began to cry. I whispered her not to look up, and to continue at her work, as if she had not observed him. Suspecting the truth of the matter, however, he soon staggered up to me in a great rage.

"What did you say to Pats?" he demanded, with an oath. I made him some evasive answer, which only had the effect of increasing his violence.

"How long have you owned this plantation, *say*, you d——d nigger?" he inquired, with a malicious sneer, at the same time taking hold of my shirt collar with one hand, and thrusting the other into his pocket. "Now I'll cut your black throat; that's what I'll do," drawing his knife from his pocket as he said it. But with one hand he was unable to open it, until finally seizing the blade in his teeth, I saw he was about to succeed, and felt the necessity of escaping from him, for in his present reckless state, it was evident he was not joking, by any means. My shirt was open in front, and as I turned round quickly and sprang from him, while he still retained his gripe,* it was stripped entirely from my back. There was no difficulty now in eluding him. He would chase me until out of breath, then stop until it was recovered, swear, and renew the chase again. Now he would command me to come to him, now endeavor to coax me, but I was careful to keep at a respectful distance. In this manner we made the circuit of the field several times, he making desperate plunges, and I always dodging them, more amused than frightened, well knowing that when his sober senses returned, he would laugh at his own drunken folly. At length I observed the mistress standing by the yard fence, watching our half-serious, half-comical manœuvres. Shooting past him, I ran directly to her. Epps, on discovering her, did not follow. He remained about the field an hour or more, during which time I stood by the mistress, having related the particulars of what had taken place. Now, *she* was aroused again, denouncing her husband and Patsey about equally. Finally, Epps came towards the house, by this time nearly sober, walking demurely, with his hands behind his back, and attempting to look as innocent as a child.

* For "grip" (error in original).

As he approached, nevertheless, Mistress Epps began to berate him roundly, heaping upon him many rather disrespectful epithets, and demanding for what reason he had attempted to cut my throat. Epps made wondrous strange of it all, and to my surprise, swore by all the saints in the calendar he had not spoken to me that day.

"Platt, you lying nigger, *have* I?" was his brazen appeal to me.

It is not safe to contradict a master, even by the assertion of a truth. So I was silent, and when he entered the house I returned to the field, and the affair was never after alluded to.

Shortly after this time a circumstance occurred that came nigh divulging the secret of my real name and history, which I had so long and carefully concealed, and upon which I was convinced depended my final escape. Soon after he purchased me, Epps asked me if I could write and read, and on being informed that I had received some instruction in those branches of education, he assured me, with emphasis, if he ever caught me with a book, or with pen and ink, he would give me a hundred lashes. He said he wanted me to understand that he bought "niggers" to work and not to educate. He never inquired a word of my past life, or from whence I came.[9] The mistress, however, cross-examined me frequently about Washington, which she supposed was my native city, and more than once remarked that I did not talk nor act like the other "niggers," and she was sure I had seen more of the world than I admitted.

My great object always was to invent means of getting a letter secretly into the post-office, directed to some of my friends or family at the North. The difficulty of such an achievement cannot be comprehended by one unacquainted with the severe restrictions imposed upon me. In the first place, I was deprived of pen, ink, and paper. In the second place, a slave cannot leave his plantation without a pass, nor will a post-master mail a letter for one without written instructions from his owner. I was in slavery nine years, and always watchful and on the alert, before I met with the good fortune of obtaining a sheet of paper. While Epps was in New-Orleans, one winter, disposing of his cotton, the mistress sent me to Holmesville, with an order for several articles, and among the rest a quantity of foolscap.[1] I appropriated a sheet, concealing it in the cabin, under the board on which I slept.

After various experiments I succeeded in making ink, by boiling white maple bark, and with a feather plucked from the wing of a duck, manufactured a pen. When all were asleep in the cabin, by the light of the coals, lying upon my plank couch, I managed to complete

---

9. There is good reason to believe Northup also "carefully" minimized his literacy to avoid suspicion.
1. Large piece of paper that was commonly employed for letter writing in the nineteenth century. It was folded to make a folio.

a somewhat lengthy epistle. It was directed to an old acquaintance at Sandy Hill, stating my condition, and urging him to take measures to restore me to liberty. This letter I kept a long time, contriving measures by which it could be safely deposited in the post-office. At length, a low fellow, by the name of Armsby, hitherto a stranger, came into the neighborhood, seeking a situation as overseer. He applied to Epps, and was about the plantation for several days. He next went over to Shaw's, near by, and remained with him several weeks. Shaw was generally surrounded by such worthless characters, being himself noted as a gambler and unprincipled man. He had made a wife of his slave Charlotte, and a brood of young mulattoes were growing up in his house. Armsby became so much reduced at last, that he was compelled to labor with the slaves. A white man working in the field is a rare and unusual spectacle on Bayou Bœuf. I improved every opportunity of cultivating his acquaintance privately, desiring to obtain his confidence so far as to be willing to intrust the letter to his keeping. He visited Marksville repeatedly, he informed me, a town some twenty miles distant, and there, I proposed to myself, the letter should be mailed.

Carefully deliberating on the most proper manner of approaching him on the subject, I concluded finally to ask him simply if he would deposit a letter for me in the Marksville post-office the next time he visited that place, without disclosing to him that the letter was written, or any of the particulars it contained; for I had fears that he might betray me, and knew that some inducement must be held out to him of a pecuniary nature, before it would be safe to confide in him. As late as one o'clock one night I stole noiselessly from my cabin, and, crossing the field to Shaw's, found him sleeping on the piazza. I had but a few picayunes—the proceeds of my fiddling performances, but all I had in the world I promised him if he would do me the favor required. I begged him not to expose me if he could not grant the request. He assured me, upon his honor, he would deposit it in the Marksville post-office, and that he would keep it an inviolable secret forever. Though the letter was in my pocket at the time, I dared not then deliver it to him, but stating I would have it written in a day or two, bade him good night, and returned to my cabin. It was impossible for me to expel the suspicions I entertained, and all night I lay awake, revolving in my mind the safest course to pursue. I was willing to risk a great deal to accomplish my purpose, but should the letter by any means fall into the hands of Epps, it would be a death-blow to my aspirations. I was "perplexed in the extreme."[2]

My suspicions were well-founded, as the sequel demonstrated. The next day but one, while scraping cotton in the field, Epps seated

2. From *Othello* 5.2.

himself on the line fence between Shaw's plantation and his own, in such a position as to overlook the scene of our labors. Presently Armsby made his appearance, and, mounting the fence, took a seat beside him. They remained two or three hours, all of which time I was in an agony of apprehension.

That night, while broiling my bacon, Epps entered the cabin with his rawhide in his hand.

"Well, boy," said he, "I understand I've got a larned nigger, that writes letters, and tries to get white fellows to mail 'em. Wonder if you know who he is?"

My worst fears were realized, and although it may not be considered entirely creditable, even under the circumstances, yet a resort to duplicity and downright falsehood was the only refuge that presented itself.

"Don't know nothing about it, Master Epps," I answered him, assuming an air of ignorance and surprise; "Don't know nothing at all about it, sir."

"Wan't you over to Shaw's night before last?" he inquired.

"No, master," was the reply.

"Hav'nt you asked that fellow, Armsby, to mail a letter for you at Marksville?"

"Why, Lord, master, I never spoke three words to him in all my life. I don't know what you mean."

"Well," he continued, "Armsby told me to-day the devil was among my niggers; that I had one that needed close watching or he would run away; and when I axed him why, he said you come over to Shaw's, and waked him up in the night, and wanted him to carry a letter to Marksville. What have you got to say to that, ha?"

"All I've got to say, master," I replied, "is, there is no truth in it. How could I write a letter without any ink or paper? There is nobody I want to write to, 'cause I haint got no friends living as I know of. That Armsby is a lying, drunken fellow, they say, and nobody believes him anyway. You know I always tell the truth, and that I never go off the plantation without a pass. Now, master, I can see what that Armsby is after, plain enough. Did'nt he want you to hire him for an overseer?"

"Yes, he wanted me to hire him," answered Epps.

"That's it," said I, "he wants to make you believe we're all going to run away, and then he thinks you'll hire an overseer to watch us. He just made that story out of whole cloth, 'cause he wants to get a situation. It's all a lie, master, you may depend on't."

Epps mused awhile, evidently impressed with the plausibility of my theory, and exclaimed,

"I'm d—d, Platt, if I don't believe you tell the truth. He must take me for a soft, to think he can come it over me with them kind of yarns, musn't he? Maybe he thinks he can fool me; maybe he thinks

I don't know nothing—can't take care of my own niggers, eh! Soft soap[3] old Epps, eh! Ha, ha, ha! D—n Armsby! Set the dogs on him, Platt," and with many other comments descriptive of Armsby's general character, and his capability of taking care of his own business, and attending to his own "niggers," Master Epps left the cabin. As soon as he was gone I threw the letter in the fire, and, with a desponding and despairing heart, beheld the epistle which had cost me so much anxiety and thought, and which I fondly hoped would have been my forerunner to the land of freedom, writhe and shrivel on its bed of coals, and dissolve into smoke and ashes. Armsby, the treacherous wretch, was driven from Shaw's plantation not long subsequently, much to my relief, for I feared he might renew his conversation, and perhaps induce Epps to credit him.

I knew not now whither to look for deliverance. Hopes sprang up in my heart only to be crushed and blighted. The summer of my life was passing away; I felt I was growing prematurely old; that a few years more, and toil, and grief, and the poisonous miasmas of the swamps would accomplish their work upon me—would consign me to the grave's embrace, to moulder and be forgotten. Repelled, betrayed, cut off from the hope of succor, I could only prostrate myself upon the earth and groan in unutterable anguish. The hope of rescue was the only light that cast a ray of comfort on my heart. That was now flickering, faint and low; another breath of disappointment would extinguish it altogether, leaving me to grope in midnight darkness to the end of life.

Chapter XVII.

WILEY DISREGARDS THE COUNSELS OF AUNT PHEBE AND UNCLE ABRAM, AND IS CAUGHT BY THE PATROLLERS—THE ORGANIZATION AND DUTIES OF THE LATTER—WILEY RUNS AWAY—SPECULATIONS IN REGARD TO HIM—HIS UNEXPECTED RETURN—HIS CAPTURE ON THE RED RIVER, AND CONFINEMENT IN ALEXANDRIA JAIL—DISCOVERED BY JOSEPH B. ROBERTS—SUBDUING DOGS IN ANTICIPATION OF ESCAPE—THE FUGITIVES IN THE GREAT PINE WOODS—CAPTURED BY ADAM TAYDEM AND THE INDIANS—AUGUSTUS KILLED BY DOGS—NELLY, ELDRET'S SLAVE WOMAN—THE STORY OF CELESTE—THE CONCERTED MOVEMENT—LEW CHENEY,[*] THE TRAITOR—THE IDEA OF INSURRECTION.

The year 1850, down to which time I have now arrived, omitting many occurrences uninteresting to the reader, was an unlucky year for my companion Wiley, the husband of Phebe, whose taciturn and

3. Idiom meaning "to persuade," usually involving deception.
* The transcriber changed "LEW CHEENEY" to "LEW CHENEY".

retiring nature has thus far kept him in the background. Notwith-standing Wiley seldom opened his mouth, and revolved in his obscure and unpretending orbit without a grumble, nevertheless the warm elements of sociality were strong in the bosom of that silent "nig-ger." In the exuberance of his self-reliance, disregarding the philoso-phy of Uncle Abram, and setting the counsels of Aunt Phebe utterly at naught, he had the fool-hardiness to essay a nocturnal visit to a neighboring cabin without a pass.

So attractive was the society in which he found himself, that Wiley took little note of the passing hours, and the light began to break in the east before he was aware. Speeding homeward as fast as he could run, he hoped to reach the quarters before the horn would sound; but, unhappily, he was spied on the way by a company of patrollers.

How it is in other dark places of slavery, I do not know, but on Bayou Bœuf there is an organization of patrollers, as they are styled, whose business it is to seize and whip any slave they may find wan-dering from the plantation. They ride on horseback, headed by a captain, armed, and accompanied by dogs. They have the right, either by law, or by general consent, to inflict discretionary chastise-ment upon a black man caught beyond the boundaries of his mas-ter's estate without a pass, and even to shoot him, if he attempts to escape. Each company has a certain distance to ride up and down the bayou. They are compensated by the planters, who contribute in proportion to the number of slaves they own. The clatter of their horses' hoofs dashing by can be heard at all hours of the night, and frequently they may be seen driving a slave before them, or leading him by a rope fastened around his neck, to his owner's plantation.

Wiley fled before one of these companies, thinking he could reach his cabin before they could overtake him; but one of their dogs, a great ravenous hound, griped him by the leg, and held him fast. The patrollers whipped him severely, and brought him, a prisoner, to Epps. From him he received another flagellation still more severe, so that the cuts of the lash and the bites of the dog rendered him sore, stiff and miserable, insomuch he was scarcely able to move. It was impossible in such a state to keep up his row, and con-sequently there was not an hour in the day but Wiley felt the sting of his master's rawhide on his raw and bleeding back. His sufferings became intolerable, and finally he resolved to run away. Without dis-closing his intentions to run away even to his wife Phebe, he pro-ceeded to make arrangements for carrying his plan into execution. Having cooked his whole week's allowance, he cautiously left the cabin on a Sunday night, after the inmates of the quarters were asleep. When the horn sounded in the morning, Wiley did not make his appearance. Search was made for him in the cabins, in the corn-crib, in the cotton-house, and in every nook and corner of the premises. Each of us was examined, touching any knowledge we might have that could throw light upon his sudden disappearance or present whereabouts. Epps raved and stormed, and mounting his horse, galloped to neighboring plantations, making inquiries in all directions. The search was fruitless. Nothing whatever was elicited, going to show what had become of the missing man. The dogs were led to the swamp, but were unable to strike his trail. They would circle away through the forest, their noses to the ground, but invariably returned in a short time to the spot from whence they started.

Wiley had escaped, and so secretly and cautiously as to elude and baffle all pursuit. Days and even weeks passed away, and nothing could be heard of him. Epps did nothing but curse and swear. It was the only topic of conversation among us when alone. We indulged in a great deal of speculation in regard to him, one suggesting he might have been drowned in some bayou, inasmuch as he was a poor swimmer; another, that perhaps he might have been devoured by alligators, or stung by the venomous moccasin, whose bite is certain and sudden death. The warm and hearty sympathies of us all, however, were with poor Wiley, wherever he might be. Many an earnest prayer ascended from the lips of Uncle Abram, beseeching safety for the wanderer.

In about three weeks, when all hope of ever seeing him again was dismissed, to our surprise, he one day appeared among us. On leaving the plantation, he informed us, it was his intention to make his way back to South Carolina—to the old quarters of Master Buford. During the day he remained secreted, sometimes in the branches of a tree, and at night pressed forward through the swamps. Finally, one morning, just at dawn, he reached the shore of Red River. While standing on the bank, considering how he could cross it, a white man accosted him, and demanded a pass. Without one, and evidently a runaway, he was taken to Alexandria, the shire town of the parish of Rapides, and confined in prison. It happened several days after that Joseph B. Roberts, uncle of Mistress Epps, was in Alexandria, and going into the jail, recognized him. Wiley had worked on his plantation, when Epps resided at Huff Power. Paying the jail fee, and writing him a pass, underneath which was a note to Epps, requesting him not to whip him on his return, Wiley was sent back to Bayou Bœuf. It was the hope that hung upon this request, and which Roberts assured him would be respected by his master, that sustained him as he approached the house. The request, however, as may be readily supposed, was entirely disregarded. After being kept in suspense three days, Wiley was stripped, and compelled to endure one of those inhuman floggings to which the poor slave is so often subjected. It was the first and last attempt of Wiley to run away. The long scars upon his back, which he will carry with him to the grave, perpetually remind him of the dangers of such a step.

There was not a day throughout the ten years I belonged to Epps that I did not consult with myself upon the prospect of escape. I laid many plans, which at the time I considered excellent ones, but one after the other they were all abandoned. No man who has never been placed in such a situation, can comprehend the thousand obstacles thrown in the way of the flying slave. Every white man's hand is raised against him—the patrollers are watching for him—the hounds are ready to follow on his track, and the nature of the country is such as renders it impossible to pass through it with any safety. I thought, however, that the time might come, perhaps, when I should be running through the swamps again. I concluded, in that case, to be prepared for Epps' dogs, should they pursue me. He possessed several, one of which was a notorious slave-hunter, and the most fierce and savage of his breed. While out hunting the coon or the opossum, I never allowed an opportunity to escape, when alone, of whipping them severely. In this manner I succeeded at length in subduing them completely. They feared me, obeying my voice at once when others had no control over them whatever. Had they followed and overtaken me, I doubt not they would have shrank from attacking me.

Notwithstanding the certainty of being captured, the woods and swamps are, nevertheless, continually filled with runaways. Many of them, when sick, or so worn out as to be unable to perform their tasks, escape into the swamps, willing to suffer the punishment inflicted for such offences, in order to obtain a day or two of rest.

While I belonged to Ford, I was unwittingly the means of disclosing the hiding-place of six or eight, who had taken up their residence in the "Great Pine Woods." Adam Taydem frequently sent me from the mills over to the opening after provisions. The whole distance was then a thick pine forest. About ten o'clock of a beautiful moonlight night, while walking along the Texas road, returning to the mills, carrying a dressed pig in a bag swung over my shoulder, I heard footsteps behind me, and turning round, beheld two black men in the dress of slaves approaching at a rapid pace. When within a short distance, one of them raised a club, as if intending to strike me; the other snatched at the bag. I managed to dodge them both, and seizing a pine knot, hurled it with such force against the head of one of them that he was prostrated apparently senseless to the ground. Just then two more made their appearance from one side of the road. Before they could grapple me, however, I succeeded in passing them, and taking to my heels, fled, much affrighted, towards the mills. When Adam was informed of the adventure, he hastened straightway to the Indian village, and arousing Cascalla and several of his tribe, started in pursuit of the highwaymen.[4] I accompanied them

4. Typically a word used to describe robbers who target travelers.

to the scene of attack, when we discovered a puddle of blood in the road, where the man whom I had smitten with the pine knot had fallen. After searching carefully through the woods a long time, one of Cascalla's men discovered a smoke curling up through the branches of several prostrate pines, whose tops had fallen together. The rendezvous was cautiously surrounded, and all of them taken prisoners. They had escaped from a plantation in the vicinity of Lamourie, and had been secreted there three weeks. They had no evil design upon me, except to frighten me out of my pig. Having observed me passing towards Ford's just at night-fall, and suspecting the nature of my errand, they had followed me, seen me butcher and dress the porker, and start on my return. They had been pinched for food, and were driven to this extremity by necessity. Adam conveyed them to the parish jail, and was liberally rewarded.

Not unfrequently the runaway loses his life in the attempt to escape. Epps' premises were bounded on one side by Carey's, a very extensive sugar plantation. He cultivates annually at least fifteen hundred acres of cane, manufacturing twenty-two or twenty-three hundred hogsheads of sugar; an hogshead and a half being the usual yield of an acre. Besides this he also cultivates five or six hundred acres of corn and cotton. He owned last year one hundred and fifty three field hands, besides nearly as many children, and yearly hires a drove during the busy season from this side the Mississippi.

One of his negro drivers, a pleasant, intelligent boy, was named Augustus. During the holidays, and occasionally while at work in adjoining fields, I had an opportunity of making his acquaintance, which eventually ripened into a warm and mutual attachment. Summer before last he was so unfortunate as to incur the displeasure of the overseer, a coarse, heartless brute, who whipped him most cruelly. Augustus ran away. Reaching a cane rick on Hawkins' plantation, he secreted himself in the top of it. All Carey's dogs were put upon his track—some fifteen of them—and soon scented his footsteps to the hiding place. They surrounded the rick, baying and scratching, but could not reach him. Presently, guided by the clamor of the hounds, the pursuers rode up, when the overseer, mounting on to the rick, drew him forth. As he rolled down to the ground the whole pack plunged upon him, and before they could be beaten off, had gnawed and mutilated his body in the most shocking manner, their teeth having penetrated to the bone in an hundred places. He was taken up, tied upon a mule, and carried home. But this was Augustus' last trouble. He lingered until the next day, when death sought the unhappy boy, and kindly relieved him from his agony.

It was not unusual for slave women as well as slave men to endeavor to escape. Nelly, Eldret's girl, with whom I lumbered for a time in the "Big Cane Brake," lay concealed in Epps' corn crib three days.

At night, when his family were asleep, she would steal into the quarters for food, and return to the crib again. We concluded it would no longer be safe for us to allow her to remain, and accordingly she retraced her steps to her own cabin.

But the most remarkable instance of a successful evasion of dogs and hunters was the following: Among Carey's girls was one by the name of Celeste. She was nineteen or twenty, and far whiter than her owner, or any of his offspring. It required a close inspection to distinguish in her features the slightest trace of African blood. A stranger would never have dreamed that she was the descendant of slaves. I was sitting in my cabin late at night, playing a low air on my violin, when the door opened carefully, and Celeste stood before me. She was pale and haggard. Had an apparition arisen from the earth, I could not have been more startled.

"Who are you?" I demanded, after gazing at her a moment.

"I'm hungry; give me some bacon," was her reply.

My first impression was that she was some deranged young mistress, who, escaping from home, was wandering, she knew not whither, and had been attracted to my cabin by the sound of the violin. The coarse cotton slave dress she wore, however, soon dispelled such a supposition.

"What is your name?" I again interrogated.

"My name is Celeste," she answered. "I belong to Carey, and have been two days among the palmettoes. I am sick and can't work, and would rather die in the swamp than be whipped to death by the overseer. Carey's dogs won't follow me. They have tried to set them on. There's a secret between them and Celeste, and they wont mind the devilish orders of the overseer. Give me some meat—I'm starving."

I divided my scanty allowance with her, and while partaking of it, she related how she had managed to escape, and described the place of her concealment. In the edge of the swamp, not half a mile from Epps' house, was a large space, thousands of acres in extent, thickly covered with palmetto. Tall trees, whose long arms interlocked each other, formed a canopy above them, so dense as to exclude the beams of the sun. It was like twilight always, even in the middle of the brightest day. In the centre of this great space, which nothing but serpents very often explore—a sombre and solitary spot—Celeste had erected a rude hut of dead branches that had fallen to the ground, and covered it with the leaves of the palmetto. This was the abode she had selected. She had no fear of Carey's dogs, any more than I had of Epps'. It is a fact, which I have never been able to explain, that there are those whose tracks the hounds will absolutely refuse to follow. Celeste was one of them.

For several nights she came to my cabin for food. On one occasion our dogs barked as she approached, which aroused Epps, and induced him to reconnoitre the premises. He did not discover her, but after that it was not deemed prudent for her to come to the yard. When all was silent I carried provisions to a certain spot agreed upon, where she would find them.

In this manner Celeste passed the greater part of the summer. She regained her health, and became strong and hearty. At all seasons of the year the howlings of wild animals can be heard at night along the borders of the swamps. Several times they had made her a midnight call, awakening her from slumber with a growl. Terrified by such unpleasant salutations, she finally concluded to abandon her lonely dwelling; and, accordingly, returning to her master, was scourged, her neck meanwhile being fastened in the stocks, and sent into the field again.

The year before my arrival in the country[5] there was a concerted movement among a number of slaves on Bayou Bœuf, that terminated tragically indeed. It was, I presume, a matter of newspaper notoriety at the time, but all the knowledge I have of it, has been derived from the relation of those living at that period in the immediate vicinity of the excitement. It has become a subject of general and unfailing interest in every slave-hut on the bayou, and will doubtless go down to succeeding generations as their chief tradition. Lew Cheney, with whom I became acquainted—a shrewd, cunning negro, more intelligent than the generality of his race, but unscrupulous and full of treachery—conceived the project of organizing a company sufficiently strong to fight their way against all opposition, to the neighboring territory of Mexico.

A remote spot, far within the depths of the swamp, back of Hawkins' plantation, was selected as the rallying point. Lew flitted from one plantation to another, in the dead of night, preaching a crusade to Mexico, and, like Peter the Hermit,[6] creating a furor of excitement wherever he appeared. At length a large number of runaways were assembled; stolen mules, and corn gathered from the fields, and bacon filched from smoke-houses, had been conveyed into the woods. The expedition was about ready to proceed, when their hiding place was discovered. Lew Cheney, becoming convinced of the ultimate failure of his project, in order to curry favor with his master, and avoid the consequences which he foresaw would follow, deliberately determined to sacrifice all his companions. Departing secretly from the encampment, he proclaimed among the planters the number collected in the swamp, and, instead of stating truly the object they had in view, asserted their intention was to emerge

5. The Lew Cheney insurrection actually occurred in 1837, several years before Northup's capture.
6. Medieval French priest who rallied peasants to join the First Crusade.

from their seclusion the first favorable opportunity, and murder every white person along the bayou.

Such an announcement, exaggerated as it passed from mouth to mouth, filled the whole country with terror. The fugitives were surrounded and taken prisoners, carried in chains to Alexandria, and hung by the populace. Not only those, but many who were suspected, though entirely innocent, were taken from the field and from the cabin, and without the shadow of process or form of trial, hurried to the scaffold. The planters on Bayou Bœuf finally rebelled against such reckless destruction of property, but it was not until a regiment of soldiers had arrived from some fort on the Texan frontier, demolished the gallows, and opened the doors of the Alexandria prison, that the indiscriminate slaughter was stayed. Lew Cheney escaped, and was even rewarded for his treachery.[7] He is still living, but his name is despised and execrated by all his race throughout the parishes of Rapides and Avoyelles.

Such an idea as insurrection, however, is not new among the enslaved population of Bayou Bœuf. More than once I have joined in serious consultation, when the subject has been discussed, and there have been times when a word from me would have placed hundreds of my fellow-bondsmen in an attitude of defiance. Without arms or ammunition, or even with them, I saw such a step would result in certain defeat, disaster and death, and always raised my voice against it.

During the Mexican war[8] I well remember the extravagant hopes that were excited. The news of victory filled the great house with rejoicing, but produced only sorrow and disappointment in the cabin. In my opinion—and I have had opportunity to know something of the feeling of which I speak—there are not fifty slaves on the shores of Bayou Bœuf, but would hail with unmeasured delight the approach of an invading army.

They are deceived who flatter themselves that the ignorant and debased slave has no conception of the magnitude of his wrongs. They are deceived who imagine that he arises from his knees, with back lacerated and bleeding, cherishing only a spirit of meekness and forgiveness. A day may come—it *will* come, if his prayer is heard—a terrible day of vengeance, when the master in his turn will cry in vain for mercy.

7. Cheney was freed and given $500 to leave the state after betraying the rebellion.
8. War (1846–48) between the United States and Mexico prompted by the U.S. annexation of Texas. Opponents of slavery saw more than the border of Texas at stake; they believed the war was driven by the slave power's desire for more land.

Chapter XVIII.

O'NIEL, THE TANNER—CONVERSATION WITH AUNT PHEBE
OVERHEARD—EPPS IN THE TANNING BUSINESS—STABBING OF UNCLE
ABRAM—THE UGLY WOUND—EPPS IS JEALOUS—PATSEY IS MISSING—
HER RETURN FROM SHAW'S—HARRIET, SHAW'S BLACK WIFE—EPPS
ENRAGED—PATSEY DENIES HIS CHARGES—SHE IS TIED DOWN NAKED
TO FOUR STAKES—THE INHUMAN FLOGGING—FLAYING OF PATSEY—
THE BEAUTY OF THE DAY—THE BUCKET OF SALT WATER—THE DRESS
STIFF WITH BLOOD—PATSEY GROWS MELANCHOLY—HER IDEA OF
GOD AND ETERNITY—OF HEAVEN AND FREEDOM—THE EFFECT
OF SLAVE-WHIPPING—EPPS' OLDEST SON—"THE CHILD IS FATHER
TO THE MAN."

Wiley suffered severely at the hands of Master Epps, as has been related in the preceding chapter, but in this respect he fared no worse than his unfortunate companions. "Spare the rod,"[9] was an idea scouted by our master. He was constitutionally subject to periods of ill-humor, and at such times, however little provocation there might be, a certain amount of punishment was inflicted. The circumstances attending the last flogging but one that I received, will show how trivial a cause was sufficient with him for resorting to the whip.

A Mr. O'Niel, residing in the vicinity of the Big Pine Woods, called upon Epps for the purpose of purchasing me. He was a tanner and currier by occupation, transacting an extensive business, and intended to place me at service in some department of his establishment, provided he bought me. Aunt Phebe, while preparing the dinner-table in the great house, overheard their conversation. On returning to the yard at night, the old woman ran to meet me, designing, of course, to overwhelm me with the news. She entered into a minute repetition of all she had heard, and Aunt Phebe was one whose ears never failed to drink in every word of conversation uttered in her hearing. She enlarged upon the fact that "Massa Epps was g'wine to sell me to a tanner ober in de Pine Woods," so long and loudly as to attract the attention of the mistress, who, standing unobserved on the piazza at the time, was listening to our conversation.

"Well, Aunt Phebe," said I, "I'm glad of it. I'm tired of scraping cotton, and would rather be a tanner. I hope he'll buy me."

O'Niel did not effect a purchase, however, the parties differing as to price, and the morning following his arrival, departed homewards. He had been gone but a short time, when Epps made his

---

9. "Spare the rod and spoil the child," a saying in support of corporal punishment adapted from Proverbs and first expressed in these words in Samuel Butler's late seventeenth-century poem "Hudibras."

appearance in the field. Now nothing will more violently enrage a master, especially Epps, than the intimation of one of his servants that he would like to leave him. Mistress Epps had repeated to him my expressions to Aunt Phebe the evening previous, as I learned from the latter afterwards, the mistress having mentioned to her that she had overheard us. On entering the field, Epps walked directly to me.

"So, Platt, you're tired of scraping cotton, are you? You would like to change your master, eh? You're fond of moving round—traveler—ain't ye? Ah, yes—like to travel for your health, may be? Feel above cotton-scraping, I 'spose. So you're going into the tanning business? Good business—devilish fine business. Enterprising nigger! B'lieve I'll go into that business myself. Down on your knees, and strip that rag off your back! I'll try my hand at tanning."[1]

I begged earnestly, and endeavored to soften him with excuses, but in vain. There was no other alternative; so kneeling down, I presented my bare back for the application of the lash.

"How do you like *tanning*?" he exclaimed, as the rawhide descended upon my flesh. "How do you like *tanning*?" he repeated at every blow. In this manner he gave me twenty or thirty lashes, incessantly giving utterance to the word "tanning," in one form of expression or another. When sufficiently "tanned," he allowed me to arise, and with a half-malicious laugh assured me, if I still fancied the business, he would give me further instruction in it whenever I desired. This time, he remarked, he had only given me a short lesson in "*tanning*"—the next time he would "curry me down."

Uncle Abram, also, was frequently treated with great brutality, although he was one of the kindest and most faithful creatures in the world. He was my cabin-mate for years. There was a benevolent expression in the old man's face, pleasant to behold. He regarded us with a kind of parental feeling, always counseling us with remarkable gravity and deliberation.

Returning from Marshall's plantation one afternoon, whither I had been sent on some errand of the mistress, I found him lying on the cabin floor, his clothes saturated with blood. He informed me that he had been stabbed! While spreading cotton on the scaffold, Epps came home intoxicated from Holmesville. He found fault with every thing, giving many orders so directly contrary that it was impossible to execute any of them. Uncle Abram, whose faculties were growing dull, became confused, and committed some blunder of no particular consequence. Epps was so enraged thereat, that, with drunken recklessness, he flew upon the old man, and stabbed him in the back. It was a long, ugly wound, but did not happen to

1. Epps is punning on the expression "tanning one's hide," slang for a beating.

penetrate far enough to result fatally. It was sewed up by the mistress, who censured her husband with extreme severity, not only denouncing his inhumanity, but declaring that she expected nothing else than that he would bring the family to poverty—that he would kill all the slaves on the plantation in some of his drunken fits.

It was no uncommon thing with him to prostrate Aunt Phebe with a chair or stick of wood; but the most cruel whipping that ever I was doomed to witness—one I can never recall with any other emotion than that of horror—was inflicted on the unfortunate Patsey.

It has been seen that the jealousy and hatred of Mistress Epps made the daily life of her young and agile slave completely miserable. I am happy in the belief that on numerous occasions I was the means of averting punishment from the inoffensive girl. In Epps' absence the mistress often ordered me to whip her without the remotest provocation. I would refuse, saying that I feared my master's displeasure, and several times ventured to remonstrate with her against the treatment Patsey received. I endeavored to impress her with the truth that the latter was not responsible for the acts of which she complained, but that she being a slave, and subject entirely to her master's will, he alone was answerable.

At length "the green-eyed monster"[2] crept into the soul of Epps also, and then it was that he joined with his wrathful wife in an infernal jubilee over the girl's miseries.

On a Sabbath day in hoeing time, not long ago, we were on the bayou bank, washing our clothes, as was our usual custom. Presently Patsey was missing. Epps called aloud, but there was no answer. No one had observed her leaving the yard, and it was a wonder with us whither she had gone. In the course of a couple of hours she was seen approaching from the direction of Shaw's. This man, as has been intimated, was a notorious profligate, and withal not on the most friendly terms with Epps. Harriet, his black wife, knowing Patsey's troubles, was kind to her, in consequence of which the latter was in the habit of going over to see her every opportunity. Her visits were prompted by friendship merely, but the suspicion gradually entered the brain of Epps, that another and a baser passion led her thither—that it was not Harriet she desired to meet, but rather the unblushing libertine, his neighbor. Patsey found her master in a fearful rage on her return. His violence so alarmed her that at first she attempted to evade direct answers to his questions, which only served to increase his suspicions. She finally, however, drew herself up proudly, and in a spirit of indignation boldly denied his charges.

"Missus don't give me soap to wash with, as she does the rest," said Patsey, "and you know why. I went over to Harriet's to get a

2. Jealousy; from *Othello* 3.3.

piece," and saying this, she drew it forth from a pocket in her dress and exhibited it to him. "That's what I went to Shaw's for, Massa Epps," continued she; "the Lord knows that was all."

"You lie, you black wench!" shouted Epps.

"I *don't* lie, massa. If you kill me, I'll stick to that."

"Oh! I'll fetch you down. I'll learn you to go to Shaw's. I'll take the starch out of ye," he muttered fiercely through his shut teeth.

Then turning to me, he ordered four stakes to be driven into the ground, pointing with the toe of his boot to the places where he wanted them. When the stakes were driven down, he ordered her to be stripped of every article of dress. Ropes were then brought, and the naked girl was laid upon her face, her wrists and feet each tied firmly to a stake. Stepping to the piazza, he took down a heavy whip, and placing it in my hands, commanded me to lash her. Unpleasant as it was, I was compelled to obey him. Nowhere that day, on the face of the whole earth, I venture to say, was there such a demoniac exhibition witnessed as then ensued.

Mistress Epps stood on the piazza among her children, gazing on the scene with an air of heartless satisfaction. The slaves were huddled together at a little distance, their countenances indicating the sorrow of their hearts. Poor Patsey prayed piteously for mercy, but her prayers were vain. Epps ground his teeth, and stamped upon the ground, screaming at me, like a mad fiend, to strike *harder*.

"Strike harder, or *your* turn will come next, you scoundrel," he yelled.

"Oh, mercy, massa!—oh! have mercy, *do*. Oh, God! pity me," Patsey exclaimed continually, struggling fruitlessly, and the flesh quivering at every stroke.

When I had struck her as many as thirty times, I stopped, and turned round toward Epps, hoping he was satisfied; but with bitter oaths and threats, he ordered me to continue. I inflicted ten or fifteen blows more. By this time her back was covered with long welts, intersecting each other like net work. Epps was yet furious and savage as ever, demanding if she would like to go to Shaw's again, and swearing he would flog her until she wished she was in h—l. Throwing down the whip, I declared I could punish her no more. He ordered me to go on, threatening me with a severer flogging than she had received, in case of refusal. My heart revolted at the inhuman scene, and risking the consequences, I absolutely refused to raise the whip. He then seized it himself, and applied it with ten-fold greater force than I had. The painful cries and shrieks of the tortured Patsey, mingling with the loud and angry curses of Epps, loaded the air. She was terribly lacerated—I may say, without exaggeration, literally flayed. The lash was wet with blood, which flowed down her sides and dropped upon the ground. At length she ceased

THE STAKING OUT AND FLOGGING OF THE GIRL PATSEY.

N. ORR N.Y

Courtesy of the UNC–CH Library, The University of North Carolina at Chapel Hill.

struggling. Her head sank listlessly on the ground. Her screams and supplications gradually decreased and died away into a low moan. She no longer writhed and shrank beneath the lash when it bit out small pieces of her flesh. I thought that she was dying!

It was the Sabbath of the Lord. The fields smiled in the warm sunlight—the birds chirped merrily amidst the foliage of the trees—peace and happiness seemed to reign everywhere, save in the bosoms of Epps and his panting victim and the silent witnesses around him. The tempestuous emotions that were raging there were little in harmony with the calm and quiet beauty of the day. I could look on Epps only with unutterable loathing and abhorrence, and thought within myself—"Thou devil, sooner or later, somewhere in the course of eternal justice, thou shalt answer for this sin!"

Finally, he ceased whipping from mere exhaustion, and ordered Phebe to bring a bucket of salt and water. After washing her thoroughly with this, I was told to take her to her cabin. Untying the ropes, I raised her in my arms. She was unable to stand, and as her head rested on my shoulder, she repeated many times, in a faint voice scarcely perceptible, "Oh, Platt—oh, Platt!" but nothing further. Her dress was replaced, but it clung to her back, and was soon stiff with blood. We laid her on some boards in the hut, where she remained a long time, with eyes closed and groaning in agony. At night Phebe applied melted tallow to her wounds, and so far as we were able, all endeavored to assist and console her. Day after day she lay in her cabin upon her face, the sores preventing her resting in any other position.

A blessed thing it would have been for her—days and weeks and months of misery it would have saved her—had she never lifted up her head in life again. Indeed, from that time forward she was not what she had been. The burden of a deep melancholy weighed heavily on her spirits. She no longer moved with that buoyant and elastic step—there was not that mirthful sparkle in her eyes that formerly distinguished her. The bounding vigor—the sprightly, laughter-loving spirit of her youth, were gone. She fell into a mournful and desponding mood, and oftentimes would start up in her sleep, and with raised hands, plead for mercy. She became more silent than she was, toiling all day in our midst, not uttering a word. A care-worn, pitiful expression settled on her face, and it was her humor now to weep, rather than rejoice. If ever there was a broken heart—one crushed and blighted by the rude grasp of suffering and misfortune—it was Patsey's.

She had been reared no better than her master's beast—looked upon merely as a valuable and handsome animal—and consequently possessed but a limited amount of knowledge. And yet a faint light cast its rays over her intellect, so that it was not wholly dark. She had a dim perception of God and of eternity, and a still more dim perception of a Saviour who had died even for such as her. She entertained but confused notions of a future life—not comprehending the distinction between the corporeal and spiritual existence. Happiness, in her mind, was exemption from stripes—from labor—from the cruelty of masters and overseers. Her idea of the joy of heaven was simply *rest,* and is fully expressed in these lines of a melancholy bard:

> "I ask no paradise on high,
> With cares on earth oppressed,
> The only heaven for which I sigh,
> Is rest, eternal rest."[3]

It is a mistaken opinion that prevails in some quarters, that the slave does not understand the term—does not comprehend the idea of freedom. Even on Bayou Bœuf, where I conceive slavery exists in its most abject and cruel form—where it exhibits features altogether unknown in more northern States—the most ignorant of them generally know full well its meaning. They understand the privileges and exemptions that belong to it—that it would bestow upon them the fruits of their own labors, and that it would secure to them the enjoyment of domestic happiness. They do not fail to observe the difference between their own condition and the meanest white man's, and to realize the injustice of the laws which place it in his power not only to appropriate the profits of their industry, but to subject them to unmerited and unprovoked punishment, without remedy, or the right to resist, or to remonstrate.

Patsey's life, especially after her whipping, was one long dream of liberty. Far away, to her fancy an immeasurable distance, she knew there was a land of freedom. A thousand times she had heard that somewhere in the distant North there were no slaves—no masters. In her imagination it was an enchanted region, the Paradise of the earth. To dwell where the black man may work for himself—live in his own cabin—till his own soil, was a blissful dream of Patsey's—a dream, alas! the fulfillment of which she can never realize.

The effect of these exhibitions of brutality on the household of the slave-holder, is apparent. Epps' oldest son is an intelligent lad of ten or twelve years of age. It is pitiable, sometimes, to see him chastising, for instance, the venerable Uncle Abram. He will call the old man to account, and if in his childish judgment it is necessary, sentence him to a certain number of lashes, which he proceeds to inflict with much gravity and deliberation. Mounted on his

---

3. From the poem "Byron's Prayer" by John Malcolm. It appeared in number 5 of the *Edinburgh Literary Journal* of 1831 and was published in America in the second number of the *American Masonic Register* (1841).

pony, he often rides into the field with his whip, playing the overseer, greatly to his father's delight. Without discrimination, at such
times, he applies the rawhide, urging the slaves forward with shouts,
and occasional expressions of profanity, while the old man laughs,
and commends him as a thorough-going boy.

"The child is father to the man,"[4] and with such training, whatever
may be his natural disposition, it cannot well be otherwise than
that, on arriving at maturity, the sufferings and miseries of the
slave will be looked upon with entire indifference. The influence of
the iniquitous system necessarily fosters an unfeeling and cruel spirit,
even in the bosoms of those who, among their equals, are regarded
as humane and generous.

Young Master Epps possessed some noble qualities, yet no process of reasoning could lead him to comprehend, that in the eye of
the Almighty there is no distinction of color. He looked upon the
black man simply as an animal, differing in no respect from any
other animal, save in the gift of speech and the possession of somewhat higher instincts, and, therefore, the more valuable. To work like
his father's mules—to be whipped and kicked and scourged through
life—to address the white man with hat in hand, and eyes bent servilely on the earth, in his mind, was the natural and proper destiny
of the slave. Brought up with such ideas—in the notion that we
stand without the pale of humanity—no wonder the oppressors of my
people are a pitiless and unrelenting race.

Chapter XIX.

AVERY, OF BAYOU ROUGE—PECULIARITY OF DWELLINGS—EPPS
BUILDS A NEW HOUSE—BASS, THE CARPENTER—HIS NOBLE
QUALITIES—HIS PERSONAL APPEARANCE AND ECCENTRICITIES—
BASS AND EPPS DISCUSS THE QUESTION OF SLAVERY—EPPS' OPINION
OF BASS—I MAKE MYSELF KNOWN TO HIM—OUR CONVERSATION—
HIS SURPRISE—THE MIDNIGHT MEETING ON THE BAYOU BANK—
BASS' ASSURANCES—DECLARES WAR AGAINST SLAVERY—WHY I DID
NOT DISCLOSE MY HISTORY—BASS WRITES LETTERS—COPY OF HIS
LETTER TO MESSRS. PARKER AND PERRY—THE FEVER OF SUSPENSE—
DISAPPOINTMENTS—BASS ENDEAVORS TO CHEER ME—
MY FAITH IN HIM.

In the month of June, 1852, in pursuance of a previous contract,
Mr. Avery, a carpenter of Bayou Rouge, commenced the erection of
a house for Master Epps. It has previously been stated that there

4. From William Wordsworth's "My Heart Leaps Up When I Behold" (1802).

are no cellars on Bayou Bœuf; on the other hand, such is the low and swampy nature of the ground, the great houses are usually built upon spiles. Another peculiarity is, the rooms are not plastered, but the ceiling and sides are covered with matched cypress boards, painted such color as most pleases the owner's taste. Generally the plank and boards are sawed by slaves with whip-saws, there being no waterpower upon which mills might be built within many miles. When the planter erects for himself a dwelling, therefore, there is plenty of extra work for his slaves. Having had some experience under Tibeats as a carpenter, I was taken from the field altogether, on the arrival of Avery and his hands.

Among them was one to whom I owe an immeasurable debt of gratitude. Only for him, in all probability, I should have ended my days in slavery. He was my deliverer—a man whose true heart overflowed with noble and generous emotions. To the last moment of my existence I shall remember him with feelings of thankfulness. His name was Bass, and at that time he resided in Marksville. It will be difficult to convey a correct impression of his appearance or character. He was a large man, between forty and fifty years old, of light complexion and light hair. He was very cool and self-possessed, fond of argument, but always speaking with extreme deliberation. He was that kind of person whose peculiarity of manner was such that nothing he uttered ever gave offence. What would be intolerable, coming from the lips of another, could be said by him with impunity. There was not a man on Red River, perhaps, that agreed with him on the subject of politics or religion, and not a man, I venture to say, who discussed either of those subjects half as much. It seemed to be taken for granted that he would espouse the unpopular side of every local question, and it always created amusement rather than displeasure among his auditors, to listen to the ingenious and original manner in which he maintained the controversy. He was a bachelor—an "old bachelor," according to the true acceptation of the term—having no kindred living, as he knew of, in the world. Neither had he any permanent abiding place—wandering from one State to another, as his fancy dictated. He had lived in Marksville three or four years, and in the prosecution of his business as a carpenter; and in consequence, likewise, of his peculiarities, was quite extensively known throughout the parish of Avoyelles. He was liberal to a fault; and his many acts of kindness and transparent goodness of heart rendered him popular in the community, the sentiment of which he unceasingly combated.

He was a native of Canada, from whence he had wandered in early life, and after visiting all the principal localities in the northern and western States, in the course of his peregrinations, arrived in the unhealthy region of the Red River. His last removal was from

Illinois. Whither he has now gone, I regret to be obliged to say, is unknown to me. He gathered up his effects and departed quietly from Marksville the day before I did, the suspicions of his instrumentality in procuring my liberation rendering such a step necessary. For the commission of a just and righteous act he would undoubtedly have suffered death, had he remained within reach of the slave-whipping tribe on Bayou Bœuf.

One day, while working on the new house, Bass and Epps became engaged in a controversy, to which, as will be readily supposed, I listened with absorbing interest. They were discussing the subject of Slavery.

"I tell you what it is Epps," said Bass, "it's all wrong—all wrong, sir—there's no justice nor righteousness in it. I wouldn't own a slave if I was rich as Crœsus,[5] which I am not, as is perfectly well understood, more particularly among my creditors. *There's* another humbug—the credit system—humbug, sir; no credit—no debt. Credit leads a man into temptation. Cash down is the only thing that will deliver him from evil. But this question of *Slavery*; what *right* have you to your niggers when you come down to the point?"

"What right!" said Epps, laughing; "why, I bought 'em, and paid for 'em."

"Of *course* you did; the law says you have the right to hold a nigger, but begging the law's pardon, it *lies*. Yes, Epps, when the law says that it's a *liar*, and the truth is not in it. Is every thing right because the law allows it? Suppose they'd pass a law taking away your liberty and making you a slave?"

"Oh, that ain't a supposable case," said Epps, still laughing; "hope you don't compare me to a nigger, Bass."

"Well," Bass answered gravely, "no, not exactly. But I have seen niggers before now as good as I am, and I have no acquaintance with any white man in these parts that I consider a whit better than myself. Now, in the sight of God, what is the difference, Epps, between a white man and a black one?"

"All the difference in the world," replied Epps. "You might as well ask what the difference is between a white man and a baboon. Now, I've seen one of them critters in Orleans that knowed just as much as any nigger I've got. You'd call them feller citizens, I s'pose?"—and Epps indulged in a loud laugh at his own wit.

"Look here, Epps," continued his companion; "you can't laugh me down in that way. Some men are witty, and some ain't so witty as they think they are. Now let me ask you a question. Are all men created free and equal as the Declaration of Independence holds they are?"

5. Ancient king known for his fabled wealth.

"Yes," responded Epps, "but all men, niggers, and monkeys *ain't;*" and hereupon he broke forth into a more boisterous laugh than before.

"There are monkeys among white people as well as black, when you come to that," coolly remarked Bass. "I know some white men that use arguments no sensible monkey would. But let that pass. These niggers are human beings. If they don't know as much as their masters, whose fault is it? They are not *allowed* to know anything. You have books and papers, and can go where you please, and gather intelligence in a thousand ways. But your slaves have no privileges. You'd whip one of them if caught reading a book.[6] They are held in bondage, generation after generation, deprived of mental improvement, and who can expect them to possess much knowledge? If they are not brought down to a level with the brute creation, you slaveholders will never be blamed for it. If they are baboons, or stand no higher in the scale of intelligence than such animals, you and men like you will have to answer for it. There's a sin, a fearful sin, resting on this nation, that will not go unpunished forever. There will be a reckoning yet— yes, Epps, there's a day coming that will burn as an oven. It may be sooner or it may be later, but it's a coming as sure as the Lord is just."

"If you lived up among the Yankees in New-England," said Epps, "I expect you'd be one of them cursed fanatics that know more than the constitution, and go about peddling clocks[7] and coaxing niggers to run away."

"If I was in New-England," returned Bass, "I would be just what I am here. I would say that Slavery was an iniquity, and ought to be abolished. I would say there was no reason nor justice in the law, or the constitution that allows one man to hold another man in bondage. It would be hard for you to lose your property, to be sure, but it wouldn't be half as hard as it would be to lose your liberty. You have no more right to your freedom, in exact justice, than Uncle Abram yonder. Talk about black skin, and black blood; why, how many slaves are there on this bayou as white as either of us? And what difference is there in the color of the soul? Pshaw! the whole system is as absurd as it is cruel. You may own niggers and be hanged, but I wouldn't own one for the best plantation in Louisiana."

"You like to hear yourself talk, Bass, better than any man I know of. You would argue that black was white, or white black, if any body would contradict you. Nothing suits you in this world, and I don't

6. An educated slave was considered dangerous; many states had laws making it a crime to teach a slave to read.
7. In 1807, Eli Terry (1772–1852) developed a method of mass-producing wooden clocks. The South did not have the manufacturing infrastructure necessary to produce the clocks locally, so New England "peddlers" made a lucrative business of exporting their merchandise to other parts of the country. These salesmen often took advantage of southern ignorance of the trade by selling clocks for exorbitant prices.

believe you will be satisfied with the next, if you should have your choice in them."

Conversations substantially like the foregoing were not unusual between the two after this; Epps drawing him out more for the purpose of creating a laugh at his expense, than with a view of fairly discussing the merits of the question. He looked upon Bass, as a man ready to say anything merely for the pleasure of hearing his own voice; as somewhat self-conceited, perhaps, contending against his faith and judgment, in order, simply, to exhibit his dexterity in argumentation.

He remained at Epps' through the summer, visiting Marksville generally once a fortnight. The more I saw of him, the more I became convinced he was a man in whom I could confide. Nevertheless, my previous ill-fortune had taught me to be extremely cautious. It was not my place to speak to a white man except when spoken to, but I omitted no opportunity of throwing myself in his way, and endeavored constantly in every possible manner to attract his attention. In the early part of August he and myself were at work alone in the house, the other carpenters having left, and Epps being absent in the field. Now was the time, if ever, to broach the subject, and I resolved to do it, and submit to whatever consequences might ensue. We were busily at work in the afternoon, when I stopped suddenly and said—

"Master Bass, I want to ask you what part of the country you came from?"

"Why, Platt, what put that into your head?" he answered. "You wouldn't know if I should tell you." After a moment or two he added—"I was born in Canada; now guess where that is."

"Oh, I know where Canada is," said I, "I have been there myself."

"Yes, I expect you are well acquainted all through that country," he remarked, laughing incredulously.

"As sure as I live, Master Bass," I replied, "I have been there. I have been in Montreal and Kingston, and Queenston, and a great many places in Canada, and I have been in York State, too—in Buffalo, and Rochester, and Albany, and can tell you the names of the villages on the Erie canal and the Champlain canal."

Bass turned round and gazed at me a long time without uttering a syllable.

"How came you here?" he inquired, at length. "Master Bass," I answered, "if justice had been done, I never would have been here."

"Well, how's this?" said he. "Who are you? You have been in Canada sure enough; I know all the places you mention. How did you happen to get here? Come, tell me all about it."

"I have no friends here," was my reply, "that I can put confidence in. I am afraid to tell you, though I don't believe you would tell Master Epps if I should."

He assured me earnestly he would keep every word I might speak to him a profound secret, and his curiosity was evidently strongly excited. It was a long story, I informed him, and would take some time to relate it. Master Epps would be back soon, but if he would see me that night after all were asleep, I would repeat it to him. He consented readily to the arrangement, and directed me to come into the building where we were then at work, and I would find him there. About midnight, when all was still and quiet, I crept cautiously from my cabin, and silently entering the unfinished building, found him awaiting me.

After further assurances on his part that I should not be betrayed, I began a relation of the history of my life and misfortunes. He was deeply interested, asking numerous questions in reference to localities and events. Having ended my story I besought him to write to some of my friends at the North, acquainting them with my situation, and begging them to forward free papers, or take such steps as they might consider proper to secure my release. He promised to do so, but dwelt upon the danger of such an act in case of detection, and now impressed upon me the great necessity of strict silence and secrecy. Before we parted our plan of operation was arranged.

We agreed to meet the next night at a specified place among the high weeds on the bank of the bayou, some distance from master's dwelling. There he was to write down on paper the names and address of several persons, old friends in the North, to whom he would direct letters during his next visit to Marksville. It was not deemed prudent to meet in the new house, inasmuch as the light it would be necessary to use might possibly be discovered. In the course of the day I managed to obtain a few matches and a piece of candle, unperceived, from the kitchen, during a temporary absence of Aunt Phebe. Bass had pencil and paper in his tool chest.

At the appointed hour we met on the bayou bank, and creeping among the high weeds, I lighted the candle, while he drew forth pencil and paper and prepared for business. I gave him the names of William Perry, Cephas Parker and Judge Marvin, all of Saratoga Springs, Saratoga county, New-York. I had been employed by the latter in the United States Hotel, and had transacted business with the former to a considerable extent, and trusted that at least one of them would be still living at that place. He carefully wrote the names, and then remarked, thoughtfully—

"It is so many years since you left Saratoga, all these men may be dead, or may have removed. You say you obtained papers at the custom house in New-York. Probably there is a record of them there, and I think it would be well to write and ascertain."

I agreed with him, and again repeated the circumstances related heretofore, connected with my visit to the custom house with Brown and Hamilton. We lingered on the bank of the bayou an hour or more, conversing upon the subject which now engrossed our thoughts. I could no longer doubt his fidelity, and freely spoke to him of the many sorrows I had borne in silence, and so long. I spoke of my wife and children, mentioning their names and ages, and dwelling upon the unspeakable happiness it would be to clasp them to my heart once more before I died. I caught him by the hand, and with tears and passionate entreaties implored him to befriend me—to restore me to my kindred and to liberty—promising I would weary Heaven the remainder of my life with prayers that it would bless and prosper him. In the enjoyment of freedom—surrounded by the associations of youth, and restored to the bosom of my family—that promise is not yet forgotten, nor shall it ever be so long as I have strength to raise my imploring eyes on high.

"Oh, blessings on his kindly voice and on his silver hair,
And blessings on his whole life long, until he meet me there."[8]

He overwhelmed me with assurances of friendship and faithfulness, saying he had never before taken so deep an interest in the fate of any one. He spoke of himself in a somewhat mournful tone, as a lonely man, a wanderer about the world—that he was growing old, and must soon reach the end of his earthly journey, and lie down to his final rest without kith or kin to mourn for him, or to remember him—that his life was of little value to himself, and henceforth should be devoted to the accomplishment of my liberty, and to an unceasing warfare against the accursed shame of Slavery.

After this time we seldom spoke to, or recognized each other. He was, moreover, less free in his conversation with Epps on the subject of Slavery. The remotest suspicion that there was any unusual intimacy—any secret understanding between us—never once entered the mind of Epps, or any other person, white or black, on the plantation.

I am often asked, with an air of incredulity, how I succeeded so many years in keeping from my daily and constant companions the knowledge of my true name and history. The terrible lesson Burch taught me, impressed indelibly upon my mind the danger and uselessness of asserting I was a freeman. There was no possibility of any slave being able to assist me, while, on the other hand, there *was* a possibility of his exposing me. When it is recollected the whole current of my thoughts, for twelve years, turned to the contemplation of escape, it will not be wondered at, that I was always cautious and on my guard. It would have been an act of folly to have proclaimed my *right* to freedom; it would only have subjected me to

8. From Alfred, Lord Tennyson's "The May Queen."

severer scrutiny—probably have consigned me to some more distant and inaccessible region than even Bayou Bœuf. Edwin Epps
was a person utterly regardless of a black man's rights or wrongs—
utterly destitute of any natural sense of justice, as I well knew. It
was important, therefore, not only as regarded my hope of deliverance, but also as regarded the few personal privileges* I was permitted to enjoy, to keep from him the history of my life.

The Saturday night subsequent to our interview at the water's
edge, Bass went home to Marksville. The next day, being Sunday,
he employed himself in his own room writing letters. One he
directed to the Collector of Customs at New-York, another to Judge
Marvin, and another to Messrs. Parker and Perry jointly. The latter
was the one which led to my recovery. He subscribed my true
name, but in the postscript intimated I was not the writer. The
letter itself shows that he considered himself engaged in a dangerous undertaking—no less than running "the risk of his life, if
detected." I did not see the letter before it was mailed, but have
since obtained a copy, which is here inserted:

"Bayou Bœuf, August 15, 1852.

"Mr. WILLIAM PERRY or Mr. CEPHAS PARKER:

"Gentlemen—It having been a long time since I have seen or
heard from you, and not knowing that you are living, it is with
uncertainty that I write to you, but the necessity of the case
must be my excuse.

"Having been born free, just across the river from you, I am
certain you must know me, and I am here now a slave. I wish
you to obtain free papers for me, and forward them to me at
Marksville, Louisiana, Parish of Avoyelles, and oblige

"Yours,   SOLOMON NORTHUP.

"The way I came to be a slave, I was taken sick in Washington
City, and was insensible for some time. When I recovered my
reason, I was robbed of my free-papers, and in irons on my way
to this State, and have never been able to get any one to write
for me until now; and he that is writing for me runs the risk of
his life if detected."

The allusion to myself in the work recently issued, entitled "A
Key to Uncle Tom's Cabin,"[9] contains the first part of this letter,
omitting the postscript. Neither are the full names of the gentlemen

---

* The transcriber changed "priviliges" to "privileges".
9. Stowe published *A Key to* Uncle Tom's Cabin in 1853 to address accusations that her
   novel sensationalized the realities of slave life. The *Key* contained documents and testimonies to support Stowe's account.

to whom it is directed correctly stated, there being a slight discrepancy, probably a typographical error. To the postscript more than to the body of the communication am I indebted for my liberation, as will presently be seen.

When Bass returned from Marksville he informed me of what he had done. We continued our midnight consultations, never speaking to each other through the day, excepting as it was necessary about the work. As nearly as he was able to ascertain, it would require two weeks for the letter to reach Saratoga in due course of mail, and the same length of time for an answer to return. Within six weeks, at the farthest, we concluded, an answer would arrive, if it arrived at all. A great many suggestions were now made, and a great deal of conversation took place between us, as to the most safe and proper course to pursue on receipt of the free papers. They would stand between him and harm, in case we were overtaken and arrested leaving the country altogether. It would be no infringement of law, however much it might provoke individual hostility, to assist a freeman to regain his freedom.

At the end of four weeks he was again at Marksville, but no answer had arrived. I was sorely disappointed, but still reconciled myself with the reflection that sufficient length of time had not yet elapsed— that there might have been delays—and that I could not reasonably expect one so soon. Six, seven, eight, and ten weeks passed by, however, and nothing came. I was in a fever of suspense whenever Bass visited Marksville, and could scarcely close my eyes until his return. Finally my master's house was finished, and the time came when Bass must leave me. The night before his departure I was wholly given up to despair. I had clung to him as a drowning man clings to the floating spar, knowing if it slips from his grasp he must forever sink beneath the waves. The all-glorious hope, upon which I had laid such eager hold, was crumbling to ashes in my hands. I felt as if sinking down, down, amidst the bitter waters of Slavery, from the unfathomable depths of which I should never rise again.

The generous heart of my friend and benefactor was touched with pity at the sight of my distress. He endeavored to cheer me up, promising to return the day before Christmas, and if no intelligence was received in the meantime, some further step would be undertaken to effect our design. He exhorted me to keep up my spirits— to rely upon his continued efforts in my behalf, assuring me, in most earnest and impressive language, that my liberation should, from thenceforth, be the chief object of his thoughts.

In his absence the time passed slowly indeed. I looked forward to Christmas with intense anxiety and impatience. I had about given up the expectation of receiving any answer to the letters. They might have miscarried, or might have been misdirected. Perhaps those at

Saratoga, to whom they had been addressed, were all dead; perhaps, engaged in their pursuits, they did not consider the fate of an
obscure, unhappy black man of sufficient importance to be noticed.
My whole reliance was in Bass. The faith I had in him was continually re-assuring me, and enabled me to stand up against the tide of
disappointment that had overwhelmed me.

So wholly was I absorbed in reflecting upon my situation and pros-
pects, that the hands with whom I labored in the field often observed
it. Patsey would ask me if I was sick, and Uncle Abram, and Bob, and
Wiley frequently expressed a curiosity to know what I could be thinking about so steadily. But I evaded their inquiries with some light
remark, and kept my thoughts locked closely in my breast.

Chapter XX.

BASS FAITHFUL TO HIS WORD—HIS ARRIVAL ON CHRISTMAS EVE—
THE DIFFICULTY OF OBTAINING AN INTERVIEW—THE MEETING IN
THE CABIN—NON-ARRIVAL OF THE LETTER—BASS ANNOUNCES HIS
INTENTION TO PROCEED NORTH—CHRISTMAS—CONVERSATION
BETWEEN EPPS AND BASS—YOUNG MISTRESS M'COY,[1] THE BEAUTY OF
BAYOU BŒUF—THE "NE PLUS ULTRA" OF DINNERS—MUSIC AND
DANCING—PRESENCE OF THE MISTRESS—HER EXCEEDING BEAUTY—
THE LAST SLAVE DANCE—WILLIAM PIERCE—OVERSLEEP MYSELF—
THE LAST WHIPPING—DESPONDENCY—COLD MORNING—EPPS'
THREATS—THE PASSING CARRIAGE—STRANGERS APPROACHING
THROUGH THE COTTON-FIELD—LAST HOUR ON BAYOU BŒUF.

Faithful to his word, the day before Christmas, just at night-fall,
Bass came riding into the yard.

"How are you," said Epps, shaking him by the hand, "glad to see
you."

He would not have been *very* glad had he known the object of his
errand.

"Quite well, quite well," answered Bass. "Had some business
out on the bayou, and concluded to call and see you, and stay over
night."

Epps ordered one of the slaves to take charge of his horse, and
with much talk and laughter they passed into the house together;
not, however, until Bass had looked at me significantly, as much as
to say, "Keep dark, we understand each other." It was ten o'clock at
night before the labors of the day were performed, when I entered

---

1. This is the only place this spelling occurs; everywhere else in the text the name is
spelled "McCoy," which could signal that the original printer used the apostrophe to
squeeze a line here.

the cabin. At that time Uncle Abram and Bob occupied it with me. I laid down upon my board and feigned I was asleep. When my companions had fallen into a profound slumber, I moved stealthily out of the door, and watched, and listened attentively for some sign or sound from Bass. There I stood until long after midnight, but nothing could be seen or heard. As I suspected, he dared not leave the house, through fear of exciting the suspicion of some of the family. I judged, correctly, he would rise earlier than was his custom, and take the opportunity of seeing me before Epps was up. Accordingly I aroused Uncle Abram an hour sooner than usual, and sent him into the house to build a fire, which, at that season of the year, is a part of Uncle Abram's duties.

I also gave Bob a violent shake, and asked him if he intended to sleep till noon, saying master would be up before the mules were fed. He knew right well the consequence that would follow such an event, and, jumping to his feet, was at the horse-pasture in a twinkling.

Presently, when both were gone, Bass slipped into the cabin.

"No letter yet, Platt," said he. The announcement fell upon my heart like lead.

"Oh, *do* write again, Master Bass," I cried; "I will give you the names of a great many I know. Surely they are not all dead. Surely some one will pity me."

"No use," Bass replied, "no use. I have made up my mind to that. I fear the Marksville post-master will mistrust something, I have inquired so often at his office. Too uncertain—too dangerous."

"Then it is all over," I exclaimed. "Oh, my God, how can I end my days here!"

"You're not going to end them here," he said, "unless you die very soon. I've thought this matter all over, and have come to a determination. There are more ways than one to manage this business, and a better and surer way than writing letters. I have a job or two on hand which can be completed by March or April. By that time I shall have a considerable sum of money, and then, Platt, I am going to Saratoga myself."

I could scarcely credit my own senses as the words fell from his lips. But he assured me, in a manner that left no doubt of the sincerity of his intention, that if his life was spared until spring, he should certainly undertake the journey.

"I have lived in this region long enough," he continued; "I may as well be in one place as another. For a long time I have been thinking of going back once more to the place where I was born. I'm tired of Slavery as well as you. If I can succeed in getting you away from here, it will be a good act that I shall like to think of all my life. And I *shall* succeed, Platt; I'm *bound* to do it. Now let me tell you what I want.

Epps will be up soon, and it won't do to be caught here. Think of a great many men at Saratoga and Sandy Hill, and in that neighborhood, who once knew you. I shall make excuse to come here again in the course of the winter, when I will write down their names. I will then know who to call on when I go north. Think of all you can. Cheer up! Don't be discouraged. I'm with you, life or death. Goodbye. God bless you," and saying this he left the cabin quickly, and entered the great house.

It was Christmas morning—the happiest day in the whole year for the slave. That morning he need not hurry to the field, with his gourd and cotton-bag. Happiness sparkled in the eyes and overspread the countenances of all. The time of feasting and dancing had come. The cane and cotton fields were deserted. That day the clean dress was to be donned—the red ribbon displayed; there were to be re-unions, and joy and laughter, and hurrying to and fro. It was to be a day of *liberty* among the children of Slavery. Wherefore they were happy, and rejoiced.

After breakfast Epps and Bass sauntered about the yard, conversing upon the price of cotton, and various other topics.

"Where do your niggers hold Christmas?" Bass inquired.

"Platt is going to Tanners to-day. His fiddle is in great demand. They want him at Marshall's Monday, and Miss Mary McCoy, on the old Norwood plantation, writes me a note that she wants him to play for her niggers Tuesday."

"He is rather a smart boy, ain't he?" said Bass. "Come here, Platt," he added, looking at me as I walked up to them, as if he had never thought before to take any special notice of me.

"Yes," replied Epps, taking hold of my arm and feeling it, "there isn't a bad joint in him. There ain't a boy on the bayou worth more than he is—perfectly sound, and no bad tricks. D—n him, he isn't like other niggers; doesn't look like 'em—don't act like 'em. I was offered seventeen hundred dollars for him last week."

"And didn't take it?" Bass inquired, with an air of surprise.

"Take it—no; devilish clear of it. Why, he's a reg'lar genius; can make a plough beam, wagon tongue—anything, as well as you can. Marshall wanted to put up one of his niggers agin him and raffle for them, but I told him I would see the devil have him first."

"I don't see anything remarkable about him," Bass observed.

"Why, just feel of him, now," Epps rejoined. "You don't see a boy very often put together any closer than he is. He's a thin-skin'd cuss, and won't bear as much whipping as some; but he's got the muscle in him, and no mistake."

Bass felt of me, turned me round, and made a thorough examination, Epps all the while dwelling on my good points. But his visitor seemed to take but little interest finally in the subject, and consequently it was dropped. Bass soon departed, giving me another sly look of recognition and significance, as he trotted out of the yard.

When he was gone I obtained a pass, and started for Tanner's—not Peter Tanner's, of whom mention has previously been made, but a relative of his. I played during the day and most of the night, spending the next day, Sunday, in my cabin. Monday I crossed the bayou to Douglas Marshall's, all Epps' slaves accompanying me, and on Tuesday went to the old Norwood place, which is the third plantation above Marshall's, on the same side of the water.

This estate is now owned by Miss Mary McCoy, a lovely girl, some twenty years of age. She is the beauty and the glory of Bayou Bœuf. She owns about a hundred working hands, besides a great many house servants, yard boys, and young children. Her brother-in-law, who resides on the adjoining estate, is her general agent. She is beloved by all her slaves, and good reason indeed have they to be thankful that they have fallen into such gentle hands. Nowhere on the bayou are there such feasts, such merrymaking, as at young Madam McCoy's. Thither, more than to any other place, do the old and the young for miles around love to repair in the time of the Christmas holidays; for nowhere else can they find such delicious repasts; nowhere else can they hear a voice speaking to them so pleasantly. No one is so well beloved—no one fills so large a space in the hearts of a thousand slaves, as young Madam McCoy, the orphan mistress of the old Norwood estate.

On my arrival at her place, I found two or three hundred had assembled. The table was prepared in a long building, which she had erected expressly for her slaves to dance in. It was covered with every variety of food the country afforded, and was pronounced by general acclamation to be the rarest of dinners. Roast turkey, pig, chicken, duck, and all kinds of meat, baked, boiled, and broiled, formed a line the whole length of the extended table, while the vacant spaces were filled with tarts, jellies, and frosted cake, and pastry of many kinds. The young mistress walked around the table, smiling and saying a kind word to each one, and seemed to enjoy the scene exceedingly.

When the dinner was over the tables were removed to make room for the dancers. I tuned my violin and struck up a lively air; while some joined in a nimble reel, others patted and sang their simple but melodious songs, filling the great room with music mingled with the sound of human voices and the clatter of many feet.

In the evening the mistress returned, and stood in the door a long time, looking at us. She was magnificently arrayed. Her dark hair and eyes contrasted strongly with her clear and delicate complexion. Her form was slender but commanding, and her movement was a combination of unaffected dignity and grace. As she stood there, clad in her rich apparel, her face animated with pleasure, I thought I had never looked upon a human being half so beautiful. I dwell with delight upon the description of this fair and gentle lady, not only because she inspired me with emotions of gratitude and admiration, but because I would have the reader understand that all slave-owners on Bayou Bœuf are not like Epps, or Tibeats, or Jim Burns. Occasionally can be found, rarely it may be, indeed, a good man like William Ford, or an angel of kindness like young Mistress McCoy.

Tuesday concluded the three holidays Epps yearly allowed us. On my way home, Wednesday morning, while passing the plantation of William Pierce, that gentleman hailed me, saying he had received a line from Epps, brought down by William Varnell, permitting him to detain me for the purpose of playing for his slaves that night. It was the last time I was destined to witness a slave dance on the shores of Bayou Bœuf. The party at Pierce's continued their jollification until broad daylight, when I returned to my master's house, somewhat wearied with the loss of rest, but rejoicing in the possession of numerous bits and picayunes, which the whites, who were pleased with my musical performances, had contributed.

On Saturday morning, for the first time in years, I overslept myself. I was frightened on coming out of the cabin to find the slaves were already in the field. They had preceded me some fifteen minutes. Leaving my dinner and water-gourd, I hurried after them as fast as I could move. It was not yet sunrise, but Epps was on the piazza as I left the hut, and cried out to me that it was a pretty time of day to be getting up. By extra exertion my row was up when he came out after breakfast. This, however, was no excuse for the offence of oversleeping. Bidding me strip and lie down, he gave me ten or fifteen lashes, at the conclusion of which he inquired if I thought, after that, I could get up sometime in the *morning*. I expressed myself quite positively that I *could*, and, with back stinging with pain, went about my work.

The following day, Sunday, my thoughts were upon Bass, and the probabilities and hopes which hung upon his action and determination. I considered the uncertainty of life; that if it should be the will of God that he should die, my prospect of deliverance, and all expectation of happiness in this world, would be wholly ended and destroyed. My sore back, perhaps, did not have a tendency to render me unusually cheerful. I felt down-hearted and unhappy all day long, and when I laid down upon the hard board at night, my heart was oppressed with such a load of grief, it seemed that it must break.

Monday morning, the third of January, 1853, we were in the field betimes. It was a raw, cold morning, such as is unusual in that region. I was in advance, Uncle Abram next to me, behind him Bob, Patsey and Wiley, with our cotton-bags about our necks. Epps happened (a rare thing, indeed) to come out that morning without his whip. He swore, in a manner that would shame a pirate, that we were doing nothing. Bob ventured to say that his fingers were so numb with cold he couldn't pick fast. Epps cursed himself for not having brought his rawhide, and declared that when he came out again he would warm us well; yes, he would make us all hotter than that fiery realm in which I am sometimes compelled to believe he will himself eventually reside.

With these fervent expressions, he left us. When out of hearing, we commenced talking to each other, saying how hard it was to be compelled to keep up our tasks with numb fingers; how unreasonable master was, and speaking of him generally in no flattering terms. Our conversation was interrupted by a carriage passing rapidly towards the house. Looking up, we saw two men approaching us through the cotton-field.

Having now brought down this narrative to the last hour I was to spend on Bayou Bœuf—having gotten through my last cotton picking, and about to bid Master Epps farewell—I must beg the reader to go back with me to the month of August; to follow Bass' letter on its long journey to Saratoga; to learn the effect it produced—and that, while I was repining and despairing in the slave hut of Edwin Epps, through the friendship of Bass and the goodness of Providence, all things were working together for my deliverance.

Chapter XXI.

THE LETTER REACHES SARATOGA—IS FORWARDED TO ANNE—IS LAID BEFORE HENRY B. NORTHUP—THE STATUTE OF MAY 14, 1840—ITS PROVISIONS—ANNE'S MEMORIAL TO THE GOVERNOR—THE AFFIDAVITS ACCOMPANYING IT—SENATOR SOULE'S LETTER—DEPARTURE OF THE AGENT APPOINTED BY THE GOVERNOR—ARRIVAL AT MARKSVILLE—THE HON. JOHN P. WADDILL—THE CONVERSATION ON NEW-YORK POLITICS—IT SUGGESTS A FORTUNATE IDEA—THE MEETING WITH BASS—THE SECRET OUT—LEGAL PROCEEDINGS INSTITUTED—DEPARTURE OF NORTHUP AND THE SHERIFF FROM MARKSVILLE FOR BAYOU BŒUF—ARRANGEMENTS ON THE WAY—REACH EPPS' PLANTATION—DISCOVER HIS SLAVES IN THE COTTON FIELD—THE MEETING—THE FAREWELL.

I am indebted to Mr. Henry B. Northup and others for many of the particulars contained in this chapter.

The letter written by Bass, directed to Parker and Perry, and which was deposited in the post-office in Marksville on the 15th day of August, 1852, arrived at Saratoga in the early part of September.

Some time previous to this, Anne had removed to Glens Falls, Warren county, where she had charge of the kitchen in Carpenter's Hotel. She kept house, however, lodging with our children, and was only absent from them during such time as the discharge of her duties in the hotel required.

Messrs. Parker and Perry, on receipt of the letter, forwarded it immediately to Anne. On reading it the children were all excitement, and without delay hastened to the neighboring village of Sandy Hill, to consult Henry B. Northup, and obtain his advice and assistance in the matter.

Upon examination, that gentleman found among the statutes of the State an act providing for the recovery of free citizens from slavery. It was passed May 14, 1840, and is entitled "An act more effectually to protect the free citizens of this State from being kidnapped or reduced to slavery."[2] It provides that it shall be the duty of the Governor, upon the receipt of satisfactory information that any free citizen or inhabitant of this State, is wrongfully held in another State or Territory of the United States, upon the allegation or pretence that such person is a slave, or by color of any usage or rule of law is deemed or taken to be a slave, to take such measures to procure the restoration of such person to liberty, as he shall deem necessary. And to that end, he is authorized to appoint and employ an agent, and directed to furnish him with such credentials and instructions as will be likely to accomplish the object of his appointment. It requires the agent so appointed to proceed to collect the proper proof to establish the right of such person to his freedom; to perform such journeys, take such measures, institute such legal proceedings, &c., as may be necessary to return such person to this State, and charges all expenses incurred in carrying the act into effect, upon moneys not otherwise appropriated in the treasury.

It was necessary to establish two facts to the satisfaction of the Governor: First, that I was a free citizen of New-York; and secondly, that I was wrongfully held in bondage. As to the first point, there was no difficulty, all the older inhabitants in the vicinity being ready to testify to it. The second point rested entirely upon the letter to Parker and Perry, written in an unknown hand, and upon the letter penned on board the brig Orleans, which, unfortunately, had been mislaid or lost.

A memorial was prepared, directed to his excellency, Governor Hunt, setting forth her[3] marriage, my departure to Washington city;

2. Northup was the first New York citizen known to have been freed under this law, which was instrumental in winning the release of several other kidnapped persons later in the 1850s.
3. Anne's; memorial: a formal statement of facts, usually as part of an official appeal; Washington Hunt (1811–1867) served as Governor of New York from January 1, 1851, to December 31, 1852.

the receipt of the letters; that I was a free citizen, and such other facts as were deemed important, and was signed and verified by Anne. Accompanying this memorial were several affidavits of prominent citizens of Sandy Hill and Fort Edward, corroborating fully the statements it contained, and also a request of several well known gentlemen to the Governor, that Henry B. Northup be appointed agent under the legislative act.

On reading the memorial and affidavits, his excellency took a lively interest in the matter, and on the 23d day of November, 1852, under the seal of the State, "constituted, appointed and employed Henry B. Northup, Esq., an agent, with full power to effect" my restoration, and to take such measures as would be most likely to accomplish it, and instructing him to proceed to Louisiana with all convenient dispatch.

The pressing nature of Mr. Northup's professional and political engagements delayed his departure until December. On the fourteenth day of that month he left Sandy Hill, and proceeded to Washington. The Hon. Pierre Soule, Senator in Congress from Louisiana, Hon. Mr. Conrad, Secretary of War, and Judge Nelson,[4] of the Supreme Court of the United States, upon hearing a statement of the facts, and examining his commission, and certified copies of the memorial and affidavits, furnished him with open letters to gentlemen in Louisiana, strongly urging their assistance in accomplishing the object of his appointment.

Senator Soule[5] especially interested himself in the matter, insisting, in forcible language, that it was the duty and interest of every planter in his State to aid in restoring me to freedom, and trusted the sentiments of honor and justice in the bosom of every citizen of the commonwealth would enlist him at once in my behalf. Having obtained these valuable letters, Mr. Northup returned to Baltimore, and proceeded from thence to Pittsburgh. It was his original intention, under advice of friends at Washington, to go directly to New Orleans, and consult the authorities of that city. Providentially, however, on arriving at the mouth of Red River, he changed his mind. Had he continued on, he would not have met with Bass, in which case the search for me would probably have been fruitless.

4. Charles Magill Conrad (1804–1878), a Louisianan then serving as Secretary of War under Millard Fillmore, later a secessionist and Confederate politician. Samuel Nelson (1792–1873), a New Yorker, served as a justice on the U.S. Supreme Court from 1845 to 1872.
5. Pierre Soulé (1801–1870) was involved in a failed 1854 attempt to persuade the U.S. government to annex Cuba. He would go on to oppose Louisiana's secession from the Union, but became a supporter of the Confederacy once his state joined.

Taking passage on the first steamer that arrived, he pursued his journey up Red River, a sluggish, winding stream, flowing through a vast region of primitive forests and impenetrable swamps, almost wholly destitute of inhabitants. About nine o'clock in the forenoon, January 1st, 1853, he left the steamboat at Marksville, and proceeded directly to Marksville Court House, a small village four miles in the interior.

From the fact that the letter to Messrs. Parker and Perry was post-marked at Marksville, it was supposed by him that I was in that place or its immediate vicinity. On reaching this town, he at once laid his business before the Hon. John P. Waddill, a legal gentleman of distinction, and a man of fine genius and most noble impulses. After reading the letters and documents presented him, and listening to a representation of the circumstances under which I had been carried away into captivity, Mr. Waddill at once proffered his services, and entered into the affair with great zeal and earnestness. He, in common with others of like elevated character, looked upon the kidnapper with abhorrence. The title of his fellow parishioners and clients to the property which constituted the larger proportion of their wealth, not only depended upon the good faith in which slave sales were transacted, but he was a man in whose honorable heart emotions of indignation were aroused by such an instance of injustice.

Marksville, although occupying a prominent position, and standing out in impressive italics on the map of Louisiana, is, in fact, but a small and insignificant hamlet. Aside from the tavern, kept by a jolly and generous boniface,[6] the court house, inhabited by lawless cows and swine in the seasons of vacation, and a high gallows, with its dissevered rope dangling in the air, there is little to attract the attention of the stranger.

Solomon Northup was a name Mr. Waddill had never heard, but he was confident that if there was a slave bearing that appellation in Marksville or vicinity, his black boy Tom would know him. Tom was accordingly called, but in all his extensive circle of acquaintances there was no such personage.

The letter to Parker and Perry was dated at Bayou Bœuf. At this place, therefore, the conclusion was, I must be sought. But here a difficulty suggested itself, of a very grave character indeed. Bayou Bœuf, at its nearest point, was twenty-three miles distant, and was the name applied to the section of country extending between fifty and a hundred miles, on both sides of that stream. Thousands and thousands of slaves resided upon its shores, the remarkable richness and fertility of the soil having attracted thither a great number of

6. Inn or tavern keeper.

planters. The information in the letter was so vague and indefinite as to render it difficult to conclude upon any specific course of proceeding. It was finally determined, however, as the only plan that presented any prospect of success, that Northup and the brother of Waddill, a student in the office of the latter, should repair to the Bayou, and traveling up one side and down the other its whole length, inquire at each plantation for me. Mr. Waddill tendered the use of his carriage, and it was definitely arranged that they should start upon the excursion early Monday morning.

It will be seen at once that this course, in all probability, would have resulted unsuccessfully. It would have been impossible for them to have gone into the fields and examine all the gangs at work. They were not aware that I was known only as Platt; and had they inquired of Epps himself, he would have stated truly that he knew nothing of Solomon Northup.

The arrangement being adopted, however, there was nothing further to be done until Sunday had elapsed. The conversation between Messrs. Northup and Waddill, in the course of the afternoon, turned upon New-York politics.

"I can scarcely comprehend the nice distinctions and shades of political parties in your State," observed Mr. Waddill. "I read of soft-shells and hard-shells, hunkers and barnburners,[7] woolly-heads and silver-grays,[8] and am unable to understand the precise difference between them. Pray, what is it?"

Mr. Northup, re-filling his pipe, entered into quite an elaborate narrative of the origin of the various sections of parties, and concluded by saying there was another party in New-York, known as free-soilers or abolitionists.[9] "You have seen none of those in this part of the country, I presume?" Mr. Northup remarked.

"Never, but one," answered Waddill, laughingly. "We have one here in Marksville, an eccentric creature, who preaches abolitionism as vehemently as any fanatic at the North. He is a generous, inoffensive man, but always maintaining the wrong side of an argument. It affords us a deal of amusement. He is an excellent mechanic, and almost indispensable in this community. He is a carpenter. His name is Bass."

7. Leading up to the election of 1848, the New York Democratic Party divided into the Barnburners, who supported slavery, and the Hunkers, who opposed it. After the election, the Hunkers themselves split into Soft-shells, who advocated for reconciliation with the Barnburners, and Hard-shells, who wanted to maintain the division.
8. Rough Whig Party equivalent of Hunkers and Barnburners. On the national political scene, woolly-heads and their counterparts in other states were more commonly referred to as "Conscience Whigs."
9. Although the Free-Soil Party, created by an alliance between anti-slavery Democrats and Whigs, opposed slavery, it was not actively abolitionist. Rather, its goal was stopping slavery's expansion into the western United States territories. While the Free-Soil Party originated in New York, it was a national party, fielding candidates in the 1848 and 1852 elections. Many Free-Soilers were absorbed into the Republican Party in 1854.

Some further good-natured conversation was had at the expense of Bass' peculiarities, when Waddill all at once fell into a reflective mood, and asked for the mysterious letter again.

"Let me see—l-e-t m-e s-e-e!" he repeated, thoughtfully to himself, running his eyes over the letter once more. "'Bayou Bœuf, August 15.' August 15—post-marked here. 'He that is writing for me—' Where did Bass work last summer?" he inquired, turning suddenly to his brother. His brother was unable to inform him, but rising, left the office, and soon returned with the intelligence that "Bass worked last summer somewhere on Bayou Bœuf."

"He is the man," bringing down his hand emphatically on the table,* "who can tell us all about Solomon Northup," exclaimed Waddill.

Bass was immediately searched for, but could not be found. After some inquiry, it was ascertained he was at the landing on Red River. Procuring a conveyance, young Waddill and Northup were not long in traversing the few miles to the latter place. On their arrival, Bass was found, just on the point of leaving, to be absent a fortnight or more. After an introduction, Northup begged the privilege of speaking to him privately a moment. They walked together towards the river, when the following conversation ensued:

"Mr. Bass," said Northup, "allow me to ask you if you were on Bayou Bœuf last August?"

"Yes, sir, I was there in August," was the reply.

"Did you write a letter for a colored man at that place to some gentleman in Saratoga Springs?"

"Excuse me, sir, if I say that is none of your business," answered Bass, stopping and looking his interrogator searchingly in the face.

"Perhaps I am rather hasty, Mr. Bass; I beg your pardon; but I have come from the State of New-York to accomplish the purpose the writer of a letter dated the 15th of August, post-marked at Marksville, had in view. Circumstances have led me to think that you are perhaps the man who wrote it. I am in search of Solomon Northup. If you know him, I beg you to inform me frankly where he is, and I assure you the source of any information you may give me shall not be divulged, if you desire it not to be."

A long time Bass looked his new acquaintance steadily in the eyes, without opening his lips. He seemed to be doubting in his own mind if there was not an attempt to practice some deception upon him. Finally he said, deliberately—

"I have done nothing to be ashamed of. I am the man who wrote the letter. If you have come to rescue Solomon Northup, I am glad to see you."

* The transcriber removed quotation marks before "bringing" and after "table,".

"When did you last see him, and where is he?" Northup inquired.

"I last saw him Christmas, a week ago to-day. He is the slave of Edwin Epps, a planter on Bayou Bœuf, near Holmesville. He is not known as Solomon Northup; he is called Platt."

The secret was out—the mystery was unraveled. Through the thick, black cloud, amid whose dark and dismal shadows I had walked twelve years, broke the star that was to light me back to liberty. All mistrust and hesitation were soon thrown aside, and the two men conversed long and freely upon the subject uppermost in their thoughts. Bass expressed the interest he had taken in my behalf—his intention of going north in the Spring, and declaring that he had resolved to accomplish my emancipation, if it were in his power. He described the commencement and progress of his acquaintance with me, and listened with eager curiosity to the account given him of my family, and the history of my early life. Before separating, he drew a map of the bayou on a strip of paper with a piece of red chalk, showing the locality of Epps' plantation, and the road leading most directly to it.

Northup and his young companion returned to Marksville, where it was determined to commence legal proceedings to test the question of my right to freedom. I was made plaintiff, Mr. Northup acting as my guardian, and Edwin Epps defendant. The process to be issued was in the nature of replevin,[1] directed to the sheriff of the parish, commanding him to take me into custody, and detain me until the decision of the court. By the time the papers were duly drawn up, it was twelve o'clock at night—too late to obtain the necessary signature of the Judge, who resided some distance out of town. Further business was therefore suspended until Monday morning.

Everything, apparently, was moving along swimmingly, until Sunday afternoon, when Waddill called at Northup's room to express his apprehension of difficulties they had not expected to encounter. Bass had become alarmed, and had placed his affairs in the hands of a person at the landing, communicating to him his intention of leaving the State. This person had betrayed the confidence reposed in him to a certain extent, and a rumor began to float about the town, that the stranger at the hotel, who had been observed in the company of lawyer Waddill, was after one of old Epps' slaves, over on the bayou. Epps was known at Marksville, having frequent occasion to visit that place during the session of the courts, and the fear entertained by Mr. Northup's adviser was, that intelligence would be conveyed to him in the night, giving him an opportunity of secreting me before the arrival of the sheriff.

1. Legal action to recover items of property.

This apprehension had the effect of expediting matters considerably. The sheriff, who lived in one direction from the village, was requested to hold himself in readiness immediately after midnight, while the Judge was informed he would be called upon at the same time. It is but justice to say, that the authorities at Marksville cheerfully rendered all the assistance in their power.

As soon after midnight as bail could be perfected, and the Judge's signature obtained, a carriage, containing Mr. Northup and the sheriff, driven by the landlord's son, rolled rapidly out of the village of Marksville, on the road towards Bayou Bœuf.

It was supposed that Epps would contest the issue involving my right to liberty, and it therefore suggested itself to Mr. Northup, that the testimony of the sheriff, describing my first meeting with the former, might perhaps become material on the trial. It was accordingly arranged during the ride, that, before I had an opportunity of speaking to Mr. Northup, the sheriff should propound to me certain questions agreed upon, such as the number and names of my children, the name of my wife before marriage, of places I knew at the North, and so forth. If my answers corresponded with the statements given him, the evidence must necessarily be considered conclusive.

At length, shortly after Epps had left the field, with the consoling assurance that he would soon return and *warm* us, as was stated in the conclusion of the preceding chapter, they came in sight of the plantation, and discovered us at work. Alighting from the carriage, and directing the driver to proceed to the great house, with instructions not to mention to any one the object of their errand until they met again, Northup and the sheriff turned from the highway, and came towards us across the cotton field. We observed them, on looking up at the carriage—one several rods in advance of the other. It was a singular and unusual thing to see white men approaching us in that manner, and especially at that early hour in the morning, and Uncle Abram and Patsey made some remarks, expressive of their astonishment. Walking up to Bob, the sheriff inquired:

"Where's the boy they call Platt?"

"Thar he is, massa," answered Bob, pointing to me, and twitching off his hat.

I wondered to myself what business he could possibly have with me, and turning round, gazed at him until he had approached within a step. During my long residence on the bayou, I had become familiar with the face of every planter within many miles; but this man was an utter stranger—certainly I had never seen him before.

"Your name is Platt, is it?" he asked.

"Yes, master," I responded.

Pointing towards Northup, standing a few rods distant, he demanded—"Do you know that man?"

I looked in the direction indicated, and as my eyes rested on his countenance, a world of images thronged my brain; a multitude of well-known faces—Anne's, and the dear children's, and my old dead father's; all the scenes and associations of childhood and youth; all the friends of other and happier days, appeared and disappeared, flitting and floating like dissolving shadows before the vision of my imagination, until at last the perfect memory of the man recurred to me, and throwing up my hands towards Heaven, I exclaimed, in a voice louder than I could utter in a less exciting moment—

"*Henry B. Northup!* Thank God—thank God!"

In an instant I comprehended the nature of his business, and felt that the hour of my deliverance was at hand. I started towards him, but the sheriff stepped before me.

"Stop a moment," said he; "have you any other name than Platt?"

"Solomon Northup is my name, master," I replied.

"Have you a family?" he inquired.

"I *had* a wife and three children."

"What were your children's names?"

"Elizabeth, Margaret and Alonzo."

"And your wife's name before her marriage?"

"Anne Hampton."

"Who married you?"

"Timothy Eddy, of Fort Edward."

"Where does that gentleman live?" again pointing to Northup, who remained standing in the same place where I had first recognized him.

"He lives in Sandy Hill, Washington county, New-York," was the reply.

He was proceeding to ask further questions, but I pushed past him, unable longer to restrain myself. I seized my old acquaintance by both hands. I could not speak. I could not refrain from tears.

"Sol," he said at length, "I'm glad to see you."

I essayed to make some answer, but emotion choked all utterance, and I was silent. The slaves, utterly confounded, stood gazing upon the scene, their open mouths and rolling eyes indicating the utmost wonder and astonishment. For ten years I had dwelt among them, in the field and in the cabin, borne the same hardships, partaken the same fare, mingled my griefs with theirs, participated in the same scanty joys; nevertheless, not until this hour, the last I was to remain among them, had the remotest suspicion of my true name, or the slightest knowledge of my real history, been entertained by any one of them.

Not a word was spoken for several minutes, during which time I clung fast to Northup, looking up into his face, fearful I should awake and find it all a dream.

"Throw down that sack," Northup added, finally; "your cotton-picking days are over. Come with us to the man you live with."

I obeyed him, and walking between him and the sheriff, we moved towards the great house. It was not until we had proceeded some distance that I had recovered my voice sufficiently to ask if my family were all living. He informed me he had seen Anne, Margaret and Elizabeth but a short time previously; that Alonzo was also living, and all were well. My mother, however, I could never see again. As I began to recover in some measure from the sudden and great excitement which so overwhelmed me, I grew faint and weak, insomuch it was with difficulty I could walk. The sheriff took hold of my arm and assisted me, or I think I should have fallen. As we entered the yard, Epps stood by the gate, conversing with the driver. That young man, faithful to his instructions, was entirely unable to give him the least information in answer to his repeated inquiries of what was going on. By the time we reached him he was almost as much amazed and puzzled as Bob or Uncle Abram.

Shaking hands with the sheriff, and receiving an introduction to Mr. Northup, he invited them into the house, ordering me, at the same time, to bring in some wood. It was some time before I succeeded in cutting an armful, having, somehow, unaccountably lost the power of wielding the axe with any manner of precision. When I entered with it at last, the table was strewn with papers, from one of which Northup was reading. I was probably longer than necessity required, in placing the sticks upon the fire, being particular as to the exact position of each individual one of them. I heard the words, "the said Solomon Northup," and "the deponent further says," and "free citizen of New-York," repeated frequently, and from these expressions understood that the secret I had so long retained from Master and Mistress Epps, was finally developing. I lingered as long as prudence permitted, and was about leaving the room, when Epps inquired,

"Platt, do you know this gentleman?"

"Yes, master," I replied, "I have known him as long as I can remember."

"Where does he live?"

"He lives in New-York."

"Did you ever live there?"

"Yes, master—born and bred there."

"You was free, then. Now you d——d nigger," he exclaimed, "why did you not tell me that when I bought you?"

SCENE IN THE COTTON FIELD, SOLOMON DELIVERED UP.

Courtesy of the UNC–CH Library, The University of North Carolina at Chapel Hill.

"Master Epps," I answered, in a somewhat different tone than the one in which I had been accustomed to address him—"Master Epps, you did not take the trouble to ask me; besides, I told one of my owners—the man that kidnapped me—that I was free, and was whipped almost to death for it."

"It seems there has been a letter written for you by somebody. Now, who is it?" he demanded, authoritatively. I made no reply.

"I say, who wrote that letter?" he demanded again.

"Perhaps I wrote it myself," I said.

"You haven't been to Marksville post-office and back before light, I know."

He insisted upon my informing him, and I insisted I would not. He made many vehement threats against the man, whoever he might be, and intimated the bloody and savage vengeance he would wreak upon him, when he found him out. His whole manner and language exhibited a feeling of anger towards the unknown person who had written for me, and of fretfulness at the idea of losing so much property. Addressing Mr. Northup, he swore if he had only had an hour's notice of his coming, he would have saved him the trouble of taking me back to New-York; that he would have run me into the swamp, or some other place out of the way, where all the sheriffs on earth couldn't have found me.

I walked out into the yard, and was entering the kitchen door, when something struck me in the back. Aunt Phebe, emerging from the back door of the great house with a pan of potatoes, had thrown one of them with unnecessary violence, thereby giving me to understand that she wished to speak to me a moment confidentially. Running up to me, she whispered in my ear with great earnestness,

"Lor a' mity, Platt! what d'ye think? Dem two men come after ye. Heard 'em tell massa you free—got wife and tree children back thar whar you come from. Goin' wid 'em? Fool if ye don't—wish I could go," and Aunt Phebe ran on in this manner at a rapid rate.

Presently Mistress Epps made her appearance in the kitchen. She said many things to me, and wondered why I had not told her who I was. She expressed her regret, complimenting me by saying she had rather lose any other servant on the plantation. Had Patsey that day stood in my place, the measure of my mistress' joy would have overflowed. Now there was no one left who could mend a chair or a piece of furniture—no one who was of any use about the house— no one who could play for her on the violin—and Mistress Epps was actually affected to tears.

Epps had called to Bob to bring up his saddle horse. The other slaves, also, overcoming their fear of the penalty, had left their work and come to the yard. They were standing behind the cabins, out

of sight of Epps. They beckoned me to come to them, and with all
the eagerness of curiosity, excited to the highest pitch, conversed
with and questioned me. If I could repeat the exact words they
uttered, with the same emphasis—if I could paint their several
attitudes, and the expression of their countenances—it would be
indeed an interesting picture. In their estimation, I had suddenly
arisen to an immeasurable height—had become a being of immense
importance.

The legal papers having been served, and arrangements made
with Epps to meet them the next day at Marksville, Northup and
the sheriff entered the carriage to return to the latter place. As I
was about mounting to the driver's seat, the sheriff said I ought to
bid Mr. and Mrs. Epps good bye. I ran back to the piazza where
they were standing, and taking off my hat, said,

"Good-bye, missis."

"Good-bye, Platt," said Mrs. Epps, kindly.

"Good-bye, master."

"Ah! you d—d nigger," muttered Epps, in a surly, malicious tone
of voice, "you needn't feel so cussed tickled—you ain't gone yet—
I'll see about this business at Marksville to-morrow."

I was only a "*nigger*" and knew my place, but felt as strongly as if
I had been a white man, that it would have been an inward comfort,
had I dared to have given him a parting kick. On my way back to
the carriage, Patsey ran from behind a cabin and threw her arms
about my neck.

"Oh! Platt," she cried, tears streaming down her face, "you're goin'
to be free—you're goin' way off yonder where we'll neber see ye any
more. You've saved me a good many whippins, Platt; I'm glad you're
goin' to be free—but oh! de Lord, de Lord! what'll become of me?"

I disengaged myself from her, and entered the carriage. The driver
cracked his whip and away we rolled. I looked back and saw Patsey,
with drooping head, half reclining on the ground; Mrs. Epps was on
the piazza; Uncle Abram, and Bob, and Wiley, and Aunt Phebe stood
by the gate, gazing after me. I waved my hand, but the carriage
turned a bend of the bayou, hiding them from my eyes forever.

We stopped a moment at Carey's sugar house, where a great
number of slaves were at work, such an establishment being a curiosity to a Northern man. Epps dashed by us on horseback at full
speed—on the way, as we learned next day, to the "Pine Woods," to
see William Ford, who had brought me into the country.

Tuesday, the fourth of January, Epps and his counsel, the Hon. H.
Taylor, Northup, Waddill, the Judge and sheriff of Avoyelles, and
myself, met in a room in the village of Marksville. Mr. Northup stated
the facts in regard to me, and presented his commission, and the

affidavits accompanying it. The sheriff described the scene in the cotton field. I was also interrogated at great length. Finally, Mr. Taylor assured his client that he was satisfied, and that litigation would not only be expensive, but utterly useless. In accordance with his advice, a paper was drawn up and signed by the proper parties, wherein Epps acknowledged he was satisfied of my right to freedom, and formally surrendered me to the authorities of New-York. It was also stipulated that it be entered of record in the recorder's office of Avoyelles.

Mr. Northup and myself immediately hastened to the landing, and taking passage on the first steamer that arrived, were soon floating down Red River, up which, with such desponding thoughts, I had been borne twelve years before.

Chapter XXII.

ARRIVAL IN NEW-ORLEANS—GLIMPSE OF FREEMAN—GENOIS, THE RECORDER—HIS DESCRIPTION OF SOLOMON—REACH CHARLESTON— INTERRUPTED BY CUSTOM HOUSE OFFICERS—PASS THROUGH RICHMOND—ARRIVAL IN WASHINGTON—BURCH ARRESTED— SHEKELS AND THORN—THEIR TESTIMONY—BURCH ACQUITTED— ARREST OF SOLOMON—BURCH WITHDRAWS THE COMPLAINT—THE HIGHER TRIBUNAL—DEPARTURE FROM WASHINGTON—ARRIVAL AT SANDY HILL—OLD FRIENDS AND FAMILIAR SCENES—PROCEED TO GLENS FALLS—MEETING WITH ANNE, MARGARET, AND ELIZABETH— SOLOMON NORTHUP STAUNTON—INCIDENTS—CONCLUSION.

As the steamer glided on its way towards New-Orleans, *perhaps* I was not happy—*perhaps* there was no difficulty in restraining myself from dancing round the deck—perhaps I did not feel grateful to the man who had come so many hundred miles for me—perhaps I did not light his pipe, and wait and watch his word, and run at his slightest bidding. If I didn't—well, no matter.

We tarried at New-Orleans two days. During that time I pointed out the locality of Freeman's slave pen, and the room in which Ford purchased me. We happened to meet Theophilus in the street, but I did not think it worth while to renew acquaintance with him. From respectable citizens we ascertained he had become a low, miserable rowdy—a broken-down, disreputable man.

We also visited the recorder, Mr. Genois, to whom Senator Soule's letter was directed, and found him a man well deserving the wide and honorable reputation that he bears. He very generously furnished us with a sort of legal pass, over his signature and seal of office, and as it contains the recorder's description of my personal appearance, it may not be amiss to insert it here. The following is a copy:

> "*State of Louisiana—City of New-Orleans*:
> Recorder's Office, Second District.

"To all to whom these presents shall come:—

"This is to certify that Henry B. Northup, Esquire, of the county of Washington, New-York, has produced before me due evidence of the freedom of Solomon, a mulatto man, aged about forty-two years, five feet, seven inches and six lines,[2] woolly hair, and chestnut eyes, who is a native born of the State of New-York. That the said Northup, being about bringing the said Solomon to his native place, through the southern routes, the civil authorities are requested to let the aforesaid colored man Solomon pass unmolested, he demeaning well and properly.

"Given under my hand and the seal of the city of New-Orleans this 7th January, 1853.

> "TH. GENOIS, Recorder."

[L. S.]

On the 8th we came to Lake Pontchartrain, by railroad, and, in due time, following the usual route, reached Charleston. After going on board the steamboat, and paying our passage at this city, Mr. Northup was called upon by a custom-house officer to explain why he had not registered his servant. He replied that he had no servant—that, as the agent of New-York, he was accompanying a free citizen of that State from slavery to freedom, and did not desire nor intend to make any registry whatever. I conceived from his conversation and manner, though I may perhaps be entirely mistaken, that no great pains would be taken to avoid whatever difficulty the Charleston officials might deem proper to create. At length, however, we were permitted to proceed, and, passing through Richmond, where I caught a glimpse of Goodin's pen, arrived in Washington January 17th, 1853.

We ascertained that both Burch and Radburn were still residing in that city. Immediately a complaint was entered with a police magistrate of Washington, against James H. Burch, for kidnapping and selling me into slavery. He was arrested upon a warrant issued by Justice Goddard, and returned before Justice Mansel,[3] and held to bail in the sum of three thousand dollars. When first arrested, Burch was much excited, exhibiting the utmost fear and alarm, and before reaching the justice's office on Louisiana Avenue, and before knowing the precise nature of the complaint, begged the police to permit him to

---

2. Obsolete unit of measurement equal to approximately 1/12th of an inch.
3. Actually Benjamin K. Morsell.

consult Benjamin O. Shekels, a slave trader of seventeen years' standing, and his former partner. The latter became his bail.

At ten o'clock, the 18th of January, both parties appeared before the magistrate. Senator Chase, of Ohio, Hon. Orville Clark, of Sandy Hill, and Mr. Northup acted as counsel for the prosecution, and Joseph H. Bradley[4] for the defence.

Gen. Orville Clark was called and sworn as a witness, and testified that he had known me from childhood, and that I was a free man, as was my father before me. Mr. Northup then testified to the same, and proved the facts connected with his mission to Avoyelles.

Ebenezer Radburn was then sworn for the prosecution, and testified he was forty-eight years old; that he was a resident of Washington, and had known Burch fourteen years; that in 1841 he was keeper of Williams' slave pen; that he remembered the fact of my confinement in the pen that year. At this point it was admitted by the defendant's counsel, that I had been placed in the pen by Burch in the spring of 1841, and hereupon the prosecution rested.

Benjamin O. Shekels was then offered as a witness by the prisoner. Benjamin is a large, coarse-featured man, and the reader may perhaps get a somewhat correct conception of him by reading the exact language he used in answer to the first question of defendant's lawyer. He was asked the place of his nativity, and his reply, uttered in a sort of rowdyish way, was in these very words—

"I was born in Ontario county, New-York, and *weighed fourteen pounds!*"

Benjamin was a prodigious baby! He further testified that he kept the Steamboat Hotel in Washington in 1841, and saw me there in the spring of that year. He was proceeding to state what he had heard two men say, when Senator Chase raised a legal objection, to wit, that the sayings of third persons, being hearsay, was improper evidence. The objection was overruled by the Justice, and Shekels continued, stating that two men came to his hotel and represented they had a colored man for sale; that they had an interview with Burch; that they stated they came from Georgia, but he did not remember the county; that they gave a full history of the boy, saying he was a bricklayer, and played on the violin; that Burch remarked he would purchase if they could agree; that they went out and brought the boy in, and that I was the same person. He further testified, with as much unconcern as if it was the truth, that I represented[*] I was

4. Salmon P. Chase (1808–1873), one of the founders of the Free-Soil Party, also served as Governor of Ohio, Secretary of the Treasury, and Chief Justice of the U.S. Supreme Court. Orville Clarke was a layer and New York State senator. Joseph H. Bradley was later well known for the successful defense of John H. Surratt, one of the men accused of conspiring with John Wilkes Booth to assassinate Abraham Lincoln. The trial resulted in Bradley being temporarily disbarred, apparently for challenging the judge to a duel.
* The transcriber changed "reppresented" to "represented".

born and bred in Georgia; that one of the young men with me was my master; that I exhibited a great deal of regret at parting with him, and he believed "got into tears!"—nevertheless, that I insisted my master had a right to sell me; that he *ought* to sell me; and the remarkable reason I gave was, according to Shekels, because he, my master, "had been gambling and on a spree!"

He continued, in these words, copied from the minutes taken on the examination: "Burch interrogated the boy in the usual manner, told him if he purchased him he should send him south. The boy said he had no objection, that in fact he would like to go south. Burch paid $650 for him, to my knowledge. I don't know what name was given him, but think it was not Solomon. Did not know the name of either of the two men. They were in my tavern two or three hours, during which time the boy played on the violin. The bill of sale was signed in my bar-room. It was a *printed blank, filled up by Burch*. Before 1838 Burch was my partner. Our business was buying and selling slaves. After that time he was a partner of Theophilus Freeman, of New-Orleans. Burch bought here—Freeman sold there!"

Shekels, before testifying, had heard my relation of the circumstances connected with the visit to Washington with Brown and Hamilton, and therefore, it was, undoubtedly, he spoke of "two men," and of my playing on the violin. Such was his fabrication, utterly untrue, and yet there was found in Washington a man who endeavored to corroborate him.

Benjamin A. Thorn testified he was at Shekels' in 1841, and saw a colored boy playing on a fiddle. "Shekels said he was for sale. Heard his master tell him he should sell him. The boy acknowledged to me he was a slave. I was not present when the money was paid. Will not swear positively this is the boy. The master *came near shedding tears: I think the boy did*! I have been engaged in the business of taking slaves south, off and on, for twenty years. When I can't do that I do something else."

I was then offered as a witness, but, objection being made, the court decided my evidence inadmissible. It was rejected solely on the ground that I was a colored man—the fact of my being a free citizen of New-York not being disputed.

Shekels having testified there was a bill of sale executed, Burch was called upon by the prosecution to produce it, inasmuch as such a paper would corroborate the testimony of Thorn and Shekels. The prisoner's counsel saw the necessity of exhibiting it, or giving some reasonable explanation for its non-production. To effect the latter, Burch himself was offered* as a witness in his own behalf. It was

---

* The transcriber changed "offer" to "offered".

contended by counsel for the people, that such testimony should not be allowed—that it was in contravention of every rule of evidence, and if permitted would defeat the ends of justice. His testimony, however, was received by the court! He made oath that such a bill of sale had been drawn up and signed, *but he had lost it, and did not know what had become of it!* Thereupon the magistrate was requested to dispatch a police officer to Burch's residence, with directions to bring his books, containing his bills of sales for the year 1841. The request was granted, and before any measure could be taken to prevent it, the officer had obtained possession of the books, and brought them into court. The sales for the year 1841 were found, and carefully examined, but no sale of myself, by any name, was discovered!

Upon this testimony the court held the fact to be established, that Burch came innocently and honestly by me, and accordingly he was discharged.

An attempt was then made by Burch and his satellites, to fasten upon me the charge that I had conspired with the two white men to defraud him—with what success, appears in an extract taken from an article in the New-York Times, published a day or two subsequent to the trial: "The counsel for the defendant had drawn up, before the defendant was discharged, an affidavit, signed by Burch, and had a warrant out against the colored man for a conspiracy with the two white men before referred to, to defraud Burch out of six hundred and twenty-five dollars. The warrant was served, and the colored man arrested and brought before officer Goddard. Burch and his witnesses appeared in court, and H. B. Northup appeared as counsel for the colored man, stating he was ready to proceed as counsel on the part of the defendant, and asking no delay whatever. Burch, after consulting privately a short time with Shekels, stated to the magistrate that he wished him to dismiss the complaint, as he would not proceed farther with it. Defendant's counsel stated to the magistrate that if the complaint was withdrawn, it must be without the request or consent of the defendant. Burch then asked the magistrate to let him have the complaint and the warrant, and he took them. The counsel for the defendant objected to his receiving them, and insisted they should remain as part of the records of the court, and that the court should endorse the proceedings which had been had under the process. Burch delivered them up, and the court rendered a judgment of discontinuance by the request of the prosecutor, and filed it in his office."

There may be those who will affect to believe the statement of the slave-trader—those, in whose minds his allegations will weigh heavier than mine. I am a poor colored man—one of a down-trodden and degraded race, whose humble voice may not be heeded by the oppressor—but *knowing* the truth, and with a full sense of my accountability, I do solemnly declare before men, and before God, that any charge or assertion, that I conspired directly or indirectly with any person or persons to sell myself; that any other account of my visit to Washington, my capture and imprisonment in Williams' slave pen, than is contained in these pages, is utterly and absolutely false. I never played on the violin in Washington. I never was in the Steamboat Hotel, and never saw Thorn or Shekels, to my knowledge, in my life, until last January. The story of the trio of slave-traders is a fabrication as absurd as it is base and unfounded. Were it true, I should not have turned aside on my way back to liberty for the purpose of prosecuting Burch. I should have *avoided* rather than sought him. I should have known that such a step would have resulted in rendering me infamous. Under the circumstances— longing as I did to behold my family, and elated with the prospect of returning home—it is an outrage upon probability to suppose I would have run the hazard, not only of exposure, but of a criminal prosecution and conviction, by voluntarily placing myself in the position I did, if the statements of Burch and his confederates contain a particle of truth. I took pains to seek him out, to confront him in a court of law, charging him with the crime of kidnapping; and the only motive that impelled me to this step, was a burning sense of the wrong he had inflicted upon me, and a desire to bring him to justice. He was acquitted, in the manner, and by such means as have been described. A human tribunal has permitted him to escape; but there is another and a higher tribunal, where false testimony will not prevail, and where I am willing, so far at least as these statements are concerned, to be judged at last.

We left Washington on the 20th of January, and proceeding by the way of Philadelphia, New-York, and Albany, reached Sandy Hill in the night of the 21st. My heart overflowed with happiness as I looked around upon old familiar scenes, and found myself in the midst of friends of other days. The following morning I started, in company with several acquaintances, for Glens Falls, the residence of Anne and our children.

As I entered their comfortable cottage, Margaret was the first that met me. She did not recognize me. When I left her, she was but seven years old, a little prattling girl, playing with her toys. Now she was grown to womanhood—was married, with a bright-eyed boy standing by her side. Not forgetful of his enslaved, unfortunate grand-father, she had named the child Solomon Northup Staunton.

ARRIVAL HOME, AND FIRST MEETING WITH HIS WIFE AND CHILDREN

Courtesy of the UNC–CH Library, The University of North Carolina at Chapel Hill.

When told who I was, she was overcome with emotion, and unable to speak. Presently Elizabeth entered the room, and Anne came running from the hotel, having been informed of my arrival. They embraced me, and with tears flowing down their cheeks, hung upon my neck. But I draw a veil over a scene which can better be imagined than described.

When the violence of our emotions had subsided to a sacred joy—when the household gathered round the fire, that sent out its warm and crackling comfort through the room, we conversed of the thousand events that had occurred—the hopes and fears, the joys and sorrows, the trials and troubles we had each experienced during the long separation. Alonzo was absent in the western part of the State. The boy had written to his mother a short time previous, of the prospect of his obtaining sufficient money to purchase my freedom. From his earliest years, that had been the chief object of his thoughts and his ambition. They knew I was in bondage. The letter written on board the brig, and Clem Ray himself, had given them that information. But where I was, until the arrival of Bass' letter, was a matter of conjecture. Elizabeth and Margaret once returned from school—so Anne informed me—weeping bitterly. On inquiring the cause of the children's sorrow, it was found that, while studying geography, their attention had been attracted to the picture of slaves working in the cotton-field, and an overseer following them with his whip. It reminded them of the sufferings their father might be, and, as it happened, actually *was*, enduring in the South. Numerous incidents, such as these, were related—incidents showing they still held me in constant remembrance, but not, perhaps, of sufficient interest to the reader, to be recounted.

My narrative is at an end. I have no comments to make upon the subject of Slavery. Those who read this book may form their own opinions of the "peculiar institution."[5] What it may be in other States, I do not profess to know; what it is in the region of Red River, is truly and faithfully delineated in these pages. This is no fiction, no exaggeration. If I have failed in anything, it has been in presenting to the reader too prominently the bright side of the picture. I doubt not hundreds have been as unfortunate as myself; that hundreds of free citizens have been kidnapped and sold into slavery, and are at this moment wearing out their lives on plantations in Texas and Louisiana. But I forbear. Chastened and subdued in spirit by the sufferings I have borne, and thankful to that good Being through whose mercy I have been restored to happiness and liberty, I hope henceforward to lead an upright though lowly life, and rest at last in the church yard where my father sleeps.

---

5. Common euphemism for slavery.

ROARING RIVER.

A REFRAIN OF THE RED RIVER PLANTATION.

"Harper's creek and roarin' ribber,
Thar, my dear, we'll live forebber;
Den we'll go to de Ingin nation,
All I want in dis creation,
Is pretty little wife and big plantation.

CHORUS.

Up dat oak and down dat ribber,
Two overseers and one little nigger."

APPENDIX.

A.

Chap. 375.

An act more effectually to protect the free citizens of this State from being kidnapped, or reduced to Slavery.

[Passed May 14, 1840.]

The People of the State of New-York, represented in Senate and Assembly, do enact as follows:

§ 1. Whenever the Governor of this State shall receive information satisfactory to him that any free citizen or any inhabitant of this State has been kidnapped or transported away out of this State, into any other State or Territory of the United States, for the purpose of being there held in slavery; or that such free citizen or inhabitant is wrongfully seized, imprisoned or held in slavery in any of the States or Territories of the United States, on the allegation or pretence that such a person is a slave, or by color of any usage or rule of law prevailing in such State or Territory, is deemed or taken to be a slave, or not entitled of right to the personal liberty belonging to a citizen; it shall be the duty of the said Governor to take such measures as he shall deem necessary to procure such person to be restored to his liberty and returned to this State. The Governor is hereby authorized to appoint and employ such agent or agents as he shall deem necessary to effect the restoration and return of such person; and shall furnish the said agent with such credentials and instructions as will be likely to accomplish the object of his appointment. The Governor may determine the compensation to be allowed to such agent for his services besides his necessary expenses.

§ 2. Such agent shall proceed to collect the proper proof to establish the right of such person to his freedom, and shall perform such journeys, take such measures, institute and procure to be prosecuted such legal proceedings, under the direction of the Governor, as shall be necessary to procure such person to be restored to his liberty and returned to this State.

§ 3. The accounts for all services and expenses incurred in carrying this act into effect shall be audited by the Comptroller, and paid by the Treasurer on his warrant, out of any moneys in the treasury of this State not otherwise appropriated. The Treasurer may advance, on the warrant of the Comptroller, to such agent, such sum or sums as the Governor shall certify to be reasonable advances to enable him to accomplish the purposes of his appointment, for which advance such agent shall account, on the final audit of his warrant.

§ 4. This act shall take effect immediately.

APPENDIX.

B.

Memorial of Anne.

To His Excellency, the Governor of the State of New-York:

The memorial of Anne Northup, of the village of Glens Falls, in the county of Warren, State aforesaid, respectfully sets forth—

That your memorialist, whose maiden name was Anne Hampton, was forty-four years old on the 14th day of March last, and was married to Solomon Northup, then of Fort Edward, in the county of Washington and State aforesaid, on the 25th day of December, A.D. 1828, by Timothy Eddy, then a Justice of the Peace. That the said Solomon, after such marriage, lived and kept house with your memorialist in said town until 1830, when he removed with his said family to the town of Kingsbury in said county, and remained there about three years, and then removed to Saratoga Springs in the State aforesaid, and continued to reside in said Saratoga Springs and the adjoining town until about the year 1841, as near as the time can be recollected, when the said Solomon started to go to the city of Washington, in the District of Columbia, since which time your memorialist has never seen her said husband.

And your memorialist further states, that in the year 1841 she received information by a letter directed to Henry B. Northup, Esq., of Sandy Hill, Washington county, New-York, and post-marked at New-Orleans, that said Solomon had been kidnapped in Washington, put on board of a vessel, and was then in such vessel in New-Orleans, but could not tell how he came in that situation, nor what his destination was.

That your memorialist ever since the last mentioned period has been wholly unable to obtain any information of where the said Solomon was, until the month of September last, when another letter was received from the said Solomon, post-marked at Marksville, in the parish of Avoyelles, in the State of Louisiana, stating that he was held there as a slave, which statement your memorialist believes to be true.

That the said Solomon is about forty-five years of age,[1] and never resided out of the State of New-York, in which State he was born, until the time he went to Washington city, as before stated. That the said Solomon Northup is a free citizen of the State of New-York, and is now wrongfully held in slavery, in or near Marksville, in the parish of Avoyelles, in the State of Louisiana, one of the United States of America, on the allegation or pretence that the said Solomon is a slave.

And your memorialist further states that Mintus Northup was the reputed father of said Solomon, and was a negro, and died at Fort Edward, on the 22d day of November, 1829; that the mother of said Solomon was a mulatto, or three quarters white, and died in the county of Oswego, New-York, some five or six years ago, as your memorialist was informed and believes, and never was a slave.

That your memorialist and her family are poor and wholly unable to pay or sustain any portion of the expenses of restoring the said Solomon to his freedom.

Your excellency is entreated to employ such agent or agents as shall be deemed necessary to effect the restoration and return of said Solomon Northup, in pursuance of an act of the Legislature of the State of New-York, passed May 14th, 1840, entitled "An act more effectually to protect the free citizens of this State from being kidnappd or reduced to slavery." And your memorialist will ever pray.

(Signed,)   ANNE NORTHUP.

Dated November 19, 1852.

———

STATE OF NEW-YORK:
Washington county, ss.[2]

Anne Northup, of the village of Glens Falls, in the county of Warren, in said State, being duly sworn, doth depose and say that she signed the above memorial, and that the statements therein contained are true.

(Signed,)   ANNE NORTHUP.

Subscribed and sworn before me this
19th November, 1852.
CHARLES HUGHES, Justice Peace.

———

1. Anne Northup's affidavit here suggests Solomon Northup was born in 1807, which is in contrast to the year given in Northup's memoir (1808; see p. 16 of this volume).
2. A contraction of the Latin *scilicet*, "ss." means "to wit" or "namely."

We recommend that the Governor appoint Henry B. Northup, of the village of Sandy Hill, Washington county, New-York, as one of the agents to procure the restoration and return of Solomon Northup, named in the foregoing memorial of Anne Northup.

Dated at Sandy Hill, Washington Co., N. Y.,

November 20, 1852.   (Signed.)

PETER HOLBROOK,	DANIEL SWEET,
B. F. HOAG,	ALMON CLARK,
CHARLES HUGHES,	BENJAMIN FERRIS,
E. D. BAKER,	JOSIAH H. BROWN,
ORVILLE CLARK.	

STATE OF NEW-YORK:
Washington County, ss:

Josiah Hand, of the village of Sandy Hill, in said county, being duly sworn, says, he is fifty-seven years old, and was born in said village, and has always resided there; that he has known Mintus Northup and his son Solomon, named in the annexed memorial of Anne Northup, since previous to the year 1816; that Mintus Northup then, and until the time of his death, cultivated a farm in the towns of Kingsbury and Fort Edward, from the time deponent first knew him until he died; that said Mintus and his wife, the mother of said Solomon Northup, were reported to be free citizens of New-York, and deponent believes they were so free; that said Solomon Northup was born in said county of Washington, as deponent believes, and was married Dec. 25th, 1828, in Fort Edward aforesaid, and his said wife and three children—two daughters and one son—are now living in Glens Falls, Warren county, New-York, and that the said Solomon Northup always resided in said county of Washington, and its immediate vicinity, until about 1841, since which time deponent has not seen him, but deponent has been credibly informed, and as he verily believes truly, the said Solomon is now wrongfully held as a slave in the State of Louisiana. And deponent further says that Anne Northup, named in the said memorial, is entitled to credit, and deponent believes the statements contained in her said memorial are true.

(Signed,)   JOSIAH HAND.

Subscribed and sworn before me this
   19th day of November, 1852,
      CHARLES HUGHES, Justice Peace.

State of New-York:
Washington County, ss:

Timothy Eddy, of Fort Edward, in said county, being duly sworn, says he is now over—years old, and has been a resident of said town more than—years last past, and that he was well acquainted with Solomon Northup, named in the annexed memorial of Anne Northup, and with his father, Mintus Northup, who was a negro,—the wife of said Mintus was a mulatto woman; that said Mintus Northup and his said wife and family, two sons, Joseph and Solomon, resided in said town of Fort Edward for several years before the year 1828, and said Mintus died in said town A.D. 1829, as deponent believes. And deponent further says that he was a Justice of the Peace in said town in the year 1828, and as such Justice of the Peace, he, on the 25th day of Dec'r, 1828, joined the said Solomon Northup in marriage with Anne Hampton, who is the same person who has subscribed the annexed memorial. And deponent expressly says, that said Solomon was a free citizen of the State of New-York, and always lived in said State, until about the year A.D. 1840, since which time deponent has not seen him, but has recently been informed, and as deponent believes truly, that said Solomon Northup is wrongfully held in slavery in or near Marksville, in the parish of Avoyelles, in the State of Louisiana. And deponent further says, that said Mintus Northup was nearly sixty years old at the time of his death, and was, for more than thirty years next prior to his death, a free citizen of the State of New-York.

And this deponent further says, that Anne Northup, the wife of said Solomon Northup, is of good character and reputation, and her statements, as contained in the memorial hereto annexed, are entitled to full credit.

(Signed,)   TIMOTHY EDDY.

Subscribed and sworn before me this
19th day of November, 1852,
    Tim'y Stoughton, Justice.

State of New-York:
Washington County, ss:

Henry B. Northup, of the village of Sandy Hill, in said county, being duly sworn, says, that he is forty-seven years old, and has always lived in said county; that he knew Mintus Northup, named in the annexed memorial, from deponent's earliest recollection until the time of his death, which occurred at Fort

Edward, in said county, in 1829; that deponent knew the children of said Mintus, viz, Solomon and Joseph; that they were both born in the county of Washington aforesaid, as deponent believes; that deponent was well acquainted with said Solomon, who is the same person named in the annexed memorial of Anne Northup, from his childhood; and that said Solomon always resided in said county of Washington and the adjoining counties until about the year 1841; that said Solomon could read and write; that said Solomon and his mother and father were free citizens of the State of New-York; that sometime about the year 1841 this deponent received a letter from said Solomon, post-marked New-Orleans, stating that while on business at Washington city, he had been kidnapped, and his free papers taken from him, and he was then on board a vessel, in irons, and was claimed as a slave, and that he did not know his destination, which the deponent believes to be true, and he urged this deponent to assist in procuring his restoration to freedom; that deponent has lost or mislaid said letter, and cannot find it; that deponent has since endeavored to find where said Solomon was, but could get no farther trace of him until Sept. last, when this deponent ascertained by a letter purporting to have been written by the direction of said Solomon, that said Solomon was held and claimed as a slave in or near Marksville, in the parish of Avoyelles, Louisiana, and that this deponent verily believes that such information is true, and that said Solomon is now wrongfully held in slavery at Marksville aforesaid.

(Signed,)   HENRY B. NORTHUP.

Subscribed and sworn to before me
    this 20th day of November, 1852,
        CHARLES HUGHES, J. P.

STATE OF NEW-YORK:
    Washington County, ss

Nicholas C. Northup, of the village of Sandy Hill, in said county, being duly sworn, doth depose and say, that he is now fifty-eight years of age, and has known Solomon Northup, mentioned in the annexed memorial of Ann Northup, ever since he was born. And this deponent saith that said Solomon is now about forty-five years old, and was born in the county of Washington aforesaid, or in the county of Essex, in said State, and always resided in the State of New-York until about the year 1841, since which time deponent has not seen him or known where he was, until a few weeks since, deponent was informed, and believes

truly, that said Solomon was held in slavery in the State of Louisiana. Deponent further says, that said Solomon was married
in the town of Fort Edward, in said county, about twenty-four
years ago, and that his wife and two daughters and one son
now reside in the village of Glens Falls, county of Warren, in
said State of New-York. And this deponent swears positively that
said Solomon Northup is a citizen of said State of New-York, and
was born free, and from his earliest infancy lived and resided in
the counties of Washington, Essex, Warren and Saratoga, in the
State of New-York, and that his said wife and children have
never resided out of said counties since the time said Solomon
was married; that deponent knew the father of said Solomon
Northup; that said father was a negro, named Mintus Northup,
and died in the town of Fort Edward, in the county of Washington, State of New-York, on the 22d day of November, A.D. 1829,
and was buried in the grave-yard in Sandy Hill aforesaid; that
for more than thirty years before his death he lived in the counties of Essex, Washington and Rensselaer and State of New-
York, and left a wife and two sons, Joseph and the said Solomon,
him surviving; that the mother of said Solomon was a mulatto
woman, and is now dead, and died, as deponent believes, in
Oswego county, New-York, within five or six years past. And this
deponent further states, that the mother of the said Solomon
Northup was not a slave at the time of the birth of said Solomon Northup, and has not been a slave at any time within the
last fifty years.

(Signed,)   N. C. NORTHUP.

Subscribed and sworn before me this 19th day
of November, 1852. CHARLES HUGHES, Justice Peace.

STATE OF NEW-YORK:
Washington County, ss.

Orville Clark, of the village of Sandy Hill, in the county of
Washington, State of New-York, being duly sworn, doth depose
and say—that he, this deponent, is over fifty years of age; that
in the years 1810 and 1811, or most of the time of those years,
this deponent resided at Sandy Hill, aforesaid, and at Glens
Falls; that this deponent then knew Mintus Northup, a black or
colored man; he was then a free man, as this deponent believes
and always understood; that the wife of said Mintus Northup,
and mother of Solomon, was a free woman; that from the year
1818 until the time of the death of said Mintus Northup, about
the year 1829, this deponent was very well acquainted with the
said Mintus Northup; that he was a respectable man in the

community in which he resided, and was a free man, so taken and esteemed by all his acquaintances; that this deponent has also been and was acquainted with his son Solomon Northup, from the said year 1818 until he left this part of the country, about the year 1840 or 1841; that he married Anne Hampton, daughter of William Hampton, a near neighbor of this deponent; that the said Anne, wife of said Solomon, is now living and resides in this vicinity; that the said Mintus Northup and William Hampton were both reputed and esteemed in this community as respectable men. And this deponent saith that the said Mintus Northup and his family, and the said William Hampton and his family, from the earliest recollection and acquaintance of this deponent with him (as far back as 1810) were always reputed, esteemed, and taken to be, and this deponent believes, truly so, free citizens of the State of New-York. This deponent knows the said William Hampton, under the laws of this State, was entitled to vote at our elections, and he believes the said Mintus Northup also was entitled as a free citizen with the property qualification. And this deponent further saith, that the said Solomon Northup, son of said Mintus, and husband of said Anne Hampton, when he left this State, was at the time thereof a free citizen of the State of New-York. And this deponent further saith, that said Anne Hampton, wife of Solomon Northup, is a respectable woman, of good character, and I would believe her statements, and do believe the facts set forth in her memorial to his excellency, the Governor, in relation to her said husband, are true.

(Signed,)   ORVILLE CLARK.

Sworn before me, November
   19th, 1852.
   U. G. PARIS, Justice of the Peace.

STATE OF NEW-YORK:
   Washington County, ss.

Benjamin Ferris, of the village of Sandy Hill, in said county, being duly sworn, doth depose and say—that he is now fifty-seven years old, and has resided in said village forty-five years; that he was well acquainted with Mintus Northup, named in the annexed memorial of Anne Northup, from the year 1816 to the time of his death, which occurred at Fort Edward, in the fall of 1829; that he knew the children of the said Mintus, namely, Joseph Northup and Solomon Northup, and that the said Solomon is the same person named in said memorial; that said Mintus resided in the said county of Washington to the time of his death, and was, during all that time, a free citizen of the said State of New-York, as deponent verily believes; that said memorialist, Anne Northup, is a woman of good character, and the statement contained in her memorial is entitled to credit.

(Signed,)　BENJAMIN FERRIS.

Sworn before me, November
　19th, 1852.
　　U. G. Paris, Justice of the Peace.

————

State of New-York:
Executive Chamber, Albany, Nov. 30, 1852.

I hereby certify that the foregoing is a correct copy of certain proofs filed in the Executive Department, upon which I have appointed Henry B. Northup an Agent of this State, to take proper proceedings in behalf of Solomon Northup, there in mentioned.

(Signed,)　WASHINGTON HUNT.

By the Governor.
　J. F. R., Private Secretary.

————

State of New-York:
Executive Department.

Washington Hunt, *Governor of the State of New-York,*
to whom it may concern, greeting:

Whereas, I have received information on oath, which is satisfactory to me, that Solomon Northup, who is a free citizen of this State, is wrongfully held in slavery, in the State of Louisiana:

And whereas, it is made my duty, by the laws of this State, to take such measures as I shall deem necessary to procure any citizen so wrongfully held in slavery, to be restored to his liberty and returned to this State:

Be it known, that in pursuance of chapter 375 of the laws of this State, passed in 1840, I have constituted, appointed and employed Henry B. Northup, Esquire, of the county of Washington, in this State, an Agent, with full power to effect the restoration of said Solomon Northup, and the said Agent is hereby authorized and empowered to institute such proper and legal proceedings, to procure such evidence, retain such counsel, and finally to take such measures as will be most likely to accomplish the object of his said appointment.

He is also instructed to proceed to the State of Louisiana with all convenient dispatch, to execute the agency hereby created.

[L.S.]

In witness whereof, I have hereunto subscribed my name, and affixed the privy seal of the State, at Albany, this 23d day of November, in the year of our Lord 1852.

(Signed,)   WASHINGTON HUNT.

JAMES F. RUGGLES, Private Secretary.

APPENDIX.

C.

STATE OF LOUISIANA:
Parish of Avoyelles.

Before me, Aristide Barbin, Recorder of the parish of Avoyelles, personally came and appeared Henry B. Northup, of the county of Washington, State of New-York, who hath declared that by virtue of a commission to him as agent of the State of New-York, given and granted by his excellency, Washington Hunt, Governor of the said State of New-York, bearing date the 23d day of November, 1852, authorizing and empowering him, the said Northup, to pursue and recover from slavery a free man of color, called Solomon Northup, who is a free citizen of the State of New-York, and who was kidnapped and sold into slavery, in the State of Louisiana, and now in the possession of Edwin Epps, of the State of Louisiana, of the Parish of Avoyelles; he, the said agent, hereto signing, acknowledges that the said Edwin has this day given and surrendered to him as such agent, the said Solomon Northup, free man of color, as aforesaid, in order that he be restored to his freedom, and carried back to the said State of New-York, pursuant to said commission, the said Edwin Epps being satisfied from the proofs produced by said agent, that the said Solomon Northup is entitled to his freedom. The parties consenting that a certified copy of said power of attorney be annexed to this act.

Done and signed at Marksville, parish of Avoyelles, this fourth day of January, one thousand eight hundred and fifty-three, in the presence of the undersigned, legal and competent witnesses, who have also hereto signed.

(Signed,)   HENRY B. NORTHUP.
EDWIN EPPS.
ADE. BARBIN, Recorder.

Witnesses:
  H. TAYLOR,
  JOHN P. WADDILL.

STATE OF LOUISIANA:
  Parish of Avoyelles.

I do hereby certify the foregoing to be a true and correct copy of the original on file and of record in my office.

[L. S.]

Given under my hand and seal of office as Recorder in and for the parish of Avoyelles, this 4th day of January, A.D. 1853.

(Signed,)   ADE. BARBIN, Recorder.

THE END

CONTEXTS

Contemporary Sources,
1853–62

NEW YORK TIMES

The Kidnapping Case[†]

Narrative of the Seizure and Recovery of Solomon Northrup.[1]

INTERESTING DISCLOSURES.

We have obtained from Washington the subjoined statement of the circumstances attending the seizure and recovery of the negro man SOLOMON NORTHROP, whose case had excited so high a degree of interest. The material facts in the history of the transaction have already been given, but this narrative will be found a more complete and authentic record than has yet appeared:

SOLOMON NORTHROP, the subject of the following narrative, is a free colored citizen of the United States; was born in Essex County, New-York, about the year 1808; became early a resident of Washington County, and married there in 1829. His father and mother resided in the County of Washington about fifty years, till their decease, and were both free. With his wife and children he resided at Saratoga Springs in the Winter of 1841, and while there was employed by two gentlemen to drive a team South, at the rate of a dollar a day. In fulfilment of his employment he proceeded to New-York, and having taken out free papers, to show that he was a citizen, he went on to Washington City, where he arrived the second day of April, the same year, and put up at Gadsby's Hotel. Soon after he arrived, he felt unwell and went to bed.

While suffering with severe pain some persons came in, and, seeing the condition he was in, proposed to give him some medicine

---

† *New York Times*, Jan. 20, 1853.
1. In a correction issued 161 years later, the *New York Times,* on March 4, 2014, acknowledged misspelling Solomon Northup's name variously as "Northrup" and "Northrop" in the original 1853 article. There were various minor inaccuracies in the *Times'* original 1853 article, including misspellings of names and Northup's marriage date (1828). The editors of this volume have left them untouched to give readers a sense of the article as it appeared.

and did so. That is the last thing of which he had any recollection until he found himself chained to the floor of WILLIAMS' slave pen in this City, and handcuffed. In the course of a few hours, JAMES H. BURCH, a slave dealer, came in, and the colored man asked him to take the irons off from him, and wanted to know why they were put on. BURCH told him it was none of his business. The colored man said he was free and told where he was born. BURCH called in a man by the name of EBENEZER RODBURY, and they two stripped the man and laid him across a bench, RODBURY holding him down by his wrists. BURCH whipped him with a paddle until he broke that, and then with a cat-o'-nine tails, giving him a hundred lashes, and he swore he would kill him if he ever stated to any one that he was a free man. From that time forward the man says he did not communicate the fact from fear, either that he was a free man, or what his name was, until the last summer. He was kept in the slave pen about ten days, when he, with others was taken out of the pen in the night, by BURCH, handcuffed and shackled, and taken down the river by a steamboat, and then to Richmond, where he with forty-eight others was put on board the brig *Orleans*. There BURCH left them. The brig sailed for New-Orleans, and on arriving there, before she was fastened to the wharf, THEOPHILUS FREEMAN, another slave dealer, belonging in the city of New-Orleans, and who in 1838 had been a partner with BURCH in the slave trade, came to the wharf and received the slaves as they were landed, under his direction. This man was immediately taken by FREEMAN and shut up in his pen in that city. He was taken sick with the small pox immediately after getting there, and was sent to a Hospital where he lay two or three weeks. When he had sufficiently recovered to leave the hospital, FREEMAN declined to sell him to any person in that vicinity, and sold him to a Mr. FORD, who resided in Rapides parish, in Louisiana, where he was taken and lived a little more than a year, and worked as a carpenter, working with FORD at that business.

FORD became involved and had to sell him. A Mr. TIBAUT became the purchaser. He in a short time sold him to EDWIN EPPES in Bayou Beouf, about one hundred and thirty miles from the mouth of Red River, where EPPES has retained him on a Cotton plantation since the year 1843.

To go a back a step in the narrative, the man wrote a letter in June 1841 to HENRY B NORTHROP, of the State of New-York, dated and postmarked at New-Orleans, stating that he had been kidnapped and was on board a vessel, but was unable to state what his destination was; but requesting Mr. N. to aid him in recovering his freedom, if possible. Mr. N. was unable to do anything in his behalf in consequence of not knowing where he had gone, and not being able to find any trace of him. His place of residence remained unknown until the month of September last, when the following letter was received by his friends:

Bayou Beouf, August, 1852.

Mr. Wm. Peny, or Mr. Lewis Parker:

Gentlemen: It having been a long time since I have seen or heard from you, and not knowing that you are living, it is with uncertainty that I write to you; but the necessity of the case must be my excuse. Having been born free just across the river from you, I am certain you must know me; and I am here now a slave. I wish you to obtain free papers for me, and forward them to me at Marksville, La., Parish of Avoyelles, and oblige

Yours,   SOLOMON NORTHROP.

On receiving the above letter, Mr. N. applied to Governor Hunt, of New-York, for such authority as was necessary for him to proceed to Louisiana, as an agent to procure the liberation of Solomon, Proof of his freedom was furnished to Governor Hunt, by affidavits of several gentlemen, General Clarke among others. Accordingly, in pursuance of the laws of New-York, Henry B. Northrop was constituted an agent to take such steps, by procuring evidence, retaining counsel, &c., as were necessary to secure the freedom of Solomon, and to execute all the duties of his agency. He left Sandy Hill, in New-York, on the 14th of December last, and came to the city of Washington, and stated the facts of the case to Hon. Pierre Soulé, of Louisiana; Hon. Mr. Conrad, Secretary of War, from New-Orleans, and Judge Nelson, of the Supreme Court of the United States, and other gentlemen. They furnished Mr. N. with strong letters to gentlemen residing in Louisiana, urging their assistance in accomplishing the object of restoring the man to freedom.

From Washington, Mr. N. went, by the way of Pittsburg and the Ohio and Mississippi rivers, to the mouth of the Red River, and thence up that river to Marksville, in the parish of Avoyelles, where he employed Hon. John P. Waddill, an eminent lawyer of that place, and consulted with him as to the best means of finding and obtaining possession of the man. He soon ascertained there was no such man at Marksville, nor in that vicinity. Bayou Beouf, the place where the letter was dated, was twenty-three miles distant, at its nearest point, and is seventy miles in length. For reasons which it is unnecessary to give, the very providential manner in which the residence of the man was ascertained, cannot now be given, although the circumstances would add much to the interest of the narrative. But he was found without great difficulty, and legal proceedings commenced. A process was placed in the hands of a Sheriff, directing him to proceed to Bayou Beouf and take the colored man into his possession, and wait the order of the Court in regard to his right to freedom. The next day, the owner, with his counsel, came to Marksville and called upon Mr. N., who exhibited to them the commission which he had received from the Governor of New-York, and the evidence in his possession relating to the man's being a free citizen of New-York.

EPPES' counsel, after examining it, stated to his client, that the evidence was ample and satisfactory; that it was perfectly useless to litigate the question further, and advised him by all means to deliver the colored man up, in order that he might he carried back to the State of New-York, in pursuance of the Governor's requisition. An article was drawn up between the claimant and Mr. NORTHRUP, the counsel for the colored man, and recorded in accordance with the laws of the place, showing that the colored man was free. Having settled everything satisfactorily, the agent and the rescued man started for Now-Orleans on the 4th of January instant, and on arriving there, traced the titles of the colored man from TIBAUT to EPPES, from LORD to TIBAUT, and from FREEMAN to FORD—all the titles being recorded in the proper books kept for that purpose.

Having traced the titles back as far as possible in New Orleans, the party then proceeded to the City of Washington, where BIRCH[2] lived; and on making inquiry, found who was the keeper of the slave pen in that City in 1841; and also ascertained from the keeper, upon the colored man (SOLONON N.,) being pointed out to him— that he was placed in that pen in the Spring of 1811, and then kept for a short period by BURCH.

Immediately upon the receipt of this information, complaint was made before the Police of Washington against BURCH, for kidnapping and selling into slavery this free colored man. The warrant for his arrest was issued on the 17th instant by Justice GODDARD, and returned before Justice MANSELL. BURCH was arrested and held to bail in the sum of $3,000, SHEKELS, a slave-trader of seventeen years standing, going his bail.

It is but justice to say that the authorities of Avoyelles, and indeed at New-Orleans, rendered all the assistance in their power to secure the establishment of the freedom of this unfortunate man, who had been snatched so villainously from the land of freedom, and compelled to undergo sufferings almost inconceivable in this land of heathenism, where slavery exists with features more revolting than those described in "Uncle Tom's Cabin."

2. While the author of this article and Solomon Northup, in *Twelve Years a Slave*, generally referred to this man as James H. "Burch," in their book *Solomon Northup: The Complete Story of the Author of* Twelve Years a Slave (Praeger, 2013), David Fiske, Clifford W. Brown, Jr., and Rachel Seligman point out inconsistent spellings in the historical record, including that Burch signed his name "Birch" in court records and that it is spelled "Birch" on his grave. Thus, the printer of this article was also correct, if unwittingly so, in this single instance of "Birch." Fiske et al., p. 186, n. 75.

On the 18th instant, at 10 o'clock, both parties appeared before the magistrate. Senator CHASE from Ohio, Gen. CLARK and HENRY B. NORTHRUP, being counsel for the plaintiff, and J. H. BRADLEY for the defendant. Gen. CLARK and E. H. NORTHRUP, who were sworn as witnesses on the part of the prosecution, and established the foregoing facts: On the part of the defendant, BENJAMIN SHEKELS and B. A. THORN were sworn. The prosecution offered the colored man who had been kidnapped, as a witness on the part of the prosecution, but it was objected to, and the Court decided that it was inadmissable. The evidence of this colored man was absolutely necessary to prove son a facts on the part of the prosecution, as he alone was cognizant of them.

Mr. SHEKELS, who had been, as before-stated a slave trader in the City of Washington seventeen years, testified that some ten or twelve years ago he was keeping public house in this city; that BURCH boarded at the house and carried on the business of buying and selling slaves; that in that year, two white men came into his barroom and stated that they had a slave for sale. Mr. BURCH immediately entered into a negotiation for his purchsae. The white men stated that they were from Georgia; had brought the negro with them from that State, and wished to sell him to be carried back to that State; that the negro expressed a willingness to be sold in order to return to Georgia; SHEKELS, however, was unable to state the names of either of the white men, or the name of the colored man; was unacquainted with either of them previous to that time, and had never seen either since that transaction; that he saw them execute a bill of sale to BURCH, saw BURCH pay him $625 and take the bill of sale, and that he read that bill, but could not tell who was the vendor nor who was the person sold, as appeared by the bill of sale.

Mr. THORN was next called upon the stand, and testified that he was in this tavern in the Spring of the year 1841, and saw a white man negotiating a trade with BURCH for a colored man; but whether this was the colored man or not, he could not tell—for he never saw either white man or colored man but that once, and did not know whether or not BURCH bought and paid for him.

BURCH himself was next offered as a witness in his own behalf, to prove the loss of the bill of sale. His evidence was objected to by the prosecution, but was allowed by the Court. He testified that he had the bill of sale and had lost it, and did not know what had become of it. The counsel for the prosecution requested the Court to send a police officer to bring the books of BURCH, containing his bills of sales of negroes for the year 1841 and previous years. They were fortunately procured, but no bill of sale was found of this colored man by any name. Upon this positive evidence that the man had been in the possession of BURCH and that he had been in slavery for a period of more than eleven years, the Court decided that the testimony of the slave trader established the fact that BURCH came honestly by him, and consequently discharged the defendant. The counsel for the defendant had drawn up, before the defendant was discharged, an affidavit signed by BURCH, and had a warrant out against the colored man, for a conspiracy with the two white men before referred to, to defraud BURCH out of $625. The warrant was served, and the colored man arrested and brought before Officer GODDARD. BURCH and his witnesses appeared in Court, and H. B. NORTHRUP appeared as counsel for the colored man, stating that he was ready to proceed as counsel on the part of the defendant, and asking no delay whatever. BURCH, after consulting privately for a short time with SHEKELS, stated to the Magistrate that he wished him to dismiss the complaint, as he would not proceed further with it. Defendant's counsel stated to the Magistrate that, if the complaint was withdrawn, it must be withdrawn without the request or consent of the defendant. BURCH then asked the Magistrate to let him have the complaint and the warrant, and he took them. The counsel for the defendant objected to his receiving them, and insisted that they should remain as a part of the records of the Court, and that the Court should indorse the proceedings which had been had under the process. BURCH delivered them up, and the Court rendered a judgment of discontinuance by the request of the prosecutor, and filed it in his office.

The condition of this colored man during the nine years that he was in the hands of EPPES, was of a character nearly approaching that described by Mrs. STOWE, as the condition of "Uncle Tom" while in that region. During that whole period his hut contained neither a floor, nor a chair, nor a bed, nor a mattrass, nor anything for him to lie upon except a board about twelve inches wide, with a block of wood for his pillow, and with a single blanket to cover him, while the walls of his hut did not by any means protect him from the inclemency of the weather. He was sometimes compelled to perform acts revolting to humanity, and outrageous in the highest degree. On one occasion, a colored girl belonging to EPPES, about 17 years of age, went one Sunday without the permission of her master, to the nearest plantation, about half a mile distant, to visit another colored girl of her acquaintance. She returned in the course of two or three hours, and for that offence she was called up for punishment, which SOLOMON was required to inflict. EPPES compelled him to drive four stakes into the ground at such distances that the hands and ancles of the girl might be tied to them, as she lay with her face upon the ground; and having thus fastened her down, he compelled him while standing by himself, to inflict one hundred lashes upon her bare flesh, she being stripped naked. Having inflicted the hundred blows, SOLOMON refused to proceed any further. EPPES tried to compel him to go on, but he absolutely set him at defiance and refused to murder the girl. EPPES then seized the whip and applied it until he was too weary to continue it. Blood flowed from her neck to her feet, and in this condition she was compelled the next day to go into the field to work as a field hand. She bears the marks still upon her body, although the punishment was inflicted four years ago.

When Solomon was about to leave, under the care of Mr. NORTHRUP, this girl came from behind her but, unseen by her master, and throwing her arms around the neck of SOLOMON congratulated him on his escape from slavery, and his return to his family, at the same time in language of despair exclaiming, "But, Oh, God! what will become of me?"

These statements regarding the condition of SOLOMON while with EPPES, and the punishment and brutal treatment of the colored girls, are taken from SOLOMON himself. It has been stated that the nearest plantation was distant from that of EPPES a half mile, and of course there could be no interference on the part of neighbors in any punishment however cruel, or however well disposed to interfere they might be.

By the laws of Louisiana no man can be punished there for having sold SOLOMON into slavery wrongfully, because more than two years had elapsed since he was sold; and no recovery can be had for his services, because he was bought without the knowledge that he was a free citizen.

NEW ORLEANS BEE

A Striking Contrast[†]

The *Villager*, published at Marksville, Avoyelles parish, in this State, in its edition of the 13th inst., notices the arrival in that parish of H. B. Northrop, Esq., of New York, and gives the following account of the occasion of his visit and his reception by the citizens of Avoyelles parish. The striking contrast between the treatment he received, and that accorded to Southern gentlemen who visit the North for the purpose of recovering their property, is well set forth in the concluding paragraph:

> A free negro of New York having, some twelve years ago, gone to Washington, D.C., in pursuance of his calling as a musician, was, while there, kidnapped by some villains, sent South and

[†] *New Orleans Bee* (LA), Jan. 22, 1853. Unless noted, misspellings have been left uncorrected to avoid distortion.

sold as a slave. After passing through the hands of several masters, he eventually came into the possession of a planter of our parish. As he knew how to read and write, he either personally, or by others, made his friends at the North acquainted with his condition and his residence. His friends at once communicated the intelligence to Mr. N., to whose ancestors the negro's ancestors formerly belonged, who had himself appointed as agent of the State of New York and came South in that capacity.

Mr. Northrop, on his arrival here, after taking legal advice, commenced suit by having the negro sequestered. Mr. Epps, in whose possession the negro was, on being served with the writ, declared that he would offer no opposition if satisfactory proofs were adduced. Mr. Northrop having proved the freedom of the negro to the satisfaction of Mr. Epps and his legal adviser, Mr. E. declined all opposition, although he loses the amount he paid for him. On the next day Mr. Northrop, accompanied by the negro, left for his home, Sandy Hill, New York.

This gentleman remained in the midst of a slaveholding population for four days, without being, although his object was known, subjected to the slightest affronts or inconvenience; on the contrary received every facility and attention that he required. What a contrast this presents to the treatment which Southerners receive at the hands of the people of the North, when in pursuit of their fugitive slaves. How different it is from the Gorsuch, Kennedy, Lemmon, and other cases, which are so common in Pennsylvania, New York, Massachusetts and other free States. Well may the South boast of its justice and loyalty.

SALEM PRESS

Recovery of a Free Negro[†]

Twelve years ago, a colored man, who had lived a long time in the family of H. B. NORTHUP, Esq., of Washington county, suddenly disappeared. Suspicions were excited by some concurrent circumstances, which led to the belief that he had been kidnapped and sold, but no traces could be found of him. Some time subsequently, Mr. NORTHUP received a Letter from him, in which he said he had finally succeeded in finding a friend who promised to mail that Letter. The Letter gave the name and residence of his Master.

† *Salem Press* (NY), Jan. 25, 1853. Unless noted, misspellings have been left uncorrected to avoid distortion.

The Legislature of this State, in 1840, during Gov. SEWARD's administration, passed the following enactment, intended to meet just such cases as this:—

§ 21. Whenever the Governor of this State shall receive information satisfactory to him, that any free citizen, or any inhabitant of this State, has been kidnapped and transported away out of this State, into any other State or Territory of the United States, for the purpose of being held in slavery; or that such free citizen or inhabitant is wrongfully seized, imprisoned or held in slavery in any of the States or Territories of the United States, on the allegation or pretence that such person is a slave, or by color of any usage or rule of law prevailing in such State or Territory, is deemed or taken to be a slave, or not entitled of right to the personal liberty belonging to a citizen; it shall be the duty of the said Governor to take such measures as he shall deem necessary to procure such person to be restored to his liberty and returned to this State. The Governor is hereby authorized to appoint and employ such agent or agents as he shall deem necessary to effect the restoration and return of such person, and shall furnish the said agent with such credentials and instructions as will be likely to accomplish the object of his appointment. The Governor may determine the compensation to be allowed to such agent for his services, besides his necessary expenses.—[*Sec.* 1 *of chap.* 876, *laws of* 1840].

Under this law Mr. Northup applied to Gov. HUNT last month for a commission to recover the stolen "property." It was promptly issued, and he started on his journey southward. We now find by the telegraphic reports, that he has reached Washington on his return, *bringing the man with him.* He found him at a settlement on the Red River, near the Arkansas frontier, almost beyond the reach of civilization, and entirely beyond the reach, as his captors thought, of freedom.

It is further stated that Mr. N. expresses his obligations to Senator SOULE and other Southern citizens, who aided him by every means in their power; a fact that we can readily believe, for however much we may condemn their political blindness upon the subject of Slavery, or their sensitiveness to Northern intrusion upon it, the sympathies of the mass of the Southern people are always quite as warmly aroused and their aid quite as effectively given in behalf of the unfortunate victims of kidnapping and slave-dealing as those of our own citizens.

It is quite necessary that this part of the story should be fully understood, for if it is not, some of the worthy gentlemen in the red free-stone edifice at the head of State-street, with a view to preserve the "comity of States," will, in a day or two, introduce a bill "to provide for the repeal of section first of chapter three hundred and seventy-five of the laws of 1840."

We congratulate Mr. NORTHUP on the successful termination of his benevolent mission; and full of confidence in the comity of our sister States, hope, at an early day, to lay before our readers the intelligence that the merchants, ship-owners, stock-jobbers and other influential citizens of Arkansas have contributed a generous purse of—say $5200—to "indemnify" this colored man in part for his twelve years of unpaid for servitude, and to enable him to retire comfortably to a farm in Washington county, or Texas, or Virginia, if he should prefer it.—*Alb. Eve. Journal.*

LATER.—A correspondent under date of Washington, Jan. 18, says:—

The kidnapping case grows in interest. James H. Burch, of this city, was arrested to-day, and an examination before Chief Justice Morsell, showed that the accused had had the kidnapped man in his possession at a negro-pen, and sold him to go to New Orleans. The man says he was drugged at night and carried into the pen, and was whipped severely when, on awaking, he attempted to assert his freedom. Burch brings a slave trader to prove that he (Burch,) bought the negro of some man whom he did not know. The bill of sale was not produced by the defendant, although he brought out his bill-book for the year in question. After hearing the testimony Justice Morsell decided that the evidence of the slave trader upset the testimony of the complainant, and refused to hold the accused to answer.—BURCH then got out a warrant against the negro, whose name is Solomon Northup, charging him with conspiracy to defraud, by bargaining with white men to sell him and divide the proceeds.—Mr. H. B. NORTHUP appeared in court, and declared his readiness to defend the negro, but the complainant withdrew his charge. Senator CHASE and Mr. TOWNSEND of Ohio, and many others, were present during the proceedings, and were much interested. Mr. NORTHUP and the liberated man will leave for New York tomorrow. Solomon has a wife and a large family of children at Sandy Hill. His discovery by Mr. N., was most providential. It appears that when NORTHUP reached the vicinity where he supposed he should find the man, he lost all trace of his [whereabouts], and then determined to scour the country till he found him. Presently he encountered a person who, it was believed, had written a letter for Solomon, apprising his friends of his locality. Mr. NORTHUP taxed this man with writing the letter. He replied that he was not in the habit of doing anything which he needed to be ashamed of; acknowledged the fact, and on request, told where the man was to be found.—He was with Mr. EPPS, whose counsel, on examining the evidence, advised that no resistance should be made, and the man was freed at once. Solomon tells a thrilling story of personal wrongs and cruelties inflicted on the plantations. In a few days he will make a full statement of his case.

SANDY HILL HERALD

Uncle Sol[†]

UNCLE SOL.—We are informed that an extensive publishing house in this state has offered Northup, the kidnapped slave, recently returned to this village, $3,000 for the copyright of his book, which is now being prepared by a member of the bar of this county. We hope Sol. will get rich, for we have a liking for the fellow, because he used to fiddle so finely for us when a boy.

NATIONAL ERA

A Thrilling Narrative of Slavery! Twelve Years a Slave![‡]

THE NARRATIVE OF SOLOMON NORTHUP, a Citizen of New York, Kidnapped and Sold into Slavery, in Washington City, in 1841, and Rescued in 1853, from a Cotton Plantation near the Red River, in Louisiana, with *six illustrations*, representing—

1. Portrait of Solomon in his plantation suit.
2. Scene in the slave pen at Washington.
3. Night scene in the Tocondie Swamp, pursued by hounds.
4. The staking out and flogging of the girl Patsey.
5. Scene of the Rescue in the cotton field.
6. Arrival home, and first meeting with his wife and children.

The above work is now in press, and will contain upwards of 300 pages, in one 12mo volume, and sold at the price of $1. A large portion of the net proceeds is secured to Solomon.

Orders from the Trade solicited. Copies sent by mail, soon as ready, post paid. Price to be remitted in advance. Address

DERBY & MILLER, Publishers,
Auburn, NY.; or
DERBY, ORTON, & MULLIGAN,
Buffalo, NY

---

† *Sandy Hill Herald* (NY), Mar. 22, 1853.
‡ *National Era* (Washington, D.C.), Apr. 21, 1853. Unless noted, misspellings have been left uncorrected to avoid distortion.

SALEM PRESS

Uncle Tom's Cabin—No. 2[†]

The rescue of SOLOMON NORTHUP, a Free Man who was Kidnapped and sold into Slavery, of which he had TWELVE YEARS experience, has given the public another view of the practical workings of that peculiar Institution. NORTHUP's Narrative is "Uncle Tom's Cabin" without its Romance.

Of SOLOMON NORTHUP's birth in Hoosic, Rensselaer county, and his residence at Sandy-Hill, Saratoga Springs, &c., his subsequent confinement in the Slave Pen at Washington, and his sale by BURCH, a Slave Dealer now residing in that city, there is no question. All this is of record. And his "Narrative" of what occurred during his Twelve Years of bondage bears the impress of truth. It is, we doubt not, a simple, straight forward story of his servitude, and one which we hope will find its way back to "Bayou Boeux."

NORTHUP owes his deliverance, finally, to the fact that during his long and severe ordeal, he kept the secret of his being a Free born Man locked up in his own bosom. For this the Master whom he served for ten years when his Deliverers came, reproached him.—Had the truth been known he would have been out of the reach of Friends and Laws.

In this Book, Slavery is undoubtedly revealed, as it exists in the interior of Louisiana, Arkansas, &c. NORTHUP will be believed, because, instead of indiscriminate accusations, he gives you the good and evil of Slavery just as he found it. All kindnesses are remembered with gratitude. Masters and Overseers who treated Slaves humanely are commended;—for there, as here, were good and bad men. If "Tibeats" and "Epps" were coarse, cruel and brutal, "Master FORD" and "Madam M'COY" were so just, considerate, humane as to be obeyed, honored, and beloved.

NORTHUP's sad experience shows how difficult it is for kidnapped persons to regain their Freedom. They are taken far into the interior where they are only known by an arbitrary name. Had not Mr. NORTHUP, who went with Gov. HUNT's requisition, Providentially encountered the man who wrote the Letter for "Sol," his long journey would have proved fruitless, for to no one else was he known by any other name than that of "Platt Eppes."

This Book strongly confirms what is regarded as the most revolting feature of Slavery, viz:—the separation of Families. In this there is cruelty which disgraces a Christian Nation in an age of civilization. And these bereavements fall generally upon a class of Slaves whose

[†] *Salem Press* (NY), July 26, 1853. Previously published in the *Albany Evening Journal*. Unless noted, misspellings have been left uncorrected to avoid distortion.

intelligence enables them to comprehend and realize all its bitterness. These separations occur among the Slaves of Maryland and Virginia, whose Owners, by improvidence or misfortune, are compelled to sell them to Planters farther South, where Slave labor pays better. If the inter-State Slave Trade could be prohibited, so that Virginia, &c, &c, would cease to be Slave Growing States, one of the great evils of the system would be mitigated.

This book, though less exciting than that of Mrs. STOWE, is deeply interesting, and will be extensively read. It is to be hoped that it will fall into the hands of those of whom it speaks.—Most of them, we are quite sure, would admit that "Platt" has told his story truthfully.—*Albany Eve. Journal.*

FREDERICK DOUGLASS' PAPER

Literary Notices[†]

TWELVE YEARS A SLAVE. Narrative of Solomon Northup. Auburn: Derby & Miller

What an episode in the life of a man, who from his birth had breathed the free air of the Empire State, and known no master save the God who made him.

It is a strange history, its truth far stranger than fiction. Think of it! For thirty years *a man*, with all a man's hopes, fears and aspirations—with a wife and children to call him by the endearing names of husband and father—with a home, humble it may be, but still a *home*, beneath the shelter of whose roof none had a right to molest or make him afraid—then for twelve years a *thing*, a chattel personal, classed with mules and horses, and treated with less consideration than they, torn from his home and family and the free labor by which he earned their bread and driven to unremitting, unrequited toil in a cotton field, under a burning Southern sun, by the lash of an inhuman master. Oh! It is horrible. It chills the blood to think that such things are.

The Narrative of Solomon Northup, recently issued from the press of Derby & Miller of Auburn, is a plain unvarnished history of those twelve years, during which, though a true born American [illegible in original, as captured on microfilm] held in bondage on American soil. There was no need of invoking the aid of the imagination to adorn this tale of horrors. The hero needed only to tell "what he did know, and testify of what he had seen." We are tempted to give one

† *Frederick Douglass' Paper,* Aug. 5, 1853. Unless noted, misspellings have been left uncorrected to avoid distortion.

extract, which our readers will agree with us, presents a picture of hopeless desolation rarely equalled.

On arriving at New Orleans, Solomon's first owner was William Ford, a Baptist minister of whose kindness and moral worth, he speaks in the highest terms. Owing to pecuniary embarrassments, Ford was compelled to sell Solomon to John M. Tibeats, and while under his iron rule, the following events occurred. One day, in the faithful discharge of his duties, Solomon was so unfortunate as to offend his brutal master. Finding his life in danger, he broke from the infuriated man, and ran away. Calling hounds and men to his aid, Tibeats pursued. The narrative runs thus [the author includes an excerpt from Chapter X]:

* * *

We have not space for further extracts—Our readers will be abundantly repaid for the perusal of the book. There are bright lines even in the dark picture which it presents of American slavery. But one cannot rise from its perusal without a renewed conviction of the iniquity of the system; and with a quickened sympathy for its suffering victims, he will exclaim, "How long, O Lord, how long?"

AMERICAN AND FOREIGN ANTI-SLAVERY SOCIETY

From The Thirteenth Annual Report[†]

It is cheering to notice that in the State of New-York, the region of Anti-slavery Conventions, colored editors, colored clergymen, church agitation, and Anti-slavery churches—the birth-place of distinctly-organized political Abolitionism, where slaveholding and pro-slavery voting are extensively regarded as heinous sins, it is not quite as easy as in California, Illinois, and Missouri, to enslave free citizens, without public protection or redress.

SOLOMON NORTHROP, a free colored citizen of the United States, born of free parents in Essex county, N. Y., married in 1829, and residing with his wife and children at Saratoga, found occasion, in 1841, to go to Washington City to drive a team. He took the precaution to provide himself with written testimonials of his freedom. On his arrival at Washington, he put up at Gadsby's Hotel, retired, sick, to bed, and took medicine at the hands of some persons. The next thing

† From *The Thirteenth Annual Report of the American & Foreign Anti-slavery Society, Presented at New-York, May 11, 1853; with the Addresses and Resolutions* (New York: The Am. & For. Anti-slavery Society, 1853), pp. 42–43. Unless noted, misspellings have been left uncorrected to avoid distortion.

he remembers is, that he found himself chained to the floor of Williams' slave-pen, in that city, and in possession of James H. Burch, a noted slave-dealer. In spite of all remonstrances, he was conveyed down the river, by steamboat, to Richmond, put on board the brig Orleans, carried to Louisiana and sold as a slave. After having been sold several times, he fell into the hands of Edwin Eppes, in Bayou Bœuf, about 130 miles from the mouth of Red river, in the parish of Avoyelles, La. Here he found opportunity to send a letter home, in August, 1852. Application being made to Governor Hunt, of New-York, with proper proofs of his freedom, the requisite authority of the State was obtained; Mr. H. B. Northrop, of Washington county, proceeded to Washington City, where he received testimonials from Hon. Mr. Conrad, Secretary of War, and other distinguished gentlemen. Arriving in Louisiana, a legal process was commenced, and the testimony was so complete, that the defense was relinquished and the captive restored to his freedom. On their way home through Washington City, they caused Burch to be arrested; but, owing to the rejection of the testimony of Solomon, the victim of his villany, because he was *colored*, while the testimony of Burch in his own case was allowed by the Court, he was discharged. Burch then commenced a suit against Solomon for a conspiracy to defraud him! Mr. H. B. Northrop promptly offered himself as counsel for Solomon, and asked that the trial might immediately proceed. Burch was intimidated, and discontinued the suit.[1]

A narrative of Solomon Northrop's captivity is just published, and is expected to make an important addition to the "peculiar" literature of America.

HARRIET BEECHER STOWE

From A Key to Uncle Tom's Cabin[†]

Chapter VIII. Kidnapping.

The principle which declares that one human being may lawfully hold another as property leads directly to the trade in human beings; and that trade has, among its other horrible results, the temptation to the crime of kidnapping.

1. *National Era*, Feb. 3, 1853 [Society's note].
† From *A Key to* Uncle Tom's Cabin; *Presenting the Original Facts and Documents Upon Which the Story is Founded. Together with Corroborative Statements Verifying the Truth of the Work* (Cleveland: Jewett, Proctor & Worthington, 1853), pp. 173–174. This source abridges the original *New York Times* article (January 20, 1853), reprinted in this volume. It also differs in minor details. Unless noted, misspellings have been left uncorrected to avoid distortion.

The trader is generally a man of coarse nature and low associations, hard-hearted, and reckless of right or honor. He who is not so
is an exception, rather than a specimen. If he has anything good
about him when he begins the business, it may well be seen that he
is in a fair way to lose it.

Around the trader are continually passing and repassing men and
women who would be worth to him thousands of dollars in the way
of trade,—who belong to a class whose rights nobody respects, and
who, if reduced to slavery, could not easily make their word good
against him. The probability is that hundreds of free men and
women and children are all the time being precipitated into slavery
in this way.

The recent case of *Northrop*, tried in Washington, D. C., throws
light on this fearful subject. The following account is abridged from
the *New York Times:*

> Solomon Northrop is a free colored citizen of the United States;
> he was born in Essex county, New York, about the year 1808;
> became early a resident of Washington county, and married
> there in 1829. His father and mother resided in the county of
> Washington about fifty years, till their decease, and were both
> free. With his wife and children he resided at Saratoga Springs
> in the winter of 1841, and while there was employed by two
> gentlemen to drive a team South, at the rate of a dollar a day. In
> fulfilment of his employment, he proceeded to New York, and,
> having taken out free papers, to show that he was a citizen, he
> went on to Washington city, where he arrived the second day of
> April, the same year, and put up at Gadsby's Hotel. Soon after
> he arrived he felt unwell, and went to bed.
>
> While suffering with severe pain, some persons came in,
> and, seeing the condition he was in, proposed to give him some
> medicine, and did so. This is the last thing of which he had any
> recollection, until he found himself chained to the floor of Wil-
> liams' slave-pen in this city, and handcuffed. In the course of a
> few hours, James H. Burch, a slave-dealer, came in, and the col-
> ored man asked him to take the irons off from him, and wanted
> to know why they were put on. Burch told him it was none of his
> business. The colored man said he was free, and told where he
> was born. Burch called in a man by the name of Ebenezer Rod-
> bury, and they two stripped the man and laid him across a
> bench, Rodbury holding him down by his wrists. Burch whipped
> him with a paddle until he broke that, and then with a cat-o'-
> nine-tails, giving him a hundred lashes; and he swore he would
> kill him if he ever stated to any one that he was a free man.
> From that time forward the man says he did not communicate
> the fact from fear, either that he was a free man, or what his
> name was, until the last summer. He was kept in the slave-pen
> about ten days, when he, with others, was taken out of the pen

in the night by Burch, handcuffed and shackled, and taken down the river by a steamboat, and then to Richmond, where he, with forty-eight others, was put on board the brig *Orleans*. There Burch left them. The brig sailed for New Orleans, and on arriving there, before she was fastened to the wharf, Theophilus Freeman, another slave-dealer, belonging in the city of New Orleans, and who in 1833 had been a partner with Burch in the slave-trade, came to the wharf, and received the slaves as they were landed, under his direction. This man was immediately taken by Freeman and shut up in his pen in that city. He was taken sick with the small-pox immediately after getting there, and was sent to a hospital, where he lay two or three weeks. When he had sufficiently recovered to leave the hospital, Freeman declined to sell him to any person in that vicinity, and sold him to a Mr. Ford, who resided in Rapides Parish, Louisiana, where he was taken and lived more than a year, and worked as a carpenter, working with Ford at that business.

Ford became involved, and had to sell him. A Mr. Tibaut became the purchaser. He, in a short time, sold him to Edwin Eppes, in Bayou Beouf, about one hundred and thirty miles from the mouth of Red river, where Eppes has retained him on a cotton plantation since the year 1843.

To go back a step in the narrative, the man wrote a letter, in June, 1841, to Henry B. Northrop, of the State of New York, dated and postmarked at New Orleans, stating that he had been kidnapped and was on board a vessel, but was unable to state what his destination was; but requesting Mr. N. to aid him in recovering his freedom, if possible. Mr. N. was unable to do anything in his behalf, in consequence of not knowing where he had gone, and not being able to find any trace of him. His place of residence remained unknown until the month of September last, when the following letter was received by his friends:

> Bayou Beouf, August, 1852.

MR. WILLIAM PENY, or MR. LEWIS PARKER.

GENTLEMEN: It having been a long time since I have seen or heard from you, and not knowing that you are living, it is with uncertainty that I write to you; but the necessity of the case must be my excuse. Having been born free just across the river from you, I am certain you know me; and I am here now a slave. I wish you to obtain free papers for me, and forward them to me at Marksville, Louisiana, Parish of Avovelles, and oblige Yours, SOLOMON NORTHROP.

On receiving the above letter, Mr. N. applied to Governor Hunt, of New York, for such authority as was necessary for him to proceed to Louisiana as an agent to procure the liberation of Solomon. Proof of his freedom was furnished to Governor Hunt by affidavits of several gentlemen, General Clarke among others. Accordingly, in pursuance of the laws of New York, Henry B. Northrop was constituted an agent, to take such steps, by procuring evidence, retaining counsel, &c., as were necessary to secure the freedom of Solomon, and to execute all the duties of his agency.

The result of Mr. Northrop's agency was the establishing of the claim of Solomon Northrop to freedom, and the restoring him to his native land.

It is a singular coincidence that this man was carried to a plantation in the Red river country, that same region where the scene of Tom's captivity was laid; and his account of this plantation, his mode of life there, and some incidents which he describes, form a striking parallel to that history. We extract them from the article of the *Times:*

> The condition of this colored man during the nine years that he was in the hands of Eppes was of a character nearly approaching that described by Mrs. Stowe as the condition of "Uncle Tom" while in that region. During that whole period his hut contained neither a floor, nor a chair, nor a bed, nor a mattress, nor anything for him to lie upon, except a board about twelve inches wide, with a block of wood for his pillow, and with a single blanket to cover him, while the walls of his hut did not by any means protect him from the inclemency of the weather. He was sometimes compelled to perform acts revolting to humanity, and outrageous in the highest degree. On one occasion, a colored girl belonging to Eppes, about seventeen years of age, went one Sunday, without the permission of her master, to the nearest plantation, about half a mile distant, to visit another colored girl of her acquaintance. She returned in the course of two or three hours, and for that offence she was called up for punishment, which Solomon was required to inflict. Eppes compelled him to drive four stakes into the ground at such distances that the hands and ankles of the girl might be tied to them, as she lay with her face upon the ground; and, having thus fastened her down, he compelled him, while standing by himself, to inflict one hundred lashes upon her bare flesh, she being stripped naked. Having inflicted the hundred blows, Solomon refused to proceed any further. Eppes tried to compel him to go on, but he absolutely set him at defiance, and refused to murder the girl. Eppes then seized the whip, and applied it until he was too weary to continue it. Blood flowed from her neck to her feet, and in this condition she was compelled the next day to go into the field to work as a field-hand. She bears the marks still upon her body, although the punishment was inflicted four years ago.

When Solomon was about to leave, under the care of Mr. Northrop, this girl came from behind her hut, unseen by her master, and, throwing her arms around the neck of Solomon, congratulated him on his escape from slavery, and his return to his family; at the same time, in language of despair, exclaiming, "But, O God! what will become of me?"

These statements regarding the condition of Solomon while with Eppes, and the punishment and brutal treatment of the colored girls, are taken from Solomon himself. It has been stated that the nearest plantation was distant from that of Eppes a half-mile, and of course there could be no interference on the part of neighbors in any punishment, however cruel, or however well disposed to interfere they might be.

Had not Northrop been able to write, as few of the free blacks in the slave states are, his doom might have been sealed for life in this den of misery.

Two cases recently tried in Baltimore also unfold facts of a similar nature.

FREDERICK DOUGLASS' PAPER

Letter to Frederick Douglass from Sigma[†]

BUFFALO, Jan. 13, 1854.

FREDERICK DOUGLASS: DEAR SIR:—Buffalo flourishes. To-day is celebrated the completion of the railroad running thence to Brantford. Channels of communication so increases and multiplies, and commerce so largely showers down golden rewards to industry and enterprise—that it would not be problematical if within ten years our favored town should rival the commercial marts of the Atlantic.

Last night I had the pleasure of hearing Solomon Northup narrate his trials and experiences as a kidnapped slave. The lecture was in American Hall; but owing to the inclement weather, the attendance was small. His story is full of romantic interest and painful adventures, and gives as clear an insight to the practical workings and *beauties* of American Slavery, as any other exposition ever gives to the world. In following the windings of his career, from liberty to slavery, with all its attendant horrors, and thence back to life again, one cannot but feel impressed with the flagrant enormities of that system of oppression now existing in a land of self-styled republicanism and equality, which so

† *Frederick Douglass' Paper*, Jan. 27, 1854. The identity of "Sigma" is unknown. Unless noted, misspellings have been left uncorrected to avoid distortion.

degrades men in respective ranks of life, as not only to curse them—to refuse to let the clacking of chains to be stilled forever, and the bondman go free—but also to forfeit every title to humanity, by robbing a man born on untainted soil, of his life, liberty, and pursuit of happiness, so expressly defined and guaranteed in the American Constitution.

Northup tells his story in plain and candid language, and intermingles it with flashes of genuine wit. It is a sure treat to hear him give some hazardous adventure, with so much *sans froid*, that the audience is completely enraptured and the "house brought down." . . .

Yours truly,

SIGMA

SYRACUSE DAILY JOURNAL

[Solomon Northup][†]

Solomon Northop, the colored man, the interesting account of whose experiences as a slave of twelve years has been published and excited a great deal of empathy throughout the country, will lecture in this city on Thursday evening next. We happen to be somewhat acquainted with "Sol." He is a man—every inch of him. He will lecture at the City Hall.

FREDERICK DOUGLASS' PAPER

A Speech by a "Chattel"[‡]

Solomon Northrop, the rescued slave, related his experience of the tender mercies of slavery, at the Court House in St. Albans, on Saturday evening last. He talked pretty well for "a Chattel," "a thing," as our government regards him. His unaffected simplicity, directness, and gentlemanly bearing impressed us far more than many fervid appeals to which we have listened. Here was a free-born, respectable citizen of the State of New York, who was seized, while in pursuit of a lawful business, within sight of the Capitol at Washington, brutally beaten for saying that he was free, hurried on board a brig bound for New Orleans, sold from the slave pen to a

---

[†] *Syracuse Daily Journal* (NY), Jan. 31, 1854. Unless noted, misspellings have been left uncorrected to avoid distortion.

[‡] *Frederick Douglass' Paper*, Mar. 3, 1854. Unless noted, misspellings have been left uncorrected to avoid distortion.

planter of the Red River, endured twelve years of bondage, flogging and unrequited toil, sought in vain to communicate with his wife and children in New York, and at last by his own ingenious and careful management, was rescued from that 'worst of hells upon earth,' a Southern plantation—This is the plain tale in brief, of the wrongs of, this one man. And for all this injury he has no redress. Who can give back to him those years of unpaid toil? Who shall avenge his imprisonment and cruel scourgings? Had a white man, the meanest in the land, suffered one tithe of this man's injuries, would not the nation have cried aloud for vengeance?

And it is of such devilish deeds that the old parties tell us that we must not speak! Verily is it not time that the people should wake?—*Vt. Tribune.*

SARATOGA WHIG

The Northrup Kidnapping Case[†]

In the matter of Alexander Merrill and Joseph Russell, arrested for inveigling Solomon Northrup, a free colored man, from Saratoga Springs to the City of Washington, and selling him into slavery.

An examination held before Abel Meeker and David W, Maxwell Esqs., Justices of the Peace, at Ballston Spa, on Tuesday, July 11, 1854.

Wm. T. Odell, District-Attorney, and Henry B. Northrup and Geo. G. Scott, appearing for the prosecution;[1] and Wm. Wait appearing for prisoner Merrill, and John Brotherson for Russell.

Solomon Northrup, sworn—Says he was 47 on the 10th of this month;[2] resided at Saratoga Springs in the month of March, 1841; had a family at that place consisting of wife and three children; knows the prisoner now in Court; first saw him at Saratoga Springs in 1841, latter part of March; there was another man with him, an associate, who is now sitting beside him; one now known as Merrill called his name Merrill Brown, and the other called his Abraham Hamilton; he first saw them at Mr. Moon's tavern at Saratoga Springs; they did not appear to have any particular business; they wished to hire witness to go to New-York with them to drive their carriage and play fiddle in a circus company to which they said they belonged; they offered him one dollar per day and expenses from the time he left until he returned; they had a carriage and span of horses there at the time; he drove their horses attached to the

---

[†] *Saratoga Whig* (NY), July 13, 1854. Unless noted, misspellings and typos have been left uncorrected to avoid distortion.

1. The district attorney in the case was assisted by Scott and Henry B. Northup.

2. Northup's testimony about his age suggests he was born in 1807, which is at odds with the year given in his memoir (1808; see p. 16 of this volume).

carriage to Albany by Cohoes, and thence to New-York City; after his arrival in New-York he wished to leave, but prisoners wanted him to stay and go to Washington with them; he finally concluded to go with them, and accordingly went to the Custom-House and obtained free papers, as he was afraid to go to Washington without them; prisoners went with him to what they called the Custom-House, and got what witness supposed to be free papers; having obtained free papers they took the horses and carriage and went to Baltimore through New-Jersey; the horses and carriage were left at Baltimore; saw Thaddeus St. John in Baltimore; from Baltimore went to Washington in the railroad car; said they were going to meet the circus and would come back with it; arrived in Washington the night before Gen. Harrison's funeral; stopped at Gadsby Hotel; was around with the prisoners during the day, and drank with them frequently, and smoked with them. They charged him particularly to not leave them; was taken sick during the afternoon and got worse during the evening so that he was insensible; don't know how long before he recovered, but found himself next in Williams's Slave Pen, in Washington, with handcuffs and fetters, and fetters fastened to ring in the floor; the first white persons that came in were James Birch and Ebenezer Radburn; one asked him how he felt; told him he was sick, didn't know what was the matter, and asked the reason why he was fettered and handcuffed there; Birch said he had bought witness; told Birch he was a free man, and Birch said he was a liar, and that he had run away from Georgia; told him never had been in Georgia, and could get evidence from New-York that he was born free and had always been free man; Birch said he would not hear any of his lies and if he denied having run away from Georgia would flog him; had no coat or hat on, nor money, they having been taken from him during the night; told Birch that if he ever got free would know the reason of his treatment; and Birch told Radburn to get paddle and cat-o'-nine-tails; Radburn held him across a bench with his feet on his handcuffs, and then Birch broke the paddle on him, after which he took the cat-o'-nine tails and whipped him with that until Radburn told him to stop, as he would be too sore to go to New-Orleans. Remained in the slave-pen awhile and was then taken with other negroes by steamboat a piece and thence by railroad to Norfolk, VA.; was taken from thence with other negroes to New-Orleans in a brig; at New-Orleans was claimed by a man named Freeman, who came on board the vessel and took him to a slave-pen, whence he was sold to a Wm. P. Ford to go up to Red River; was next sold to John Tibbetts,[3] and then to

3. Tibbets here is misspelled; it should be Tibaut. Similarly, in the text of *Twelve Years a Slave*, Northup and his editor, David Wilson, recorded Tibaut's surname as Tibeats, a spelling that readers of the text carried forth in their writing.

Edwin Epps, who lived at Bayou Boef. He was kept in Slavery for nearly twelve years, up to January 3, 1853. He was on that day set at liberty and returned to his family. He has never seen either of the prisoners from the time he was taken sick in Washington until last week. He first saw Merrill in Fulton Co., two miles from Fonda's Bush; first saw him in bed at the house of prisoner's father.

[The counsel here wished to ask as to the weapons found with prisoner's clothes by the side of his bed, but prisoner's counsel objected, when an argument was held upon the subject, during which Mr. Northup asserted that he should attempt to prove that the prisoners had been for a long time engaged in kidnapping and other crimes, and that he always went armed for offense and defense.]

In a belt were found a bowie-knife and revolver loaded with six charges. Was informed that he arrived from the South on the Monday previous. First saw Merrill on Monday, July 11, at Schenectady, in custody of officers Wendell and Harlow. Was informed that one of the prisoners was known in Fulton County as Alexander Merrill and the other as Joseph Russell.

On Cross-Examination—Witness said, could not recollect of having been in Albany during the winter previous to his being kidnapped; thinks he stayed at the Eagle Tavern in Albany with prisoners; could not recollect the names of stopping places between Albany and New-York; has forgotten how many days they were in going to New-York; stopped at a hotel on the North River side of the City in New-York; cannot tell which of the prisoners spoke to him about going farther than New-York, but think that it was Russell; both were together and offered him one dollar per day and his expenses to continue on to Washington; it was Merrill or Russell that poured out the liquor for him to drink the last time he drank with them; saw Thaddeus St. John at Washington, and thinks the last time he drank with prisoners St. John drank with them; after he went to bed felt so bad that he thought his liquor had been drugged, people came to his room and he told them of his sickness, and asked them to go and get him some medicine; was advised to go to a doctor; thinks the slave pen in which he found himself less than a quarter of a mile from Gadsby's Hotel; has not seen St. John from the time he drank with him at Washington until one day last week, when he saw him at Fonda; he recognized St. John at once when he saw him at Fonda in the bar room of the hotel.

Thaddeus St. John being sworn, says he resides at Fonda, Montgomery Co.; was brought up in the town of Northampton, Fulton Co., and resided there until 1841; knows both the prisoners; their names are Alexander Merrill and Joseph Russell; has known them both from infancy; Merrill was brought up in Northampton, and Russell in Edinburgh, Saratoga Co.; was in Washington in the spring of 1841, also at Baltimore; met Merrill and Russell at Baltimore; they were together; had a colored man with them, recognized as Solomon Northrup; saw them the afternoon previous to Gen. Harrison's funeral; went to Baltimore by railroad; stopped at the Indian Queen Hotel; saw the prisoners at Gadsby's Hotel in Washington, and Solomon with them; they shook hands with him and asked him to drink, but he declined; saw them last time about 8 o'clock in the evening, and did not see them at Washington again after that day; never saw Solomon from the time he met him at Washington until last week at Fonda; had some talk with the prisoners in Baltimore; was rather surprised to meet Russell there, but knew of Merrill's having been south before; addressed them by name, and said to Russell, "What are you doing here Jo.?" Merrill then spoke to him in presence of Russell and requested him not to call them by their proper names; I spoke to him again and he put his hands together and pointed to the negro; when he left Washington to return north met Russell and Merrill on board the boat at Havre de Grace; their appearance was entirely changed from what it was when he saw them a few days previous in Baltimore and Washington; when he saw them first, Russell had long hair and whiskers and clothes pretty well worn, and when he met him on the boat his hair was cut short and whiskers cut off, was well dressed with new clothes and broadcloth cloak, had an ivory cane and a gold watch chain; Merrill also had long hair when he saw him first, and on the boat it was short cut and his appearance was changed for the better outwardly; expressed surprise at meeting them there, and said to Russell, "Jo, you have made a victim somewhere;" told him he had sold the negro or something worse; should watch the papers and see if anyone had been murdered; if so should know who did it; Russell laughed and walked away; remarked to Merrill that they had changed their appearance for some object; when they got across the river they entered the cars; Russell sat in seat by his side, and Merrill behind him; commenced conversation with Russell by asking what he should tell his venerable and pious old father; Russell said, "tell him I am "the best looking son he has got by a d—d sight;" Russell then threw off his cloak and exhibited a splendid gold watch; then put his hand into his pantaloons and drew out a handful of gold; when asked where he got so much, made motions as though he had been gambling; told him if it was gambling money it must belong to Aleck, as he was not smart enough to win money from southern gamblers; he opened the case of the watch and showed him three bank bills, one of which was denomination of $1,000, apparently; told him again he was carrying Aleck's money; Merrill set by listening; nothing else occurred that he remembers until they were met on the steamboat from New-York to Albany; it was a very stormy night and they kept company with him;

said they were going west; witness afterward moved to Fonda, and about four years ago Russell moved there and commenced butchering, with a shop for selling his meat near witness's residence; often joked Russell about his southern trip; when he exhibited the money witness wrote $3,000, put negro at $500, and Merrill told him to add $150; to that Russell said, "That is more money than you often see a Sacandaga boy have."

Norman Prindle sworn, says: He is fifty-four years of age; was at Saratoga Springs in March, 1841, employed as stage driver by G. W. Wilcox; has known Solomon Northup since 1826 or '27; Northrup lived at Saratoga Springs in 1841; identifies Merrill, and says he saw him on Montgomery Hall stoop at Saratoga Springs, and a day or two after saw him in a carriage there; another man in carriage who had long hair and large whiskers saw Solomon Northrup drive away the carriage containing the two men; had some conversation with Solomon before he started, told him that he had not better go off with those men as they would not know him when they got away south; others told Solomon the same story.

On cross-examination says he remembers having prisoners pointed out to him as from the South and about to buy Mr. Seaman's horses; Solomon told witness that he would risk the prisoners selling him; told him again he had not better go South with them; meant to slave States; next time he saw Merrill from the time he saw him at Saratoga, was in jail here at Ballston; recognized Merrill at first glance when he stood at the light; thinks he would have no difficulty in recollecting him if he should have talked with him; does not recollect of having said anything on the subject from the time Solomon left until he heard of Esq. Northrup's going after him; said then that he had told Solomon before he left how it would be; says he is not positive that Merrill is the man he saw at Saratoga, in 1841; he is very confident, however; could not be fully positive as to his own father after so long a time; has no positive recollection of Russell; there was something more striking in the appearance of Merrill than in that of Russell, to make him recollect him at the time he saw [him] at Saratoga; Merrill was more talkative and lively; first saw Solomon in H. B. Northrup's kitchen, the morning after he returned from the South; there was a great crowd present at the time; is not positive, but thinks he told Northrup before he went after Solomon, that he knew of the persons who took him.

John S. Enos sworn—Reside at Johnstown, and is the District-Attorney of Fulton County; is acquainted with Merrill by sight, and has seen Russell, but not to know him particularly; saw Merrill in Johnstown Jail last Saturday; conversed with him in relation to the arms found upon him at the time of his arrest; Merrill said he had been in California for the last three years, and south on the Mississippi;

asked him where he had been since 1841, and his reply was the same; asked him particularly whether he had resided in the State since 1841, and he said he had not, coming only occasionally to visit his father; has had no acquaintance or correspondence with H. B. Northrup before Tuesday, July 11.

On cross-examination, says—Did not go to jail for purpose of getting confession; part of information in regard to residence was in answer to questions, and part voluntary; Merrill said he had been about all over the world; told him that witness was the prosecuting attorney of the county, and did not wish to extort any confession from him.

On reexamination, says—His motive for conversing with Merrill was, that the name had excited his curiosity, on account of a relative of his wife's having married James Merrill of Saratoga County; and then asked him if he was at James Merrill's in July or August, 1841, and whether he had ever staid at J Merrill's in 1841? Said he passed through Ballston Spa in the spring of 1841.

Re-cross-examined—Merrill was brought to the jail the night previous to the interview, as he understood.

Reexamined—Merrill said the people of that part of the country seemed to be down on him, and if he could have had any notice of this they could not have caught him. In conversation about the arms found with him, said that he had led rather a bad life, had formerly been a gambler, but had given that up of late years; he seemed to feel rather bad at being in jail.

Re-cross-examined—Merrill said he understood the negro told his story at Gloverville the night before; witness asked him if he had read the life of Solomon Northrup, or seen him before; he said he had seen the d—d nigger before, somewhere; said he had no doubt Solomon had been kidnapped and sold; denied having done it himself, but expressed fears about getting out of the scrape.

People rested. The revolver taken from Merrill when arrested was shown in Court.

Mr. Wait, counsel for Merrill, waived calling any witnesses in his behalf or having him examined.

Counsel for Russell also waived any witnesses or having him examined, but claimed his discharge on account of the statute of limitations requiring an indictment to be found within three years of the commission of the offense.

District-Attorney Odell contended that the power of the magistrates was only to say whether any offense had probably been committed, and then they must send their evidence to the proper tribunal for indictment and trial. He also contended that the offense was committed during all the time he was held in Slavery and until he was finally released, and the statute of limitations would run only from January, 1853, when Solomon was set free in Louisiana. The law provided that if a man was stabbed and death did not ensue until 364 days after the stabbing, it might be murder, as the law provided it might be murder if death ensued in a year and a day.

The magistrates decided to hold the prisoners, and they were accordingly committed to jail, it not being within the power of a Justice of the Peace to fix bail for an offense of that magnitude.

The prisoners were taken in a civil suit on Tuesday and held to bail in the sum of $5,000 each to answer Solomon Northrup for his personal damages in being sold into slavery.

The punishment for kidnapping and selling into slavery is imprisonment in the State Prison not less than two nor over ten years. It seems to us that the law should hold them as long for punishment as their victim was held in slavery.

FREDERICK DOUGLASS' PAPER

The Northup Kidnappers[†]

The Northup Kidnappers are likely "to do the State some services." The evidence against them appears to be conclusive; and they are likely to end their base career by TEN YEARS OF SLAVERY in the penitentiary. The case presents many remarkable features. A worthy, intelligent and industrious citizen of this State,

"Guilty of a skin not colored like our own,"

is decoyed to the capital of the nation, is there drugged, and while insensible is draged to a slave pen, sold, cruelly beaten, and ultimately consigned to the obscurest section of the Red River region. *Twelve years* he is subjected to the severe rigors of the slave system; when by a concurrence of the most singular events, he is found out and rescued by an agent acting under a commission from the Governor of this State.

He returns, publishes a most interesting narrative of the scenes and sufferings thro' which he had passed entitled, SOLOMON NORTHUP: or, "TWELVE YEARS A SLAVE," which is read by hundreds of thousands of his fellow citizens and which enlists their warmest sympathies in his behalf. No one, however, expects to find the guilty perpetrators of the base outrage. But they *are* found, and a host of the most creditable witnesses rise up as if by magic to prove their identity and their guilt. The whole case is certainly the most remarkable upon record, and it can only be appreciated by reading the "narrative" in connexion with the incidents of the arrest and detention of the kidnappers.—*Auburn Daily Advertiser.*

† *Frederick Douglass' Paper*, Aug. 4, 1854. Unless noted, misspellings have been left uncorrected to avoid distortion.

DAILY PICAYUNE

More Uncle Tom[†]

MORE UNCLE TOM.—Some few years ago, it was discovered that a black man who was held in slavery in the upper part of this State had been unjustly deprived of his rights as a free negro of the State of New York. It did not appear that this was by any fault of the holder of the negro, who had bought him in good faith, as a slave. On the showing of the facts in the case by an agent appointed by the Governor of New York, he was promptly set at liberty and returned to the place from whence he came.

When Mrs. Harriet Beecher Stowe published what she called her "Key" to the abolition novel she had palmed off upon the world as a true history, but which was the most absurd farrago of exaggerated romance, she chanced to allude to this case as having occurred somewhere in the neighborhood of the locality selected from some of the scenes in her "Uncle Tom." Whereupon, one of those obscure but canny firms in the book-selling trade, which fatten on getting up this sort of treasonable and blasphemous trash, bethought then that here was a good chance of turning a penny, by the publication of yet another "Uncle Tom." Why should Jewett & Co. carry off all the plunder to be made out of the credulous old women of the North, and the hypocritical *habitués* of Exeter Hall, while Miller, Orton and Mulligan, of Auburn, (Wm. H. Seward's place of residence,) stood ready to do the same dirty work, just as dirtily, and for the same price? Forbid it, humbug!

So Solomon Northup was engaged to cook up a narrative of his experiences on a Louisiana plantation, which having been swelled into a volume of some 300 pages, was profusely decorated with bugaboo wood cuts, representing "more horrors than vast hell could hold," and dedicated, of course, to Harriet Beecher Stowe, by tying themselves to whose petticoats this enterprising publishing firm hoped to be lifted into a future equal to that achieved by their Boston *confrères*.

This was all in the year before last, and now, the book having had its little day, and been forgotten, together with the rest of that kind of mimick of which it is a fair, or rather a foul type, some fanatical dullard, who inscribes "From B. Coates, Philadelphia," on the wrapper, sends us through the post office, a copy of the wretched catchpenny.

Who B. Coates, of Philadelphia, may be we know not, neither do we care. But what he is, insolently presuming as he does to send us

---

† *Daily Picayune* (New Orleans, LA), Jan. 26, 1855. Unless noted, misspellings have been left uncorrected to avoid distortion.

such a mendacious libel upon the public and the institutions of this section of the country, we could tell him, in very plain and unmistakable terms, had we the mind to do so. We hold the book subject to his order, and would advise him that when he has any more such presents to make us, he had better do it in person.

HENRY C. WRIGHT

Letter to the Editor[†]

DEAR GARRISON:[1] Allow me to call the attention of the abolitionists of Boston and vicinity to SOLOMON NORTHUP, now in this city. He is here to relate his twelve years experience in slavery. It is well known that he was kidnapped in 1840[2]—taken from his wife and three children in Saratoga, N.Y.—taken to Washington—there confined and whipped under the very eyes of the national capitol—sold to a New Orleans slave-dealer—taken to that city—sold to a planter living on the Red River, near the borders of Texas—taken to his destination, and there whipped and worked twelve years, under the most frightful form of slavery—and at length, by the requisition of the Governor of New York, restored to his family.

His experience, as detailed in the volume entitled "Solomon Northup, Twelve Years a Slave," is one of thrilling interest, and has been widely read in New England. No narrative of man's experience as a slave, a chattel, is more touching, or better calculated to expose the true character and designs of slaveholders. But it is far more potent to see the man, and hear him, in his clear, manly, straight-forward way, speak of slavery as he experienced it, and as he saw it in others. Those who have read his Narrative can scarce fail to desire to see the man, thus kidnapped and tortured in body and soul, for twelve years, and to hear his story from his own lips.

I heard him relate his experience in the Meionnon,[3] on the evening of the 15th, and last evening; in a private social circle. To-morrow evening he is to lecture in the Bethel on Commercial street. But he should have an opportunity to tell his experience in the country towns and villages. I understand that he intends to be at Worcester, at the Non-Resistance Convention. Cannot arrangements be made for him to relate what he has felt, seen and heard in the land of whips and chains, in the towns and villages of Massachusetts?

† *The Liberator*, Mar. 23, 1855. Henry Clark Wright (1797–1870) was a fervent abolitionist.
1. Abolitionist crusader William Lloyd Garrison (1805–1879) began publishing *The Liberator* in 1831. It became the country's longest-running antislavery newspaper, ending publication after the close of the Civil War in 1865.
2. Northup was kidnapped in 1841, not 1840.
3. This should be Melonaon, according to Northup biographer David Fiske.

His two kidnappers are now in prison, at Ballston, N. Y., awaiting their trial in May, before the Supreme Court of New York. They own to the deed, but plead exemption from guilt and punishment on the ground that the suit was not brought against them within three years—the time fixed by law—after the deed was done. A strange plea of innocence that! Who was to prosecute them? Their victim was being flogged and worked 1200 miles from the scene of their outrage, where to assert that he was a free citizen of New York exposed him to the merciless lash, and where the word and oath of a black man are never received against a white man. Under such circumstances, his kidnappers plead innocence and exemption from punishment, because he did not arrest them within three years after they sold him! Will the people of New York allow that plea?

What is this Union to Solomon Northup? Literally a confederacy of kidnappers. Where is the Church or political party that will refuse to open the way to give this victim of slavery a hearing, and repay him for the suffering this Union has inflicted on him? But there are 4,000,000 of kidnapped men, women and children still under the *American* lash. Who will help to redeem them, and pay for their sufferings? WHO CAN?

HENRY C. WRIGHT.
Boston, March 20, 1855.

SUPREME COURT OF NEW YORK

The People vs. Alexander Merrill and Joseph Russell[†]

Essex General Term. July, 1855.
C. L. *Allen,* James and *Bockes, Justices.*

THE PEOPLE vs. ALEXANDER MERRILL AND JOSEPH RUSSELL.

A state has no jurisdiction of crimes committed beyond its territorial limits.

Every statute is presumed to be enacted with reference to the local jurisdiction of the legislature of each state.

Section 32 of 2 R. S. 665, which provides for the punishment, as for a felony, of every person who shall sell, or in any manner transfer, for any term, the services or labor of any black, mulatto

† From *Reports of Decisions in Criminal Cases Made at Term, in Chambers, and in the Courts of Oyer and Terminer of the State of New York,* compiled by Amasa J. Parker, Vol. II (Albany, NY: Banks, Gould, and Co., 1856), pp. 590–605. Unless noted, misspellings have been left uncorrected to avoid distortion.

or other person of color, who shall have been forcibly taken, inveigled or kidnapped from this state to any other state, place or country is not applicable to a sale or transfer made in another state of a black inveigled in this state.

To give to it a broader construction, and make it applicable to a sale or transfer made in another state, would make it repugnant to the constitution of the United States, (amendment, art. 6) which delares that in criminal prosecutions, the accused shall enjoy the right to a speedy and public trial by an impartial jury *of the state and district wherein the crime shall have been committed*, and also to art. 4, sec. 2 of the constitution of the United States, which declares that the citizens of each state shall be entitled to all the immunities of the citizens of the several states; and provides that a person charged in any state with treason, or felony, or other crime, who shall flee from justice, or shall be found in another state, shall, on demand of the executive authority of the state from which he fled, be delivered up to be removed to the state having jurisdiction of the crime.

Forms of an indictment for kidnapping, with intent to sell, under sec. 28 of 2 R. S. 664 and of an indictment for inveigling a person of color and selling him as a slave under section 32,— and of demurrer and joinder in demurrer.

This was a writ of error to the Saratoga Oyer and Terminer, in which court the defendants were tried on the following indictment:

SARATOGA COUNTY, ss. *Be it remembered:* That at a court of General Sessions, holden at the court house, in the village of Ballston Spa, in and for the county of Saratoga, on the 28th day of August, 1854, before John A. Corey, county judge of the county of Saratoga, David Maxwell and Abram Sickler, justices of the peace for sessions, in and for said county, and James W. Horton, clerk:

It is presented upon the oaths of the jurors, of the people of the state of New York, in and for the body of the county aforesaid, good and lawful men of the county aforesaid, then and there sworn and charged to inquire for the said people, for the body of the county aforesaid:—

First.—That Alexander Merrill and Joseph Russell, late of the town of Saratoga Springs, in the county of Saratoga aforesaid, on or about the tenth day of March, in the year of our Lord one thousand eight hundred and forty-one, with force and arms, at the said town of Saratoga Springs, in the county of Saratoga aforesaid, without lawful authority, one Solomon Northup, he, the said Solomon Northup, there living a free negro and a citizen of the state of New York, and in the peace of God and the people of said state, then and there being, did unlawfully and feloniously inveigle and kidnap with intent, him, the said Samuel Northup, unlawfully and feloniously against his will and without his consent, to cause to be sold as a slave. And him, the said Solomon Northup, unlawfully and feloniously and against his will, did sell as a slave, against the statute in such case made and provided, and against the peace of the people of the state of New York, and their dignity, and the jurors aforesaid, upon their oaths aforesaid, do further present: that from the time the said Alexander Merrill and Joseph Russell, had so inveigled and kidnapped the said Solomon Northup, to wit: the tenth day of March, 1841, during and until the first day of July, 1854, they, the said Alexander Merrill and Joseph Russell, have not been the inhabitants of the state of New York.

Second.—And the jurors aforesaid, upon their oaths aforesaid, do further present:

That the said Alexander Merrill and Joseph Russell, late of the town of Saratoga Springs, in the county of Saratoga aforesaid, afterwards, to wit: on the said tenth day of March, in the year of our Lord one thousand eight hundred and forty-one, with force and arms, at the said town of Saratoga Springs, in the county of Saratoga aforesaid, without lawful authority, one Solomon Northup, he, the said Solomon Northup, then being a free negro and a citizen of the state of New York, and in the peace of God and of the people of the said state, then and there being, did unlawfully and feloniously inveigle to accompany them, the said Alexander Merrill and Joseph Russell, to the District of Columbia, with intent unlawfully and feloniously to cause the said Solomon Northup to be sold as a slave; and him, the said Solomon Northup, did then and there without his consent sell as a slave, to the great damage of the said Solomon Northup, against the statute in such case made and provided, and against the peace of the people of the state of New York and their dignity.

And the jurors aforesaid, upon their oaths aforesaid, do further present:

That from the time the said Alexander Merrill and Joseph Russell had inveigled the said Solomon Northup, and him, the said Solomon Northup, sold as a slave aforesaid, to wit: the tenth day of March, 1841, during and until the first day of July, 1854, they, the said Alexander Merrill and Joseph Russell, were not usually resident within the state of New York.

Third.—And the jurors aforesaid, upon their oaths aforesaid, do further present:

That heretofore, to wit: on the tenth day of March, in the year of our Lord one thousand eight hundred and forty-one, at the town of Saratoga Springs, in the county of Saratoga aforesaid, one Solomon Northup, who was then a free negro and an inhabitant of the state of New York, was unlawfully and feloniously and without lawful authority, inveigled from this state to the city of Washington, in the district of Columbia, by the above mentioned Alexander Merrill and Joseph Russell. That the said Alexander Merrill and Joseph Russell, late of the said town of Saratoga Springs, in the said county of Saratoga, afterwards, to wit: on or about the first day of January, in the year of our Lord one thousand eight hundred and fifty-three, with force and arms, at the said city of Washington, unlawfully and feloniously sold and transferred the services and labor convicted of the said Solomon Northup, without his consent, to some person or persons to the jurors aforesaid unknown, for a term to the jurors aforesaid unknown, to the great damage of the said Solomon Northup, and against the statute in such case made and provided, and against the peace of the people of the state of New York, and their dignity.

Fourth.—And the jurors aforesaid, upon their oaths aforesaid, do further present:

That Alexander Merrill and Joseph Russell, late of the town of Saratoga Springs, in the county of Saratoga aforesaid, afterwards, to wit: on or about the first day of January, in the year of our Lord one thousand eight hundred and fifty-three, with force and arms, at the said town of Saratoga Springs, in the county of Saratoga aforesaid, without lawful authority, one Solomon Northup, then being a free negro and an inhabitant of the state of New York, and in the peace of God and of the people of the state of New York, then and there being, did unlawfully and feloniously inveigle from the state of New York to the city of Washington, in the District of Columbia, with intent, then and there, to cause the said Solomon Northup to be sold as a slave. And the said Alexander Merrill and Joseph Russell, him, the said Solomon Northup, did, then and there, with force and arms, unlawfully and feloniously sell as a slave to some person or persons to the jurors aforesaid unknown, to the great damage of him, the said Solomon Northup; against the statute in such case made and provided, and against the peace of the people of the state of New York, and their dignity.

To the first count the defendants pleaded not guilty.

To the second count the defendants demurred as follows:

And the said Alexander Merrill and Joseph Russell in their own proper persons, come into court here, having heard the second count of the said indictment read and say:

That the said count and the matters therein contained, in manner and form as the same are above stated and set forth, are not sufficient in law, and that the said Alexander Merrill and Joseph Russell are not bound by the law of the land to answer the same, and this they are ready to verify; wherefore, for want of a sufficient indictment in this behalf, the said Alexander Merrill and Joseph Russell pray judgment, and that by the court they may be dismissed and discharged from the said premises in the said second count specified."

Similar demurrers were interposed to the third and fourth counts. The public prosecutor joined in demurrer as follows;

And William T. Odell, district attorney of Saratoga county, who prosecutes for the people of the state of New York in this behalf, saith:

"That the said second count in the said indictment, and the matters therein contained in manner and form as the same are above stated and set forth, are sufficient in law to compel the said Alexander Merrill and Joseph Russell to answer the same; and the said William T. Odell, who prosecutes as aforesaid, is ready to verify and prove the same as the court here shall direct and award; therefore, inasmuch as the said Alexander Merrill and Joseph Russell have not answered to the said count in the said indictment, nor hitherto in any manner denied the same, the said William T. Odell, for the said people, prays judgment on the said count, and that the said Alexander Merrill and Joseph Russell may be convicted of the premises in the said count specified."

Similar joinders were put in to the other demurrers. Judgment upon the demurrers to the second, third and fourth counts was given for the defendants, whereupon a writ of error was prosecuted by the district attorney to this court.

W. T. Odell (District Attorney) for the people.

Beach, Cochrane and *Wait*, for defendants.

By the Court, C. L. ALLEN, J.—There is no objection to the count under the thirtieth section, and to this count the defendants pleaded not guilty. That section enacts, that any person the felony there declared, shall, upon conviction, be punished by imprisonment in a state prison not exceeding ten years. The offence there created and declared, is one arising upon the *intent* of the party *formed in this state,* and which constitutes the crime committed within the state, and to punish which, on conviction, the tribunals of the state have exclusive and perfect jurisdiction. The duelling act, so called, (2 *R. S.* 686,) provides for the punishment of those who shall thereafter fight a duel within the state, declaring the offence to be a felony; and then follows the fifth section against the same act, declaring, that if any inhabitant of the state shall leave the same for the purpose of eluding the operation of its provisions, *with the intent* of giving or receiving any challenge therein prohibited, or of aiding or abetting in giving or receiving such challenge, and shall give or receive any such challenge or shall aid or abet in giving and receiving the same without the state, he shall be deemed as guilty, *and shall be subject to the like punishment as if the offence had been committed within this state.*

Here, again, the *intent conceived* in this state, was made to constitute
the crime, the giving and receiving the challenge *without* the state
being made evidence of *such* intent;—and the concluding part of
the section declaring that *the punishment*, upon conviction of such
intent, shall be the same *as if the offence had been committed within
the state*, was a legislative construction or *adjudication*, if proper so to
speak, that if the act were committed *without* the state, unaccom-
panied by the intent *conceived* by the *inhabitant* of the state *before
leaving it*, our courts would have no jurisdiction over it.

But the thirty-fourth section of the act under which the objection-
able counts in this case were framed, is somewhat broader in its
terms as to assertion of jurisdiction than the section of the duelling
act just adverted to. It declares that "every person who shall sell, or
in any manner transfer, for any term, the services or labor of any
black, mulatto, or other person of color, *who shall have been forcibly
taken, inveigled or kidnapped* from this state, to any other state,
place or country, shall, upon conviction, be punished by imprisonment in a state prison not exceeding ten years, or in a county jail
not exceeding one year, or by a fine not exceeding $1,000, or by both
such fine or imprisonment."

It must be presumed, in construing this section, that the intention of the legislature was to confine the courts of the state, to the
offences or felonies over which it had jurisdiction, and to them
alone. It can not be pretended or assumed that a state has jurisdiction over crimes committed beyond its territorial limits. The first
section of the 2 R. S., 697, (4 *ed.* 881,) declares that the several courts
of justice organized under the constitution and laws of this state,
possess the sole and exclusive jurisdiction of trying and punishing
in the manner prescribed by law, all persons for offences and crimes
committed *within the boundaries of this state*, and excepting only
such as are exclusively cognizable by the courts deriving their jurisdiction under the laws and constitution of the United States. This
enactment is in conformity to the law as always understood from
the earliest period. (*Vattel's Law of Nations*, 108, Story's *Conflict of
Laws*, 516, 518, 619, *et seq.*)

It was early adjudicated that our courts had no jurisdiction over
offences committed in other states. In the case of *The People v.
Wrights*, (2 *Caines' R.*, 213,) the defendants were in custody of the
sheriff on heavy civil process, and while thus in custody a warrant
was issued upon an indictment against them found in Massachusetts for a crime committed there. The court refused to comit them,
saying they had no jurisdiction—and that the constitution pointed
out the mode by which offenders could be claimed by a foreign
state. The case of *The People v. Gardiner*, (2 *J. R.*, 477,) was one
where the prisoner was indicted and convicted of felony at the

General Sessions, in Washington county, for stealing a horse. It turned out in evidence that the original taking was in Vermont, but that the prisoner was arrested in Washington county with the horse in his possession. The court decided that the prisoner could not be tried for the offence in this state, the original taking having been without its jurisdiction, and that the offence did not continue and accompany the possession of the thing stolen, as it did when property was stolen in one county in the state, and the thief was found in another county with the stolen property in his possession. In *The People v. Schenck* (2 *J. R.*, 479,) the prisoner was discharged because it turned out that the gun, which he was charged with stealing, was taken in New Jersey, and brought into New York, and there offered for sale by him. But the court caused him to be detained in custody for thirteen weeks to enable the executive of New Jersey to apply for his delivery to the proper officers of that state It is not improbable that these decisions, particularly the two latter, somewhat aided in the enactment, (2 *R. S.*, 698, § 4,) by which it is declared that "every person who shall feloniously steal the property of another, in any other state or country, and shall bring the same into this state, may be convicted and punished in the same manner as if such larceny had been committed in this state;" and in every such case, such larceny may be charged to have been committed in any town or city into, or through which, such stolen property shall have been brought."

The case of the *People agt. Burke*, (11 *Wend.* 129,) was decided after the passage of this section. It appeared in evidence in that case, that the prisoner, who was indicted for grand larceny, and charged with having stolen money in the town of Gates, in the county of Monroe, stole the money in Upper Canada and came into Gates, where a part of the stolen money was found in his possession. The case, as was correctly remarked by the Chief Justice, Savage, came precisely within the statute, which was, in his opinion, constitutional, and was not justly liable to the objection, that the legislature undertook to punish offences committed against another government. Why? Because it was not the larceny in Canada which the court of this state undertook to punish, but that committed in the state of New York, in every place into which the stolen property had been brought. That the statute was only recognizing the common law, (*Sec.* 1. *Ch. Crim. Law, p.* 179; 13 *Coke*, 53,) by which the possession of stolen property, in contemplation of law, remains in the owner, and the thief is guilty of theft in every place into which he carries the stolen goods.

The offence is committed in this state by bringing the stolen property into it; "for being in possession of the stolen property;" *animo furandi*. The statute was likened to that for punishing persons having in their possession forged bank notes. "No one ever doubted," remarks the learned judge, "the propriety of a conviction if it appealed (as it generally does in such cases,) that the notes were actually forged in Canada. The offence is complete in this state by having them in *possession with intent to pass them.*" So in the statute we are now considering, inveigling or enticing a colored man, in this state, out of its limits, with *intent* to sell him, constitutes the crime here, as before intimated.

The doctrine that a person can not be punished for a crime committed without the state, is not only not denied, but broadly admitted in the case in 11 Wend., as it was also in the cases of the *People* agt. *Sturdevant*, (23 *Wend.* 418,) and the *People* agt. *Charles*, (3 *Denio*, 212.) In both those cases the offence was complete by the publication of, or the sale of lottery tickets, *in this state*, though the lotteries in which they were sold, were authorized by the laws of other states.

The case also of the *People* agt. *Adams*, (3 *Denio*, 190,) affirms the same principles. The defendant was a resident of the state of Ohio, and in that state made and executed the false receipts and drafts by which the money was fraudulently, and by false pretences, obtained from the house in New York, the papers having been presented to the firm in New York by agents of the defendant, he having remained during the transaction in the state of Ohio.

The court held that the offence was committed where the false pretence was used, and where the money was obtained; and Beardsley, J., after a very able review of all the cases bearing upon the question, remarked, in delivering the opinion of the court, that the crime was committed in the city of New York, and not elsewhere; that the defendant, although acting through his innocent agents there, and not personally present within this state, was here in purpose and design, and acted by those agents; "*qui facit per alium facit per se.*" That the crime was perpetrated within this state, and that, therefore, our courts had an undoubted jurisdiction; that jurisdiction over the criminal necessarily followed, "*crimen trahit personam,*" and the offender should be held responsible when afterwards found within the state; and the conclusion arrived at finally, was that, although civil redress for this violation of a statute of our state would be afforded by the courts of Ohio, as well as New York, yet that the law of this state creating the offence for which the defendant was indicted, could only be enforced by its own tribunals. The judgment in this case was affirmed by the Court of Appeals, (1 *Comst. R.* 173.) The court there reiterating the averment that the crime was committed *within the state*, and through the instrumentality of the defendant though absent from it, and a resident of another state at the time. One of the court remarked, that it was a matter of little consequence under the circumstances of the case, whether the defendant owed allegiance to the state or not; that there were only two cases where the question of allegiance could have any thing to do with the criminal prosecution, one was, where the accused was charged with a breach of the duty of allegiance, as in cases of treason; and the other was, *where the government purposes to punish offences committed by its own citizens, beyond the territorial limits of the state*, almost exactly defining and deciding, in my judgment, the question in the case now under consideration. The same doctrine is recognized in Massachusetts, as well as in this state. (2 *Mass. R.* 132, 134; 13 *Mass.* 4,) and also in Pennsylvania, (5 *Bin.* 617.)

Thus it will be seen, that the several cases above referred to, uniformly agree, that the several offences considered in them were committed *in this state*, and that therefore, our courts had jurisdiction over them, and over the persons committing them, when found within the state; and that they all admit, that the courts could have had no jurisdiction, if those offences had been perpetrated without the limits of the state. "The different states," it has been truly remarked, by an eminent judge, "are altogether as independent of each other, in point of jurisdiction, as any two nations," and an offence committed in one state, can not be tried in another.

The precedents and authorities in England, cited by the counsel for the prosecution, all grew out of special statutes of that realm. As has been already remarked, by the common law, offences were local, and could only be tried in the county where committed. (*See* 1 *Ch. Crim. Law*, 150, 177, 179.) The several acts of parliament are there cited and commented upon which provide for the trial in one county of certain offences committed in another. Under the statute of 33 Henry VIII, c. 23, arose the case of *Ney* agt. *Sawyer*, (61 *c. L. R.* 100,) cited by the counsel on both sides, on the argument of this demurrer; it was held in that case that a British subject was triable in that country for the murder of another British subject, committed on land within the territory of a foreign independent kingdom. The argument in that case, in support of the jurisdiction was the same that is urged here; that there is a mutual contract between the government and its citizens; that the citizen is bound to yield obedience to the laws, and that the government is bound to protect the citizen, and the additional argument in the case in England, was derived from the preamble of the act of Henry VIII, that persons guilty of murder or manslaughter, committed out of the realm, and not upon the high seas, might, without the remedy afforded by the act, escape punishment. It is to be observed, in passing, that the statute under which this conviction was had, was repealed by that of 9 Geo. IV, c. 31, and other provisions instituted in its stead. The counsel for the people in this case, while he admits that a similar jurisdiction to that which he claims here, was derived in England by special statute, contends that our statute is sufficiently broad to sustain the counts demurred to.

I have already intimated that every statute is presumed to be enacted with reference to the local jurisdiction of the legislature of each state. The section is very general.

"*Every person* who shall sell *or in any manner transfer the services* of any black, who *shall have been* forcibly taken, inveigled or kidnapped from this state to any other state, place or country, shall, upon conviction, be punished." It does not confine the offence to persons who shall be residents of the state at the time of the perpetration of it, nor does it confine its commission against citizens of the state alone, for the protection of which it is supposed to be intended to provide. The phraseology, however, is like that of most, if not all the other sections and statutes in relation to crimes and misdemeanors For instance, the 29th section of the act, (2 *R. S.* 664,) to punish for *mayhem*, uses the same general language, when it declares that *every person*, who from premeditated design, shall cut off or disable any limb or member, shall, upon conviction, be punished by imprisonment in a state prison; and so the statutes respecting murder and manslaughter, and the accessories thereto, are equally general in their phraseology. Yet no one can contend that a citizen of this state, who is guilty of the murder of another citizen in the state of New Jersey, can be tried for that crime in this state. The district attorney has indeed put forth the averment, that if an *alien* should be guilty of mayhem upon a citizen of the state, beyond its territorial limits, and the courts had obtained jurisdiction of his person, by his voluntarily coming within the state, he could be tried and punished; but the authority which he cites (*Story's Conflict of Laws*, § 5, *p.* 625, 626) does not support his position. Story remarks, in a note to one of the sections quoted, that "the more common usage in modern times is to remand the criminal to the country or state where the crime was committed, the practice of most countries being to surrender up fugitives from justice, who escape into their territories, and seek an asylum from punishment." It may, therefore, be argued that the section is to be limited in its application to a sale within the state, and the description "who shall have been forcibly taken," &c, is referable to the time of indictment and trial, and not to the time of sale; and that the offence probably aimed at by the legislature, was a sale within the state, with intent forcibly to remove; and it might refer to removing and selling afterwards. At all events, whatever may have been the doctrine in England under their special statutes, our courts are governed by the common law in our own state, and by comparing all those statutes together, it is evident that their jurisdiction is limited to offences within the state; (2 *R. S.*, *4th ed.*, *p.* 881; 1 *Kent Com.*, *note R*) and the cases cited and commented on above, show what offences shall be considered as having been committed in the state, and do not include the one embraced in the counts demurred to in this case.

It is argued that there is an obvious necessity for the power of the state to pass the section which it is insisted supports these counts. That the state can not protect its citizens without it; that the state must have such power and right. To this, it may be answered:

First. That this state, as a sovereign and independent member of the confederacy, can not protect its citizens beyond its own territorial limits.

Suppose a citizen is imprisoned in Europe, or in Cuba, to whom is he to apply for protection? Undoubtedly to the general government. The right to arrest and try offences out of the state, is founded upon its duty and power to protect; and it can not protect beyond its boundaries. The doctrine, therefore, can hardly be said to apply to the individual states, but to the government of the union. If an individual passes the boundaries of his own state, and enters another, he retains his rights and high character as an American citizen, but he subjects himself, at the same time, to the laws of the state to which he removes or in which he abides. The great inquiry when the general government interferes in behalf of this citizen, is whether his personal rights have been violated, and whether he has or not, committed an offence against the laws of the government which is assuming to punish him. If he has, he is left subject to the laws, and can obtain no further redress.

Again, this argument may be answered, secondly, by remarking that the section is general, and not confined to the punishment of or protection of residents within the state. It embraces *every person* who shall sell any black, who may have been *forcibly taken or inveigled* from the state, by another, without the knowledge of the seller, who may be doing an act entirely consistent with and in obedience to the laws of the state in which he makes the sale. This could never be tolerated, and was never intended. The conclusion is this, that the legislature intended to provide against kidnapping; that they created an offence cognizable by the laws, when they enacted the 31st section, declaring that if any person should inveigle a person of color out of the *state* with *intent* to sell and dispose of him as a slave, it should be a felony. The actual sale, or attempt to sell, out of the state, would undoubtedly be evidence of the felonious intent, and would in all courts be so received; conviction would probably follow, and the whole object of the statute be fully answered by the infliction of deserved punishment upon the culprit.

Second. But whatever construction we give to this statute, and if it is indeed to be considered as broad and comprehensive in its terms, as is contended for by the counsel for the people, it is then, in my judgment, repugnant to the constitution of the United States.

The 6th article of the amendments to that instrument, declares that in all criminal prosecutions, the accused shall enjoy the right to a speedy and public trial by an impartial jury, *of the state and district wherein the crime shall have been committed.*

The penal acts of one state can have no operation in another state. The courts of this state, have no power to enforce here the criminal laws of another state. Here, laws are local, and affect nothing more than they can reach. (*Story's Conflict of Laws*, 516, 517; *Sears*, 619, 620, 621; 14 *J. R.* 338, 340; *Taylor N. C. R.* 65.)

It is also not in accordance with the 2d section of the 4th article of the same constitution. That declares that the citizens of each shall be entitled to all the immunities of the citizens in the several states, and provides that a person charged in any state with treason or felony or other crime, who shall flee from justice, or shall be found in another state, shall, on demand of the executive authority of the state from which he fled, be delivered up to be removed to the state having jurisdiction of the crime. The third and fourth counts of the indictment charge substantially that Northup, on the 10th day of March, 1841, was a free negro, and inhabitant of the state of New York; that he was on that day, unlawfully and feloniously, and without lawful authority, inveigled from this state to the city of Washington, in the District of Columbia, by the defendants, and that they, on the first day of January, 1853, at the city of Washington, unlawfully and feloniously sold him as a slave. Now the act of selling was a lawful one in the District of Columbia, for congress, though often invoked so to do, have not assumed to prohibit the sale of slaves in that district. The defendants therefore had the right to sell, by the laws of the district, and for that act alone were not punishable there. Suppose any other person, who had not participated at all in enticing Northup from this state, had found him at Washington, and claimed and sold him there, could he have been indicted and tried here, if caught, for such sale? Undoubtedly not. And yet the section, if the construction is given to it which is contended for here, includes just such a case. Could such a person when indicted, have been demanded here as a fugitive from justice, under the 2d subdivision of article four? There is but one reply, it appears to me, that can properly be given to these questions. It is no answer to say that the persons selling were guilty of inveigling or kidnapping; that is another distinct offence, and is provided for by the 30th section.

The inveigling with *intent* to sell there constitutes the crime, and is properly and clearly punishable as already shown. It is the sale alone, for which the defendants are indicted, under the counts we are now considering, and that sale in a district where it was perfectly lawful.

It can not be said that the constitution of the United States is not operative upon a case of this character. It is the supreme law of the land, and binding upon all states and upon all state courts. It is insisted that the state is an independent sovereignty in every thing except what is granted to the United States by the articles of confederation, and provided for by the constitution. This may be conceded, and yet that instrument may be binding in this particular case; our statute coming in conflict with two of its particular provisions. The constitution was intended to be binding, as it regards the rights of the citizens of the several states, upon the people of the whole union. It was never intended that a legislature should violate state comity, or national rights, as the section in question does, by assuming to punish as a felony, a sale of property in a state or district where the right exists, by the laws of the locality, to make such sale; and when the seller may have no knowledge whatever of the forcible abduction from the state which claims to punish him.

It can not be seriously, at all events, contended, in my judgment, that one selling a slave in a foreign state, where it is lawful, can be held criminally responsible for the act of another, in removing such slave from the state without any knowledge of such removal. "Every man shall answer for his own sins," is a correct maxim in morals, as well as law, and no legislative body possesses the power, in my judgment, to alter it.

I am happy, in thus feeling myself required to come to the conclusion that the judgment in this case must be affirmed, that the defendants, if guilty, are not to escape trial and conviction. The 30th section makes ample provision, within constitutional limits, for their punishment, and if convicted, under the first count, which is framed under that section, the whole object of the law will be answered, state sovereignty will be maintained, the rights of the citizens protected, and no principle will be violated.

No state can ask more than this, and no wise legislature will ever be disposed to grant it.

Judgment of the Oyer and Terminer should be affirmed.

DAILY SARATOGIAN

The Solomon Northrup Case[†]

—*The Sol. Northrup Case.*—The *Tribune* of this morning says that the Court of Appeals has overruled the demurrer to the indictment against Merrill and Russell, for abducting Solomon Northrup, and that the case is remanded back to this county for

---

† *Daily Saratogian* (NY), July 11, 1856. Unless noted, misspellings have been left uncorrected to avoid distortion.

trial. They will, therefore, probably be tried in September, if they choose to stand trial.

BALLSTON JOURNAL

Court Proceedings[†]

* * *

The People agst Henry Merrill and Joseph Russell, under an indictment for kidnapping Solmon Northup. Case discharged.

DAILY PICAYUNE

Letter from Mississippi[‡]

[Special Correspondence of the Picayune.]
WASHINGTON, MISS., *May* 20, 1857.

Eds. Pic.—I met with many anxious inquirers on the subject of hedging and of pasture and meadow of Bermuda grass, during my late ride from Alexandria to the mouth of Red River: and that, notwithstanding all that has been published on this subject, I promised additional information through the columns of the Pic. So here goes:

. . . I was strongly urged to take contracts to hedge several plantations during the coming fall; and may perhaps do so. Few seemed to understand what would be required of the party owning the plantation or property to be hedged. Whether they plant for themselves, or another does it on contract, the hedge-row to be planted next fall should be thoroughly and deeply broken up during the summer, removing everything in the shape of tree, bush or vine, and harrowing well: and that to the width of six feet *at least*, and better if from eight to ten feet. It should then be ploughed over, ridging towards the middle; when it may be planted in cow peas, tended and kept clean. When the pea vine is removed, it should again be ploughed over, ridging to the middle, so as to insure yet more perfect drainage. The hedge is then planted by the contractor, during from first of October to middle of February. And it is well to give him any farther aid he may want, in the more thorough preparation of the hedge-row, as it would be after labor saved. The planter or

---

† *Ballston Journal* (NY), May 26, 1857. Unless noted, misspellings have been left uncorrected to avoid distortion.
‡ *Daily Picayune* (LA), May 27, 1857. Unless noted, misspellings have been left uncorrected to avoid distortion.

owner of the land must tend the hedge precisely as he does a row or
rows of cotton, keeping it clean and the ground well stirred. In the
fall the contractor again takes it in hand, pruning properly, filling
up missing places, &c. And again the hedge must be tended as
before. The second fall the contractor brings the young hedge into
shape, and leaves it in proper condition, with instructions for its
after treatment, surrendering it to the owner. For all this he charges
his so much per rod or mile. . . .

During my cruise in that bayou region, I first met with that precious production, entitled "Solomon Northup, or twelve years a
slave." The copy I saw had evidently done good service; having been
loaned from hand to hand, to those who wished to read it, so as to
avoid buying more copies. A good idea with such a book. The scene
is laid in that region—on Bayou Rouge. I found that much of Solomon or Platt's account of himself was true, that he was no doubt a
native of New York and free. But, it is also clear, that Solomon was
one of those cute Yankee niggers who permit themselves to be sold
occasionally, pocketing half the proceeds, and then claiming and
proving their freedom, under the plea of having been kidnapped.
Solomon was not so wise as his name would indicate, and allowed
himself to be thus sold once too often. He is spoken of on the bayou
as a very decent and generally well behaved negro. And, as in "Uncle
Tom's Cabin," just enough of truth has been worked up, to give the
abundance of lies a *vraisemblance*,[1] it is evident that some most
unprincipled scoundrel, possessed of considerable ability as a cross-
examiner and writer, has led the negro on, and has worked up his
simple tale in the most plausible manner, without the slightest reference to actual truth. For instance, he speaks of a girl Patsy, as having
been most cruelly punished at the instigation of her mistress—cut
most fearfully. Master Solomon's own gallantries lead the poor girl
repeatedly into trouble, it seems. But I had the assurance of the resident physician, whose statement no one would pretend to doubt, that
six or twelve months before Solomon's removal, and long after the
time that he pretends these severe punishments were given, he had
occasion to cup[2] this girl, and found her back without a scar. What
a consummate and unprincipled scoundrel must be he who could
work up such a book as that, introducing as he has the names of
respectable and excellent families.

But again I must close.
Yours &c.,   T. A.

1. *Vraisemblance* is the French word for verisimilitude, meant to convey having the
appearance or likelihood of truth.
2. "Cup" in this sense refers to the physician's practice of placing a cup on the back of a
patient—in this case, allegedly, the slave Patsey—and, with heat, creating a vacuum of
air that would relieve a boil or other skin abscess by pulling the blood to the surface.

P.S. By the way, I have before me three requests to aid the writers in inducing practical market gardeners to go to three different growing towns in the South, and establish market gardens. The parties applying, have all negroes and land, and propose as I understand them, to join with the gardeners in the business, or otherwise aid them. To quote one from Camden, Ouachita county, Ark., dated 8th May, inst.: "The growing population of our little city is such, I think, as would pay a good kitchen gardener. If you could send me a kitchen gardener, I think I could build up a market for a large quantity of vegetables. I hardly know what proposal to make a gardener; but if you know of one that you would make a proposition to, to come here, you would add, &c., &c."

Men who feel themselves competent, and would like to attempt a thing of the kind, may communicate with me. There are such openings near all of our Southern towns of any size, and for market and dairy farms. The great difficulty is, that the parties must either own labor of their own, or be connected in the business with some one that can supply the requisite labor. To hire it, or to rely upon white labor, will be found alike unprofitable.

THE FREE PRESS

[Merrill and Russell Indictment][†]

The *Saratoga Press* (Republican) in reply to inquiries of the Albany Evening *Journal*, in regard to the *nolle prosequi*[1] entered in the case of Merrill and Russell, the alleged kid-nappers of Sol. Northup, at the last Oyer and Terminer, says: "We would answer by saying that since the indictment was found, the District Attorney was placed in possession of facts that whilst proving their guilt in a measure, would prevent a conviction. To speak more plainly, it is more than suspected that Sol Northup was an accomplice in the sale, calculating to slip away and share the spoils, but that the purchaser was too sharp for him, and instead of getting the cash he got something else."

---

† *The Free Press* (Glens Falls, NY), June 13, 1857. Misspellings have been left uncorrected to avoid distortion.
1. *Nolle prosequi* is a legal term, derived from Latin for "to not wish to pursue." Prosecutors enter it in criminal matters to signal their unwillingness to prosecute.

WILLIAM COOPER NELL

The Taney Hunt Against Colored Americans[†]

We hazard nothing by asserting, at the outset, that ninety-nine per cent. of the outrages daily committed against freedom, including the indignities heaped upon the unoffending colored man in these United States, are directly or indirectly the work of those connected with the Administration party—and all, too, in the name of American Democracy.

The infamous decision of Judge Taney,[1] that colored men have no rights that white men are bound to respect, is already acknowledged as the key-note to which these democratic hunters of men—

'Priests, warriors and statesmen, from Georgia to Maine,
Are mounting the saddle and grasping the rein;
Right merrily hunting the black man, whose sin
Is the curl of his hair and the hue of his skin.'

The first blast came from Rhode Island, where, at the Gloucester elections, colored citizens were driven from the ballot-box. To be sure, since then, the city of Providence has, by political chance—not by intent—elected a colored man as Warden—and his fulfillment of the official duties thereby imposed has done something to offset, and perhaps to rightly settle, the pending question of Rhode Island colored citizenship.

In Maine a colored man has recently been refused, by the authorities at Bath, his customary license as skipper of a fishing vessel. He was accompanied by the owner when the application was made, but it availed nothing. King Slavery is on the throne.

The New York Legislature last year advanced a step in securing equal suffrage to colored citizens, and unless democratic wire-pulling prevails, the right so long withheld will soon be conceded. But the heavy hand of proscription still presses upon them in the several departments of society, as at 'the Normal School for Girls, which had a grand exhibition a few days since at the Academy of Music, when the graduating class received their diplomas amid the cheers of an admiring crowd. Two young women, (Miss Helen Appo and Miss Elizabeth Jennings,) who passed a successful examination, were denied the privilege of appearing with their fellow-pupils, and sharing with

---

† *The Liberator*, Aug. 28, 1857. Misspellings have been left uncorrected to avoid distortion.
1. The author is here referring to *Dred Scott v. Sandford*, the controversial pro-slavery decision issued by the U.S. Supreme Court on March 6, 1857. The opinion for the Court in *Dred Scott* was written by Chief Justice Roger B. Taney (b. 1777), a Maryland native and former Attorney General and Treasury Secretary nominated to the bench by the president he had served, Andrew Jackson. Confirmed by the Senate in 1836, Taney served as Chief Justice until his death in 1864.

them the pleasures and honors of the occasion, for no reason, except that God had given them a darker complexion than that of their sisters. On this account, they were compelled to receive their diplomas in private. This fact is disgraceful to the Board of Education, and a reproach to the city which does not with one voice protest against it.'

How stands it with Solomon Northup, a colored citizen of the Empire State, as certified by His Excellency, Washington Hunt? He was kidnapped and carried into slavery, and held for twelve years, but finally found his way back to his family. 'He brought suit some time ago against his kidnappers, whom he knew, and who certainly would have fared hard under an investigation; but since the Dred Scott decision, he has been obliged to abandon all hope of bringing them to justice, because he cannot sue in the United States courts. This is democratic *equal* justice and equal rights.'[1]

Even Wisconsin, the State which has given such promise of resisting, to the limit of disunion, all Federal usurpation in Fugitive Slave Law cases, has just been disgraced by the withholding of a Notary Public's commission from a colored citizen, though signed by Governor Bashford, the Secretary of State, Colonel Jones refusing to sign it, on the pretext that the appointment was in violation of the Constitution.

In Iowa, where the people are to decide by vote whether colored men shall enjoy the elective franchise, to make it certain that they shall not, all who do not vote at all are to be considered as if they voted in the negative! If this is not the concentration of Democratic infernalism, where can it be found?

Ohio yet shoots down the fugitive who seeks her soil *en route* to freedom—enforces her black laws against voting—and also prohibits the colored citizens from equal enrolment in the State militia.

Illinois, too, horribly mangles to death a man who was trying to declare his independence from slavery, and by Judge McLean's decision in the Mitchell case, concedes the right of colored men to State citizenship, but affords no defence of their rights as United States citizens.

The first Republican Convention held in Minnesota declared that there should be no civil disabilities on account of color, birthplace, or religious belief; but the Convention just held for the purpose of amending the Constitution, reveals the fact, that despite all Republican pretensions, a bargain had been made with the Democrats, which culminated in retaining the word *white*, and 'crushing out' the colored man's right to vote. One member, Hon J.W. NORTH, made a manly speech in favor of equal suffrage, but their disregard of his appeal proves that, as a body, 'No North' exists among them. Southward this free Western State points her political vane.

If report speaks truly, Mr. HALL, who defended the colored man's rights in the California Legislature, has acted with the Democrats; but if consistent with himself, he will soon leave their ranks for more congenial spirits. But where will he find them, practically, if Republicans are not reliable?

In New Hampshire, where just now Buchanan Democracy is not in the ascendant, equality of militia privileges has been granted to colored men.

California is legislating to prevent colored men from becoming residents; Minnesota officials forbid them the exercise of the right of pre-emption, and Free State men in Kansas deny him a constitutional home; while at Washington, Newfoundland dogs are being trained to carry the United States mail—a service from which colored American citizens are by express regulation prohibited. A more *dog*matic development of Democratic colorphobia the pages of history cannot furnish.

The recent 17th of June demonstration on Bunker Hill, and some associations connected therewith, suggest the grouping together a few facts and comments, historical and otherwise, in further illustration of the characteristic crowding out and 'crushing out' policy exhibited toward the cause of freedom, sacrificing white men and colored men alike on the same altar of Democratic America's 'peculiar institution.'

Swett, the early historian of Bunker Hill battle, gives a graphic account of the signal act of Peter Salem, a colored American, who shot Major Pitcairn, and thus helped essentially to turn the tide of events on that memorable day. A contribution was made in the army for the colored soldier, and he was formally presented to General Washington, with special reference to having performed this feat.

In some engravings of this battle, Salem occupies a prominent position, but in more recent editions, his figure is not to be seen—a significant, but inglorious occasion. On some bills, however, of the Monumental Bank, Charlestown, and Freeman's Bank, Boston, his presence is manifest. Yet, when Mr. Frothingham, junior editor of the *Boston Post,* publishes his version of Bunker Hill battle, no mention is made of Peter Salem and his deed, which, had he been a white man, would have been immortalized by this Democratic writer as the most gallant American of them all. But in contradistinction from Democratic abnegation of the colored man's patriotism and bravery, Hon. Edward Everett, in his oration, gave utterance to the following tribute, which, being loudly applauded, was evidently appreciated by the multitude:—

'No name adorns the shaft, but ages hence, though our alphabet may become as obscure as those which cover the monuments of Nineveh and Babylon, its uninscribed surface, on which monarchs might be proud to engrave their titles, will perpetuate the memory of the 17th of June. It is the monument of the day, of the event, of the battle of Bunker Hill, of all the brave men who shared its perils—*alike* of

Prescott and Putnam and Warren, the chiefs of the day, and the *colored man, Salem,* who is reported to have shot the gallant Pitcairn as he mounted the parapet. Cold as the clods on which it rests, still as the silent heavens to which it soars, it is yet vocal, eloquent in *their individual praise.'*

In commemoration of Peter Salem, Titus Coburn, Alexander Ames, Barzillai Low, Cato Howe, and other colored Americans who performed duty on Bunker Hill, it was anticipated that a delegation, including some descendants of these colored pensioners, would have formed part of the procession from Boston to Charlestown, in the late celebration, but a combination of unlooked-for causes prevented. The colored Masons, too, but for independent obstacles, would have augmented the procession. As Gen. Warren was a Mason, and the celebration was under Masonic auspices, the whole would have been in harmony with the occasion. The banner they intended to display contained the names of the above colored men, with brief mention of their individual positions during the battle, while the reverse read as follows:—'Extract from Gen. Warren's speech, March 5th, 1772, in commemoration of the Boston Massacre: *"The voice of your father's blood cries to you from the ground: My sons, scorn to be slaves!"'*

Apropos to this extract may be noted the late news from Washington, that Joseph Warren Newcomb, the only lineal descendant and family representative of the revolutionary Warren living, has been turned out from a clerkship, because he was supposed not to recognize the nationality and divinity of slavery, as expounded by the Democratic party and Fugitive Slave Law Mason. Because he will not be a slave, the government will not employ him. And this proscription, be it remembered, was coincident with the celebration on Bunker Hill. Of what real significance are monuments erected to the dead fathers, when their living sons are ostracised for most remotely imitating the very deeds which emblazoned the name and fame of the fathers with imperishable renown? It is said that when the proposition was made to Mr. Newcomb to deny any affinity with free soil politics, he replied, 'Tell the Secretary that I will see him in the bottom of the bottomless pit before I will so degrade myself.' Answered in the spirit fit for the descendant of him who said, 'My sons, scorn to be slaves!'

Hon. Robert C. Winthrop, in his recent speech at the Musical Festival, referred to the negotiation at Ghent, where the band master, in a dilemma, had recourse to the colored servant of Mr. Clay, who whistled 'Yankee Doodle,' which being jotted down as he whistled, was then played by the orchestra, thus affording edification to the allied sovereigns. 'Whether that boy was bond or free,' continued Mr. Winthrop, 'I know not; but I think both South and North would agree that he earned his liberty, and his citizenship too, on that occasion.' Suppose, in the spirit which seemingly prompted this admission, Mr. Winthrop had, on Bunker Hill, submitted some such extract as the following, from Gen. Warren's speech in Boston, March 5th, 1772:—

'That *personal freedom is the natural right of every man*, and that property or an exclusive right to dispose of what he has honestly acquired by his own labor, necessarily arises therefrom, are truths which common sense has placed beyond the reach of contradiction. And no man or body of men can without being guilty of flagrant injustice, claim a right to dispose of the persons or acquisitions of any other men or body of men, unless it has arisen from some compact between the parties, in which it has been explicitly and freely granted.'

To be sure, Senator Mason would not have applauded these sentiments to the echo, but the liberty-loving masses would have glorified and gratefully remembered the deed, which is more than can be predicted of Mr. W's deferential tribute to the slaveholding and slave-hunting Senator.

The Senator from Georgia once threatened to call the roll of his slaves on Bunker Hill. The presence at this celebration of a Senator from Virginia, the author of the Fugitive Slave Law—the menace and the face—corroborating the predominant influence that slavery exerts over public men at the North, foreshadows what some already prophecy, that instead of Liberty being sacred, even at her shrine on Bunker Hill, this *Mason* and his accomplices may soon so subjugate white freemen that the monument may give place to the *To(o)mbs*.

But to return from this digression. The Masonic order claim to be preeminently a band of brothers, recognising, in their mystic tie, all at home or abroad, who, by grip, sign or password, give proof of initiation; and yet, as an organization, they have never, in the United States, fraternized with colored Masons. A veteran anti-slavery man, and, withal, one high in Masonic authority, informs me that Primus Hall, Boston Smith, Thomas Saunderson, and others, endeavored to obtain a charter from the Grand Lodge of Massachusetts, but did not succeed. The refusal is said to have been founded on the color of the applicants. This denial prompted them to seek a charter from England in the year 1683, through the medium of a sea captain by the name of Scott, said to have been a brother-in-law of revolutionary John Hancock, and the said charter, with Constitution, was forwarded from London, Sept. 19, 1784, and signed by Lord Howard, Earl of Effingham, (acting Grand Master under His Royal Highness, Henry Frederick, Duke of Cumberland, who was then head of the Masonic body in England), Wm. White as Secretary, and Rolland Holt, D. G. M.; and thus originated the Prince Hall Lodge,—the first colored lodge in the United States. Prince Hall and other colored Americans received their degrees in English lodges, and colored Masons visiting them to this day are always received as Brethren.

On the last 4th of July, these words were suspended across State street—'Reader, within your view is the sacred spot where fell the first martyrs in the cause of American Independence.' How many passers-by were conscious that among that pioneer party of American revolutionists, Crispus Attucks, a colored man, was the first to attack, and was himself the first martyr? Henry Q. Smith, of Boston, has issued a large and handsome lithograph (executed by Champney) of this scene, which gives due *color* to the occasion, by assigning Attucks his true and leading position; but J. F. Schroeder, D. D., is now publishing the life and times of Washington, with illustrations by Chappel, and in part six has an engraving of the Boston Massacre, from which Attucks has been wholly omitted. Whether any reference will be made to him in subsequent numbers, we have not now the means of judging. And yet Botta, Hewes—of tea-party reminiscence—Goodrich and other historians, in substance concur with John Adams, in his plea for the British soldiers, that 'Attucks appeared to be the hero of the night, and to lead the people;' in acknowledgment of which, he was buried with great honor from Faneuil Hall, and John Hancock, on March 5th, 1774, invoked the injured shades of the slain, including Attucks; and Judge Dawes, with a galaxy of successors—Lovell, Church, Austin, Tudor, Mason, Minot, and others—eulogised the 5th of March martyrs for thus ushering in the day which history has selected as the dawn of the American Revolution.

General Washington had none of this Democratic squeamishness about colored men and their patriotism. He not only slept under the same blanket with Primus Hall, but throughout the war, he specially rewarded the valor and integrity of many other colored soldiers; and to William Lee he left an annuity 'as a testimony of my [his][2] sense of attachment to me, and for his faithful services during the Revolutionary War.' In view of these facts, it would seem that there was a constant struggle of his better nature to do that which, neglected, has left

> —'Posterity's sad eye to run
> Along one line, with slave and Washington.'

Some one has described that to be a Republic where love of freedom and love of country, together with the execration of despotism, are predominant. In this self-styled 'model republic,' 'bright Eden-land of nations,' and 'proud home of liberty,' systematic and persistent measures are put forth to persecute and outrage one seventh of the

2. Author's note.

population, and to ignore every act performed by them which win for white men everlasting fame and honor. But let it be kept in constant remembrance by the colored American and his friends, and by them held up before the people, that some of the most signal and brilliant examples of patriotic heroism have been exhibited by colored men on every revolutionary battle-field, from Bunker Hill to Yorktown; and the military and naval records exhibit equal evidences of the colored man's valor and patriotism. Indeed, this last war was undertaken because of the impressment of three seamen, two of whom were colored—satisfactory proof, at least, that they were American citizens. And yet, with all these facts written on the page of impartial history, American democracy, now grown rabid by high judicial encouragement in the Dred Scott decision, 'though the foxes have holes, and the birds of the air have nests,' would leave us no place to lay our heads; for by their bearing are they constantly taunting colored Americans, asking—

'What right have *they* here in the home of the white,
Shadowed o'er by *our* banner of freedom and right?'

If there is any remedy for these stupendous wrongs, it is to be found in the faithfulness of word and action of the true-hearted of all parties, whose exertions will be rewarded by a regenerated state of public opinion, declaring that colored American citizens have rights that all mankind are bound to respect.
Boston, August 1857.   W. C. N.[3]

THOMAS W. MacMAHON

From Cause and Contrast: An Essay on the American Crisis[†]

* * *

Here, then, is the race—or the branch of a race, rather—in whose name and behalf a terrible, unnatural, and devastating civil war has been fomented—reclaimed as they are, from the barbarism, not only of their origin and ancestors, but from that of their innate nature; and elevated, in the scales of moral and doctrinal Christianity and civilization, to a degree never known before to any equal number of their family. But for many long years this crusade of

---

3. William Cooper Nell (1816–1874), the influential, Boston-based black abolitionist and historian.
† From *Cause and Contrast: An Essay on the American Crisis* (Richmond: West & Johnson, 1862), pp. 83–87. Unless noted, misspellings have been left uncorrected.

aggression upon the constitutional rights of the South, and of revolution in the Federal Union, has been assiduously prosecuted by the politicians and intellectual classes in the abolition section of the States. Their journals teemed with malignant vilification of the South—with studied and exaggerated misrepresentation of Southern institutions, resources, and even Christianity. The family relations, the unimpeachable virtue of females, the honor and courage of brave and heroic men—all and each formed the staple theme of Northern scurrility, libel, and wilful falsehood. Popular applause greeted the labors of the infamous slanderer; and, like the informer who measures his gains by the corpses of his victims, he advanced in popular favor in proportion as he became the successful traducer of his country. Even the most respectable publishing houses became infected with this vile disease. A few years since, all meritorious or standard literature was repulsed from their presses, and negro tales and romances, written from the stand-point of Caucasian sentimental sympathy, could only hope to meet with success. Books like "Dred," "Solomon Northrup," and "Ida May," became the fashion of the day. Publishers who but recently had been bankrupt, rose to opulence, and in one instance retired from business, upon the profits of such publications.

Yet, during the continuance of this aggressive and pragmatical carnival, crime prospered; and squalid wretchedness surrounded those who were sounding the trumpet of freedom and servile insurrection in the negro's ear. Misery, drunkenness, pollution, degradation, barbarism, irreligiousness, lawlessness, and utter obliviousness of shame, virtue, manliness, Briarean and Hydra-headed, stalked forth through Anne street of Boston, and the Five Points of New York.

* * *

What, then, could have been the motive of all this agitation—of all these slanders—of all this belligerent literature? * * * [T]he negroes upon behalf of whom Mrs. Stowe and her abolition coadjutors had written, and spoken, and done so much, were already prosperous and contented, relatively civilized and christianized. If their love for this species of mankind was exemplary, all Africa, in full and primeval barbarism, and semi-civilized and degenerate Hayti, Jamaica, Guiana, were open to their zeal.

* * *

A Genealogy of Secondary
Sources, 1881–2015

PUBLISHERS' PREFACE

From Twelve Years a Slave (c. 1881)†

Slavery is now one of the institutions of the past. It is so interwoven in the history of our country, that, undesirable as a reference or recollection of this particular bygone custom may be, it is nevertheless necessary to be studied in order to form some adequate idea of our Nation's progress and growth. To take in, or to understand the exact social status of such a people in all its bearings, we can pursue no better course than to live among them, to become for a time one of them, to fall from a condition of freedom to one of bondage, to feel the scourge, to bear the marks of the brands, and the outrage of manacles. To experience all this was the misfortune of Mr. Northup; and his story, simple and artless, affords an insight and enlists a sympathy far deeper than any work of fiction which genius can produce.

It is on this account that the publishers have undertaken to issue a new edition of this work. And surely, at this time—when the exciting questions of color, of race, and of social standing are forever settled on American soil by the Magna Charta of our common rights, the Constitution—surely, now, a reprint of the story of a slave, thrilling in its details, calls for no apology. It can be taken for what it is worth—a personal narrative of personal sufferings and keenly felt and strongly resented wrongs; but, in our opinion, the individual will be lost or merged in the general interest, and the work will be regarded as a history of an institution which our political economy has now happily superseded, but which, however much its existence may be regretted, should be studied—indeed, must be studied—by every one

† From *Twelve Years a Slave: The Thrilling Story of a Free Colored Man, Kidnapped in Washington in 1841, Sold into Slavery, and after a Twelve Years' Bondage, Reclaimed by State Authority from a Cotton Plantation in Louisiana*, by S. Northup (Philadelphia: J. E. Potter and Company, 18[?]), pp. xv–xvi. In their book *Solomon Northup: The Complete Story of the Author of* Twelve Years a Slave (Praeger, 2013), David Fiske, Clifford W. Brown, Jr., and Rachel Seligman posit that this edition was published after Northup's copyright expired, likely in 1881.

whose interest in our country incites him to obtain a correct knowledge of her past existence.

And that the narrative may be the more interesting, we have made
no changes from the original; we have left unmodified every observation, changed no statement, nor tried, in a single instance, to
modernize or explain allusions which, viewed from the present, may
not be so apparent. It may be interesting for the reader to notice the
remarkable fulfillments which time has brought to the unconscious
prophecies of events, or to measure the estimate of the past with
what history has actually proven them. In any event, the flavor of a
past era must add piquancy to the enjoyment of the perusal.

GEORGE WASHINGTON WILLIAMS

From History of the Negro Race in America from 1619 to 1880†

* * *

Anti-slavery literature wrought mightily for God in its field.[1] Frederick Douglass's book, "My Bondage and My Freedom"; Bishop
Loguen's, "As a Slave and As a Freeman"; "Autobiography of a Fugitive Negro," by the Rev. Samuel Ringgold Ward; "Twenty-two Years
a Slave, and Forty Years a Freeman," by the Rev. Austin Stewart;
"Narrative of Solomon Northup," "Walker's Appeal,"—all by eminent
Negroes, exposed the true character of slavery, informed the public
mind, stimulated healthy thought, and touched the heart of two
continents with a sympathy almost divine.

But the uncounted millions of anti-slavery tracts, pamphlets,
journals, and addresses of the entire period of agitation were little
more than a paper wad compared with the solid shot "Uncle Tom's
Cabin" was to slavery. Written in vigorous English, in scintillating,
perspicuous style; adorned with gorgeous imagery, bristling with
living "facts", going to the lowest depths, mounting to the greatest
altitudes, moving with panoramic grandeur, picturing humanity
forlorn and outraged; giving forth the shrillest, most despairing
cries of the afflicted, and the sublimest strains of Christian faith;
the struggle of innocent, defenceless womanhood, the subdued sorrow of chattel-babyhood, the yearnings of fettered manhood, and
the piteous sobs of helpless old age,—made Mrs. Harriet Beecher
Stowe's "Uncle Tom's Cabin" the magnifying wonder of enlightened

---

† From History of the Negro Race in America from 1619 to 1880, vol. 2 (New York: G. P.
Putnam's Sons, 1883), pp. 59–61.
1. Judge Stroud, William Goodell, Wendell Phillips, William Jay, and hundreds of other
   white men contributed to the anti-slavery literature of the period [Williams's note].

Christendom! It pleaded the cause of the slave in twenty different languages; it engrossed the thought of philosophers, and touched the heart of youth with a strange pity for the slave. It covered audiences with the sunlight of laughter, wrapt them in sorrow, and veiled them in tears. It illustrated the power of the Gospel of Love, the gentleness of Negro character, and the powers and possibilities of the race. It was God's message to a people who had refused to listen to his anti-slavery prophets and priests; and its sad, weird, and heart-touching descriptions and dialogues restored the milk of human kindness to a million hearts that had grown callous in an age of self-seeking and robbery of the poor.

In a political and sectional sense, the "Impending Crisis," by Helper,[2] exerted a wide influence for good. It was read by merchants and politicians.

Diverse and manifold as were the methods of the friends of universal freedom, and sometimes apparently conflicting, under God no honest effort to rid the Negro and the country of the curse of slavery was lost. All these agencies, running along different lines, converged at a common centre, and aimed at a common end—the ultimate extinction of the foreign and domestic slave-trade.

*   *   *

JAMES CEPHAS DERBY

From Fifty Years among Authors, Books and Publishers[†]

*   *   *

While Mr. Seward was Governor of the State of New York, a law was enacted on his recommendation for the recovery of colored citizens of the State, kidnapped into slavery. It was under the provisions of this act, that in January, 1853, H. B. Northrup, of Washington County, N. Y., procured the liberty of Solomon, a colored man, formerly living as a member of his family, who twelve years previous had been inveigled to the City of Washington and there kidnapped and sold into slavery.

Although a freeman, Solomon was sold under the hammer by slave-traders and taken south as far as Louisiana. His whereabouts

2. White North Carolina native Hinton R. Helper (1829–1909) authored the politically charged anti-slavery book *The Impending Crisis of the South: How to Meet It* (1857), which was banned in several southern states. In 1861, President Abraham Lincoln appointed him U.S. consul in Buenos Aires, Argentina.

† From *Fifty Years among Authors, Books and Publishers* (New York: G. W. Carleton, 1884), pp. 62–63. Unless noted, misspellings have been left uncorrected to avoid distortion.

were providentially discovered and immediate measures were taken to restore him to freedom. On his return north, by the aid of his former employer, he prepared a narrative, relating to his twelve years of captivity, under the title of "Twelve Years a Slave," by Solomon Northrup.

This book was brought out by my firm, and Solomon's thrilling experiences caused quite a sensation among the reading community, the book meeting with a rapid and large sale.

*   *   *

DANIEL BARCLAY WILLIAMS

From Freedom and Progress[†]

*   *   *

The interesting and instructive literature of the colored people since emancipation constitute one of the grandest fruits of their progress. Prior to emancipation, the following works formed almost the entire literary productions of the Colored-American: Poems, by Phillis Wheatley; Light and Truth, by R. B. Lewis; Volume of Poems, by J. M. Whitfield; Volume of Poems, by D. A. Payne; Principia of Ethnology: The Origin of Races and Color, by M. R. Delaney; The Colored Patriots of the American Revolution, by W. C. Nell; Autobiography of a Fugitive Negro, by S. R. Ward; Narrative of the Life of an American Slave, My Bondage and my Freedom, by Frederick Douglass; Narrative of Solomon Northup, Twenty-two Years a Slave and Forty Years a Freeman, by Rev. Austin Stewart; and The Black Man, by Wm. Wells Brown.

*   *   *

MARION GLEASON McDOUGALL

From Fugitive Slaves, 1619–1865[‡]

§ 38. **Solomon Northup case.**—Sometimes, if they feared to enter their case in court, slave hunters could find opportunity, by watching a negro for a while, to carry out their plans through some small deception. One of the most striking of these cases is that of Solomon Northup, who has written an account of his experiences as freeman and as slave. He was born in 1808 in New York State. His father had

---

[†] From *Freedom and Progress* (Petersburg, VA: Daniel B. Williams, 1890), pp. 28–29.
[‡] From *Fugitive Slaves, 1619–1865* (Boston: Ginn & Company, 1891), pp. 37–38. Unless noted, misspellings have been left uncorrected to avoid distortion.

been made a free man by the provisions of his master's will. Thus Solomon was brought up under the influences of freedom, and knew little of slavery. After his marriage, he lived for some years in Saratoga. Here he earned a comfortable livelihood. During the day he worked about the hotels, and in the evenings he was often engaged to play the violin at parties. One day, two men, apparently managers of a travelling circus company, met him and offered him good pay if he would go with them as a violinist to Washington. He consented. Their behavior seemed to him peculiar, but he remained in their service, only to find himself one morning in a slave pen in Washington. How he got there remained always a mystery, but it is evident that he must have been drugged. Resistance was useless. He was carried South and sold to Mr. Epps, a hard master, with whom he remained for twelve years.

After he had long given up all hopes of escape, a friend was found in a Northern man who was working on the same plantation. Mr. Bass consented, though at a great risk to himself, to write some letters, telling Solomon's story to his Northern friends. The letters reached their destination, and, under the law of 1840 against kidnapping, a memorial was prepared to the Governor of New York. He became interested, and immediately sent a man South to find Northrup. After a long search, the agent was directed to Mr. Epps's plantation. Much to the disappointment of the master, who used every means to prevent his return, Solomon was identified at last, and went back to New York again a free man. Efforts were made to prosecute the kidnappers; but as sufficient evidence could not be obtained, no case was made out.

ALBERT BUSHNELL HART

From Slavery and Abolition 1831–1841[†]

* * *

For it must not be forgotten that if a slave could become free, a free negro could also become a slave, and that without fault or neglect on his own part. This reversion to slavery came about in many different methods, all acting steadily and effectively. In the first place, persons who had been set free for years and had no reason to suppose that they were anything else, might be seized upon for defects in the legal process of manumission. There were instances where successful suits were brought for the possession of families who had lived in freedom unmolested for thirty years.[1]

[†] From *Slavery and Abolition 1831–1841* (New York: Harper & Brothers, 1906), pp. 88–89, 340. Unless noted, all notes are Hart's.

1. E.g., Rhame *vs.* Ferguson and Dangerfield, in Buckingham, *Slave States*, II., 32; Adams, *Southside View*, 154.

The second method was by kidnapping, which was frequent in the north and south throughout the slavery period. One of the most striking cases, that of Peter Still,[2] was revealed in all its enormity by the return of the stolen person to Philadelphia after more than twenty years' captivity.[3] Of course, a grown man or woman thus kidnapped might find means of communicating with his friends; but Solomon Northup was in bondage twelve years before he could attract the attention of the legal authorities to his undoubted claim to freedom.[4] In the south the offence was a little more dangerous, because it was closely akin to slave stealing, which was one of the most atrocious of all crimes against slave property.

A still more common case was the sale of free negroes for their jail fees, a thing which could hardly be believed but for the accumulation of evidence. In several of the southern states a negro who incurred a fine which he could not pay might be sold as a slave. In Maryland a free negro under certain circumstances might be sold as a perpetual slave, simply for the offence of coming into the state.[5] The practice attracted great attention in the north because of the revelation in 1829 that it was steadily going on in the District of Columbia.[6] The practice of the District authorities was to arrest any colored person who could not give an account of himself, to advertise him, and, if nobody appeared to establish a claim, to sell him in order to reimburse the jailers their fees. In five cases reported the marshal had not only recovered his fees, but about three hundred dollars more. The desperate injustice of condemning a man to slavery because of a failure to prove him a slave was one of the most effective arguments of the abolitionists.

* * *

SLAVE NARRATIVES.—Many fugitives who escaped to the north told their stories, which were often put into literary form by anti-slavery friends. Such books are: Charles Stearns, *Narrative of Henry Box Brown* (1849); Frederick Douglass, *My Bondage and My Freedom* (1855); W. G. Eliot, *The Story of Archer Alexander* (1885); *Narrative of Events in the Life of William Green* (1853); *Life of J. Henson, Formerly a Slave* (1849); *Experiences of Thomas Jones, who was a Slave for Forty-Three Years* (1850); W. G. Hawkins, *Lunsford Lane* (1863); R. Hildreth, *The Slave, or Memoirs of Archy Moore* (2 vols.,

---

2. According to William Still, Peter had not actually been "kidnapped." See William Still, *The Underground Rail Road* (Philadelphia: Porter & Coates, 1872), p. 38. The editors thank David Fiske for pointing this out [Editors' note].
3. Pickard, *Kidnapped and Ransomed*, 248.
4. McDougall, *Fugitive Slaves*, §38; Chambers, *Am. Slavery and Colour*, 192.
5. Case of Ned Davis in Maryland, 1851, Chambers, *Am. Slavery and Colour*, 186–188.
6. *Debates of Congress*, 20 Cong., 2 Sess., 167, 175–187, 191; *House Reports*, 20 Cong, 2 Sess, No. 60; *Niles' Register*, XXXIV., 191; Tremain, *Slavery in District of Columbia*, 42–49.

1836); Solomon Northup, *Twelve Years a Slave, Narrative of Solomon Northup* (1853); *Narrative of the Adventures and Escape of Moses Roper* (1837); L. W. Paine, *Six Years in a Georgia Prison* (1852); Kate E. R. Pickard, *The Kidnapped and the Ransomed* [Peter Still] (1846); *Narrative of Sojourner Truth* (1850); *Narrative of Henry Watson, a Fugitive Slave* (1845); Booker T. Washington, *Up from Slavery, an Autobiography* (1901).

JOHN HERBERT NELSON

The Heroic Fugitive[†]

*   *   *

Curiously enough, of the many slave autobiographies, or biographies—for they were often "edited" by friends of the slave— all but three or four seem to be forgotten. For this neglect students of literature are easily excusable, because the narratives are seldom works of art; not so the historians, however, whose need is always for just such illuminating documents. Although filled with the most vociferous propaganda, in parts embittered and untrue, even the worst of them record as nothing else does the workaday life of the *ante-bellum* South. A reader soon learns to distinguish, in the large, the true portions from the falsified, and having done so, he finds himself confronted with pictures of slavery as it was; he discovers how both slaves and masters of the old South actually talked, dressed, carried on their occupations, amused themselves—in short, what their social background was, the world in which they moved.

In the two decades preceding the Civil War, the vogue of slave narratives was enormous. As propaganda they won thousands of friends for the Southern bondsmen, and as gripping stories they rivalled contemporary novels, some "far excelling fiction in their touching pathos." Romantic and thrilling, they interested by the sheer horror of their revelations, and they satisfied in the reading public a craving for the sensational. Needless to say, most slave narratives were hopelessly partisan, telling, except by implication, only one side of the story, and grossly overdrawing that, but what mattered far more at the time, they interested readers and won friends for the slaves.

Nothing could more clearly show their popularity than that some of them sold at all, for often they were trivial indeed. By 1850 practically any writing by or about a negro was in demand, even if he had never been a slave. The only requisites were a black skin and a grievance. Destitute blacks of both sexes energetically demanded

† From *The Negro Character in American Literature* (Lawrence, KS: Department of Journalism Press, 1926), pp. 60–63. All notes are Nelson's but have been edited.

help from the "charitable reader," who was admonished, in the name of humanity, to buy their books.[1] Northern negro preachers who had never in their lives set foot on slave soil rushed confidently into print, begging for assistance or extolling their good work.[2] Ex-slaves like Frederick Douglass, Father Henson, and Sojourner Truth found it profitable to publish more than one story of their experiences. Northern—sometimes British—"editors" came gladly to the aid of the newly arrived fugitive who wished to write his life history. Even publishers shared in the general enthusiasm: once at least a publisher imposed on his credulous public by reissuing an old story under a new title. Twenty-two years after it first appeared, the excellent narrative of Charles Ball was seized upon, condensed slightly, bound in a fiery red cover, with great wavering gilt letters staring out at the reader, and handed out to an eager public under the astonishing title, *Fifty Years in Chains*. The public was told, moreover, that the slave thus held for fifty years was still alive, and that revealing his name would make him liable to capture—this although his name had been blazoned abroad on title-pages for two decades—and whereas the brief preface intimated quite clearly that this was the first printing of the story, it had gone through at least two editions before.

It is now impossible to ascertain the number of separately published narratives, but a conservative estimate would put it at more than a hundred. This leaves out of account numerous briefer sketches which appeared in *The Liberator* and antislavery anthologies. A number of narratives, too, were published in England by fugitives escaped thither, but these may be counted among our own, for not only were they intended to sell here as in the British Isles, but their subject matter and authors were American. The narratives became common in this country about 1840, then increased steadily in number till the Civil War, after which, naturally enough, few new ones appeared.

When one comes to examine the troop of fugitives here presented, he is struck by the vivid personalities among them and their variation

1. See especially Frances H. Greene and Elleanor Eldridge, *Memoirs of Elleanor Eldridge* (Providence: B.T. Albro, 1838); Frances H. Greene and Elleanor Eldridge, *Elleanor's Second Book* (Providence: B. T. Albro, 1839); Nancy Prince, *A Narrative of the Life and Travels of Mrs. Nancy Prince* (Boston: The Author, 1850—third edition, 1856); Harriet E. Wilson, *Our Nig: or, Sketches from the life of a free Black, in a two-story white house, North, Showing that slavery's shadows fall even there* (Boston: GEO. C. Rand & Avery, 1859); and Mary W. Thompson, *Sketches of the History, Character, and Dying Testimony, of Beneficiaries of the Colored Home, in the City of New-York* (New York: John F. Trow, 1851)—the latter composed of sketches of negroes, written to aid the inmates of the Colored Home of the City of New York.
2. See Jeremiah Asher, *Incidents in the Life of the Rev. J. Asher, pastor of Shiloh (Coloured) Baptist Church, Philadelphia, U.S.* (London: Charles Gilpin, 1850); Daniel H. Peterson, *The Looking-Glass: Being a True Report and Narrative of the Life, Travels, and Labors of the Rev. Daniel H. Peterson* (New York: Wright, 1854); and more readable than either, Noah Davis, *A Narrative of the Life of Rev. Noah Davis, a Colored Man* (Baltimore: John F. Weishampel, Jr., 1859). Davis had once been a slave.

in type. Not a few of these escaped slaves show the negro at his best, with virtues almost peculiar to the race and an intelligence far above that of the usual plantation menial. Such a man was Charles Ball, such was Solomon Northup, such was old Father Henson—the original of Mrs. Stowe's Uncle Tom. Charles Ball's narrative was one of the earliest, as well as one of the most pithy, informative, and unbiased.[3] A slave for years, sold hither and yon, suffering the whip, starvation, insult, and excessive tasking, Ball could yet write of his experiences fairly and without bitterness, and this not through mere servility or obsequiousness, but because of never-failing patience and a forbearance seemingly proof against all misfortune; the whole account is in a straightforward, manly vein. Northup's performance appears still more remarkable—as nothing short of astounding, in fact.[4] This man, a free citizen of New York State, was kidnapped and sold into slavery on the notorious Red River of Louisiana. Here for twelve years he was driven, flogged, and kicked about by brutal planters until rescued by a Northern friend and restored to his family. In spite of this horrible ordeal in the South, however, he still found it possible to recount his misfortunes with fairness and justice—a feat of no small magnitude, and one of which few men, certainly few white men, would be capable. Nor was this calm and unresentful attitude the result of simplicity, for though possessing the yielding disposition of his race, Northup was nevertheless highly intelligent. The shrewd observations in the book and Northup's calm estimates make *Twelve Years a Slave* a superior and unique treatment of Southern slavery. As a historical document it is worth more than the charmingly simple and unaffected history of Father Henson, although Father Henson himself has an appeal all his own.[5] Patient, reliable, without malice, a Christian through and through, he is today far more appealing than Mrs. Stowe's martyr, and in the flesh a stronger argument against slavery than mountains of argumentative pamphlets and ethical discourses.

* * *

3. Charles Ball, *Slavery in the United States: A Narrative of the Life and Adventures of Charles Ball* (Lewistown: John W. Shugert, 1836). The book went into a second edition in 1837, and in 1858 was republished as Charles Ball, *Fifty Years in Chains; or The Life of an American Slave* (New York: H. Dayton Publishers, 1859).
4. Solomon Northup, *Twelve Years a Slave: Narrative of Solomon Northup, a Citizen of New-York* (Auburn: Derby and Miller, 1853). The work was copiously reprinted. Other narratives to be compared with Ball's and Northup's are Hannah Farnham Saywer Lee, *Memoir of Pierre Toussaint, Born a Slave in St. Domingo* (Boston: Crosby, Nicholas, and Company, 1854) and Austin Steward, *Twenty-Two Years a Slave, and Forty Years a Freeman* (Rochester: William Alling, 1857).
5. Josiah Henson, *Formerly a Slave, Now an Inhabitant of Canada, as Narrated by Himself* (Boston: Arthur D. Phelps, 1849). Henson himself wrote the account later. See Harriet Beecher Stowe, *Truth Stranger than Fiction: Father Henson's Story of His Own Life* (Boston: John P. Jewett and Company, 1858).

ULRICH B. PHILLIPS

Some Virginia Masters[†]

Many travelers made Southern tours and wrote of what they saw. Basil Hall carried a "camera lucida" by which he made some pre-photographic pictures; and using his mind's eye, which was that of a British naval captain, he found the lot of the slaves in some regards comparable to that of sailors in Her Majesty's service. Bartram, Lyell and Robert Russell went as observers of plants, rocks and weather, but made good notes of human life. Louis Tasistro was an actor on tour, and Tyrone Power likewise; but William Chambers went merely for a "change of air and scene." Paulding, Miss Martineau and Miss Bremer were professional writers, seeking something with which to employ their pens. J. S. C. Abbott was a more or less literary compiler who took ship and train and put forth a book subtitled *Impressions received during a trip to Cuba and the South*; though he might more fittingly have styled it "Impressions retained despite a trip." Philo Tower was an abolitionist who put so much plagiarism and fabrication into his account as to raise a doubt whether he ever left the closet of his New England parsonage. So the list might run much further. Olmsted and William H. Russell are among the few to be classed as expert observers. Solon Robinson, another such, is almost the only one who gave himself to the description of individual plantations; and his accounts have the merit, as compared with Olmsted's, of naming the estates to which they apply. Regrettably his writings remain as yet scattered in the periodicals to which he sent them.[1]

As a rule sojourners wrote more illuminatingly than tourists, because more intimately and with some continuity of experience. Philip Fithian, J. H. Ingraham, A. de Puy Van Buren, Emily Burke and Catherine Hopley went as teachers, Nehemiah Adams and T. D. Ozanne as preachers. Solomon Northup went as a Negro kidnaped into slavery, and wrote a vivid account of plantation life from the under side. But ex-slave narratives in general, and those of Charles Ball, Henry Box Brown and Father Henson in particular, were issued with so much abolitionist editing that as a class their authenticity is doubtful.

Many of every ilk who wrote for the press were propagandists of one cause and another, and as such they set their spectacles upon their readers' noses. And travelers' accounts as a body, while indispensable,

[†] From *Life and Labor in the Old South* (1929; rpt. Columbia: University of South Carolina Press, 2007), pp. 218–20. Reprinted by permission of the publisher.
1. They are now being assembled and edited by Herbert A. Kellar for publication by the Indiana Historical Commission.

have essential defects and shortcomings. They are jottings of strangers likely to be most impressed by the unfamiliar, and unable to distinguish what was common in the régime from what was unique in some special case; furthermore they yield mere glimpses here and there from time to time, permitting no steady view of any one's experience or life history. But a present-day student may in a sense make a tour of his own through the South of a century ago, at least a mental journey through the plantation records; and though he may not ask questions at will he may find that planters, overseers and even slaves have more or less unconsciously answered questions of interest and drawn sketches almost as if by interview and request. Some of these records have been printed as they stand, some have been analyzed in detail, some are here used for the first time, and many are no doubt still awaiting discovery. Among those available there is great diversity in form and content. In one case nothing will have survived but a diary of routine, in another financial records only, in a third overseers' reports, in a fourth a miscellany of letters, legal documents and vouchers, often of course mingled with a mass of trivial rubbish. Never do they give singly a view of experience in all phases; but in combination they exhibit personalities, operations, problems and adjustments perhaps as well as do the vestiges of past régimes in other parts of the world.

The Carters, who being lowland Virginians pronounced their name *Kyahta*, may be followed in their scattered plantation records for at least four generations. The chief architect of the family fortune was Robert, born in 1663. His large patrimony was hugely increased by vigorous use of the many devices prevalent among the magnates of the time; and his domineering demeanor in public office gave him the nickname of "King" Carter.[2] By 1700 he was already one of the greatest freeholders in the Northern Neck; and when he made his will in 1726 he designated plantations in groups rather than singly, to be inherited by each of his nine children then living. Upon his death six years later the inventory of his estate made a prodigious catalogue. Along with the furniture of his many-chambered mansion, it embraced a copious library, great stores of cloth, buttons, medicines, nails, tools, groceries, spare sails and miscellaneous impedimenta. In the personnel at his homestead, "Corotoman", there were seventeen indentured white servants (including sailors, tailors and carpenters, a glazier, a bricklayer and a blacksmith) and thirty-three slaves. And on outlying lands in perhaps a dozen counties there were nearly seven hundred slaves, a hundred or so horses, upwards of a thousand cattle, a like number of swine, and some hundreds of sheep. These slaves, with small quotas of livestock, were distributed

2. Memorandum of Governor Nicholson in 1705.—*Virginia Magazine*, VIII, 56.

in half a hundred "quarters" as working groups with a white overseer
and a slave foreman at the head of each unit. In size the groups
ranged from as few as six slaves to more than thirty.[3] This scheme of
operation in small units was maintained in some part by descendants
to the third generation, as will shortly appear.

* * *

VERNON LOGGINS

From The Negro Author: His Development in America[†]

* * *

[O]f all the narratives of this class the least dull perhaps is the work
of an anonymous biographer, whose unusual subject matter is suggested by the full title of his book, *Twelve Years a Slave; Narrative of
Solomon Northrup, a Citizen of New York, Kidnapped in Washington
City in 1841, and Rescued in 1853, from a Cotton Plantation near the
Red River in Louisiana*. The book, published in 1853, does not seem
too long, even though it contains more than three hundred pages. A
perusal of it makes one realize that the narratives of fugitives would
have been more effective if they had been written as pure biographies and not as "dictated" or "edited" autobiographies. * * *

Biography, Poetry, and Miscellaneous Writings, 1840–1865

A. BIOGRAPHY

* * *

ANONYMOUS. Aunt Sally; or, The Cross the Way of Freedom. A Nar-
    rative of the Slave-life and Purchase of the Mother of Rev. Isaac
    Williams, of Detroit, Michigan. 216 pp. Cincinnati, 1858.

———— Glorying in Tribulation; a Brief Memoir of Hannah Carson,
    for Thirteen Years Deprived of the Use of All Her Limbs. 56 pp.
    Philadelphia, 1864.

---

3. The will and inventory, the latter in condensed form, are printed in the *Virginia Magazine*, V–VII, *passim*.
† From *The Negro Author: His Development in America* (New York: Columbia University
   Press, 1931), pp. 228, 434. Copyright © 1931 Columbia University Press. Reprinted by
   permission of the publisher. Vernon Loggins (1893–1968), for much of his career,
   taught in the English department at Columbia University in the City of New York. The
   fact that such a distinguished scholar misspelled Northup's name and suggested *Twelve
   Years a Slave* was not a "'dictated' or 'edited'" work suggests Professor Loggins may
   have not had a copy of the book at hand when he was writing this passage. (Since
   Northup's editor, David Wilson, included an Editor's Preface in the 1853 text, no one
   looking at it carefully would have called *Twelve Years a Slave* the work of "an

———— The Rev. J. W. Loguen, as a Slave and as a Freeman; a Narrative of Real Life. 444 pp. Syracuse, 1859.

———— Narrative of Sojourner Truth, Northern Slave, Emancipated from Bodily Servitude by the State of New York, in 1828. 144 pp. Boston, 1850.

———— Same, with an Introduction by Harriet Beecher Stowe. iv, 144 pp. New York, 1855.

———— Twelve Years a Slave; Narrative of Solomon Northrup, a Citizen of New York, Kidnapped in Washington City in 1841, and Rescued in 1853, from a Cotton Plantation near the Red River in Louisiana. 336 pp. Auburn, 1853.

*   *   *

HERBERT APTHEKER

The Negro in the Abolitionist Movement[†]

*   *   *

Of the antislavery books produced by Negroes (largely, though by no means wholly, autobiographical) one can here select for notice only a few of those which were most influential in creating and molding public opinion, for an attempt at compiling merely a list of all that flooded the bookstores would require many pages.[1] Restricting ourselves to a dozen autobiographical works that were not equaled by any other single piece of writing so far as depicting the essence of the institution of slavery is concerned, we may note the narratives of Charles Ball,[2] Henry Bibb,[3] William Wells Brown[4] (this former slave also produced, prior to the Civil War, a travel book, a collection of antislavery songs, a

---

anonymous biographer.") That said, it would have been an easy mistake for a scholar in Loggins's position to make in 1931, given that Northup's memoir had fallen out of print after 1900 and was not reissued until 1968, sadly, the year of Loggins's death. Thus, it would have been a challenge for Professor Loggins to purchase his own copy of the book; instead, and more likely, he would have needed to rely on a library's collection and, therefore, may have been working from research notes when he himself sat down to write. Of course, this, too, is speculation, offered only to clarify for the reader that *Twelve Years a Slave* is noteworthy for many reasons but being the work of an "anonymous biographer" is not one of them.

† From *Science & Society* 5.2 (Spring 1941): 163–64. © 1941 Guilford Press. Reprinted with permission of The Guilford Press. Aptheker's notes have been edited.

1. For a partial list see M. A. Howe and R. E. Lewis, *A Classified Catalogue of the Negro Collection in the Huntington Library of Hampton Institute* (mimeographed, Hampton, 1940), especially pp. 66–69.

2. Charles Ball, *Slavery in the United States: A Narrative of the Life and Adventures of Charles Ball* (Lewistown: John W. Shugert, 1836); reprinted as Charles Ball, *Fifty Years in Chains; or The Life of an American Slave* (New York: H. Dayton Publishers, 1859).

3. Henry Bibb, *Narrative of the Life and Adventures of Henry Bibb, an American Slave, Written by Himself* (New York: Author, 1849).

4. William Wells Brown, *Narrative of William W. Brown, a Fugitive Slave. Written by Himself* (Boston: The Anti-Slavery Office, 1847).

novel, and a play), Lewis and Milton Clarke,[5] Josiah Henson[6] (his work so moved a lady named Harriet Beecher Stowe that in 1850 she visited and conversed with him in Boston—an important force behind the production, in 1852, of her epoch-making *Uncle Tom's Cabin*[7]), Jeremiah W. Loguen,[8] Solomon Northup,[9] James W. C. Pennington[1] (the first edition of 6,000 copies of the life of this fugitive slave and militant Abolitionist, who earned the degree of Doctor of Divinity from Heidelberg University, was sold within the year), Austin Steward,[2] Sojourner Truth,[3] Samuel R. Ward,[4] and, in a class by itself in this literature or any literature, the perfectly forthright and magnificently moving autobiography of Frederick Douglass, first published in Boston in 1845.

✻   ✻   ✻

STERLING ALLEN BROWN, ARTHUR PAUL DAVIS, AND ULYSSES LEE

From The Negro Caravan[†]

Little is known of Solomon Northup except what he tells in the book *Twelve Years a Slave* (1893).[1] The title page announces him as "a citizen of New York, kidnapped in Washington City in 1841 and rescued in 1853, from a cotton plantation near the Red River in Louisiana." In the year of his rescue David Wilson took down his story as "a correct

5. Lewis Garrard Clarke and Milton Clarke, *Narratives of the Sufferings of Lewis and Milton Clarke, Sons of a Soldier of the Revolution, During a Captivity of More than Twenty Years Among the Slaveholders of Kentucky, One of the So-Called Christian States of North America* (Boston: Bela Marsh, 1846).
6. Josiah Henson, *Formerly a Slave, Now an Inhabitant of Canada, as Narrated by Himself* (Boston: Arthur D. Phelps, 1849).
7. Aileen Ward, "In Memory of 'Uncle Tom,'" in *Dalhousie Review* (1940), XX, 335–38.
8. J. W. Loguen, *The Rev. J. W. Loguen, as a Slave and as a Freeman, A Narrative of Real Life* (Syracuse: J. G. K. Truair & Co., 1859).
9. Solomon Northup, *Twelve Years a Slave: Narrative of Solomon Northup, a Citizen of New-York* (Auburn: Derby and Miller, 1853).
1. James W. C. Pennington, *The Fugitive Blacksmith; or, Events in the History of James W. C. Pennington, Pastor of a Presbyterian Church, New York, Formerly a Slave in the State of Maryland, United States* (London: Charles Gilpin, 1849).
2. Austin Steward, *Twenty-Two Years a Slave, and Forty Years a Freeman* (Rochester: William Alling, 1857).
3. Olive Gilbert, *Narrative of Sojourner Truth, a Northern Slave, Emancipated from Bodily Servitude by the State of New York, in 1828* (Boston: Printed for the Author, 1850).
4. Samuel Ringgold Ward, *Autobiography of a Fugitive Negro: His Anti-Slavery Labours in the United States, Canada, & England* (London: John Snow, 1855).
† From *The Negro Caravan*, ed. Sterling A. Brown, Arthur P. Davis, and Ulysses Lee (1941; rpt. New York: Arno Press and the *New York Times*, 1969), pp. 714–19. This excerpting of the memoir shows what Brown thought was a representative and affecting Northup passage (about Christmas on Bayou Bœuf). Unless noted, misspellings have been left uncorrected.
1. *Twelve Years a Slave* was originally published in 1853.

picture of slavery." An appendix contains letters establishing the authenticity of Solomon Northup's kidnapping and of the many efforts, finally successful, to redeem him from the Red River plantation.

[Christmas on Bayou Boeuf]

The only respite from constant labor the slave has through the whole year, is during the Christmas holidays. Epps allowed us three— others allow four, five and six days, according to the measure of their generosity. It is the only time to which they look forward with any interest or pleasure. They are glad when night comes, not only because it brings them a few hours repose, but because it brings them one day nearer Christmas. It is hailed with equal delight by the old and the young; even Uncle Abram ceases to glorify Andrew Jackson, and Patsy forgets her many sorrows, amid the general hilarity of the holidays. It is the time of feasting, and frolicking, and fiddling— the carnival season with the children of bondage. They are the only days when they are allowed a little restricted liberty, and heartily indeed do they enjoy it.

It is the custom for one planter to give a "Christmas supper," inviting the slaves from neighboring plantations to join his own on the occasion; for instance, one year it is given by Epps, the next by Marshall, the next by Hawkins, and so on. Usually from three to five hundred are assembled, coming together on foot, in carts, on horseback, on mules, riding double and triple, sometimes a boy and girl, at others a girl and two boys, and at others again a boy, a girl and an old woman. Uncle Abram astride a mule, with Aunt Phebe and Patsy behind him, trotting towards a Christmas supper, would be no uncommon sight on Bayou Boeuf.

Then, too, "of all days i' the year," they array themselves in their best attire. The cotton coat has been washed clean, the stump of a tallow candle has been applied to their shoes, and if so fortunate as to possess a rimless or a crownless hat, it is placed jauntily on the head. They are welcome with equal cordiality, however, if they come bare-headed and bare-footed to the feast. As a general thing, the women wear handkerchiefs tied about their heads, but if chance has thrown in their way a fiery red ribbon, or a cast-off bonnet of their mistress' grandmother, it is sure to be worn on such occasions. Red— the deep blood red—is decidedly the favorite color among the enslaved damsels of my acquaintance. If a red ribbon does not encircle the neck, you will be certain to find all the hair of their woolly heads tied up with red strings of one sort or another.

The table is spread in the open air, and loaded with varieties of meat and piles of vegetables. Bacon and corn meal at such times are dispensed with. Sometimes the cooking is performed in the kitchen on the plantation, at others in the shade of wide branching trees. In the latter case, a ditch is dug in the ground, and wood laid in and burned until it is filled with glowing coals, over which chickens, ducks, turkeys, pigs, and not unfrequently the entire body of a wild ox, are roasted. They are furnished also with flour, of which biscuits are made, and often with peach and other preserves, with tarts, and every manner and description of pies, except the mince, that being an article of pastry as yet unknown among them. Only the slave who has lived all the years on his scanty allowance of meal and bacon, can appreciate such suppers. White people in great numbers assemble to witness the gastronomical enjoyments.

They seat themselves at the rustic table—the males on one side, the females on the other. The two between whom there may have been an exchange of tenderness, invariably manage to sit opposite; for the omnipresent Cupid disdains not to hurl his arrows into the simple hearts of slaves. Unalloyed and exulting happiness lights up the dark faces of them all. The ivory teeth, contrasting with their black complexions, exhibit two long, white streaks the whole extent of the table. All around the bountiful board a multitude of eyes roll in ecstacy. Giggling and laughter and the clattering of cutlery and crockery succeed. Cuffee's elbow hunches his neighbor's side, impelled by an involuntary impulse of delight; Nelly shakes her finger at Sambo and laughs, she knows not why, and so the fun and merriment flows on.

When the viands have disappeared, and the hungry maws of the children of toil are satisfied, then, next in the order of amusement, is the Christmas dance. My business on these gala days always was to play on the violin. The African race is a music-loving one, proverbially; and many there were among my fellow-bondsmen whose organs of tune were strikingly developed, and who could thumb the banjo with dexterity; but at the expense of appearing egotistical, I must, nevertheless, declare, that I was considered the Ole Bull of Bayou Boeuf. My master often received letters, sometimes from a distance of ten miles, requesting him to send me to play at a ball or festival of the whites. He received his compensation, and usually I also returned with many picayunes jingling in my pockets—the extra contributions of those to whose delight I had administered. In this manner I became more acquainted than I otherwise would, up and down the bayou. The young men and maidens of Holmes-ville always knew there was to be a jollification somewhere, whenever Platt Epps was seen passing through the town with his fiddle in his hand. "Where are you going now, Platt?" and "What is coming off to-night, Platt?" would be interrogations issuing from every door and window, and many a time when there was no special hurry, yielding to pressing importunities, Platt would draw his bow, and sitting astride his mule, perhaps, discourse musically to a crowd of delighted children, gathered around him in the street.

Alas! had it not been for my beloved violin, I scarcely can conceive how I could have endured the long years of bondage. It introduced me to great houses—relieved me of many days' labor in the field—supplied me with conveniences for my cabin—with pipes and tobacco, and extra pairs of shoes, and oftentimes led me away from the presence of a hard master, to witness scenes of jollity and mirth. It was my companion—the friend of my bosom—trumphing loudly when I was joyful, and uttering its soft, melodious consolations when I was sad. Often, at midnight, when sleep had fled affrighted from the cabin, and my soul was disturbed and troubled with the contemplation of my fate, it would sing me a song of peace. On holy Sabbath days, when an hour or two of leisure was allowed, it would accompany me to some quiet place on the bayou bank, and, lifting up its voice, discourse kindly and pleasantly indeed. It heralded my name round the country—made me friends, who, otherwise would not have noticed me—gave me an honored seat at the yearly feasts, and secured the loudest and heartiest welcome of them all at the Christmas dance. The Christmas dance! Oh, ye pleasure-seeking sons and daughters of idleness, who move with measured step, listless and snail-like, through the slow winding cotillon, if ye wish to look upon the celerity, if not the "poetry in motion"—upon genuine happiness, rampant and unrestrained—go down to Louisiana, and see the slaves dancing in the starlight of a Christmas night.

On that particular Christmas I have now in my mind, a description whereof will serve as a description of the day generally, Miss Lively and Mr. Sam, the first belonging to Stewart, the latter to Roberts, started the ball. It was well known that Sam cherished an ardent passion for Lively, as also did one of Marshall's and another of Carey's boys; for Lively was *lively* indeed, and a heartbreaking coquette withal. It was a victory for Sam Roberts, when, rising from the repast, she gave him her hand for the first "figure" in preference to either of his rivals. They were somewhat crestfallen, and, shaking their heads angrily, rather intimated they would like to pitch into Mr. Sam and hurt him badly. But not an emotion of wrath ruffled the placid bosom of Samuel as his legs flew like drum-sticks down the outside and up the middle, by the side of his bewitching partner. The whole company cheered them vociferously, and, excited with the applause, they continued "tearing down" after all the others had become exhausted and halted a moment to recover breath. But Sam's superhuman exertions overcame him finally, leaving Lively alone, yet whirling like a top. Thereupon one of Sam's rivals, Pete Marshall, dashed in, and, with might and main, leaped and shuffled and threw himself into every conceivable shape, as if determined to show Miss Lively and all the world that Sam Roberts was of no account.

Pete's affection, however, was greater than his discretion. Such violent exercise took the breath out of him directly, and he dropped like an empty bag. Then was the time for Harry Carey to try his hand; but Lively also soon out-winded him, amidst hurrahs and shouts, fully sustaining her well-earned reputation of being the "fastest gal" on the bayou.

One "set" off, another takes its place, he or she remaining longest on the floor receiving the most uproarious commendation, and so the dancing continues until broad daylight. It does not cease with the sound of the fiddle, but in that case they set up a music peculiar to themselves. This is called "patting," accompanied with one of those unmeaning songs, composed rather for its adaption to a certain tune or measure, than for the purpose of expressing any distinct idea. The patting is performed by striking the hands on the knees, then striking the hands together, then striking the right shoulder with one hand, the left with the other—all the while keeping time with the feet, and singing, perhaps, this song:

> "Harper's creek and roarin' ribber,
> Thar, my dear, we'll live forebber;
> Den we'll go to de Ingin nation,
> All I want in dis creation,
> Is pretty little wife and big plantation.
>
> *Chorus.* Up dat oak and down dat ribber,
>   Two overseers and one little nigger."

Or, if these words are not adapted to the tune called for, it may be that "Old Hog Eye" *is*—a rather solemn and startling specimen of versification, not, however, to be appreciated unless heard at the South. It runneth as follows:

> "Who's been here since I've been gone?
>   Pretty little gal wid a josey on.
>   Hog Eye!
>   Old Hog Eye!
>   And Hosey too!
>
>   Never see de like since I was born,
>   Here comes a little gal wid a josey on.
>   Hog Eye!
>   Old Hog Eye!
>   And Hosey too!"

Or, may be the following, perhaps, equally nonsensical, but full of melody, nevertheless, as it flows from the negro's mouth:

> "Ebo Dick and Jurdan's Jo,
>   Them two niggers stole my yo'.
>
> *Chorus.* Hop Jim along,
>   Walk Jim along,
>   Talk Jim along," &c.
>
> Old black Dan, as black as tar,
> He dam glad he was not dar.
>   Hop Jim along," &c.

During the remaining holidays succeeding Christmas, they are provided with passes, and permitted to go where they please within a limited distance, or they may remain and labor on the plantation, in which case they are paid for it. It is very rarely, however, that the latter alternative is accepted. They may be seen at these times hurrying in all directions, as happy looking mortals as can be found on the face of the earth. They are different beings from what they are in the field; the temporary relaxation, the brief deliverance from fear, and from the lash, producing an entire metamorphosis in their appearance and demeanor. In visiting, riding, renewing old friendships, or, perchance, reviving some old attachment, or pursuing whatever pleasure may suggest itself, the time is occupied. Such is "southern life as it is," *three days in the year,* as I found it—the other three hundred and sixty-two being days of weariness, and fear, and suffering, and unremitting labor.

Marriage is frequently contracted during the holidays, if such an institution may be said to exist among them. The only ceremony required before entering into that "holy estate," is to obtain the consent of the respective owners. It is usually encouraged by the masters of female slaves. Either party can have as many husbands or wives as the owner will permit, and either is at liberty to discard the other at pleasure. The law in relation to divorce, or to bigamy, and so forth, is not applicable to property, of course. If the wife does not belong on the same plantation with the husband, the latter is permitted to visit her on Saturday nights, if the distance is not too far. Uncle Abram's wife lived seven miles from Epps', on Bayou Huff Power. He had permission to visit her once a fortnight, but he was growing old, as has been said, and truth to say, had latterly well nigh forgotten her. Uncle Abram had no time to spare from his meditations on General Jackson—connubial dalliance being well enough for the young and thoughtless, but unbecoming a grave and solemn philosopher like himself.

MARION WILSON STARLING

From The Slave Narrative: Its Place in American History[†]

Solomon Northup's experience was ideal for a slave narrative thriller. He was born to free Negroes living in Essex County, New York, about 1808. In 1829 he married[1] and, in the winter of 1841, moved his wife and children to Saratoga Springs. Two men approached him with the offer of a job driving a team South for a dollar a day. Northup accepted the offer, not being averse to seeing more of the country than his own state, which he had never left before, and took out free papers when he got as far as New York City to show that he was not a slave. He then drove the team on down to Washington City, putting up for the night at Gadsby's Hotel. This was on April 2, 1841.

Taken sick with severe pains in the stomach soon after arriving at the hotel, Northup went to bed. When some persons came into his room with some medicine they were offering to ease his pain, he took it. This was the last thing he had any recollection of until he discovered himself lying handcuffed and chained to the floor of a slave pen run by a Mr. Williams in Washington City. A few hours after he had made this unbelievable discovery, a slave dealer named James Burch came in. Northup asked him why the irons had been put on him and told Burch that he wanted them off. He was told he had no business to ask questions. Northup answered that he was a free man, born in New York State. Burch then called in a man by the name of Ebenezer Rodbury. The two men stripped Northup and then administered a severe beating of more than a hundred lashes. Burch swore that he would kill him if he were ever to tell anyone that he was a free man. He remained in the slave pen about ten days, while it was being filled with others like himself. Then they were all taken away by night, handcuffed and shackled, down to Richmond by river-boat. At Richmond he was loaded, with forty-eight others, onto the brig *Orleans*, bound for the city of New Orleans. Before the brig docked at that city, they were unloaded by one Theophilus Freeman, a former partner with Burch, and whisked away to a slave pen. Northup was taken sick with smallpox and sent to a hospital, where he remained two or three weeks. He was sold soon after he left the hospital to a Mr. Ford of Rapides Parish, Louisiana. He lived with Mr. Ford for about a year, working in his business as a carpenter, and

---

[†] From *The Slave Narrative: Its Place in American History*, 2nd ed. (Washington, D.C.: Howard University Press, 1988), pp. 173–74. Originally published as a Ph.D. dissertation at New York University in 1946. Starling's notes have been edited. Unless noted, misspellings in the main text have been left uncorrected.

1. See note regarding Northup's marriage date on p. 17 of this volume [Editors' note].

was fairly well treated. But Ford encountered financial difficulties and had to sell Northup. A Mr. Tibaut became his second owner. Tibaut sold him in a short time to the "Mr. Gooch" of Northup's narrative. His real name was Mr. Edwin Eppes, of Bayou Beouf, Louisiana, the owner of a cotton plantation about one hundred and thirty miles from the mouth of Red River. There Northup was to spend nine harrowing years in a "perpetual nightmare" of slave life.

It was a plantation on the same order as Francis Whitfield's in Henry Bibb's narrative, with the same type of accommodations for the workers as we have found the slaves "enjoying" where Grandy lived, and Henson, and Curry, and many, many others: no floor, no chair, no bed, no mattress, no clothes, and almost no food. The slaves were driven from sunup to sundown, beaten fiendishly to extract labor from them, no matter how hungry or how sick they were, and punished even more dreadfully for any manifestations of normal desires for social contacts—visiting one's mother on an adjoining plantation or going to prayer meeting. Northup "worked up to" the position of overseer, which proved more revolting to him than his position in the ranks, as he was forced by Eppes to beat the slaves "to order," their bodies tied and hung up or stretched taut between stakes or worse. He had tried, whenever possible, to get word to Northern friends to tell them where he was, but he had no luck. One letter, however, finally made its way out of the dangerous labyrinth in which he was confined. Sent from Bayou Beouf in August, 1842, it told of his plight:

> Mr. William Penny, or Mr. Lewis Parker.
> Gentlemen: It having been a long time since I have seen or heard from you, and not knowing that you are living, it is with uncertainty that I write to you; but the necessity of the case must be my excuse. Having been born free just across the river from you, I am certain you know me; and I am here now a slave. I wish you to obtain free papers for me, and forward them to me at Marksville, Louisiana, Parish of Avoelles . . . [2]

His friends received the letter and straightway set about applying to Governor Hunt of New York State for permission to send an agent to Louisiana for the purpose of procuring Solomon Northup's freedom. That freedom was finally obtained when the case was tried before the court in Washington, D.C. Northup's story of his experience was written at once in order to take advantage of the publicity that had come to the case through reports in the New York *Times* and other public journals, as well as in the antislavery press. Then began Northup's tour of the Northern States as a lecturer on his experience. A typical reaction to the tour can be found in a letter to

2. Solomon Northup, *Twelve Years a Slave: Narrative of Solomon Northup, a Citizen of New-York* (Auburn: Derby and Miller, 1853), p. 275.

Garrison two years after the first appearance of *Twelve Years a Slave*:

> *Twelve Years a Slave* has been widely read in New England, and no narrative of man's experience as a slave . . . is more touching, or better calculated to expose the true character and designs of slave-holders. But it is far more potent to see the man, and hear him, in his clear, manly, straightforward way, speak of slavery as he experienced it, and as he saw it in others. Those who have read his Narrative can scarce fail to desire to see the man . . . and to hear his story from his own lips.[3]

KENNETH STAMPP

From The Peculiar Institution: Slavery in the Ante-Bellum South[†]

Mammy Harriet had nostalgic memories of slavery days: "Oh, no, we was nebber hurried. Marster nebber once said, 'Get up an' go to work,' an' no oberseer ebber said it, neither. Ef some on 'em did not git up when de odders went out to work, marster nebber said a word. Oh, no, we was nebber hurried."[1] Mammy Harriet had been a domestic at "Burleigh," the Hinds County, Mississippi, estate of Thomas S. Dabney. She related her story of slave life there to one of Dabney's daughters who wrote a loving volume about her father and his cotton plantation.

Another slave found life less leisurely on a plantation on the Red River in Louisiana: "The hands are required to be in the cotton field as soon as it is light in the morning, and, with the exception of ten or fifteen minutes, which is given them at noon to swallow their allowance of cold bacon, they are not permitted to be a moment idle until it is too dark to see, and when the moon is full, they often times labor till the middle of the night." Work did not end when the slaves left the fields. "Each one must attend to his respective chores. One feeds the mules, another the swine—another cuts the wood, and so forth; besides the packing [of cotton] is all done by candle light. Finally, at a late hour, they reach the quarters, sleepy and overcome with the long day's toil."[2] These were the bitter memories of Solomon

---

3. *Liberator* 25 (March 23, 1855): 57.
† From *The Peculiar Institution: Slavery in the Ante-Bellum South* (New York: Knopf, 1956), pp. 73–75. Copyright © 1956, copyright renewed 1984 by Kenneth M. Stampp. Used by permission of Alfred A. Knopf, an imprint of the Knopf Doubleday Publishing Group, a division of Penguin Random House LLC. All rights reserved. Stampp's notes have been edited.
1. Susan Dabney Smedes, *Memorials of a Southern Planter* (Baltimore, 1887), p. 57.
2. Solomon Northup, *Twelve Years a Slave: Narrative of Solomon Northup, a Citizen of New-York* (Auburn: Derby and Miller, 1853), pp. 167–68.

Northup, a free Negro who had been kidnapped and held in bondage for twelve years. Northup described his experiences to a Northerner who helped him prepare his autobiography for publication.

Mammy Harriet's and Solomon Northup's disparate accounts of the work regimen imposed upon slaves suggest the difficulty of determining the truth from witnesses, Negro and white, whose candor was rarely uncompromised by internal emotions or external pressures. Did Dabney's allegedly unhurried field-hands (who somehow produced much cotton and one of whom once tried to kill the overseer) feel the same nostalgia for slavery days? How much was Northup's book influenced by his amanuensis and by the preconceptions of his potential northern readers?

And yet there is nothing in the narratives of either of these ex-slaves that renders them entirely implausible. The question of their complete accuracy is perhaps less important than the fact that both conditions actually did exist in the South. Distortion results from exaggerating the frequency of either condition or from dwelling upon one and ignoring the other.

No sweeping generalization about the amount of labor extracted from bondsmen could possibly be valid, even when they are classified by regions, or by occupations, or by the size of the holdings upon which they lived. For the personal factor transcended everything else. How hard the slaves were worked depended upon the demands of individual masters and their ability to enforce them. These demands were always more or less tempered by the inclination of most slaves to minimize their unpaid toil. Here was a clash of interests in which the master usually, but not always, enjoyed the advantage of superior weapons.

* * *

STANLEY ELKINS

From Slavery: A Problem in American Institutional and Intellectual Life†

Kenneth Stampp made one side of this point in an article published in 1952. "The traveler in the South who viewed slavery with an entirely open mind was rare indeed," he said, "but it does not necessarily follow that the only accurate reporters among them were those who viewed it sympathetically." "The Historian and Southern Negro Slavery,"

† From Slavery: A Problem in American Institutional and Intellectual Life (Chicago: University of Chicago Press, 1959), note 3 on pp. 3–5. © 1959 by the University of Chicago. Reprinted by permission of the publisher. Unless noted, misspellings have been left uncorrected.

American Historical Review, LVII (April, 1952), 615. One must not only fully indorse this proposition but also reverse it; it does not follow that the only accurate reporters were the unsympathetic ones either.

Among the most useful of the travelers' and other eyewitness accounts are Nehemiah Adams, *A South-Side View of Slavery* (Boston: T. R. Marvin, and Sanborn, Carter, and Brazin); Frederika Bremer, *The Homes of the New World* (2 vols.; New York: Harper, 1853); J. S. Buckingham, *Slave States of America* (2 vols.; London: Fisher, Son & Co., 1842); William Chambers, *Things as They Are in America* (London: W. & R. Chambers, 1854) and *American Slavery and Colour* (London: W. & R. Chambers, 1857); George W. Featherstonhaugh, *Excursion through the Slave States* (New York: Harper, 1844); Basil Hall, *Travels in North America in the Years 1827 and 1828* (Edinburgh: Cadell, 1829); Joseph H. Ingraham, *The South-West, by a Yankee* (2 vols.; New York: Harper, 1835); Frances Anne Kemble, *Journal of a Residence on a Georgian Plantation in 1838–1839* (New York: Harper, 1863); Sir Charles Lyell, *A Second Visit to the United States of North America* (New York: Harper, 1849); Harriet Martineau, *Society in America* (2 vols., London: Saunders & Otley, 1837); Frederick Law Olmsted, *A Journey in the Seaboard Slave States, with Remarks on Their Economy* (New York: Putnam, 1904); *A Journey Through Texas* (New York: Edwards, 1857), *A Journey in the Back Country* (New York: Mason, 1860), and *The Cotton Kingdom: A Traveller's Observations of Cotton and Slavery in the American Slave States* (2 vols.; New York: Mason, 1861); James K. Paulding, *Slavery in the United States* (New York: Harper, 1836); William H. Russell, *My Diary North and South* (Boston: T. O. H. P. Burnham, 1863); Susan Dabney Smedes, *Memorials of a Southern Planter* (Baltimore: Cushings & Bailey, 1888).

To this material should be added whatever is dependable from the reminiscences and narratives of slaves themselves. Two such narratives are particularly convincing: David Wilson (ed.), *Narrative of Solomon Northrup* (Buffalo: Derby, Orton & Mulligan, 1853); and Kate E. R. Pickard, *The Kidnapped and the Ransomed, Being the Personal Recollections of Peter Still and His Wife Vina after Forty Years of Slavery* (Syracuse: W. T. Hamilton, 1856). Charles Stearns's *Narrative of Henry Box Brown* (1849) and *Life of J. Henson, Formerly a Slave* (Boston: A. D. Phelps, 1849) are heavily edited by abolitionists, though not entirely undependable. Frederick Douglass' *My Bondage and My Freedom* (New York: Miller, Orton & Mulligan, 1855) is obviously not the work of an ordinary slave, but some of the author's insights into the slave system are very valuable. Two latter-day efforts to tell the story of slavery through interviews with former slaves are John B. Cade, "Out of the Mouths of Slaves," *Journal of Negro History*, XX (July, 1935), 294–337, and B. A. Botkin (ed.), *Lay My Burden Down* (Chicago: University of Chicago Press, 1945).

GILBERT OSOFSKY

From The Significance of Slave Narratives[†]

The slave narratives are tales of bondage and freedom written or told by former slaves. There are many thousands of such narratives if one includes the stories of fugitives collected by antislavery advocates and published in the abolitionist press, or those gathered for publication in nineteenth- and twentieth-century documentary accounts. Brief descriptions of slavery from the mouths of those who lived it appear in many nineteenth-century books, such as William Still's *The Underground Rail Road* (1883), Levi Coffin's *Reminiscences* (1876), Benjamin Drew's *North-Side View of Slavery* (1856), Lydia Maria Child's *Isaac T. Hopper: A True Life* (1854), Wilson Armistead's *A Tribute for the Negro* (1848). The WPA slave-narrative collection in the Library of Congress runs to seventeen volumes.[1] Perhaps most remarkable of this extensive literature are the fourscore full-length autobiographies of slaves published before the Civil War. These books are the main focus of this essay.[2]

A literature so diffuse obviously varies widely in style, purpose, and competence. Some books are works of enduring value from a literary as well as "protest" perspective. The autobiographies of Frederick Douglass, Henry Bibb, and Solomon Northup fuse imaginative style with keenness of insight. They are penetrating and self-critical, superior autobiography by any standards. The quality of mind and spirit of their authors is apparent.

Because the best narratives reflect the imaginative minds of the most gifted and rebellious slaves, their value as reliable sources for the study of slavery has been questioned.[3] To doubt the relevancy of autobiographies written by exceptional slaves, however, is a specious argument in its inception. The great slave narrative, like all great

---

† From *Puttin' on Ole Massa: The Slave Narratives of Henry Bibb, William Wells Brown, and Solomon Northup*, ed. Gilbert Osofsky (New York: Harper & Row, 1969), pp. 9–11, 44. Reprinted by permission of the Estate of Gilbert Osofsky.

1. Federal Writers' Project, "Slave Narratives: A Folk History of Slavery in the United States from Interviews with Former Slaves" (Typescripts, Washington, D.C., 1941), 17 vols.; Norman R. Yetman, "The Background of the Slave Narrative Collection," *American Quarterly*, XIX (Fall, 1967), 534–553; Benjamin A. Botkin, *Lay My Burden Down: A Folk History of Slavery* (Chicago, 1945).

2. Two invaluable doctoral dissertations in the field of American literature provide an overview of the subject: Charles H. Nichols, Jr., "A Study of the Slave Narrative" (doctoral dissertation, Brown University, 1948); and Margaret Young Jackson, "An Investigation of Biographies and Autobiographies of American Slaves Published Between 1840 and 1860: Based upon the Cornell Special Slavery Collection (doctoral dissertation, Cornell University, 1954). Each contains a solid bibliography.

3. This question has arisen with deadening regularity each time I've lectured on the subject. The argument generally made is that men like Douglass were so unusual that their experiences emphasize only the atypical aspects of slavery.

autobiography, is the work of the especially perceptive viewer and writer. In describing his personal life, the sensitive and creative writer touches a deeper reality that transcends his individuality. Frederick Douglass, for example, was certainly an exceptional man, but his autobiography has much to teach us about the slaves around him, his friends and enemies on the plantation and in the city, and many other typical aspects of American slavery. Douglass is gibingly critical of the weaknesses of many of his fellow slaves. He derides those who adopted the master's code of behavior, those who fought for the baubles and goodies used as rewards and bribes, and those who dissipated their energy in wild sports and drinking bouts during holidays.[4] Douglass presents a many-sided depiction of the slave experience— his is no papier-mâché book or antislavery tract. The historians who fail to use such a book or the narratives of a Bibb, a Brown, a Northup, or a Samuel Ringgold Ward because they are "exceptional" men might as well argue that Claude Brown and Eldridge Cleaver are unsuitable commentators on today's ghetto. To exclude the "exceptional" is to eliminate all strong autobiography as a distortion of the events of its time. Yet it is these writers whose books are most likely to interpret reality with insight and clarity.

* * *

The volumes reprinted here are chosen for reasons of judgment and preference. They are fascinating slave narratives. Northup, Brown, and Bibb, as their autobiographies demonstrate, were men of creativity, wisdom and talent. Each was capable of writing his life story with sophistication. Brown and Bibb became leading figures in the anti-slavery movement immediately upon their escapes. Brown was a well-known novelist, playwright, and professional lecturer. He was one of the most militant and astute Garrisonians in the country. Bibb settled in Canada, helped establish a colony for fugitives and free blacks, and edited the influential *Voice of the Fugitive* until his untimely death at the age of thirty-eight in 1854. Northup was less active in the organized anti-slavery movement, but he too toured the country telling people of his days of bondage.[5] These three books differ from one another in style and content, yet exemplify the slave-narrative literature in its most representative forms.

4. Frederick Douglass, *Life and Times of Frederick Douglass* (New York, 1962), pp. 145–148.
5. A recent study of the Northup volume attests to its authenticity. See: Sue Eakin and Joseph Logsdon, eds., *Twelve Years a Slave* (Baton Rouge, 1968), pp. ix–xxiv.

BENJAMIN QUARLES

From Black Abolitionists[†]

* * *

Unquestionably the slave narratives were propagandistic—they were, after all, a weapon in the warfare. But if they were to be believed, they had to be as accurate as possible. Hence, aside from a few hoaxes, most of the slave narratives were soundly buttressed in fact. The abolitionists preferred to have former slaves write their own stories, not only to counter the notion of Negro inferiority but to give them the stamp of authenticity. When the abolitionist societies found it necessary to employ ghost writers, they sought persons with a high sense of integrity, such as Lydia Maria Child, John Greenleaf Whittier, and Edmund Quincy.

Whatever their relative admixture of social reality and sensationalism, slave narratives moved well in the book marts. No Negroes, before or since, have ever experienced less difficulty in getting published. Four editions of the biography of William Wells Brown made their appearance in less than two years. In a similar span, over twenty-seven thousand copies had been sold of the narrative of Solomon Northrup, a free Negro who had spent twelve years in slavery after having been kidnapped and put on the auction block as a runaway.

Slave narratives made a deep impression in the North, most readers finding their testimony quite persuasive. To Giles B. Stebbins the narrative by Douglass was "a voice coming up from the prison-house, speaking like a thousand-voiced psalm." Another reader said that she had wept over *Oliver Twist*, that her tears had moistened whole chapters of Eugène Sue's *Mysteries of Paris*, but that Douglass's narrative had "entered so deep into the chambers of my soul, as to entirely close the safety valve." In December 1855 Lewis Tappan wrote Douglass that his wife had read "your history" over and over again: "Its contents will be laid up in our hearts."[1]

A Boston newspaperman defied anyone to have any patience with slavery after reading Bibb's book. The Unitarian clergyman, William H. Furness, confessed to picking up Solomon Northrup's narrative reluctantly, feeling that it would "show the marks of

† From *Black Abolitionists* (New York: Oxford University Press, 1969), pp. 65–67, 265. © 1962 by Oxford University Press, Inc. Renewed 1990 by Benjamin Quarles. Reprinted by permission of Oxford University Press. Unless noted, misspellings have been left uncorrected.
1. *North Star*, Apr. 21, 1848. *Liberator*, June 6, 1845. Tappan to Douglass, Dec. 21, 1855, Tappan Papers.

book-making." But what he found was a work that rivetted the reader from beginning to end, giving him a deeper impression of slavery's savage spirit.[2]

The influence of the slave narratives was widened by the abolitionist weeklies, which reprinted extracts from them or ran them in serial form. Chief among the items likely to be selected for reproduction was a slave's letter to his former master. A long letter to one's erstwhile owner berating him for his sins of omission and commission was found to be an effective device. "I intend to make full use of you," wrote Douglass to his former master, "as a weapon with which to assail the system of slavery."[3] Bibb, Brown, and the clergyman, orator, and underground railroad operator, Jermain Wesley Loguen of Syracuse, were among the other more prominent correspondents whose letters to former masters were displayed over and over in the columns of the antislavery weeklies. And if the master could be goaded into making a reply, as in the case of Bibb and Loguen, his letter was gratefully pounced upon by the abolitionist sheets.

Harriet Beecher Stowe praised slave narratives for the vigor, shrewdness, and originality that their characters exhibited, and for their clear portrayal of the slave's own viewpoint. Well might the author of *Uncle Tom's Cabin* speak such words of commendation. Far more than she could ever sense, the vast audience that responded to her classic tale of Uncle Tom was an audience that had already been conditioned and prepared by the life stories of runaway slaves. For, as the knowledgeable Frederick Law Olmsted pointed out, most Northerners got their impressions of slavery from having read slave narratives.[4] Hence if President Lincoln could greet Mrs. Stowe as "the little lady who made this big war," certainly some of this credit might be shared by those former slaves whose stories had been dinned in the public mind, creating an adverse image of slavery that helped make possible the emergence of a Mrs. Stowe and an Abraham Lincoln.

* * *

2. Boston *Chronotype*, in *Bugle*, Nov. 3, 1849. Furness to editor of *Standard*, Mar. 9, 1854, in *Pennsylvania Freeman* (Philadelphia), Mar. 23, 1854.
3. Douglass to his former master, Sept. 22, 1848, in *Liberator*, Sept. 14, 1849.
4. Mrs. Stowe's appraisal of slave narratives in *Douglass' Paper*, Mar. 14, 1856, copied from *The Independent*. Frederick Law Olmsted, *A Journey in the Seaboard States* (2 vols., New York, 1904), I, 198–99.

WILLIAM L. ANDREWS

From To Tell a Free Story: The First Century of
Afro-American Autobiography, 1760–1865[†]

* * *

About a year after *Uncle Tom's Cabin* was published, the narrative
of Solomon Northup, a free-born black New Yorker who had been
kidnapped in Washington, D.C., and sold to a succession of Louisiana slaveowners, became the first of several slave autobiographies
to promise to outdo Stowe in the full factual reportage of slavery.
The kidnapping and sale of free blacks had been protested in the
Liberator for two decades,[1] but *Twelve Years a Slave* was unique in its
detailed, unchallenged account of not only the outrage but also the
restoration of the abused black man to his family. Moreover, the
book was dedicated to Mrs. Stowe and invited comparision to *Uncle
Tom's Cabin*, as several reviewers were quick to note, if for no other
reason than that the Red River plantation where Northup had been
a captive was located in the same region in which Uncle Tom had
suffered and died under the lash of Simon Legree.[2] Northup's ghost-
writer, David Wilson, did not let the first page of the narrative go by
without both capitalizing on the fame of Stowe's novel and using it
as a precedent that his own book would try to surpass. The narrator
of *Twelve Years a Slave* remarks approvingly on "the increasing
interest throughout the Northern States, in regard to the subject of
Slavery. Works of fiction [such as *Uncle Tom's Cabin*], professing to
portray its features in their more pleasing as well as more repugnant
aspects, have been circulated to an extent unprecedented, and, as I
understand, have created a fruitful topic of comment and discussion." Against the background of this discussion based on "works of
fiction," the narrator's object, he claims, is simply "to repeat the
story of my life, without exaggeration, leaving it for others to determine, whether even the pages of fiction present a picture of more
cruel wrong or a severer bondage."

Hard at work on *The Key to Uncle Tom's Cabin* when *Twelve Years
a Slave* came out, Stowe cited the new narrative, as she had most of

---

† From *To Tell a Free Story: The First Century of Afro-American Autobiography, 1760–
1865* (Urbana: University of Illinois Press, 1986), pp. 181–83, 318. Copyright 1986 by
the Board of Trustees of the University of Illinois. Used with permission of the University
of Illinois Press. Andrews's notes have been edited.
1. See Marion Wilson Starling, *The Slave Narrative: Its Place in American History* (Boston: G. K. Hall, 1981), pp. 171–72.
2. Reviews of *Twelve Years a Slave* are discussed in Sue Eakin and Joseph Logsdon's carefully edited reprint of *Twelve Years a Slave* (Baton Rouge: Louisiana State University
Press, 1968), pp. xii, xiv. Further quotations from *Twelve Years a Slave* are taken from
this edition.

the other famous slave autobiographies, as further proof of the reliability of her novel. She stressed that Northup's account of Red River plantation life formed "a striking parallel to that history" of slave suffering that she had recorded in the latter pages of *Uncle Tom's Cabin*. It is equally striking to notice that in comparing Northup's autobiography to her work of fiction, Stowe labeled the latter "that history." To the difficult task of verifying "that history," the slave narrative was crucial, for narratives like Northup's contained the facts that would support and vindicate Mrs. Stowe's fictions. Thus, in *The Key to Uncle Tom's Cabin* she encouraged the reading of black autobiography as a gloss on her own novel, the more to convince people that her novel could be treated "as a reality."[3] In the process she treated the slave narrative in the familiar, circumscribed manner of her era—as a source of facts best employed as signifiers of some prior reality (slavery) or some higher reality (myths about slavery valorized by white writing). The first page of *Twelve Years a Slave*, however, suggests that this story would not play merely a supportive role in the drama of Mrs. Stowe's literary defense. Wilson virtually guarantees his reader that the memory of Solomon Northup will outstrip the imagination of Harriet Beecher Stowe in the depiction of cruel wrongs done to a slave. *Twelve Years a Slave* would challenge Stowe's capacity to tell the whole truth about slavery.

In *The Key to Uncle Tom's Cabin* Stowe admits that "for the purposes of art" she had deliberately avoided telling the entire ugly truth about slavery in her novel. The artist who wishes to "succeed" must "draw a veil" over the most "dreadful" features of slavery; the book that failed to do so "could not be read."[4] However, Northup's narrative asked to be read as "a candid and truthful statement of facts," not a work of art, implying in the process that the black autobiographer would not be inhibited in the way that the white novelist was. That is, one could assume Northup's narrative to be more accurate than Stowe's because the former implicitly promised not to "draw a veil" or otherwise observe the proprieties that Mrs. Stowe felt obliged to abide by. This statement by Wilson on Northup's behalf anticipates a new discursive contract that evolves in the autobiographies of the 1850s and 1860s. For decades the slave narrator had asked to be believed on the basis, at least in part, of his ability to restrain himself, to keep to the proprieties of discourse that required the ugliest truths of slavery to be veiled. At mid-century, however, the black autobiographer would begin to claim credibility *because* he or she had violated those same proprieties of discourse. The further this new autobiographer placed himself or herself outside the conventions of the standard discourse on

3. Harriet Beecher Stowe, *The Key to Uncle Tom's Cabin* (Boston: J. P. Jewett, 1853), pp. 342, 1.
4. Ibid., p. 1.

slavery, the more truthful this autobiographer claimed to be. I am to be trusted, this new black narrator seemed to be saying, because what I tell you is shocking and ought not to be said. That which "could not be read" would no longer be suppressed out of a fear of its being dismissed as a lie. An ever-heightening severity of subject or tone would now be invested with the illocutionary force of authentication itself.

*　　*　　*

ROBERT B. STEPTO

From "I Rose and Found My Voice": Narration, Authentication, and Authorial Control in Four Slave Narratives[†]

While I am not prepared to classify Solomon Northup's *Twelve Years a Slave* (1854)[1] as an autobiography, it is certainly a more sophisticated text than Henry Bibb's, principally because its most important authenticating document is integrated into the tale as a voice and character. *Twelve Years a Slave* is, however, an integrated narrative unsure of itself. Ultimately, its authenticating strategy depends as much upon an appended set of authenticating texts as upon integrated documents and voices.

In comparison to the Bibb "Introduction," the Northup introductory materials appear purposely short and undeveloped. Northup's editor and amanuensis, a Mr. David Wilson, offers a one-page "Preface," not a full-blown "Introduction," and Northup's own introductory words are placed in the first chapter of his tale, rather than in a discrete entry written expressly for that purpose. Wilson's "Preface" is, predictably, an authenticating document, formulaically acknowledging whatever "faults of style and of expression" the narrative may contain while assuring the reader that he, the editor and a white man, is convinced of Northup's strict adherence to the truth. Northup's own contributions, like Bibb's, are not so much authenticating as they are reflective of what a slave may have been forced to consider while committing his tale to print.

Northup's first entry is simply and profoundly his signature—his proof of literacy writ large, with a bold, clear hand. It appears beneath a pen-and-ink frontispiece portrait entitled "Solomon in His Plantation Suit." His subsequent entries quite self-consciously

---

† From *From Behind the Veil: A Study of Afro-American Narrative*, 2nd ed. (Urbana: University of Illinois Press, 1991), pp. 11–16. Copyright 1979, 1991 Board of Trustees of the University of Illinois. Used with permission of the University of Illinois Press.
1. *Twelve Years a Slave* was originally published in 1853 [Editors' note].

place his narrative amid the antislavery literature of the era, in particular, with Harriet Beecher Stowe's *Uncle Tom's Cabin* (1852) and *Key to Uncle Tom's Cabin* (1853). If one wonders why Northup neither establishes his experience among those of other kidnapped and enslaved blacks nor positions his narrative with other narratives, the answer is provided in part by his dedicatory page. There, after quoting a passage from *Key to Uncle Tom's Cabin* which, in effect, verifies his account of slavery because it is said to "form a striking parallel" to Uncle Tom's, Northup respectfully dedicates his narrative to Miss Stowe, remarking that his tale affords "another *Key to Uncle Tom's Cabin*."

This is no conventional dedication; it tells us much about the requisite act of authentication. While the Bibb narrative is authenticated by documents provided by the Detroit Liberty Association, the Northup narrative begins the process of authentication by assuming kinship with a popular antislavery novel. Audience, and the former slave's relationship to that audience, are the key issues here: authentication is, apparently, a rhetorical strategy designed not only for verification purposes, but also for the task of initiating and insuring a readership. No matter how efficacious it undoubtedly was for Northup (or his editor) to ride Miss Stowe's coattails and share in her immense notoriety, one cannot help wondering about the profound implications involved in authenticating personal history by binding it to historical fiction. In its way, this strategy says as much about a former slave's inability to confirm his existence and "cast his shadow" as does the more conventional strategy observed in the Bibb narrative. Apparently, a novel may authenticate a personal history, especially when the personal history is that of a former slave.

While not expressing the issue in these terms, Northup seems to have thought about the dilemma of authentication and that of slave narratives competing with fictions of both the pro- and antislavery variety. He writes:

> Since my return to liberty, I have not failed to perceive the increasing interest throughout the Northern states, in regard to the subject of Slavery. Works of fiction, professing to portray its features in their more pleasing as well as more repugnant aspects, have been circulated to an extent unprecedented, and, as I understand, have created a fruitful topic of comment and discussion.
>
> I can speak of Slavery only so far as it came under my own observation—only so far as I have known and experienced it in my own person. My object is, to give a candid and truthful statement of facts: to repeat the story of my life, without exaggeration, leaving it for others to determine, whether even the pages of fiction present a picture of more cruel wrong or a severer bondage.

Clearly, Northup felt that the authenticity of his tale would not be taken for granted, and that, on a certain peculiar but familiar level enforced by rituals along the color line, his narrative would be viewed as a fiction competing with other fictions. However, in this passage Northup also inaugurates a counter-strategy. His reference to his own observation of slavery may be a just and subtle dig at the "arm-chair sociologists" of North and South alike, who wrote of the slavery question amid the comforts of their libraries and verandas. But more important, in terms of plot as well as point of view, the remark establishes Northup's authorial posture as a "participant-observer" in the truest and (given his bondage) most regrettable sense of the phrase. In these terms, then, Northup contributes personally to the authentication of *Twelve Years a Slave*: he challenges the authenticity of the popular slavery fictions and their power of authenticating his own personal history by first exploiting the bond between them and his tale and then assuming the posture of an authenticator. One needn't delve far into the annals of American race relations for proof that Northup's rhetorical strategy is but a paradigm for the classic manipulation of the master by the slave.

As the first chapter of *Twelve Years a Slave* unfolds, Northup tells of his family's history and circumstances. His father, Mintus Northup, was a slave in Rhode Island and in Rensselaer County, New York, before gaining his freedom in 1803 upon the death of his master. Mintus quickly amassed property and gained suffrage; he came to expect the freedoms that accompany self-willed mobility and self-initiated employment, and gave his son, Solomon, the extraordinary advantage of being born a free man. As a result, Solomon writes of gaining "an education surpassing that ordinarily bestowed upon children in our condition," and he recollects leisure hours "employed over my books, or playing the violin." Solomon describes employment (such as lumber-rafting on Lake Champlain) that was not only profitable but also, in a way associated with the romance of the frontier, adventurous and even manly. When Solomon Northup married Anne Hampton on Christmas Day of 1829,[2] they did not jump over a broomstick, as was the (reported) lot of most enslaved black Americans; rather, the two were married by a magistrate of the neighborhood, Timothy Eddy, Esq. Furthermore, their first home was neither a hovel nor a hut but the "Fort House," a residence "lately occupied by Captain Lathrop" and used in 1777 by General Burgoyne.

This saga of Solomon's heritage is full of interest, and it has its rhetorical and strategical properties as well. Northup has begun to establish his authorial posture removed from the condition of the black masses in slavery—a move which, as we have indicated,

2. See note regarding Northup's marriage date on p. 17 of this volume [Editors' note].

is as integral to the authenticating strategy as to the plot of his tale. In addition to portraying circumstances far more pleasant and fulfilling than those which he suffers in slavery, Northup's family history also yields some indication of his relations with whites in the district, especially the white Northups. Of course, these indications also advance both the plot and the authenticating strategy. One notes, for example, that while Mintus Northup did indeed migrate from the site of his enslavement once he was free, he retained the Northup surname and labored for a relative of his former master. Amid his new prosperity and mobility, Mintus maintained fairly amicable ties with his past; apparently this set the tone for relations between Northups, black and white. One should be wary of depicting New York north of Albany as an ideal or integrated area in the early 1800's, but the black Northups had bonds with whites—perhaps blood ties. To the end Solomon depends on these bonds for his escape from slavery and for the implicit verification of his tale.

In the first chapter of *Twelve Years a Slave*, Henry B. Northup, Esq., is mentioned only briefly as a relative of Mintus Northup's former master; in the context of Solomon's family history, he is but a looming branch of the (white) Northup family tree. However, as the tale concludes, Henry Northup becomes a voice and character in the narrative. He requests various legal documents essential to nullifying Solomon's sale into bondage; he inquires into Solomon's whereabouts in Bayou Boeuf, Louisiana; he presents the facts before lawyers, sheriffs, and Solomon's master, Edwin Epps; he pleads Solomon's case against his abductors before a District of Columbia court of law; and, most important, after the twelve years of assault on Solomon's sense of identity, Henry Northup utters, to Solomon's profound thanksgiving, Solomon's given name—not his slave name. In this way Henry Northup enters the narrative, and whatever linguistic authentication of the tale Solomon inaugurated by assuming the rather objective posture of the participant-observer-authenticator is concluded and confirmed, not by appended letter, but by Henry Northup's presence.

This strategy of authentication functions hand in hand with the narrative's strategy of reform. Like the carpenter, Bass, who jeopardizes his own safety by personally mailing Solomon's appeals for help to New York, Henry Northup embodies the spirit of reform in the narrative. In terms of reform strategy, Henry Northup and Bass—who, as a Canadian, represents a variation on the archetype of deliverance in Canada—are not only saviors but also models whose example might enlist other whites in the reform cause. Certainly abolitionists near and far could identify with these men, and that was important. Slave narratives were often most successful when they were as subtly pro-abolition as they were overtly anti-slavery—a consideration which could only have exacerbated the former slave's already sizeable problems with telling his tale in such a way that he, and not his editors or guarantors, controlled it.

But Henry Northup is a different kind of savior from Bass: he is an American descended from slaveowners, and he shares his sur-name with the kidnapped Solomon. Furthermore, his posture as a family friend is inextricably bound to his position in the tale as a lawyer. At the end of *Twelve Years a Slave*, Henry Northup appears in Louisiana as an embodiment of the law, as well as of Solomon Northup's past (in all its racial complexity) come to reclaim him. In this way, Solomon's *tale* assumes the properties of an integrated narrative—the authenticating texts (here, the words and actions of Henry Northup) are integrated into the former slave's tale. * * * Whereas the Bibb narrative begins with a discrete set of authenti-cating texts, the Northup narrative ends with such a set—an "Appendix."

The Northup Appendix contains three types of documents. First comes the New York state law, passed May 14, 1840, employed by Henry Northup and others to reclaim Solomon Northup from bondage in Louisiana. There follows a petition to the Governor of New York from Solomon's wife, Anne Northup, replete with legal language that persists in terming her a "memorialist." The remain-ing documents are letters, mostly from the black Northups' white neighbors, authenticating Solomon's claim that he is a free Negro. Despite our initial disappointment upon finding such an orthodox authenticating strategy appended to what had heretofore been a refreshingly sophisticated slave narrative (the narrative does not need the Appendix to fulfill its form), the Appendix does have its points of interest. Taken as a whole, it portrays the unfolding of a law; the New York law with which it begins precipitates the texts that follow, notably, in chronological order. On one level, then, Northup's Appendix is, far more than Bibb's Introduction, a story in epistolary form that authenticates not only his tale but also those voices within the tale, such as Henry Northup's. On another level, however, the Appendix becomes a further dimension to the reform strategy sub-sumed within the narrative. Just as Bass and Henry Northup posture as model reformers, the narrative's Appendix functions as a primer, complete with illustrative documents, on how to use the law to retrieve kidnapped free Negroes. Thus, the Appendix, as much as the tale itself, can be seen (quite correctly) as an elaborate rhetorical strategy against the Fugitive Slave Law of 1850.

In the end, the Northup narrative reverts to primitive authenti-cating techniques, but that does not diminish the sophistication and achievement of the tale within the narrative. We must now ask:

To what end does the immersion of authenticating documents and strategies within the texture of Northup's tale occur? Furthermore, is this goal literary or extraliterary? In answering these questions we come a little closer, I think, to an opinion on whether narratives like Northup's may be autobiographies.

Northup's conscious or unconscious integration and subsequent manipulation of authenticating voices advances his tale's plot and most certainly advances his narrative's validation and reform strategies. However, it does little to develop what Albert Stone has called a literary strategy of self-presentation. The narrative renders an extraordinary experience, but not a remarkable self. The two need not be exclusive, as Frederick Douglass's 1845 *Narrative* illustrates, but in the Northup book they appear to be distinct entities, principally because of the eye or "I" shaping and controlling the narration. Northup's eye and "I" are not so much introspective as they are inquisitive; even while in the pit of slavery in Louisiana, Northup takes time to inform us of various farming methods and of how they differ from practices in the North. Of course, this remarkable objective posture results directly from Northup assuming the role of a participant-observer for authentication purposes. But it all has a terrible price. Northup's tale is neither the history nor a metaphor for the history of his life; and because this is so, his tale cannot be called autobiographical.

* * *

CAROL WILSON

"From Their Free Homes into Bondage": The Abduction of Free Blacks into Slavery[†]

The possibility of being kidnapped and sold into slavery was shared by the entire American free black community, whether young or old, freeborn or freed slave, northerner or southerner. Certainly, however, some were at greater risk than others. Geography may have been the most important factor influencing the degree of risk. Although the practice occurred throughout the nation, residents of the states bordering the Mason-Dixon line were especially vulnerable. The large numbers of free blacks in Delaware, Maryland, and southern Pennsylvania, as well as proximity to the South, probably attracted kidnappers to this area.

† From *Freedom at Risk: The Kidnapping of Free Blacks in America, 1780–1865* (Lexington, KY: The University Press of Kentucky, 1994), pp. 9–18, 123–25. Reprinted by permission of the publisher. Wilson's notes have been edited.

Several factors other than geography determined the frequency of kidnapping. Age was another element. Children, presumably because they were easier to abduct than adults, were a favored target of kidnappers. Poverty was a third factor. Impoverished adults, desperate for income, were vulnerable to a kidnapper's deceptive offer of work. But again, no one was safe from the crime. Even several free blacks among the elite—financially secure and respected in their communities—encountered the specter of kidnapping.

The crime was pervasive partly because of the potential for great profits from a successful kidnapping and sale of a free black into slavery, which made many kidnappers willing to take the risks. In any case, kidnappers may have perceived no great risk, as the racism of the majority of American whites rendered it unlikely that kidnappers would be prosecuted to the full extent of the law. Although kidnapping was a crime in most states, it was a crime committed against blacks and therefore ignored by many whites.

Thus, kidnapping occurred throughout the country. One of the northernmost recorded kidnappings occurred in Sanbornton, New Hampshire, in 1836. The victim was a ten-year-old boy who had been placed with Noah Rollins by the overseers of the poor. For fifty dollars Rollins sold the child to an Alabama man named Bennett. Although the purchaser escaped, Rollins was jailed for kidnapping, and the boy was rescued.[1]

Possibly the southernmost known kidnapping occurred in Baton Rouge in 1860. Marguerite S. Fayman, a Creole girl from "people of wealth and prestige," was kidnapped at age ten. She had been living on a farm where her family raised pelicans, and she had attended a private school run by French nuns. The Sisters often took their young charges for walks around the port of Baton Rouge. Walking along the wharf on the Mississippi River one day, Marguerite became separated from the other children. A man grabbed her, took her aboard a nearby ship, and kept her in a cabin until the vessel sailed for Louisville. She remained a slave in Kentucky until her escape in 1864.[2]

The vast majority of kidnappings, however, took place not along the nation's perimeters but in the border states of Pennsylvania, Delaware, and Maryland. As Underground Railroad conductor Levi Coffin remembered, "Free negroes in Pennsylvania were frequently kidnapped or decoyed into these states [Virginia and Maryland], then hurried away to Georgia, Alabama, Louisiana and sold."[3] Lawyer and antislavery pamphleteer Jesse Torrey declared in 1818 that it would take a book to record all the incidences of kidnapping

1. *Courier and Enquirer* (New Hampshire), 25 Nov. 1836.
2. Norman Yetman, ed., *Voices from Slavery* (New York: Holt and Rinehart, 1970), 121.
3. Levi Coffin, *Reminiscences of Levi Coffin* (1876; New York: Arno Press, 1968), 12.

that had occurred in Delaware. Two years earlier, Torrey had testified before a U.S. House of Representatives committee about the
numerous kidnappings in Delaware and Maryland of which he had
personal knowledge.[4]

There are several reasons for the primacy of this area. Pennsylvania, Delaware, and Maryland combined had a greater free black
population than the rest of the country combined from 1790 to 1860.
Especially in the early nineteenth century, when many tobacco
farmers in the Upper South began diversifying their crops and
manumitting or selling their slaves, the free black populations of
these states increased. Cities, particularly Philadelphia, saw a large
percentage of this increase.[5]

Proximity to the Mason-Dixon line made it easy to transport victims into the South. Some kidnappers carried their victims southward by land, but many also took advantage of the Delaware River
and the network of rivers leading into the Chesapeake Bay.[6] Moreover, the anonymity of the port cities of Philadelphia, Wilmington,
and Baltimore facilitated kidnapping.

Kidnappers used a variety of methods. The most obvious means
of enslaving a free person was direct, forceful abduction. Kidnappers simply took their victims by incapacitating them or by threatening violence. As earlier indicated, children were especially
vulnerable in this regard. Henry Edwards, for example, as a young
boy was spirited away by two kidnappers from Newtown, New Jersey, hidden in a wagon. In Bordentown, several miles away, the victim managed to gain the attention of passersby by kicking the wagon's
side. They rescued him and the kidnappers fled.[7] Two free black men
from Illinois were not so fortunate. Forced across the Mississippi
River from Cairo by a Missouri gang, one escaped by swimming back
across the river. He managed to find his way home, bleeding and
"mangled about the head." As in numerous other cases, what happened to the second victim is unknown.[8]

Deceit was a ubiquitous element in adult kidnappings. Adults
were frequently lured into a kidnapper's company by some pretext,
then forcibly restrained and taken into slavery. Some kidnapping
victims were attracted by the promise of a job. The case of Solomon
Northup, probably the most famous kidnapping case, involved such
deception. Northup was a free black man well known in New York

4. Jesse Torrey, A Portraiture of Domestic Slavery in the United States, 2d ed. (Ballston
   Spa, N.Y.: Privately published, 1818), 95.
5. U.S. Bureau of the Census, Negro Population in the United States, 1790–1915 (Washington, D.C.: Government Printing Office, 1918), 57.
6. William M. Wiecek, The Sources of Antislavery: Constitutionalism in America, 1760–
   1848 (Ithaca: Cornell Univ. Press, 1977), 88.
7. National Anti-Slavery Standard, 14 Nov. 1857.
8. Cincinnati Gazette, 25 July 1857.

state for his skill as a musician. Invited by two white entertainers to join their act, he traveled about the East Coast. Reaching the nation's capital, he was drugged by his companions and awakened in a slave jail. Sold to a dealer, Northup was sent to Louisiana, where he labored as a slave for more than a decade before he could get word to his wife, Anne. She secured the aid of Washington Hunt, the governor of New York, in freeing her husband. En route to his home, Northup and his lawyer stopped in Washington, D.C., and initiated prosecution of the slave trader who had sold Northup to New Orleans. James Burch was acquitted.[9] But the Cleveland *Leader* reported in 1854 that it was thought that Northup's kidnapper (presumably one of the men who had lured him to Washington) had been captured. "If so, let the law deal with the scoundrel in its utmost severity!"[1]

The offer of a job was not the only means kidnappers used to lure victims, as antislavery writer Jesse Torrey heard from one of several blacks he discovered chained in an attic in Washington, D.C. (As a slave-trading center, the nation's capital was an especially threatening spot for people of color.) One of the people he encountered there was a twenty-one-year-old indentured servant, who had been decoyed from his home in Delaware by the prospect of hunting possum with his master. Once he was in the fields, two strangers seized, bound, and threatened him with pistols. Eventually he was taken to Washington and sold, being beaten several times for insisting he was not a slave.[2]

Blacks as well as whites were guilty of kidnapping. Two especially tragic accounts of kidnappings performed by blacks involved men who lured women with romantic advances. Jesse Torrey described "a monster in human shape," a Philadelphia man who apparently married black women for the purpose of selling them into slavery. When the city's black population discovered his treachery, a mob attacked him, but the police saved him from certain death by incarcerating him.[3]

A similar story was that of a woman known only as Lucinda, a young domestic in a small Illinois town about fifty miles from the Missouri border. Formerly a slave in Kentucky, she had "legally secured her freedom." Lucinda had been seeing a barber in the town, although she had been warned about him. He was described as "a decidedly dandyish fellow" who was believed to be part black, although he claimed to be part Indian. Early one summer, a man who said he was from Maryland arrived in the Illinois town looking

9. Solomon Northup, *Twelve Years a Slave* (New York: Miller, Orton, and Mulligan, 1854), 3, 9, 12–20, 48, 61, 212–214, 225–228, 242, 243–251, 256–266. *New York Times*, 20 Jan. 1854.
1. *Cleveland Leader*, 10 July 1854.
2. Torrey, *Portraiture of Slavery*, 81–83; deposition of Jesse Torrey, 29 April 1816, in Papers of the Select Committee to Inquire into the Existence of an Inhuman and Illegal Traffic in Slaves . . . in the District of Columbia, National Archives.
3. Torrey, *Portraiture of Slavery*, 97.

for a summer home. "And to those of us who were boys he 'looked exactly like a southerner,'" recalled resident George Murray McConnel, "but the real southerners by birth who lived in the village smiled, and said he was rather too tropical in style."[4]

The stranger made Lucinda's acquaintance and claimed he was a friend of her former master in Kentucky. She was also warned about him, but paid no heed. One day the barber took Lucinda for a drive. When they had not returned by sunset as expected, no one worried, thinking that the barber was proposing marriage. That night, however, an alarm was raised after the barber returned to town alone on horseback. One man said that the wagon in which the two had gone for a ride belonged to the southerner. Three men, including McConnel's father, confronted the barber, who first claimed that he had returned with Lucinda but changed his story when they threatened him. The barber said that several miles out of town he had gone into the woods for some sassafras root and when he returned, Lucinda and the wagon were gone. He had not notified the police because he thought she had abandoned him, and he was angry with her.[5]

Eventually the men caught up with Lucinda and the Marylander several miles outside of town. Others, having heard the story, joined them, and they all returned home, "a little triumphal procession." Lucinda backed up the barber's story, saying that she had been kidnapped after her escort went into the woods. No one believed the barber's innocence, and he left town shortly thereafter.[6]

As mentioned earlier, children were particularly vulnerable to kidnapping. Many were enslaved after being hired out by their parents, a common and economically necessary practice in the poor black community. Ira Berlin has argued that many blacks, especially children, were virtually enslaved under apprenticeship agreements. Even worse, these arrangements left children open to actual enslavement when they were sold by an unscrupulous employer.[7] Young Sarah Taylor (or Harrison) was begging in the streets of New York City when she came to the attention of Haley and Anna Howard in 1858. They persuaded her parents to let Sarah go with them to live in Newark, New Jersey, as their servant. Instead, they took the girl to Washington, D.C., where they attempted to sell her for six hundred dollars. When she related her story to the owner of the hotel where they were staying, Sarah won his protection. Sarah's case was brought to the attention of the mayor of New York City, who had her restored to her family. The Howards (their names turned

4. George Murray McConnel, "Illinois and Its People," *Transactions of the Illinois Historical Society*, no. 7 (Springfield, Ill., 1902), 80–81.
5. Ibid., 81–82.
6. Ibid.
7. Ira Berlin, *Slaves without Masters: The Free Negro in the Antebellum South* (New York: Pantheon Books, 1974), 226.

out to be aliases) fled to Baltimore, but authorities caught up with and arrested them, and Haley Howard eventually served several months in prison for kidnapping.[8]

Another case involved six-year-old Peter Still and his eight-year-old brother, Levin, who were kidnapped in the early nineteenth century. Playing at their home near Philadelphia, the boys became concerned as the day wore on and their mother did not return home as expected. Deciding to go to the church to look for her, they accepted a ride with a stranger in a gig. He took them not to their mother but to Versailles, Kentucky. In nearby Lexington, they were taken to their new master's cook and told, "There is your mother." The boys were struck when they protested, and they quickly learned not to contradict their owner. They thought about their former home and freedom frequently, however, and although afraid to run away, they hoped to buy their freedom someday. Levin died a slave, but Peter Still eventually purchased his freedom and returned home after about forty years.[9]

Children were targets of kidnappers because they were easier to abduct forcibly than adults. William Wells Brown, abolitionist and author, wrote to National Anti-Slavery Standard editor Sydney Gay; apprising him of a kidnapping in Georgetown, Ohio, in 1844. Traveling through the town on his way to Mount Pleasant, Brown encountered "the citizens standing upon the corners of the streets talking as though something had occurred during the night." They told him that the night before, five or six men had broken into the home of John Wilkinson, beating him and his wife before carrying away their fourteen-year-old son. With the help of neighbors, Wilkinson pursued the kidnappers, who crossed the Ohio River into Virginia. It is not known whether the boy was recovered.[1]

If kidnapped at a very early age, a free black child might grow up a slave never knowing that he or she had been born free. Such was the case with Lavinia Bell. She was kidnapped as an infant in Washington, D.C., along with numerous others, by Tom Watson, who was eventually sentenced to life imprisonment in the Richmond Penitentiary. Bell learned of her free status from her mistress in Galveston, Texas, where she was brutally abused. After numerous attempts, Bell eventually escaped to Montreal, where her story was recorded.[2]

Another vulnerable group was blacks held as contraband during the Civil War. Legally slaves, they had been freed in effect by

8. National Anti-Slavery Standard, 3 April 1858, 29 Jan. 1859; Niles National Register, 24 March 1858.
9. Kate E. R. Pickard, The Kidnapped and Ransomed (1856; New York: Negro Universities Press, 1968).
1. National Anti-Slavery Standard, 7 Nov. 1844.
2. Montreal Gazette, 31 Jan. 1861.

advancing Union troops, yet they existed in a legal limbo between free and slave status, a very precarious position. As nonslaves, they had no masters to protect them, but not being free they did not enjoy protection of the law. They were at the mercy of the Union soldiers, some of whom found selling them an easy way to make money.

Blacks held as contraband faced danger from soldiers of both sides during the Civil War. The abduction of sixteen-year-old Charles Amos and his younger cousin was not unusual. The two had hired out as servants to officers of the Forty-second Massachusetts Infantry Regiment, traveling with them to Galveston, Texas, late in 1862. After Confederate forces recaptured the town on the first day of the new year, the invaders sold Amos and his cousin into slavery.[3]

Cavalry units of the Army of Northern Virginia also kidnapped blacks, both slave and free, during the Pennsylvania campaign in June of 1863. By some accounts, this practice affected large numbers of black residents of southern parts of the state. Edwin Coddington, author of a study of the Gettysburg campaign, claimed that "thousands" of free blacks fled the Cumberland Valley into Harrisburg seeking refuge from the troops. At least fifty Pennsylvania blacks were sent into slavery as a result of the campaign.[4]

While the kidnapping of blacks by Confederate soldiers is not surprising, their northern counterparts were guilty of the same crime. The activities of the Ninety-ninth Regiment, New York Volunteers, stationed near Deep Creek, Virginia, provide one illustration. Residents there had been suspicious for some time that the soldiers had been "capturing stray contrabands . . . and selling them to parties who run them South." These suspicions were confirmed by the testimony of one man who reported to the provost marshal that he had been the victim of an attempted kidnapping. Two soldiers seized him while he was returning from market one day, bound and gagged him, and drove him some distance in a cart. They then "offered horse, cart, and man for three hundred dollars." When the soldiers retired to a bar for drinks, he managed to escape. As proof of his story, the victim's watch and some of his money were found on one of the soldiers. Although a reporter wrote that the men of the regiment felt "the utmost abhorrence of such barbarous and inhuman outrages," it is not known whether the kidnappers suffered any punishment.[5]

What motivated people to commit such a crime? Racism was a contributing factor. Had the rights of people of color been respected

3. *Liberator*, 27 March 1863 (from the *Dedham [Massachusetts] Gazette*); Paul M. Angle and Earl Schenck Miers, *Tragic Years, 1860–1865* (New York: Simon and Schuster, 1960), 2:463.
4. Otto Eisenschiml and Ralph Newman, *The American Iliad* (Lexington: Univ. of Kentucky Press.), 136; Edwin B. Coddington, *The Gettysburg Campaign: A Study in Command* (New York: Charles Scribner's Sons, 1968), 150, 161.
5. *Liberator*, 27 March 1863 (from *Correspondence of the Fond du Lac (Wisconsin) Commonwealth*); Reid Mitchell, *Civil War Soldiers* (New York: Viking, 1988), 123.

as much as those of whites, kidnapping could not have occurred, at least not to the extent that it did. As the free black population increased, so did racism and discrimination against blacks.[6] In 1790, slightly more than 27,000 free blacks lived in the North; by the time of the Civil War, this figure had increased tenfold, to nearly a quarter of a million.[7] Scholars of free black life such as Gary Nash have shown that whites felt threatened when the free black population of their area grew, and increased racism was often the result.[8]

Racism not only helped perpetuate the crime but also stalled prosecution. While abducting a white person usually resulted in action to rescue the victim and punish the kidnappers, the same crime committed against blacks met with apathy among most of the white community. This indifference was noticeable in the careless treatment that white newspaper reporters and letter writers often accorded black people. Sometimes the newspaper item identified a black only by first name, sometimes not even that. When names were given, little effort was made to standardize spelling. The cavalier attitude of most whites toward blacks made it possible for kidnappers to operate almost openly, with private citizens and government officials generally doing nothing to stop them.

At the root of the kidnapping of free blacks was the legality of slavery itself. The *African Observer* noted in 1827, "Where a traffic in slaves is thus actively carried on, and sanctioned by existing laws, those coloured persons who are legally free must necessarily hold their freedom by a very precarious tenure."[9] Slavery was supported by state laws, by the federal fugitive slave laws of 1793 and 1850, and by court cases such as *Prigg v. Pennsylvania* (1842), creating a climate that engendered kidnapping of free blacks. Although other laws existed to protect free blacks, they were only sporadically enforced and were not an effective counterweight to the laws that allowed for enslavement of free blacks. American law, beginning as early as the Constitution, generally served to protect slaveowners' property at the expense of black rights.

In the end, the primary motivation behind kidnapping was probably greed. Kidnapping free blacks and selling them into slavery could bring great financial reward. The prevailing motive of kidnappers was, as the Delaware Abolition Society termed it, "that fruitful source of evil—'the love of money.'"[1] According to abolitionist

6. Delaware Abolition Society (hereafter DAS). Minutes, 4 Jan. 1816, Historical Society of Pennsylvania (hereafter HSP).
7. Kenneth M. Stampp, *The Peculiar Institution: Slavery in the Ante-Bellum South* (New York: Vintage Books, 1956), 415–16.
8. Gary B. Nash, "Forging Freedom: The Emancipation Experience in the Northern Seaport Cities, 1775–1820," in Ira Berlin and Ronald Hoffman, eds., *Slavery and Freedom in the Age of the American Revolution* (Charlottesville: Univ. of Virginia Press, 1983), 11.
9. *African Observer*, July 1827.
1. DAS Minutes, 4 Jan. 1816, HSP.

Edward Needles, the idea of making money in this fashion appealed to "the lower classes," as well as "some inferior magistrates and constables."[2] Free blacks, already vulnerable because of their race and socioeconomic disabilities, were further victimized by the profit motive. The prices that slaves generally brought were bolstered by the growth of cotton production after the invention of the cotton gin, by the close of the African slave trade, and by the expansion of slavery into the Southwest. By the 1850s, slave prices had soared, with good field hands usually bringing at least a thousand dollars and some artisans selling for more than twice that amount.[3] As long as the legal system and popular opinion tacitly permitted kidnapping and as long as slaves brought a good price on the market, there would be people unscrupulous enough to make money in this manner.

Some kidnappers of free blacks were members of professional gangs who often engaged in various other extralegal activities, particularly horse thieving and other forms of robbery. Others were average citizens who joined the ranks of kidnappers only when the opportunity to make money arose unexpectedly. Still other kidnappers were slave catchers who hunted fugitives for slaveowner clients. Slave catchers occasionally strayed beyond the law, accidentally or intentionally, by claiming free blacks as fugitives. As noted, not all kidnappers were white. Sometimes blacks worked with white abductors, often as lures. There is evidence that they worked alone as well.

One thing that kidnappers had in common, though, was the fear which they engendered in the black population, another element that made kidnapping possible. At the 1828 American Convention of Abolition Societies, Thomas Shipley, chair of the committee reporting on the internal slave trade, noted, "Individuals are well known, who have decoyed free people of color on board their vessels, . . . selling them as slaves."[4] Two Kentucky kidnappers, when arrested, threatened to "burn the city of Frankfort for interrupting their business."[5] The impunity with which kidnappers acted indicates that blacks were not alone in their fear of the criminals. It was common in some parts of the country for kidnapping to be practiced openly, without interference from authorities or from neighbors who feared retribution if they spoke out. Even those who were horrified

2. Edward Needles, *An Historical Memoir of the Pennsylvania Society for Promoting the Abolition of Slavery* (1848; New York: Arno Press and New York Times, 1969), 62.
3. U.S. Bureau of the Census, *Negro Population in the United States, 1790–1915* (Washington, D. C.: Government Printing Office, 1918), 55.
4. Minutes of the American Convention, 1828, in "Reports of the American Convention of Abolition Societies on Negroes and Slavery, Their Appeals to Congress, and Their Addresses to the Citizens of the United States," *Journal of Negro History* 6 (July 1921): 327.
5. *Frankfort Yeoman*, 18 Nov. 1854.

at the kidnapping of free blacks into slavery were generally unwilling
to endanger their own lives by assisting a person of color. As a
result, many kidnappers escaped prosecution. Slaveowner-turned-
abolitionist James G. Birney wrote in 1842, "No grand inquest has for
years had the courage or virtue to find a bill of indictment against a
kidnapper, however plain and undeniable the proof of his guilt."[6]

* * *

SAM WORLEY

Solomon Northup and the Sly Philosophy of the Slave Pen[†]

Several rather sweeping assumptions about 19th-century slave narratives have made it difficult to fully understand or appreciate the
significance of Solomon Northup's 1853 autobiography, *Twelve Years
a Slave*. One assumption is that slave narratives must, as their formal telos, demonstrate "through a variety of rhetorical means that
they regard the *writing* of autobiography as in some ways uniquely
self-liberating" (Andrews xi). This romantic model of writing and
selfhood, which elegantly conflates self-expression, self-mastery,
and self-advancement, typically takes Frederick Douglass' 1845
Narrative as the foremost representative of the genre.[1] Another
assumption, to a degree consequent upon the first, is that those narratives which rely on a white amanuensis are inherently less interesting than those which do not. The argument in this latter case is
that however honorable his intentions, the amanuensis will inevitably shape the narrative to some extent, thereby undermining its
authenticity both as history and autobiography. The only other organizational scheme readers have proven capable of recognizing in
slave narratives is the providential: that found in those religiously-
driven narratives (and narrative-inspired novels) for which the
misfortunes and accidents undergone by the self achieve significance
through the unveiling of their spiritual significance or necessity.
Unlike the Douglass' paradigm which is developed primarily through
temporal figures, the providential mode chiefly utilizes spatial

6. Dwight L. Dumond, ed., *Letters of James Gillespie Birney* (1938; rpt. Gloucester, Mass.:
   Peter Smith, 1966), 2:652.
† From *Callaloo* 20.1 (Winter 1997): 243–59. Copyright © 1997 Charles H. Rowell.
   Reprinted by permission of Johns Hopkins University Press.
1. William Andrews, on the other hand, finds the second of Douglass' autobiographies,
   My Bondage and My Freedom (1855), the finest, due largely to its broader scope and
   greater complexity (218–19).

figures. *Twelve Years a Slave* conforms to neither of these models, and its reputation has suffered accordingly.

Northup's narrative, though well known, has often been treated as a narrative of the second rank, albeit one with an unusually exciting and involving story as well as, thanks to the research of its modern editors, Sue Eakin and Joseph Logsdon, one with considerable historical value. However, Northup's reliance on a white amanuensis, David Wilson, as well as the failure of the narrative to fulfill certain formal, generic expectations, has meant that analysis of the narrative patterns and philosophical perspective of the work have been almost entirely neglected. Its value has been seen as one of fact or historical record and not, as in the case of the so-called classic narratives, a matter of imposing meaningful, interpretive form on its subject matter. To the limited extent that the form of *Twelve Years* has been examined, it has been dismissed as a clichéd and none-too-skilled repetition of narrative motifs and figures from a hundred other slave stories. David Wilson, the amanuensis, too, is taken to task for the obtrusiveness of his stale, genteel diction and images.[2]

Now Wilson is, admittedly, a problem. But in his defense let it be said that, in regard to slavery at least, Wilson appears to have had no particular political agenda to whose ends he manipulates the story. A small-town lawyer, former school superintendent, and amateur writer, Wilson's only other works include *The Life of Jane McCrea, with an Account of Burgoyne's Expedition in 1777*, an account of an Indian massacre of that year, and *Henrietta Robinson*, an account of a notorious murder in 19th-century New York. There is no record indicating any activity on his part in antislavery. Instead, Wilson seems to have primarily seen Northup's adventures as merely an opportunity to tell and sell a particularly sensationalistic tale.[3] His lack of tendentiousness allows Northup's own nuanced vision of slavery to be articulated within the work without polemical oversimplification. *Twelve Years* is convincingly Northup's tale and no one else's because of its amazing attention to empirical detail and unwillingness to reduce the complexity of Northup's experience to

2. Valerie Smith writes that "the presence of an intermediary renders the majority of the narratives not artistic constructions of personal experience but illustrations of someone else's view of slavery" (9). James Olney is perhaps the most extreme in his criticism of Northup's narrative, questioning its status "as autobiography and/or literature," largely on the grounds of what he sees as Wilson's intrusive and unhelpful presence (Davis and Gates 163). Olney insists that aside from the "great one by Frederick Douglass," all slave narratives are too conventionalized and cliché-ridden to be considered seriously as literature (168). Stepto, though less harsh in his judgments overall, similarly dismisses *Twelve Years* as autobiography: "Northup's eye and 'I' are not so much introspective as they are inquisitive . . . Northup's tale is neither the history nor a metaphor for the history of his life; and because this is so, his tale cannot be called autobiographical" (Davis and Gates 237).
3. Eakin and Logsdon are similarly persuaded that Wilson was drawn primarily to the story's "publishing potential" (xiii).

a stark moral allegory. Whereas the firm, confident teleological structure of Douglass' *Narrative* reflects his intention to persuade, the
more problematic organization and emphasis of *Twelve Years* can be
most usefully seen as reflecting Northup's own difficulty in making
sense of his experiences. Even if Northup had possessed Douglass'
rhetorical prowess, it seems doubtful that he would have constructed
a narrative as assured in its judgments and analysis as Douglass'.
Twelve Years moves toward an understanding of the ironies of slavery quite unlike that of Douglass or most other antislavery writers
of the day.

Of course assigning an independent perspective to a protagonist
whom we only see second-hand through the prose of his amanuensis seems a shaky proposition at best and speculating on the narrative he might have written under other circumstances is even more
problematic. But even in its present form, *Twelve Years* does in fact
display a narrative strategy which is reducible neither to Wilson's
good story nor to the shared structures and figures of slave narratives in general. Northup's narrative offers a critical vision of slavery
which implicitly rejects two prevailing methods for understanding
both the individual slave and the institution as a whole—the rational
and the providential and their chief organizational schemes, the
temporal and the spatial. Moreover, in offering his critique, Northup displays an understanding of the nature of justice and individual identity unlike almost anything else I have seen in contemporary
narratives.

The nature of Northup's originality is evident when seen in comparison to what is probably the best-known slave narrative. The
philosophical underpinnings of Northup's narrative couldn't be farther from the rational moral idealism which structures Frederick
Douglass' *Narrative*. Criticism of Douglass' first autobiography has
repeatedly shown the extent to which it is complicit with individu-
alist bourgeois thought both through its elevation of Douglass as a
self-made man as well as its downplaying of the crucial role of the
slave community.[4] However, beyond its politically problematic
nature, this individualism is equally culpable from the standpoint
of its effect on the narrative's moral argument. Parallel to Douglass'
representation of himself as independent of community is the narrative's representation of the just or the good as radically uncondi-
tioned, independent of any social or historical context. The relative
isolation of Douglass as a moral agent denies the work the sort of

---

4. Valerie Smith, for example, writes that "the plot of the narrative offers a profound endorse-
ment of the fundamental American plot, the myth of the self-made man. His broad-based
indictments notwithstanding, by telling the story of one man's rise from slavery to the
status of esteemed orator, writer, and statesman, he confirms the myth shared by generations of American men that inner resources alone can lead to success" (27).

nuanced and complex moral vision possible only when the self is seen enmeshed in and mediated by an intricate network of social relations and contexts.

Northup's story, by contrast, emphasizes not inherently meaningful form, but its absence. *Twelve Years a Slave* sets out from the beginning to contradict and question the archetypal plot for American autobiography: the Franklinesque rise from humble beginnings to prosperity through hard work and ability. Unlike those narratives such as Douglass' where the subject's vague antecedents both emphasize the cruelty of slavery as well as the subject's absolute self-creation, what Olney calls the "sketchy account of parentage" characteristic of most narratives (153), Northup gives a comparatively extensive account of his forebears. Northup represents his family history as continuous and free from any violent breaks. Race, normally the source of discontinuity in such histories, is minimized in two different ways. Solomon Northup, black, continues to enjoy friendly relations with Henry Northup, a white man and the descendant of the family which owned Northup's ancestors. Thanks to the "persevering interest" of the latter in Solomon's well-being, Henry Northup will play a crucial role in obtaining Solomon's release and return. Solomon Northup is able to relate with considerable precision the four places in which his father lived and worked after he was set free. Reinforcing this familial continuity, Solomon recounts the various ways in which his father molded the character of his two sons. Solomon tells of his father's industry and integrity, the fact that he always remained a farmer without descending to those more demeaning occupations "which seem to be especially allotted to the children of Africa" (5). He gave his children more of an education than most Black children could expect. He owned sufficient property to entitle him to vote in New York. He taught his children morality and a degree of religion. More importantly in this context, while his father regretted slavery, he continued to express "the warmest emotions of kindness, and even of affection towards the family, in whose house he had been a bondsman" (5). Adding to the softening influence of his father's lack of racial animosity is the racial origin of Solomon's own wife, Anne Hampton, on which he places particular emphasis. He writes that

> She is not able to determine the exact line of her descent, but the blood of three races mingled in her veins. It is difficult to tell whether the red, white, or black predominates. The union of them all, however, in her origin, has given her a singular but pleasing expression, such as is rarely to be seen. Though somewhat resembling, yet she can not properly be styled a quadroon, a class to which, I have omitted to mention, my mother belonged. (7)

Both the accounts of his father and his wife allow Northup to situate his own early life in an unbroken network of family and society
that contrasts dramatically with the chaotic family relations found
in most other narratives as well as in the later portion of Northup's
own story.

The problem for the most familiar type of slave narrative is that
slavery denies the slave the very stuff of which personal narratives
are composed—origins, family identity or name, education, and
increasing self-determination leading up to the moment at which
the narrator becomes capable of writing the narrative itself. In the
archetypal slave narrative, these things are problematic. The slave
has little sense of his origins, his first name is usually given him by
his master, his true family name is unknown, he is denied education, and slavery itself restricts the extent to which the events of his
life may be said to result from his own volition. The denial of these
narrative building blocks is simply another aspect of the denial of
the slave's personhood. Keeping in mind Aristotle's crucial definition
in *The Politics* of the slave as one capable of obeying rational commands but, lacking reason himself, incapable of giving them, we can
see how to be a slave is on a profound level to be defined as a creature
whose life cannot be construed as a narrative, whose days and works
are merely submoments of the master's biography and cannot be,
according to the ideology of the slaveholder, meaningful or coherent
in themselves.

In the dynamic of most slave narratives, the absence of conventional elements of personal narrative is compensated for by making
the slave story one of how those various elements had to be created
by the subject. Douglass' 1845 narrative offers the most brilliant and
conspicuous example of this substitution and shows how, far from
being the antithesis of Bildungsroman, this variety of slave narrative
is arguably its highest form since the individual slave not only under-
goes an education in self-mastery but must create both the education
and himself. The act of writing the narrative becomes the ultimate act
of self-redemption, for by writing of his own origins the ex-slave
can make himself his own author in a sense and displace the onus of
having been merely the effect of events and becomes instead the
source of all the narrative moments. The act of reflecting upon and
representing moments of victimization or subjection allows the author
to master them, to make them, at least symbolically, the effects of his
own consciousness. Moreover, he can bestow form and meaning
upon events which were, because of their relative contingency and
unwilled nature, previously without significance or meaning.

Yet here again, Northup's narrative responds differently. *Twelve
Years a Slave* opens with a detailed recounting of Northup's early
days in New York told with explicit attention to its fulfillment of

cultural, usually white, stereotypes of hard work and social advance-
ment. Ironically, the telos of most slave narratives, freedom and
economic self-sufficiency, are the conditions from which Northup
begins. Consequently, Northup's kidnapping and descent into slavery
undermines the stability implicit in both the basic narrative model
as well as its slave narrative variant. A narrative like Douglass'
assumes that principles of justice are available anywhere, anytime to
the rational mind. As a result, his sense of injustice grows in tandem
with his developing sense of self. Implicit in this relationship is the
idea that his self results from his rational apprehension of injustice.
The Aristotelian definition of slave nature is denied through the
exercise of reason. Northup's narrative, however, directly challenges
this association. Any hope of rational narrative form is shattered by
his kidnapping. His descent into slavery brings with it a vision of the
world as a place of contingency, illusion, and disorder, neither inherently rational nor irrational. Douglass shows through the exercise of
reason, his unsuitability for slavery; Northup shows the irrationality
of slavery when he is torn from his rational existence. Douglass
works to create his own identity; Northup must be brutally trained
to deny his. Each time he fails to remember his new slave name or
inadvertently says something that suggests his life before the kidnapping, he is punished with a beating.

Northup's economic collapse similarly violates the narrative pattern characteristic of Douglass, whose first narrative operates to a
large extent as a type of Franklinesque (or, to be anachronistic,
Algeresque) rise from poverty to prosperity through the exercise of
self-discipline, self-improvement, and hard work. Douglass' economic conquest is paralleled by his mastery of linear time: to be a
successful free man is to impose the linear narrative time as the
shape or form of one's life. Meaning is bestowed on one's life by acting to guarantee that each moment of life contributes to the next
advance. The achievement of such form triumphs in the evasion of
history and contingency. Effaced in such a narrative is the possibility
of further change, the return of history, the possibility that prosperity
may be as fragile and temporary as poverty has proven to be. The
stakes of such a return are immense since in the Franklinesque
narrative form the self's value derives solely from this narrative of
economic transcendence just as the narrative is taken as the mani-
festation or realization of the subject's intrinsic value. The loss of
such value threatens to completely undermine the subject's claim
to meaning.

The first section of the narrative shows how seemingly stable and
complete Northup's prosperity was. His father, a freed slave in
Rhode Island, "was a man respected for his industry and integrity"
(5). He was an independent farmer and steadfastly refused "those

more menial positions, which seem to be especially allotted to the children of Africa." He acquired enough property to enable him to vote in New York, and he educated all of his children to a degree unheard of for a farmer's children. He taught his children the work ethic: religion, morality, and hard work. Solomon, in turn, takes up "a life of industry" (7). He moves into a building which, as he specifically points out, had played a role in the Revolutionary War, thereby further implying his connection to American life and history. Similarly, when he tells us that he worked on the construction of the Champlain Canal, he implies a connection between his personal labor and success and the national prosperity. With these wages he buys a pair of horses and tows rafts of lumber along the canal. He lists in notable detail all of his economic vicissitudes from that time forward: cutting timber, buying a farm and livestock, planting corn and oats, part-time work as a fiddle player, his wife's work in the kitchen of Sherril's Coffee House, his relocation to Saratoga Springs to work as a driver for tourists, and eventually more fiddle playing, this time for the railroad workers. Even his financial setback in Saratoga Springs is put into service as a further example of the truth of the work ethic:

> Though always in comfortable circumstances, we had not prospered. The society and associations at that world-renowned watering place, were not calculated to preserve the simple habits of industry and economy to which I had been accustomed, but, on the contrary, to substitute others in their stead, tending to shiftlessness and extravagance. (11)

But in one respect this passage deviates significantly from the Franklin narrative model: Northup concedes the disastrous effect of environment upon character; he situates his failure in a specific cultural context rather than using the episode solely as evidence of value or lack of value in character. This is not just incidental; this is a way of thinking about character that will occur again and again in his story. We can only grasp the significance of Northup's detailed accounting of his general economic prosperity when we see it in the context of the book as a whole, for where the narrative of economic transcendence usually ends, Northup begins. His is a catastrophic fall that raises questions not about his intrinsic worth but about the truth of such narratives as Douglass' and the vision of selfhood they imply.

Moving even farther away from this association of selfhood and narrative time, Northup emphasizes how when he is drugged and kidnapped he loses all sense of time: "From that moment I was insensible. How long I remained in that condition—whether only that night, or many days and nights—I do not know" (19). By bringing together the loss of access to the standard narrative of economic progress and freedom, Northup's lost sense of time, and ultimately the loss of his very identity, this passage demonstrates how the collapse of the conventional, teleological narrative destroys at once both conventional subjectivity and controlled, linear time.

   Twelve Years is particularly good at showing the irrational and brutal nature of the slavemaster's ostensible rationalization of time.[5] One of the greatest ironies of Northup's account is that while production is rationalized to absurd and frightening lengths, the time of the slave's world is increasingly disjoined from any standard sense of time. We see how the slave is initially beaten to produce the maximum amount of cotton and how that extreme quantity then becomes the standard against which all the slave's subsequent pickings will be judged. Yet alongside such passages, *Twelve Years* also tells of how slaves are made to stay up all night dancing to entertain the master, work around the clock during the cane harvest, and work on the Sabbath. The slave is expected to labor in a rationally quantifiable, predictive manner, but, in his role as a thing or possession himself, he is treated without regard to any sense of time. Emblematic of this contrast between the rationalization of labor and the irrational life of the slave, his double role as a producer of commodities and a commodity himself, is Northup's own work as overseer in which he is both the one who overworks and is himself overworked in the name of production. The absurdities and deceits practiced in the name of reason further dispels any sense of there being an objective order of rationality which can be appealed to in the name of justice. The steady unfolding of narrative time and the conception of an individual life as a matter of imposing meaningful form on that time are both explicitly undermined. Reason, both the formal and philosophical key to Douglass' narrative, appears in *Twelve Years* as merely a mask for selfishness and injustice.

   In fact, so thorough is the way in which slavery conflicts with conventional notions of time in *Twelve Years* and so thorough is the amount of coincidence and flashback and the highly literary way in which the significance of seemingly impertinent details—Northup's trip to Montreal, his ability with rafts, the name of the store where he bought his children's clothes—becomes apparent only as the story reaches its final section that it makes one suspect that the crucial influence is not the linear timeline of Franklin or Douglass but the providential mode of *Uncle Tom's Cabin*.[6]

   As is well known, Northup's work exhibits an important awareness of Harriet Beecher Stowe's *Uncle Tom's Cabin*. This is explicit

5. For the effect of the capitalist rationalization of time on slave life, see Genovese 285–94.
6. Stowe, of course, is well aware of the double nature of the slave as the title on one of her chapters suggests: "The Man Who Was a Thing."

in Northup's dedication "To Harriet Beecher Stowe / Whose Name, / Throughout the World, is Identified with the *Great Reform*; THIS NARRATIVE, AFFORDING ANOTHER KEY TO UNCLE TOM'S CABIN, / IS RESPECTFULLY DEDICATED" and only slightly less explicit in his challenge in the first chapter where he asks "whether even the pages of fiction present a picture of more cruel wrong or a severer bondage" (3).[7] If in Douglass' *Narrative*, the central feature of the plot, escape from slavery, appears as a rational development, in Stowe's work the plot reflects not reason but Providence. The diaspora-like effect in which Stowe's black characters are scattered and at least some are eventually recollected to an extent recurs in Northup as do conspicuous echoes of Stowe's own heavy irony.[8]

Admittedly, in speaking of Stowe's novel we are no longer strictly dealing with slave narratives. Stowe drew on the testimony and narratives of ex-slaves, written and oral, in the creation of both her great novel and her commentary on it in *A Key to Uncle Tom's Cabin*. The important thing in this instance is not the authority of the novel in comparison to slave autobiography, but its representative-ness of a certain mode of construing the experience of slavery and escape. That mode is, of course, providential; its cosmology, Christian. In a manner consistent with many other mid-19th century novels, *Uncle Tom's Cabin* offers a dramatic picture of lives scattered then recollected, of virtue thwarted or ignored then vindicated, of relations lost then recovered.[9] Providence displays itself like a par-lor trick, the message is written down on a piece of paper, folded neatly, shredded into a thousand pieces or tossed into the fire and then quite suddenly makes its miraculous reappearance whole and intact in the magician's gloved hand. The working of Providence, its plot, proceeds inevitably, if at times mysteriously. In place of the fire or the shredding, Stowe's characters, torn from family and home, live episodically, buffeted by a series of seemingly contingent events. They are regularly frustrated in their efforts to impose form or mean-ing on their lives—except in one crucial respect. Those characters

7. Andrews sees *Twelve Years* as an example of "a new discursive contract" that emerges in post–Uncle Tom narratives in which "the further the new autobiographer placed him-self or herself outside the conventions of the standard discourse on slavery, the more truthful this autobiographer claimed to be" (183). Andrews also discusses the relation-ship of *Twelve Years*, *Uncle Tom's Cabin*, and Stowe's *A Key to Uncle Tom's Cabin* (181–83). Robert Stepto also discusses the role of Stowe's novel as an "authenticating document" for Northup's story (232).
8. I am thinking in particular of the description of the slave trader Theophilus Freeman at the opening of chapter six or the bitterly ironic descriptions of the sadistic Epps in chapter twelve.
9. Only think of the 19th-century board game that came out in an effort to capitalize on the Uncle Tom craze. Players moved their pieces around the board through various hazards in an effort to reunite their slave family. See Gossett (164). This motif of the family providentially reunited recurs throughout post-emancipation fiction as well. Consider the almost comic opera series of improbable recognitions and reunions that occur in the postwar scenes of novels like Harper's otherwise splendid *Iola Leroy*.

which maintain a belief in God and assume a providential design at work in their lives are able to maintain some sense of purpose and direction in their lives in spite of their apparent chaos: the meaning or design is present but not visible because unlike secular narratives, here the significance is not a human creation. While it is not a particularly complex concept, the relevance and usefulness of the providential mode to narratives of slave life, fictional or true, is important enough to work out in detail.

Modern or bourgeois subjectivity is, on one crucial level, a narrative phenomenon. The life of an individual consists of a beginning, middle, and an end; the requirements of freedom and rationality are comprised of a series of causal relations between the events of a life. Self-determination is, within certain bounds, ultimately a matter of being able to write your own story. Part of the horror of slave life to the 19th-century imagination arose from the slave's inability to do just this. The absence of such agency was, for an antislavery writer such as Stowe, a result of injustice; for proslavery writers it reflected instead, the slave's imputed lack of reason (and out of this, consequent denials of family feeling, maternal feeling, introspection, a capacity for abstract thought—in short, all the stuff of novelistic character). Those who would try to offer a sympathetic representation of the character of slaves while representing the chaotic circumstances of slave life were faced with the problem of how to show the presence of the very potentiality they were arguing had been repressed: that human dignity normally expressed in the ability to make one's life an expression of one's character. The providential mode characteristically shows the failure of conventional narrative subjectivity and its replacement with a non-secular understanding of identity. Souls are revealed precisely by their resistance or inaccessibility to narrative conventions. The significance of Tom's life, for instance, is all the more dramatic for its triumph not merely over but through his apparent lack of control over his earthly destiny. The ability to work out one's salvation with fear and trembling is not significantly compromised by one's lack of control over one's worldly fate. Paradoxically, slavery is well-suited to the display of Providence precisely because the slave exercises so little control over his own life.

Within providential narratives, slavery appears as a sort of anti-narrative, disrupting continuity and linear progress. Its disruption of human aims and desires helps to shift the emphasis onto religious concerns. Yet however much *Uncle Tom's Cabin* influences *Twelve Years*, Northup's narrative also does much to revise aspects of that novel. Stowe's use of space or geography reflects her desire to tell *Uncle Tom's Cabin* as a religious allegory. It builds on the familiar image of the spiritual journey as a physical one, life as a pilgrimage. Tom's movement southward is a descent into a more and more

sinful environment and greater and greater temptations. The rigors
of this movement require a belief in providence; the author's ability
to miraculously resolve separations corresponds to the anticipated
ultimate unveiling of providential design. In short, Stowe's representation of life in spatial terms is religious and allegorical; *Twelve
Years* is neither.

Just as we saw Northup raising questions about the distorting
effects slavery has over conventional narrative time, the peculiar
institution also has peculiar effects on the representation of space.
Brown and Hamilton's deception is couched in the language of
freedom and pleasure. Northup tells us they are well-dressed circus
performers out sightseeing in the north before they return to their
troupe in Washington. As tourists, they present an image of absolute freedom as they move about the countryside at will. Crucially,
however, this will prove to be merely a front. They invite Northup to
come along and play his violin at their performances. He quickly
agrees to accompany them both for the money and the chance to see
something of the world, to share the absolute freedom they seem to
represent. They continue to lure him away with the promise of easy
money until finally they have him safely in Washington and the
domain of slavery. Then the same surreptitious drugging which made
him lose all sense of time, also makes him lose his ability to perceive
physical space. Northup's description of this event is remarkably
vivid in its emphasis on the way the drugs distort his perceptions:

> I only remember, with any degree of distinctness, that I was told
> it was necessary to go to a physician and procure medicine, and
> that pulling on my boots, without coat or hat, I followed them
> through a long passage-way, or alley, into the open street. It ran
> out at right angles from Pennsylvania Avenue. On the opposite
> side there was a light burning in a window. My impression is
> there were then three persons with me, but it is altogether indef-
> inite and vague, and like the memory of a painful dream. Going
> towards the light, which I imagined proceeded from a physi-
> cian's office, and which seemed to recede as I advanced, is the
> last glimmering recollection I can now recall. From that moment
> I was insensible. How long I remained in that condition—
> whether only that night, or many days and nights—I do not
> know; but when consciousness returned, I found myself alone,
> in utter darkness, and in chains. (19)

Northup's description of Williams' slave pen is the first of his pains-
taking accounts of specific buildings and regions that he passes
through. So meticulous are most of these descriptions that one
could easily produce a map or architectural drawing from them.
What is unique about Williams' slave pen, however, is its invisibility

to outsiders. Both physically and symbolically, Northup emphasizes how the structure defies the understanding both of geographic and ideological space:

> It was like a farmer's barnyard in most respects save it was so constructed that the outside world could never see the human cattle that were herded there . . . Its outside presented only the appearance of a quiet private residence. A stranger looking at it, would never have dreamed of its execrable uses. Strange as it may seem, within plain sight of this same house, looking down from its commanding height upon it, was the Capitol. The voices of patriotic representatives boasting of freedom and equality, and the rattling of the poor slave's chains, almost commingled. A slave pen within the very shadow of the Capitol! (22–23)

Faced with the lucidity and rationality of the enlightened values which lay behind America's political rhetoric, *Twelve Years* represents American slavery as opaque and well-nigh impossible to map. The association of freedom with individual autonomy as symbolized by the two kidnappers proves to be a vicious deception. The Capitol, which pretends to be both the symbol of democracy and, as the seat of government, its literal substance, is tainted by slavery, the reality of which is hypocritically hidden behind a seemingly innocent housefront; the Capitol itself becomes a false front for corruption. Society as represented in *Twelve Years* is not composed of autonomous individuals and discrete institutions; rather, all individuals and institutions are contingent upon one another. Slavery, though ideologically invisible, nevertheless invades the space of democracy. The symbolic confusion is reinforced by the funeral pomp of William Henry Harrison's funeral:

> The roar of the cannon and the tolling of the bells filled the air, while many houses were shrouded with crepe, and the streets were black with people. As the day advanced, the procession made its appearance, coming slowly through the Avenue, carriage after carriage, in long succession, while thousands upon thousands followed on foot—all moving to the sound of melancholy music. They were bearing the dead body of Harrison to the grave. (17)

This daytime street activity foreshadows the evening street activity when Northup and the other slaves are led from the pen to the docks. In both instances, the streets are "black with people." Similarly, the "tolling of bells" anticipates the tolling of the ship's bell as it passes Washington's grave at Mount Vernon carrying its slave cargo on to Norfolk. And the dead body, in the first instance Harrison, is to be the socially dead Northup carried off down these streets to the grave of slavery. In case there should remain any doubt about the ironic juxtaposition, Northup melodramatically underscores the irony of the slaves slipping out of Washington that night:

> So we passed, hand-cuffed and in silence, through the streets of Washington—through the Capital of a nation, whose theory of government, we were told, rests on the foundation of man's inalienable right to life, LIBERTY, and the pursuit of happiness! Hail! COLUMBIA, happy land, indeed! (34)

The emphatic references to space and geography continue through the remainder of the narrative. Occasionally they simply amount to detailed descriptions and sometimes they reflect Northup's need to hide or deny his own origins in the North (at one point he is severely beaten for telling a prospective buyer that he is from New York).[1] More typical are those instances which stress the meaninglessness and mysteriousness of Northup's movements, such as when his first letter back home fails to get him rescued because he has no idea where he is being taken and, consequently, cannot tell his friends where to find him. At the heart of *Twelve Years*'s exploration of spatial metaphors are two puzzles: the effects of all these disruptive movements on his character—typically leading at least one mistress to speculate that he has "seen more of the world than [he] admitted" (175); and the general inadequacy of spatial figures as a way of gauging or mastering life, specifically Northup's confrontation with "the limitless extent of wickedness" (27).

Related to this questioning of the categories of time and space as structuring elements in narrative is the attention *Twelve Years* pays to the effect of environment on character. Perhaps because of its antecedents in spiritual autobiography, the slave narrative ordinarily emphasizes the ability of character to master environment or the innate superiority and independence of the individual subject to its surroundings. The strange modesty, even skepticism, of Northup's vision here as elsewhere, breaks with the genre. From the early instance in which his determination and work ethic are undermined by the resort atmosphere of Saratoga Springs, Northup repeatedly reflects upon the role in which the self, far from being discrete and self-mastering, is actually subject to innumerable external influences.

Of course, many others, black and white, who wrote about slavery mentioned the deleterious effects it had upon the moral character

---

1. Another interesting reversal of the slave narrative paradigm is that where so many tell of a narrator who discards a false, white-imposed name and engages in a crucial act of self-naming, Northup starts out with a name, has it taken from him, and marks his return to freedom by, in part, reclaiming his original name. On the importance of names and self-naming in the narratives, see Sidonie Smith (19–22).

of whites. Northup certainly repeats these observations, but, more remarkably, he makes us see the moral blindness of slaveholders as itself the result of environment rather than innate evil or irrationality:

> [I]t is but simple justice to him when I say, in my opinion, there never was a more kind, noble, candid, Christian man than William Ford. The influences and associations that had always surrounded him, blinded him to the inherent wrong at the bottom of the system of Slavery. He never doubted the moral right of one man holding another in subjection. Looking through the same medium with his fathers before him, he saw things in the same light. Brought up under other circumstances and other influences, his notions would undoubtedly have been different. . . . Were all men such as he, slavery would be deprived of more than half its bitterness. (62)

Northup is equally clear, however, about the effect of environment on the character of slavers. Bass, the Canadian laborer who befriends Northup, clearly voices the antislavery view of *Twelve Years* as a whole when he says in his argument with Epps about slavery that

> These riggers are human beings. If they don't know as much as their masters, whose fault is it? They are not *allowed* to know anything. You have books and papers, and can go where you please, and gather intelligence in a thousand ways. But your slaves have no privileges. You'd whip one of them if caught reading a book. They are held in bondage, generation after generation, deprived of mental improvement, and who can expect them to possess much knowledge? If they are not brought down to a level with the brute creation, you slaveholders will never be blamed for it. If they are baboons, or stand no higher in the scale of intelligence than such animals, you and men like you will have to answer for it. (207)

One particularly strange aspect of Northup's concern for the effects of conditions upon character is that *Twelve Years* frequently includes details about slave management, though perhaps not surprisingly, given that Northup himself served as an overseer for a period during his captivity.

Northup emphasizes that while conventional owners believe that beatings and other severities like constant malnourishment keep the slaves tractable and production up, his own experience suggests the opposite: "those who treated their slaves leniently, were rewarded by the greatest amount of labor" (70). The observation itself is not as remarkable as the manner in which it is made. This, like most of his comments on discipline, is relatively free from overt moralizing.

Reflecting this general insistence on seeing character in context is the comparatively sophisticated way in which *Twelve Years* presents slavery as only one part of a vast set of social and economic arrangements. Northup does not simply describe the experience of picking cotton; he does not present cotton production as a process tangential to slave life. The cycle of cotton production is, instead, shown to shape the very contours of slave life on cotton plantations. Northup gives several pages to cotton production, from the initial preparation of the beds through the actual harvest beginning in August. The description, however, is distinguished by never being reified into a series of impersonal processes: each stage of cotton's development appears as human, specifically slave, labor. Further underlining the inseparability of production and slave life, Northup's fullest discussion of a slave's nourishment appears at the end of the cotton production description ironically sandwiched between comments about the feeding of livestock:

> This [the day's picking] done, the labor of the day is not yet ended, by any means. Each one must then attend to his respective chores. One feeds the mules, another the swine—another cuts the wood, and so forth; besides, the packing if all done by candle light. Finally, at a late hour, they reach the quarters, sleepy and overcome with the long day's toil. Then a fire must be kindled in the cabin, the corn ground in the small hand-mill, and supper, and dinner for the next day in the field, prepared. All that is allowed them is corn and bacon, which is given out at the corncrib and smoke-house every Sunday morning. Each one receives, as his weekly allowance, three and a half pounds of bacon, and corn enough to make a peck of meal. That is all— no tea, coffee, sugar, and with the exception of a very scanty sprinkling now and then, no salt. I can say, from a ten years' residence with Master Epps, that no slave of his is ever likely to suffer from the gout, superinduced by excessive high living. Master Epps' hogs were fed on *shelled* corn—it was thrown out to his 'riggers' in the ear. The former, he thought, would fatten faster by shelling, and soaking it in the water—the latter, perhaps, if treated in the same manner, might grow too fat to labor. Master Epps was a shrewd calculator, and knew how to manage his own animals, drunk or sober. (127)

He goes on to describe the procedure by which slaves grind their own corn, the material they are given for bedding, their cabins, the horn that wakes them up a few hours later, and their breakfast of "cold bacon and corn cake" (128). Even the production of the corn for slaves and livestock is described. After the last cotton picking is completed in January, slaves must then turn to harvesting the corn. Northup additionally recounts the rounding-up of hogs from the swamps, hog-killing, preservation, cattle raising, and vegetable gardening. A bit farther on in the narrative, Northup gives an almost equally detailed account of sugar cane production and the form of slave life accompanying it (159–63).

What is important about the full and complex picture of slave labor is the image it gives of slavery as a single practice taking place amidst a multitude of other practices. The same holistic perspective which refused to see individuals apart from their circumstances similarly refuses to see slavery as a discrete practice. This emphasis further distances *Twelve Years* from the theological allegory or the rational self-creation models. Neither *Uncle Tom's Cabin* nor Douglass' *Narrative* pays attention to slave life in relation to slave labor or specific practices of production.

What Northup's representation of slavery suggests is that it exists as a practice related to, though not explicitly determined by, a network of other practices with which it exists. Such a broad perspective might seem to risk leading to a sort of relativism. After all, viewing slavery as only one part of a complementary set of social relations is virtually the very same defense many white southerners offered for the peculiar institution. This sense of the seeming naturalness of slavery when viewed by the customs and standards of the South went hand in hand with the ridicule they heaped upon the sort of absolutism reflected in higher laws or moral idealism.

But it is precisely in regard to this question that *Twelve Years* distinguishes itself from run of the mill antislavery writings. The insight in question is not developed fully, but what there is of it suggests a unique strategy for arguing the injustice of slavery. At three different points in the text, Northup asserts that slavers know slavery to be wrong and know the meaning and value of freedom, but only on the last occasion does he explain why he thinks this:

> It is a mistaken opinion that prevails in some quarters, that the slave does not understand the term—does not comprehend the idea of freedom. Even on the Bayou Boeuf, where I conceive slavery exists in its most abject and cruel form—where it exhibits features altogether unknown in more northern States—the most ignorant of them generally know its full meaning. They understand the privileges and exemptions that belong to it— that it would bestow upon them the fruits of their own labors, and that it would secure to them the enjoyment of domestic happiness. They do not fail to observe the difference between their own condition and the meanest white man's, and to realize the injustice of the laws which place it in his power not only to appropriate the profits of their industry, but to subject them to unmerited, and unprovoked punishment, without remedy, or the right to exist, or to remonstrate. (200)

Slaves, who were traditionally denied their freedom by virtue of being assigned to a position on the margins or entirely outside the community, demonstrate their membership in society, their contiguity with it, through the very fact that they know what freedom is. Consequently, their knowledge of freedom, precisely because it comes about through their de facto membership in society, proves their right to freedom. The relation of freedom to slavery, an intellectual problem for Douglass, a moral one for Stowe, is here both contingent and determining. Northup uses one undeniable and unavoidable aspect of slavery—its continuity with society—to refute another part of it, its relegation of slaves to a position outside society.[2]

As this example shows, Northup can make an immanent critique of the peculiar institution because of his grasp of the way in which social practices loosely impinge upon one another. Northup represents social practices as contingent and potentially contradictory, and it is these qualities which make immanent critique possible.[3] This is not a philosophical perspective that reduces all social practices to a master code of, say, economics, and it is, as noted before, decidedly not one that calls the practice into judgment with a transcendent code of reason or religion. His picture of slavery as related to other agricultural and social practices, his destabilizing of those linear, rationalistic systems of space and time which conventionally structure individual lives, his narration of the chaotic, often disrupted, picaresque structure of his bondage instead of the focused, single-minded plot of most other slave lives, are all ultimately aspects of this uncommon perspective on society and slavery. All of these characteristics, which seem at first to undermine the narrative's ability to offer sustained moral critique, are, in fact, essential to the type of critique it offers.

But abandonment of transcendent principles in moral justification is one thing and actually knowing how to live in a world in which right conduct must be interpreted, moral guidelines created and recreated, is another. Slave narrators who rely upon rational self-initiative and those who construct their experience in religious terms have a consistent basis for moral judgment and, consequently, a basis for a morally consistent identity. But while *Twelve Years* does have its own method of moral argument, the absence of an unchanging

2. On the various ways in which slaves become aware of the nature of freedom in other narratives, see Foster (116–17).
3. My own understanding of immanent social criticism stems largely from Michael Walzer's set of lectures published as *Interpretation and Social Criticism*. Walzer contrasts immanent criticism (which endeavors to interpret or model our existing morality with all its multiple and often contradictory demands) with the path of discovery (the search for and articulation of some sort of transcendent foundation for morality) and the path of invention (the attempt to create a new moral scheme without reference to the pre-existing one). See especially the first of the lectures, "Three Paths in Moral Philosophy" (3–32).

foundation for right action requires a different model for behavior. The fluid nature of experience results in a world in which moral judgment must be made on a case by case basis; the unavailability of absolute standards outside the flux of history means that the ethical life must be constantly recreated or improvised. As William James writes in describing such a pragmatic ethics,

> Abstract rules can indeed help; but they help the less in proportion as our intuitions are more piercing, and our vocation is the stronger for the moral life. For every real dilemma is in literal strictness a unique situation; and our exact combination of ideals realized and ideals dissipated which each decision creates is always a universe without precedent, and for which no adequate previous role exists. (209)

Arguably, the awareness of such an open universe is the central fact of Northup's character. Northup's identity consists not of his allegiance to a fixed transcendent order but in his creative powers, his ability to search out and even author a new moral stance in each changing situation. Again, comparison with our other two models will help. The characteristic actions in Douglass are reading and writing, specifically learning to represent or express himself. In *Uncle Tom's Cabin*, the characteristic actions are listening and speaking, primarily the chain of evangelization and conversion, in order to turn one's own life into a sort of representation of Christ's life. But the action that epitomizes Northup's relation to the world is not representative at all: his violin playing. His ability to play triggers the ruse by which he is at first kidnapped and later is the means by which he augments his own value and gains a degree of mobility when he is permitted to play for dances at neighboring plantations. When he is called upon by the slavetrader to play in the slave pen for the other slaves, it foreshadows what is perhaps the best-known moment in the narrative, when Northup, as slave overseer, must himself whip another slave. Northup specifically contrasts his compliance with the forbearance Uncle Tom shows in a similar situation:

> At Huff Power, when I first came to Epps', Tom, one of Roberts' negroes, was driver. He was a burly fellow, and severe in the extreme. After Epps' removal to Bayou Boeuf, that distinguished honor was conferred upon myself. Up to the time of my departure I had to wear a whip about my neck in the field. If Epps was present, I dared not show any lenity, not having the Christian fortitude of a certain well-known Uncle Tom sufficiently to brave his wrath, by refusing to perform the office. In that way, only, I escaped the immediate martyrdom he suffered, and, withal, saved my companions much suffering, as it proved in the end. . . . 'Practice makes perfect,' truly;

and during my eight years' experience as a driver I learned to handle my whip with marvelous dexterity and precision, throwing the lash within a hair's breadth of the back, the ear, the nose, without, however, touching either of them. If Epps was observed at a distance, or we had reason to apprehend he was sneaking somewhere in the vicinity, I would commence plying the lash vigorously, when, according to arrangement, they would squirm and screech as if in agony, although not one of them had in fact been even grazed. Patsey would take occasion, if he made his appearance presently, to mumble in his hearing some complaints that Platt was lashing them the whole time, and Uncle Abram, with an appearance of honesty peculiar to himself, would declare roundly I had just whipped them worse than General Jackson whipped the enemy at New Orleans. (172–73)[4]

Ultimately, Northup's heroism, if that is not too grand a word for it, consists of his adaptability, quick wittedness, and ingenuity. Whether trying to foresee the probable outcome of serving as overseer or cooperating with his captors or simply manufacturing ink from white maple bark and pilfering a sheet of paper, Northup exemplifies a practical and creative heroism that acts without the reassurance of foundations.

The open nature of Northup's representation of experience is the chief cause of *Twelve Years's* seeming lack of rhetorical or aesthetic control. The rambling nature of the narrative, which lacks the framing and condensation of classic slave narratives, merely expresses the unusual but deeply reflective perspective Northup brings to his experience of race and slavery. In other words, the very characteristics that have kept *Twelve Years* from receiving the attention given to better-known narratives are, in fact, signs of its greatest distinction.

Works Cited

Andrews, William L. *To Tell a Free Story: The First Century of Afro-American Autobiography, 1760–1865*. Urbana: University of Illinois Press, 1986.

Davis, Charles T., and Henry Louis Gates, Jr., eds. *The Slave's Narrative*. New York: Oxford University Press, 1985.

Foster, Francis Smith. *Witnessing Slavery: The Development of Ante-Bellum Slave Narratives*. Westport, CT: Greenwood Press, 1979.

---

4. Northup's own ambiguous position in this equation, both as the man who attempts to work the master's will and, as much as he can, to look out for the well-being of Patsey compares interestingly with Deborah McDowell's remarks in "Making Frederick Douglass and the Afro-American Narrative Tradition" concerning the sexual bias encoded in most slave narratives' representations of female slaves being whipped.

Genovese, Eugene. *Roll Jordan Roll: The World the Slaves Made.* New York: Random House, 1974.

Gosset, Thomas. *Uncle Tom's Cabin in American Culture.* Dallas: Southern Methodist University Press, 1985.

James, William. "The Moral Philosopher and the Moral Life." *'The Will to Believe' and Other Essays in Popular Philosophy.* New York: Dover Books, 1956. 184–215.

McDowell, Deborah. "Making Frederick Douglass and the Afro-American Narrative Tradition." *African-American Autobiography: A Collection of Critical Essays.* Ed. William Andrews. Englewood Cliffs, NJ: Prentice Hall, 1993. 36–58.

Northup, Solomon. *Twelve Years a Slave.* Ed. Sue Eakin and Joseph Logsdon. Baton Rouge: Louisiana State University Press, 1968.

Olney, James, ed. *Studies in Autobiography.* New York: Oxford University Press, 1988.

Smith, Sidonie. *Where I'm Bound: Patterns of Slavery and Freedom in Black American Autobiography.* Westport, CT: Greenwood Press, 1974.

Smith, Valerie. *Self-Discovery and Authority in Afro-American Narrative.* Cambridge: Harvard University Press, 1987.

Walzer, Michael. *Interpretation and Social Criticism.* Cambridge: Harvard University Press, 1987.

JOHN ERNEST

(Auto)biography as History†

* * *

Ultimately, what I am identifying as white antislavery history here is what might be called a *docudramatic* approach to slavery. This notion of history, which assumes the possibility of objectivity and which associates history with fact, did characterize approaches to the history of slavery for many years—years in which the slave narratives were dismissed as possible historical sources. Responding to this habitual omission, Blassingame has noted that "the chief value of the autobiography lies in the fact that it is subjective, that it tells us a great deal about how blacks felt about the conditions under which they lived" (227–28).[1] But as the history of historical approaches

---

† From *Liberation Historiography: African American Writers and the Challenge of History, 1794–1861* (Chapel Hill: University of North Carolina Press, 2004), pp. 179–84, 372. Copyright © 2004 by the University of North Carolina Press. Used by permission of the publisher. All notes are Ernest's unless otherwise noted; some have been edited.
1. John W. Blassingame, *The Slave Community: Plantation Life in the Antebellum South* (New York: Oxford University Press, 1972) [Editors' note].

to slavery reveal, slave narratives are not alone in being subjective and thus revealing. In the docudramatic understanding of slavery, what matters is one's ability to re-create the conditions of slavery. Individual narratives are reduced to the status of evidence—usually questionable evidence—toward that attempted re-creation. The auto-biographical or biographical narrative becomes an individual mani-festation and a regional site of slavery.

This docudramatic approach overwhelms one of the most promi-nent of the narratives filtered through the perspective of a white amanuensis, Solomon Northup's *Twelve Years a Slave*. Northup was kidnaped in 1841, sold into slavery, and finally rescued in 1853; in the year of his rescue, his story was recorded by David Wilson, a lawyer from the upstate New York area to which Northup returned after he was rescued. The book was quite successful and was con-nected upon publication with the success of Harriet Beecher Stowe's fictional treatment of slavery, *Uncle Tom's Cabin*. Indeed, Stowe mentions Northup, and includes details and excerpts of documents of his experience, in the *Key to Uncle Tom's Cabin*, Stowe's attempt to document, after the fact, the grounds for accepting the reality behind her novel. Harriet Jacobs, famously, refused to allow her story to be reduced to the status of evidence in Stowe's *Key*; *Twelve Years a Slave*, notably, opens with a dedication to Stowe, and presents Nor-thup's narrative as "another *Key to Uncle Tom's Cabin*."[2] Even beyond Stowe's *Key*, Northup's experiences were used to validate Stowe's novel, as Stowe's reputation was used to authenticate Northup's nar-rative. In an account of Northup's enslavement and eventual return to "liberty" in the North, according to a report in the *Liberator*, the *New York Daily Times* referred to Stowe's novel to describe Northup's experiences, noting that "the condition of this colored man during the nine years that he was in the hands of Eppes, was of a character nearly approaching that described by Mrs. Stowe, as the condition of 'Uncle Tom' while in that region" ("Affecting Narration").[3]

The docudramatic approach to history is an exercise in both vision and blindness, for in the attempt to present a full picture of the past,

2. For an important reconsideration of the cultural politics involved in Stowe's *A Key to "Uncle Tom's Cabin,"* see Robert S. Levine, *Martin Delany, Frederick Douglass, and the Politics of Representative Identity* (Chapel Hill: University of North Carolina Press, 1997), 147–53.
3. The article was reprinted in the January 28, 1853, issue of *Frederick Douglass' Paper*, which is my source. That same article builds to the story of Northup being forced to whip a woman who has been "stripped naked," a typical example of the emphasis on the physical abuse of women that characterized northern commentaries on slavery. A con-densed account of this article was published in the February 18, 1853, issue of the *Liberator*. In its publication of extracts from Northup's *Twelve Years a Slave* later that year (September 9, 1853), the *Liberator* stated in its prefatory comments, "We have no doubt that it [the narrative] will obtain a wide circulation, and deepen the sympathy already existing for the 'Uncle Toms' and 'Elizas' ground into the dust beneath the heel of oppression, in this 'land of the free, and home of the brave.'"

the historian typically ignores, or dismisses as *beyond the subject*, the ideological canvas on which the portrait is constructed and the moral frame that guides the eyes of those who view the image of the past. But as anyone familiar with the misrepresentation of African American history in the U.S. system of education can attest, other images of the past will make themselves known to those who have eyes to see. Northup's narrative, in fact, concludes with a mention of an example of this unintended representation of an alternate story. Northup relates a story told to him by his wife concerning his children's awareness of his possible condition during those years when he was absent: "Elizabeth and Margaret once returned from school—so Anne informed me—weeping bitterly. On inquiring the cause of the children's sorrow, it was found that, while studying geography, their attention had been attracted to the picture of slaves working in the cotton-field, and an overseer following them with his whip. It reminded them of the sufferings their father might be, and as it happened, actually *was*, enduring in the South" (252).[4] These pictures were not intended to make a moral statement about slavery, and one can only expect that for most of the children the pictures simply represent an image of the South in a geography lesson, perhaps with an implicit claim of northern superiority. But the children find themselves living in a fundamentally different world by virtue of their connection to an absent father. This manifestation of the docudramatic approach to history realizes concretely Jacques Derrida's claim that "white mythology . . . has erased within itself the fabulous scene that has produced it, the scene that nevertheless remains active and stirring, inscribed in white ink, an invisible design covered over in the palimpsest" (qtd. in M. Wood 134).[5]

Sadly, *Twelve Years a Slave* largely offers its readers another textbook of the South, a lesson in white political geography that most readers would already know and could only reaffirm, though one that Northup seems to comment on at times. Northup ends by emphasizing that his story "is no fiction, no exaggeration," and adds, "If I have failed in anything, it has been in presenting to the reader too prominently the bright side of the picture" (252). Certainly, *Twelve Years a Slave* includes a number of eloquent denunciations of the system of slavery, though it ends by carefully limiting the book's authority to the region in which Northup was enslaved. But much of the book is a documentary of slavery, including depictions of physical

4. The page numbers Ernest cites correspond to the 1968 edition of *Twelve Years a Slave* edited by Sue Eakin and Joseph Logsdon and published by Louisiana State University Press [Editors' note].
5. Marcus Wood, *Blind Memory: Visual Representations of Slavery in England and America, 1780–1865* (New York: Routledge, 2000) [Editors' note].

abuse (depictions aided by the book's illustrations) framed by a survey of slave culture. This approach is valuable in that it can emphasize the violence inherent in the commercial and social culture of slavery—the point that Lewis Clarke underscores at the end of his narrative, when he notes that "all of the abuses which I have here related are *necessary*, if slavery must continue to exist" (60).[6] But one can hardly say that this is the unifying principle of Northup's narrative—a claim that one *might* make, for example, with Douglass's 1845 *Narrative*, and that one might make again by noting Douglass's increased emphasis on the culture of slavery in his 1855 *My Bondage and My Freedom*. Northup presents most of his glimpses into southern culture rather incidentally. Toward the beginning of chapter 12, for example, Northup pauses to note of his then master Edwin Epps, "His principal business was raising cotton, and in as much as some may read this book who have never seen a cotton field, a description of the manner of its culture may not be out of place" (123). Later, following a chapter that emphasizes the "tendency" of the system of slavery "to brutalize the humane and finer feelings" of the slaves, Northup pauses to note, "In a previous chapter the mode of cultivating cotton is described. This may be the proper place to speak of the manner of cultivating cane" (159). Northup offers as well a lengthy description of flirtation, laughter, food, music, and dance during the Christmas holidays. To be sure, he follows this holiday portrait by noting the extent to which it contrasted with everyday life, commenting implicitly on those descriptions of slave life that focus exclusively on such events. "Such is 'southern life as it is,'" Northup states, "*three days in the year*, as I found it—the other three hundred and sixty-two being days of weariness, and fear, and suffering, and unremitting labor" (169). In the end, though, the history of slavery is left behind as Northup returns to life in the North, and he concludes his narrative with a disturbing sense of resolution, as if his story is indeed over. "Chastened and subdued in spirit by the sufferings I have borne," Northup states in the narrative's concluding sentence, "and thankful to that good Being through whose mercy I had been restored to happiness and liberty, I hope henceforward to lead an upright though lowly life, and rest at last in the church yard where my father sleeps" (252). Ultimately, Northup's narrative returns its reader to the safety of the North as the sentimental site for antislavery feeling and as the site in which African American history can be

---

6. Lewis Clarke and Milton Clarke, *Narratives of the Sufferings of Lewis and Milton Clarke, Sons of a Soldier of the Revolution, during a Captivity of More than Twenty Years among the Slaveholders of Kentucky, One of the So Called Christian States of North America: Dictated by Themselves* (Boston, 1846) [Editors' note].

safely contained. In this narrative, that is the docudramatic tour of slavery disciplines black northern subjectivity.[7]

My point is not, I should emphasize, that knowledge of the daily lives and experiences of the enslaved communities is unimportant; rather, my point is that it is important to question the ways in which this knowledge is framed, and to question as well the implicit or explicit concept of historical understanding that serves as the canvas of such portraits. The limitations of knowledge of slavery's horrors are emphasized by the enormous popular and commercial response to Stowe's *Uncle Tom's Cabin*, which immediately inspired every-thing from plates to wallpaper to card games. Images of slavery's hor-rors were everywhere in white American and English culture, but they served the needs of white cultural self-definition and remained only shades away from the various racist images that were regularly featured in books, newspapers, and shopwindows.[8] As Marcus Wood has said, echoing Henry Louis Gates Jr.'s description of the cultural erasure of the reality of slavery, "The black as cultural absentee, the black as blank page for white guilt to inscribe, emerged as a neces-sary pre-condition for abolitionist polemic against the slave trade" (23). If the guiding assumption of historical study in the past has been that the story of an individual life does not constitute a his-tory of slavery, this assumption now needs to be amended, and we must recognize that detailed descriptions of slavery similarly do not constitute a history of the system of slavery.

To offer an example of this, I need here to present a rather lengthy quotation from the Introduction to the 1968 reprinting of *Twelve Years a Slave*. This is, in fact, a quotation within a quotation,

---

7. It is only fair to note that Northup's experiences were invoked to support more radical visions of social reform as well. In a letter published in the March 23, 1855, issue of the *Liberator*, for example, Henry C. Wright (one of the more radical of Garrisonian abolitionists) remarks that *Twelve Years a Slave* "has been widely read in New England" and that "no narrative of man's experience as a slave, a chattel, is more touching, or better calculated to expose the true character and designs of slaveholders." While respecting the power of the published narrative, however, Wright recommends seeing Northup in person: "But it is far more potent to see the man, and hear him, in his clear, manly, straight-forward way, speak of slavery as he experienced it, and as he saw it in others. Those who have read his Narrative can scarce fail to desire to see the man, thus kidnapped and tortured in body and soul, for twelve years, and to hear his story from his own lips." Noting the legal proceedings following Northup's rescue, and the arguments presented by his kidnappers, Wright asks, "What is this Union to Solo-mon Northup? Literally a confederacy of kidnappers." But the limits of Wright's invo-cation of Northup's story in support of radical social reform are perhaps suggested by the actual responses to the questions he raises at the end of his letter: "Where is the Church or political party that will refuse to open the way to give this victim of slavery a hearing, and repay him for the suffering this Union has inflicted on him? But there are 4,000,000 of kidnapped men, women and children still under the *American* lash. Who will help to redeem them, and pay for their sufferings?"
8. On the commercial culture inspired by *Uncle Tom's Cabin*, see Gossett, *Uncle Tom's Cabin and American Culture*; and M. Wood, chap. 4.

a framework within a framework, as editors Sue Eakin and Joseph Logsdon look back on the introduction of a previous reprinting of Northup's narrative:

> Shortly after the Civil War, Northup's narrative was republished by a Philadelphia firm. The editors made no attempt to ascertain the fate of its author. They felt that such an attempt was unnecessary since Northup's story had blended into the larger panorama of the nation's past.

>> To take in or to understand the exact status of such a people in all its bearings, we can pursue no better course than to live among them, to become one of them, to fall from a condition of freedom to one of bondage, to feel the scourge, to bear the marks of the brands, and the outrage of manacles. . . . It can be taken for what it is worth—a personal narrative of personal sufferings and keenly felt and strongly resented wrongs; but in our opinion, the individual will be lost or merged in the general interest and the work will be regarded as a history of an institution which our political economy has now happily superseded, but which, however much its existence may be regretted, should be studied—indeed, must be studied—by everyone whose interest in our country incites him to obtain a correct knowledge of her past existence.

> One hundred years later, this still constitutes a valid judgment on the significance of Solomon Northup's life and the importance of his narrative. (xv–xvi)[9]

The assumptions guiding this presentation of Northup's story would be stunning were they not so common. Northup is subsumed by a historical abstraction that stands in for African American history and identity, and the institution of slavery is left safely in the past. What remains for (white) readers of the present (be it 1853, 1869, 1968, or today) is an easy empathy available to those who read Northup's narrative—a kind of historical blackface performance by which an imagined African American identity as shaped by the system of slavery can be known and understood. White readers become "one of them" by reading a narrative of an individual life in which the individual life is "lost or merged in the general interest," a general interest marked by the treatment of slavery as an isolated

9. Sue Eakin and Joseph Logsdon, Introduction to *Twelve Years a Slave: Narrative of Solomon Northup, a Citizen of New-York, Kidnapped in Washington City in 1841, and Rescued in 1853, from a Cotton Plantation near the Red River, in Louisiana* (Baton Rouge: Louisiana State University Press, 1968) [Editors' note].

institution that can be both acknowledged and avoided, opened and contained, by "a correct knowledge" of the past.

* * *

TRISH LOUGHRAN

From The Republic in Print: Print Culture in the Age of U.S. Nation Building, 1770–1870[†]

Inside and Outside the Loop: Solomon Northup's Twelve Years a Slave

For many readers, *Uncle Tom's Cabin* dissolved into an issue of fact or fiction. Unable to stem its circulation (and thus divide the novel from its own material manifestations in rail cars, steamers, stages, and drawing rooms), *Uncle Tom's* critics sought to split the novel from itself on the grounds of faulty knowledge, interrupting its successful circulation by appealing to a discrepancy between a northern set of signifiers and a southern signified. Stowe's response was, famously, *A Key to Uncle Tom's Cabin*—an elaborate defense of the novel's characters and events based, like Weld's *Slavery as It Is*, on documentary sources.[1] The commotion over the facticity of *Uncle Tom's Cabin* indicates that for American audiences, the word *actual* never went away. The status of corrupt representation was every bit as important in the reception of Stowe's novel as it had been in the early days of republic. And while few northern abolitionists knew the South from first-hand experience, they persistently and paradoxically invoked the Revolutionary inheritance of actual representation every time they cited the language of inalienable rights and self-evident truths. In upholding these fictions, immediate abolition mapped a two-part agenda: first, it sought the fusion of all that had been alienated from itself under slavery (God and man, word and thing, the nation then and the nation now, North and South, black and white). At the same time, however, such commitments confusedly bound abolition (like other Protestant reform movements of the period) to a vision of the factual, the empirical, or what I have called throughout this book the *actual* over and against the virtualities of the nation or other regions.[2]

† From *The Republic in Print: Print Culture in the Age of U.S. Nation Building, 1770–1870* (New York: Columbia University Press, 2007), pp. 391–404, 505–06. Copyright © 2007 Columbia University Press. Reprinted by permission of the publisher.
1. Cindy Weinstein notes that the reception of *Uncle Tom's Cabin* raised questions "about the very nature of evidence itself" (85). *Family, Kinship, and Sympathy in Nineteenth-Century American Literature* (New York: Cambridge University Press, 2004).
2. On the documentary burden placed on African-American narrative by organized abolition, see William L. Andrews, "The Novelization of Voice in Early African American

Strictly speaking, these two agendas were mutually contradictory. How could abolitionists living out their lives in New York and
New England fuse their northern selves with a southern self they
had never seen firsthand? It's little wonder that southern testimony
became a key component in abolitionist discourse, which com-
pulsively amassed the conversion narratives of reformed slaveholders (like James Birney and the Grimkés); indigenous southern
"archives"—usually newspaper ads and articles; and finally, the
testimony of fugitive slaves ("native informants," as Lisa Brawley
calls them), who described their experiences in lectures and slave
narratives sponsored by both national and regional antislavery
societies. Weld, in *Slavery as It Is*, focused on the first two of these
categories, assembling a large archive of white testimony. Stowe,
in composing the *Key*, relied on all three, as well drawing on the
accruing archive of abolition itself (with Weld serving as a primary
source).

Frederick Douglass's resistance to being paraded in front of
northern audiences as "a brand new fact" is well known; so is Harriet Jacobs's refusal to be appropriated *after* the fact by Stowe.[3] We
might add to this more famous pairing the autobiographical "slave"
narrative of Solomon Northup, whose remarkable story is cited,
with a thousand others, in Stowe's *Key*. Born a free African-
American citizen of New York State, Northup was tricked in 1841
into leaving his home in Saratoga Springs by kidnappers who
engaged him to play his fiddle for a traveling circus in Washington,
DC. Once in the capital city, Northup was drugged, placed in a
slave pen, and severely whipped until he stopped claiming his freedom.[4] Transported by slave ship to New Orleans, he was eventually
sold onto a cotton plantation on the Red River in Louisiana—the
same place where Simon Legree lives (and Tom dies) in *Uncle
Tom's Cabin*. Upon returning to the North after twelve years in
slavery, Northup gave an interview about his experience that was
reprinted in numerous northern newspapers (Stowe found her
copy, for instance, in the *New York Times*). Upon resettling in New
York, Northup commenced authoring in his own right, publishing

Narrative," *PMLA* 105, no. 1 (1990): 23–34 (esp. 23–24); Barbara Foley, "History, Fiction, and the Ground Between: The Uses of the Documentary Mode in Black Literature," *PMLA* 95, no. 3 (1980): 389–403 (esp. 392); and Robert B. Stepto, *From Behind
the Veil: A Study of Afro-American Narrative* (1979; Urbana: University of Illinois Press,
1991), 3–31.
3. Douglass wryly refers to himself as "a brand new fact" when he is "introduced to the
Abolitionists" in *My Bondage and My Freedom* (New York: Miller, Orton, and Mulligan,
1855), 361. On Jacobs's resistance to Stowe, see Jean Fagan Yellin, introduction to
Incidents in the Life of a Slave Girl Written by Herself (Cambridge: Harvard University
Press, 1987), xviii–xix.
4. Kidnapping was common from the eighteenth century to the 1850s. See, for example,
Daniel E. Meaders, comp., *Kidnappers in Philadelphia: Isaac Hopper's Tales of Oppres-
sion, 1780–1843* (New York: Garland, 1994).

an extended memoir titled *Twelve Years a Slave* that went through
several large printings.[5]

Stowe gives Northup four full columns (or about two pages) in the
Key, categorizing his story under the subheading "kidnapping." Northup returns the favor of this acknowledgment by dedicating *Twelve
Years a Slave* to Stowe ("whose name, throughout the world, is identified with the great reform") and by citing his narrative as "another
Key to Uncle Tom's Cabin." But Northup's references to Stowe within
the text are less salutary. Appearing at regular intervals, these allusions are most often asides that emphasize the profound difference
between fictional accounts of slavery and its factual experience:

> Men may write fictions portraying lowly life as it is, or as it is
> not—may expatiate with owlish gravity upon the bliss of
> ignorance—discourse flippantly from arm chairs of the plea-
> sures of slave life; but let them toil with him in the field—sleep
> with him in the cabin—feed with him on husks; let them
> behold him scourged, hunted, trampled on, and they will come
> back with another story in their mouths. (158)

Northup obliquely references Stowe here (her subtitle to *Uncle
Tom's Cabin* had been "Life Among the Lowly") at the same moment
he is remarking on the truthfulness of his own account over and
against "fictions portraying lowly life as it is, or as it is not." In doing
so, he ironically deploys a critique that was usually associated with
the proslavery, or southern, side of the debate. Indeed, the phrase
"lowly life as it is" simultaneously refers to Stowe's novel and to Mary
Eastman's popular proslavery response to it, *Aunt Phillis's Cabin, or
Southern Life as It Is* (1852) (itself a pointed allusion to Weld's *Slavery as It Is*). By collapsing Stowe's title with Eastman's, Northup
manages to obfuscate the target of his critique even as he suggests
that the two might not be as different as they seem.

But many of Northup's references to *Uncle Tom's Cabin* are more
direct. On several occasions, he draws an explicit analogy between
himself and Tom in ways that suggest that Stowe has produced a
crisis for him—a need to explain why he survived the Red River
when Tom did not. In one such example, Northup is named the
driver on his plantation and pointedly remarks: "I dared not show any
lenity, not having the Christian fortitude of a certain well-known
Uncle Tom. . . . In that way, only, I escaped the immediate martyrdom
he suffered, and, withal, saved my companions much suffering" (172).
Here and elsewhere, Northup insists on his difference from Tom and
defends it, mildly reproaching Stowe for not recognizing that there
might be better ways to help one's fellow slaves (since Northup

5. Solomon Northup, *Twelve Years a Slave: Narrative of Solomon Northup* (Baton Rouge:
Louisiana State University Press, 1968).

ultimately "saved [his] companions much suffering," as Tom could not). Northup's vexed relation to *Uncle Tom* recurs later in the narrative, where he makes his most pointed criticism of Stowe, not so much targeting her portrait of southern life "as it is, or is not" as taking issue with her representation of *him*, as a brand new fact, in the supposedly factual *Key*:

> The allusion to myself in the work recently issued, entitled "A Key to Uncle Tom's Cabin," contains the first part of this letter [a document about Northup], omitting the postscript. Neither are the full names of the gentlemen to whom it is directed correctly stated, there being a slight discrepancy, probably a typographical error. To the postscript more than to the body of the communication am I indebted for my liberation, as will presently be seen. (213)

We might view this as an elaborate way for Northup to try to convince readers that they need to read both *A Key* and *Twelve Years*, except that the remark is placed near the end of the narrative and so has little selling power. Instead, this passage once again calls Stowe's facticity into question, insisting on Northup's more authentic brand of knowledge, even at the level of documentary evidence. Stowe's novel may have circulated more widely than Northup's narrative, but Northup's body had circulated more widely than Stowe's.

Here and elsewhere, Northup shows a remarkable faith in the evidence of texts, but his conception of textuality is at direct odds with Stowe's representation of it in *Uncle Tom's Cabin*. While Stowe famously declares that "mail for [Tom] had no existence," Northup can think of nothing else while in slavery. Indeed, much of *Twelve Years a Slave* documents Northup's attempt to gain control over a basic circulating representation of his situation: a letter to friends who might help locate him. Indeed, the book could well be called "Twelve Years to Post a Letter," for Northup's experience of slavery exactly coincides with his lack of access to the federal post office and to the basic materials (pen, ink, and paper) whereby any literate free American might insert himself into the disembodied circuits of national life:

> My great object always was to invent means of getting a letter secretly into the post-office, directed to some of my friends or family at the North. The difficulty of such an achievement cannot be comprehended by one unacquainted with the severe restrictions imposed upon me. In the first place, I was deprived of pen, ink, and paper. In the second place, a slave cannot leave his plantation without a pass, nor will a post-master mail a letter for one without written instructions from his owner. I was in

slavery nine years, and always watchful and on the alert, before
I met with the good fortune of obtaining a sheet of paper. (175)

In this way, the narrative recounts Northup's twelve-year odyssey
to locate a piece of paper and a pen—items not readily available to
him in either a New Orleans slave pen or a Red River cotton field.
Northup eventually "appropriates" a single sheet of foolscap, "concealing it . . . under the board on which I slept." The letter that gains
him his freedom is produced with this pilfered foolscap, ink made
from the bark of a white maple tree, and a pen "manufactured" from
the wing feathers of a duck (175). As an account of Northup's travel
across sectional boundaries (first as a body and later, in ink, as signature on a letter), *Twelve Years a Slave* serves as a rejoinder to the
geography of *Uncle Tom's Cabin*—both to its theory of national space
and to its understanding of how bodies and information circulate in
that space. Indeed, as an extended account of Northup's textual
deprivation—his inability, that is, to circulate himself as a representation through a virtual network of national information—*Twelve Years
a Slave* is a rebuke not just to *Uncle Tom's Cabin*'s representation of
"slavery as it is, or is not," but to that novel's status as an always self-
identical, because omnicirculating, object within the print network
to which Northup was, as a slave, continually denied access.

Northup goes to great lengths, for example, to show the edges of
the circuit in which Stowe's novel can be said to travel, the impenetrable locations in (and from) which certain kinds of information
have yet to be integrated. Sometimes these edges appear material
(or geographical), while at other times they appear ideological. He
speaks, for instance, of "the remoter depths of Slavery" (63)—which
he reached when living on the Red River's Bayou Boeuf, lying, as it
does, beyond "the termination of the railroad tracks" (64). In such
moments, Northup registers slavery's reach as both a vertical location in an abstract chain of power (the "depths" of slavery) and as the
horizontal edge of an empirical map ("the termination of the railroad
tracks"). Though Stowe claims to present a trustworthy representation of the Red River region, Northup goes out of his way to
emphasize the ways in which his geographic experiences elude representation—or are distorted by it. Indeed, his ultimate deliverance is
nearly foiled by the illegibility of his geographical position on a map
that his liberators have trouble reading: the town of Marksville, from
which Northup's appeal is postmarked, "although occupying a prominent position, and standing out in impressive italics on the map of
Louisiana, is, in fact, but a small and insignificant hamlet" (228–29),
while Bayou Boeuf (at which the letter was written and by-lined)
"was twenty-three miles distant [from Marksville], and was the
name applied to the section of country extending between fifty and a

hundred miles, on both sides of that stream" (229). Though seemingly legible as representations on a map (and in Stowe's novel), these Red River locales prove difficult to locate on foot or in person. Northup's ultimate release finally reads like an unlikely Cinderella story, as agents from the North arrive, only to find that the only way to locate him is to "repair to the Bayou, and traveling up one side and down the other its whole length [i.e., 150 miles], inquire at each plantation" for someone matching Northup's description (229).

But while Northup's predicament is a material one (in that he finds himself beyond the reach of pen, paper, and postage for over a decade), his narrative also emphasizes the ideological structure of emerging material infrastructures—especially the uneven access afforded to different persons inscribed within the supposedly transparent and increasingly totalizing reach of antebellum postal routes, rail lines, and telegraph wires. Northup's fellow slaves have only a vague sense of national space, not as a real-world network of places but as an imagined space of freedom. To one such slave (named Patsey), slavery "was one long dream of liberty. Far away, to her fancy an immeasurable distance, she knew there was a land of freedom. A thousand times she had heard that somewhere in the distant North there were no slaves—no masters. In her imagination it was an enchanted region, the Paradise of the earth" (200). But unlike either Uncle Tom or Patsey, Northup carries with him geographic knowledge about the place he lives in and all the other elsewheres where he once was and might one day be. He has an acute awareness of his "real situation" and "the hopelessness of any effort to escape through the wide forests" that surround the Red River region (67). But while this predicament disturbs him, he nevertheless has enough prior knowledge of the world to imagine other locations in a way that his fellow slaves do not (as when he remarks, in the same passage, that "my heart was at home in Saratoga" [67]). Indeed, Northup's deliverance is premised on his knowledge of faraway places: it is in speaking with a Canadian itinerant named Bass (the friend who ultimately helps him post his letter north) that Northup finally reveals himself as something no slave on the Red River can be: a traveler who has moved as freely through the North as Bass himself has. Northup shocks Bass with his extensive geographical knowledge:

> "Oh, I know where Canada is," said I, "I have been there myself."
>
> "Yes, I expect you are well acquainted all through that country," [Bass] remarked, laughing incredulously.
>
> "As sure as I live, Master Bass," I replied, "I have been there. I have been in Montreal and Kingston, and Queenston, and a great many places in Canada, and I have been in York State, too—in Buffalo, and Rochester, and Albany, and can tell you

the names of the villages on the Erie canal and the Champlain canal."

Bass turned round and gazed at me a long time without uttering a syllable. (208–9)

This scene points out a crucial fact of Northup's captivity: his ability to access the national network (and the freedom such circulation promises) is in some ways a material, or geographical, matter and in other ways an ideological issue shaped by the contingencies of place. It is never, however, what his master Epps thinks it is: a matter of innate biological aptitude reducible to his race (a fact I will return to in a moment).

Just as Northup is denied free circulation in his body, he is denied entrance into the circuit of national print culture while he remains in the South. His access to the world of print does not depend on his knowledge or skill but on where he happens to be at any given moment in time. He can enter the circuit of representation and experience its freedoms, in other words, only from certain distinct locations on the national map. "Beyond the reach of [Epps's] inhuman thong, and standing on the soil of the free State where I was born, thanks be to Heaven, I can raise my head once more among men. I can speak of the wrongs I have suffered, and of those who inflicted them, with upraised eyes" (138). It is place, in the end, rather than race that makes Northup free and unfree, an author or a slave, part of the circuit of representation or an outcast from it. Thus on his return North, Northup not only circulates his body and his story through the representational structures of the national book market but does so with extraordinary success, as the book's high circulation numbers and his general celebrity attest.

Frederick Douglass' Paper (among others) took special note of the discrepancy between Northup's enslavement in "the obscurest section of the Red River region" and his later celebrity as the author of "a most interesting narrative" "read by hundreds of thousands of his fellow citizens."[6] Indeed, Douglass emphasized Northup's success by reprinting at steady intervals extensive puffs from Northup's publishers trumpeting its successful circulation across a wide geographic space. After the fashion of a Stowe advertisement, the earliest ads declare that "17,000 copies have sold in 4 months" while later ones proudly announce that the "FOURTEENTH THOUSAND" copy is "NOW READY," reprinting favorable citations from twelve different reviews located in cities as diverse as Buffalo, New York, Detroit, Rochester, Cincinnati, Syracuse, Cayuga (Ohio), and

6. *Frederick Douglass' Paper*, 4 August 1854.

Pittsburgh.[7] But this only proves Northup's investment in the North as a self-making site: the book illustrates (as a plot and as an object circulating through stores in Syracuse and Pittsburgh) that Northup could be (simultaneously, it seems) a slave in the South and a celebrated author in other regions. The successful sale of the narrative across the scattered Northeast and West thus fulfills the place-based logic of his twelve-year ordeal, set as it is against the scene of textual deprivation he experiences at Bayou Boeuf.

Both in its plotline and in its circulatory afterlife as a celebrated book-object in its own right, Northup's story reveals loopholes in the model of mass circulation we associate with *Uncle Tom's Cabin*. While *Twelve Years a Slave* was frequently yoked to *Uncle Tom* in newspaper and magazine reviews, Northup actually points out one of the biggest problems in Stowe's conception of national space, for Northup's story denies the saturation (or self-sameness) of space that Stowe's novel describes, and in some sense, performs.[8] In doing so, it exposes *Uncle Tom's Cabin* as just another partial (printed) representation of slavery "as it is, or is not." To the degree that Northup fails to enter the circuit of such circulating representations (and he does fail—for twelve years), it is not because he does not know how to enter it or because it cannot reach him. It is because it is a circuit that only *seems* to saturate the world of known spaces but that is nevertheless closed to certain readers and writers (like himself) through structures of power that are hyperlocal (and thus more vertical than horizontal). In this way, Northup's narrative portrays a new kind of virtual nation: one that exists for some subjects and not for others—no matter how extensive its material structures come to be.

Northup's story is important to the argument of this book, then, for several reasons. It suggests that the nation's networks were more evenly developed in the 1850s than they had once been, but it also shows that even at the height of its self-understanding as a fused series of parts (a nation rather than a series of well-bounded sections or disaggregated state-parts), the United States was never a fully self-saturated space, even in print. Print may have emerged more evenly and produced more connections between the parts of

7. Ibid., 26 August and 9 September 1853. The book was successful enough to be cited in a magazine article about how ordinary people might become writers. Northup's circulation numbers (cited at 20,000) are listed alongside those of other antebellum best-sellers, including Fanny Fern's *Fern Leaves* (45,000) and Ik Marvel's *Reveries of a Bachelor* (70,000). The same article details how Stowe spent her writing profits. William T. Coggeshall, "Labor and Luck of Authors," *The Ladies' Repository: A Monthly Periodical, Devoted to Literature, Arts, and Religion* 19, no. 1 (1859): 20–24.

8. Journalists were especially intrigued by potential links between Northup and Uncle Tom. The *New York Daily Times* for 20 January 1853 remarks that "the condition of this colored man [while living on the Red River] was of a character nearly approaching that described by Mrs. Stowe, as the condition of 'Uncle Tom,' while in that region."

the union after 1850, but Northup's struggles to escape (back) into freedom prove that the privileges of print culture were never evenly distributed. The more actual the nation became and the more connected its parts were in 1850, 1860, and beyond, the more virtual (or hyper-) the space of national belonging became. In this way, Northup's narrative rebukes Stowe's claustrophobic fantasy of a nation so self-sutured at the ground that it needs to extract and colonize its own dark difference.

The Fulton of Indian Creek: Race and Place in Twelve Years a Slave

Throughout his narrative, Northup is invested in a place-based reading of social difference, which he explicitly opposes to a more biological reading (of the sort Stowe finally embraces)—a conflict aggressively staged in a conversation between his owner (Epps) and his "liberator"/friend (Bass). Here, Epps mouths a proslavery truism by insisting that slavery is premised on an absolute difference between the white and black races (one that he compares to the species difference "between a white man and a baboon") (206). The more sympathetic Bass, on the other hand, argues instead that the conditions of enslavement are made possible by the uneven circulation of information:

> "There are monkeys among white people as well as black, when you come to that," coolly remarked Bass. "I know some white men that use arguments no sensible monkey would. But let that pass. These niggers are human beings. If they don't know as much as their masters, whose fault is it? They are not *allowed* to know anything. You have books and papers, and can go where you please, and gather intelligence in a thousand ways. But your slaves have no privileges. You'd whip one of them if caught reading a book. They are held in bondage, generation after generation, deprived of mental improvement, and who can expect them to possess much knowledge?"
>
> . . .
>
> "If you lived up among the Yankees in New-England," said Epps, "I expect you'd be one of them cursed fanatics that know more than the constitution, and go about peddling clocks and coaxing niggers to run away."
>
> "If I was in New-England," returned Bass, "I would be just what I am here." (206–7)

In keeping with his general character, Epps lays out different rules for black and white men, suggesting they differ by virtue of race while white men differ (even from themselves) by virtue of the geographical locale (or place) that they happen to inhabit. Epps argues, in other words, that Bass's identity is likely to change based on his location, his placement in space: if Bass "lived up among the Yankees in New-England," Epps suggests, he would be an abolitionist. Bass, of course, denies this premise, insisting that he is autonomous, consistent, and self-identical no matter where he is: "If I was in New-England," he says, "I would be just what I am here." At the same time, however, he recognizes that his self-identicality is premised on his intellectual, social, and geographic mobility. As he tells Epps: "you have books and papers, and can go where you please, and gather intelligence in a thousand ways. But your slaves have no privileges. You'd whip one of them if caught reading a book."

In thinking through the question of where identity ultimately resides (in a racially marked body or in a geographic place), Northup agrees, in a sense, with Bass, suggesting that self-identicality (or consistency of character) across space is a privilege afforded largely to white men. But where Bass emphasizes the circulation of information and knowledge in the production of southern slave identities, Northup tends to emphasize the literal geographic consequences of one's placement in space. Where geography means nothing to a man like Bass (who remains the same person in New England that he is on the Red River), it means everything to Northup—who finds himself free in one state and unfree in another, even though he is every bit as learned and well traveled as either Bass or Epps. As we shall see, this recognition of his own differential identity in space ultimately leads Northup to reinvest in the very spatial construct Stowe diagnoses as lost: the sectional line dividing North from South. His reification of these regions is based, however, on a consistent understanding of how American identity is meaningfully constructed on the ground.

This may explain why an explicitly *northern* freedom becomes Northup's fetish. The lived experience of freedom is such a fundamental condition of identity for Northup that he is only able to identify and bond with those who have known it firsthand. Early in the narrative, for instance, Northup meets two falsely enslaved freemen, with whom he develops a special affective bond. One, "a man of intelligence and information," has much in common with Northup:

> His name was Robert. Like myself, he had been born free, and had a wife and two children in Cincinnati. He said he had come south with two men, who had hired him in the city of his residence. Without free papers, he had been seized at Fredericksburgh, placed in confinement, and beaten until he had learned, as I had, the necessity and the policy of silence. He had been in Goodin's pen about three weeks. To this man I became much attached. We could sympathize with, and understand each other. (38)

Northup's and Robert's fates temporarily coincide when they are literally connected by an iron chain and placed on a New Orleans-bound ship. While on this middle passage, they meet a third free-man named Arthur, who, in contrast to "the policy of silence" adopted by Northup and Robert, arrives "protest[ing], in a loud voice, against the treatment he was receiving, and demand[ing] to be released" (41). In the larger narrative, Robert and Arthur represent two potential outcomes—and affects—for Northup. Robert is "mel-ancholy" while Arthur is angry; perhaps for this reason, Robert dies quickly while Arthur lives to be rescued upon arrival in New Orleans. While on board, however, the differences between the three are collapsed in their common memory and common desire for north-ern freedom, which expresses itself in a plan, first formulated by Northup, to seize the ship:

> There was not another slave we dared to trust. Brought up in fear and ignorance as they are, it can scarcely be conceived how servilely they will cringe before a white man's look. It was not safe to deposit so bold a secret with any of them, and finally we three resolved to take upon ourselves alone the fearful responsibility of the attempt. (44–45)

Like Frederick Douglass, who, in his 1845 autobiography, describes the slave songs of his peers from a position of cultivated detachment and difference, Northup marks his difference from "real" slaves, whom he frequently describes as servile and cringing beings so damaged by their environment that they cannot be trusted. While Northup, Robert, and Arthur are men of "intelligence and informa-tion," the slaves they travel with are constructed as ignorant and untrustworthy. In this way, Northup cultivates a bond, not just with other freemen within the narrative, but with every free man who reads it.

Importantly, however, these characterizations are never elabo-rated in racial terms but are understood instead as the effects of slavery, which is in turn characterized in geographic terms as an explicitly southern institution. Northup thus rejects racial essential-isms but embraces what we might call geographic essentialisms—the idea of essences produced by location. To this end, Northup valorizes freedom—and his own status as a northern freeman—over and against the debasing and geographically based effects of southern slavery. Indeed, the terms "northern" and "freedom" are interchangeable for Northup, and he draws, throughout his years in slavery, on a base of knowledge produced by his experiences of free-dom, importing northern know-how into his everyday work-life on the Red River. At one point, he produces what he characterizes as a

"Northern" axe-handle, replacing the southern fashion of using "a round, straight stick" with the "crooked one . . . to which I had been accustomed at the North." His master responds "with astonishment, unable to determine" what it is, and Northup betrays no small amount of pride in noting that his master was "forcibly struck with the novelty of the idea" and "kept it in the house a long time, and when his friends called, was wont to exhibit it as a curiosity" (133).

"Novelty," ingenuity, efficiency, skill—not to mention the desire to produce and display "curiosities"—are all ideological productions of the northern wage economy—just as the axe-handle is a material one. Northup further reveals his investment in that economy and its values when he innovates a makeshift canal to transport his master's lumber up the Red River, an efficient alternative to moving it overland. "I ascertained the distance from the mills to the point on the latter bayou, where our lumber was to be delivered, was but a few miles less by land than by water. Provided the creek could be made navigable for rafts, it occurred to me that the expense of transportation would be materially diminished" (70). Northup's project is successful, but given his inability to circulate freely through the national network, his construction of this miniature canal might be the most ironic moment of his enslavement, expressing his faith in the very structures of commercial mobility that had both whisked him to slavery (he was moved south by both rail and boat) and that nevertheless denied him, for twelve long years, transit home. In Northup's narrative, the canal episode is meant to prove, once again, his essential difference from the southerners who surround him:

> At this business I think I was quite skillful, not having forgotten my experience years before on the Champlain canal. I labored hard, being extremely anxious to succeed, both from a desire to please my master, and to show Adam Taydem [the foreman] that my scheme was not such a visionary one as he incessantly pronounced it. (70–71)

Northup notes that the arrival of the first raft through the canal "created a sensation": "on all sides I heard Ford's Platt [Northup's slave name] pronounced the 'smartest nigger in the Pine Woods'— in fact I was the Fulton of Indian Creek" (70). Poignantly, Northup must hear himself "pronounced" worthy by a name other than his own, and he appears to respond to this enforced alienation by taking up, in turn, his own new name, dubbing himself "the Fulton of Indian Creek." Though never fully recognized for who he is, Northup revels in his ability to excel and astonish the men who surround him. But as this episode shows, the ignorance Northup describes at such moments is never racialized. Northup's white overseers and masters are as ignorant of the innovations he brings to his labor as any of their slaves are—and vice versa. Like many a northerner after 1850, Northup genuinely seems to believe in the benefits that accrue to free men through free labor—including the skill, efficiency, pride, and exceptional drive "to succeed" that he displays in building his canal. Northup learns these principles in New York but carries them with him into the South, where they serve as imports of a very local kind of knowledge and selfhood. To the degree that Northup becomes "the Fulton of Indian Creek"—the ingenious inventor who can participate fully in the densely connected circuit that is national culture (rather than remaining a slave forever excluded from that circuit)—it is because he has so fully imbibed the mores of the northern wage economy that made him what he is.

Northup's geographic essentialism is characteristic of the sectionalist identifications that mark U.S. culture in these years, and it holds within it the same paradox that would eventually undo those sectionalisms. On one hand, he takes pride in his origin as a northerner, from whence his status as a freeman derives; on the other hand, he deplores the fact that this condition is not mobile (that he cannot, in other words, be as self-identical across state lines—or sections—as Bass is). One of these positions is place-based (valorizing region of origin as the key producer of character); the other seeks to detach identity from place and make it more mobile. This contradiction suggests that there are two conflicting ways of reading identity in this period: one based on geographically conceived identity politics, and the other based on a far more mobile and highly individualized kind of identity politics in which the only border that matters is the biological border of each individual body. Of the two, geo-identity (as we might call it) would appear to be the more regressive model, rooted in the climatological theories of the Enlightenment and the social structures of a less mobile, more agrarian society. Bio-identity, on the other hand (based in the individual body), is far more suited to capitalism's mobile networks. While it is tempting, however, to link the first with the (underdeveloped) South and the second with the (developing) North, it is clear that the shift from geographic notions of identity to more biological ones actually occurred on a massive scale that, ironically, knew no geographical boundaries. The conflict between the two was, in fact, the epic cultural dilemma of Northup's era.

*   *   *

DAVID FISKE, CLIFFORD W. BROWN, JR., AND RACHEL SELIGMAN

Sharing the Story[†]

The story of Northup's rescue created a national sensation. The *New York Daily Times* ran a huge page-one story; other newspapers followed suit. The Whig press was more positive than the Democratic press, but coverage by both was extensive. The *Albany Evening Journal* reported his return to his family.[1]

Northup, barely taking time to recover from his ordeal, began making appearances at nearby antislavery rallies. On February 1, 1853, he appeared in Troy with major abolitionists like Frederick Douglass, Jermain Loguen, and Stephen Myers. Northup's description of his captivity, told "with child-like simplicity," elicited "sympathy from the audience." Afterward, Douglass asked the audience for donations for Northup, and over $18 was raised.[2] Northup appeared with Douglass again on February 4 in Albany and "stated some of the wrongs he had received." Henry Northup was there (as he had been at the Troy meeting) and spoke about his southern trip.[3]

In the course of a month, Solomon Northup had gone from living the life of a slave to being a recognized national figure. Although a publicly performing musician for most of his life, he had never experienced anything like the outpouring of attention he now received. For the next few years, he was to live the life of a celebrity while recounting, and in a sense, reliving, the extraordinary story of his kidnapping, enslavement, and rescue.

Numerous speaking engagements quickly provided a vehicle for doing so. More importantly, Northup (with the collaboration of local writer David Wilson) rapidly produced a book that told his story in a much more complete fashion than could be done on the lecture circuit. After the book was published, Northup again went on tour. He then took his story to the stage, producing two plays. Meanwhile, the book's publication led to the arrest of the kidnappers, creating a new round of publicity. His efforts throughout were designed both to help him financially and to further the antislavery cause.

---

† From *Solomon Northup: The Complete Story of the Author of* Twelve Years a Slave (Santa Barbara, CA: Praeger, 2013), pp. 111–24, 200–202. Reprinted by permission of ABC–CLIO.
1. *Albany Evening Journal* (January 21, 1853).
2. *Frederick Douglass' Paper* [cited hereafter as *FDP*] (February 18, 1853).
3. *FDP* (February 18, 1853).

The Writing of Twelve Years a Slave

The positive press coverage of Northup's tale may have provided the impetus for putting it into print. Just weeks after his early appearances, a newspaper reported that "a local gentleman in this county is engaged in writing the life of Sol. Northup."[4] This item was the first to compare Northup's book to *Uncle Tom's Cabin*, saying sarcastically "we suppose the work will be entitled 'Uncle Sol.'"

Though David Wilson was not mentioned in this early report, he doubtless was the author referred to. Wilson may have been chosen because both Henry Northup and Orville Clark had familial and professional ties to him. Though trained as an attorney (having studied in Clark's law office in Sandy Hill), Wilson's employment in that profession was short. Instead, he turned to literature, a pursuit which had perhaps interested him for some time, as he had served as the "poet" for the Kappa Alpha Society while a student at Union College. His health reportedly did not suit him for the legal profession, and was likely another factor in his decision to author books.[5]

His first book, *Life in Whitehall During the Ship Fever Times*, was published in 1850. Through the years, he wrote or edited several other books, *Life of Jane McCrea; Life of Henrietta Robinson, the Veiled Murderess* (for which he was criticized for appealing to the public's "morbid curiosity");[6] and *Narrative of Nelson Lee, a Captive among the Comanches*. However, the work which achieved the most success was *Twelve Years a Slave*. In the late 1850s, his political affiliation was with the nativist American Party[7] (called the "Know-Nothings"), which had no strong stance concerning slavery, and after the Northup book came out, one writer said of Wilson: "I believe he never was suspected of being an Abolitionist—he may be anti-slavery—somewhat conservative."[8] A few years following publication of *Twelve Years*, he moved to Albany, taking a position with the state government, and serving as Clerk of the Assembly. For the last five years of his life, Wilson adopted an entirely different line of work: he operated a brewery in Albany known as "Wilson & Company." He continued this business until his death, on June 9, 1870.[9]

Once the idea of a book had been hatched, the project came together very quickly. Over the years, readers have wondered whether Northup or Wilson did the actual writing. There is, of course, no way to tell precisely. In the "Editor's Preface" to *Twelve Years*, Wilson refers to himself as the "editor" and mentions that due

---

4. *Sandy Hill Herald* (March 8, 1853).
5. *Albany Evening Journal* (June 10, 1870); *New York Times* (June 18, 1870).
6. *[Auburn, New York] Daily American* (September 16, 1855), attributed to the *Albany Argus*.
7. *New York Times* (January 27, 1858).
8. Letter from John Thompson, *Essex County Republican* (August 13, 1853).
9. *Albany Evening Journal* (June 10, 1870).

to "all the facts which have been communicated to him," the completed book was longer than originally anticipated. His object was to give a faithful portrayal of Northup's life "as he received it from his lips." The *New York Times* described the production of the book in this way: "Some curious but no doubt competent person, has . . . been at the pains to elicit from the rescued negro a full story of his life and sufferings . . . and they fill a stout volume."[1]

Another newspaper article admitted that Northup was not the literal author, but had "dictated" the content and that "another acted as his amanuensis."[2] A letter from a relative of Henry Northup agrees with this, because he wrote that "by questions" Wilson "got enough to write a book."[3] Even if not the actual person who put pen to paper, Northup was very involved in its content. Northup, Wilson says, "invariably repeated the same story without deviating in the slightest particular, and has also carefully perused the manuscript, dictating an alteration whenever the most trivial inaccuracy has appeared." Over time—except for some extremely minor errors—Northup's account has held up to all verification efforts directed to it, indicating that the material came from a person who had actually experienced the events related.

The following elements in the book are clearly Northup's: the story line itself; the descriptions of his physical surroundings (e.g., the Great Cocodrie Swamp); the descriptions of his social surroundings; the descriptions of the agricultural and manufacturing processes in which he participated (Northup does not attempt to describe those in which he did not participate, such as the ginning of cotton); the descriptions of daily living on the plantation; and the descriptions and assessments of individual people. Northup was in a position to observe or experience all of these; Wilson was not.

Northup might be called a literalist—an author principally intent on exact narration, with little metaphor or imagery, focused on strict accuracy. The heart of Northup's story lies in the narration of facts and events, articulated by descriptive content. Much of the material is consistent with reports about his straight-forward speaking style. Details such as how a sugar mill works are recorded because Northup found them interesting, given his farming and artisan background, and he expects a worthy audience to find them interesting also. Most details included in the narrative seem to reflect his interests and thinking. But there is also a poetic voice present that can be attributed to Northup. The lyrical descriptions of both Patsey and

1. *New York Daily Times* (April 22, 1853).
2. *Syracuse Evening Journal* (January 30, 1854).
3. Letter from John Henry Northup to Edith Carman Hay, quoted in Edith Hay Wyckoff, *The Autobiography of an American Family* (Fort Edward, NY: Washington County Historical Society, 2000), p. 136.

Mary McCoy; Northup's brief but intense descriptions of the dancing at Christmas balls; and his description of Mrs. Ford's garden, where he sought emotional release following his flight through the swamp, reveal strong romantic streaks in the narrator. Finally, there is the clear human voice of a man terribly wronged, longing for home, witnessing enormities, and seeking justice. At times the syntax and word choices likely come from Wilson's initiatives, but this is Northup's book. Wilson's self-given title of "Editor" is fully appropriate and not unduly modest.

Regardless of the method of Wilson's and Northup's collaboration, the book was prepared amazingly quickly. Its publication was advertised as early as April 15, 1853.[4] Though seeking advance orders ("copies sent by mail, soon as ready"), the ad says the book is "now in Press" and would contain more than 300 pages. The volume was near enough to completion that a lengthy excerpt appeared in *Frederick Douglass' Paper* in late April.[5] Bookstores began advertising its availability in July. So, in less than five months the book had gone from concept to print, certainly quite an accomplishment. The book was published simultaneously by three firms in which three brothers were active * * *. One brother, James C. Derby of Auburn, was a life-long friend of William Seward. He specialized in printing respectable didactic and patriotic works, which would have added credibility to Northup's narrative. The illustrations were drawn by Frederick M. Coffin and engraved by Nathaniel Orr. They include the frontispiece (depicting Northup in his "plantation suit") and six other illustrations depicting dramatic moments in the tale. Coffin, a frequent illustrator of books published by the Derbys, also drew for *Harper's Magazine*. Orr was one of the country's leading wood engravers.

Reviews of Twelve Years a Slave

Press reviews were very positive. A literary notice prepared by the publisher contained excerpts from reviews printed by numerous newspapers, including the *Buffalo Courier, New York Tribune, New York Evangelist, Detroit Tribune, Buffalo Express, Cincinnati Journal, Syracuse Evening Chronicle, Syracuse Daily Journal, Cayuga Chief, Frederick Douglass' Paper, Pittsburgh Dispatch, Buffalo Commercial Advertiser,* and *New York Independent.*[6] In an item that included an extract from the book, Frederick Douglass wrote: "We think it will be difficult for any one who takes up the book in a candid and impartial spirit to lay it down until finished. . . ."[7]

4. *New York Daily Times* (April 15, 1853).
5. *FDP* (April 29, 1853).
6. *FDP* (September 9, 1853).
7. *FDP* (July 29, 1853).

William Lloyd Garrison's newspaper called the book a "deeply interesting and thrilling Narrative."[8] Though packed with exciting adventures, it was also perceived to be factual and impartial. Some reviewers were impressed by how equitable Northup's account was: "Its tone is much milder than we expected to see exhibited . . . but, while he seems to fully realize the magnitude of his sufferings, he does not condemn all."[9] "He tells apparently an honest tale, without exaggeration."[1] "NORTHUP will be believed, because, instead of indiscriminate accusations, he gives you the good and evil of Slavery just as he found it. All kindnesses are remembered with gratitude. Masters and Overseers who treated Slaves humanely are commended; for there, as here, were good and bad men. If 'Tibeats' and 'Epps' were coarse, cruel and brutal, 'Master FORD' and 'Madam McCOY' were so just, considerate, humane as to be obeyed, honored and beloved."[2]

Comparisons were of course made to the previous year's *Uncle Tom's Cabin*. That sensational book covered very similar ground, but was admittedly a work of fiction. One reader recommended Northup's book to "those persons who are so conscientious that they will not read *'Uncle Tom's Cabin'* because they say it is a Novel," but noted that Northup's narrative fully supported the degradations portrayed by Harriet Beecher Stowe.[3] Another paper observed, "Let them buy the narrative of Solomon Northup, and when they have read it, we will guarantee that they acquit Mrs. Stowe of all exaggeration."[4]

Promoting the Book

Apparently hopeful of duplicating the success of Stowe's work, an advertisement run by the publisher indicated that over 10,000 copies of Northup's book (published on July 15, 1853) had been ordered.[5] At about the same time, bookstores advertised the title's availability,[6] at a cost of $1. James C. Derby, one of the publishers, later wrote that it "caused quite a sensation among the reading community, the book meeting with a rapid and large sale."[7]

Sales were indeed strong. By mid-August 11,000 copies had been sold, even without much advertising.[8] The publisher began promoting

8. *Liberator* (September 9, 1853).
9. *Rome [New York] Citizen* (July 20, 1853).
1. *[Montpelier, Vermont] Watchman & State Journal* (January 26, 1855).
2. *Salem Press* (July 26, 1853), attributed to *Albany Evening Journal*.
3. Letter from John Thompson, *Essex County Republican* (August 13, 1853).
4. *Northern Christian Advocate* (July 13, 1853).
5. *Buffalo Daily Courier* (August 3, 1853).
6. *Syracuse Evening Chronicle* (July 18, 1853).
7. James C. Derby, *Fifty Years Among Authors, Books, and Publishers* (London: G.W. Carleton, 1884), 63.
8. *Syracuse Evening Journal* (August 12, 1853).

the book, promising a free copy to any newspaper that would run their publication announcement.[9] An additional 6,000 copies flew off the shelves over the following three months,[1] and the publisher sought 1,000 agents to handle the book, promising an annual income between $500 and $1,000.[2] A Syracuse newspaper even offered free copies of the book (for use as Christmas gifts) to individuals who recruited four new subscribers to its paper (*Uncle Tom's Cabin* could be obtained by hooking just one subscriber!).[3] Though sales fell short of the phenomenal level reached by *Uncle Tom's Cabin*, *Twelve Years* was at par with other best-sellers of the day. Publisher Miller, Orton & Mulligan announced that over 27,000 books had been sold by January 1855.[4]

Northup stood to benefit financially from the book. While it was still being prepared, there were reports that "an extensive publishing house in this State has offered Northup . . . $3,000 for the copyright of his book."[5] Notices from the publisher that appeared in newspapers mentioned that some (or all) of the profits from book sales would go to Northup. A Syracuse newspaper, offering copies for sale, added that "Northup gets a profit on all the books sold, and by helping yourselves and neighbors to some of them you will help him at the same time."[6] John Thompson, of Peru, New York, who claimed personal familiarity with Henry Northup, wrote "I understand the profits of the entire sale of the book is to be for the benefit of 'Uncle Sol,' and his family."[7]

Northup certainly saw some monetary gain. Prior to the release of his narrative, he was able to purchase real estate in Glens Falls. On May 16, 1853, he purchased property near the intersection of South and School Streets for $275.[8] This was near the property owned by his son-in-law, Philip Stanton.

The dedication in Northup's book alludes to Stowe's *A Key to Uncle Tom's Cabin*, which had come out not long before his. Stowe's book provided supporting documentation for the types of situations depicted in her blockbuster novel. Though her book referred to Northup, a direct quote from it was apparently not available for the first edition of *Twelve Years*. In 1854, however, another edition was issued, which included a short excerpt relating to Northup.

Northup's clever title was mimicked by other ex-slaves. A book which came out in 1854, just a year after his, used the long-winded

9. *National Era* (August 25, 1853); *FDP* (August 26, 1853).
1. *[Elyria, Ohio] Independent Democrat* (December 7, 1853).
2. *[Elyria, Ohio] Independent Democrat* (December 7, 1853).
3. *Wesleyan* (November 17, 1853).
4. *Syracuse Daily Standard* (January 12, 1855).
5. *Syracuse Standard* (April 4, 1853).
6. *Wesleyan* (July 20, 1854).
7. Letter from John Thompson, in *Essex County Republican* (August 13, 1853).
8. Warren County, New York, Deeds, Book U, p. 297.

title: *Experience and Personal Narrative of Uncle Tom Jones: Who Was for Forty Years a Slave. Also the Surprising Adventures of Wild Tom of the Island Retreat, a Fugitive Negro from South Carolina.* Other titles published in subsequent years included: *Twenty-two Years a Slave and Forty Years a Freeman*, by Austin Steward, in 1857, and *New Man: Twenty-Nine Years a Slave, Twenty-Nine Years a Free Man: Recollections of H. C. Bruce*, in 1859.

One indication of how widely *Twelve Years* was read can be had by noting instances where northern soldiers, on their deployment during the Civil War, described visits to locations mentioned in the book. One recalled visiting "the old slave-pen . . . where was confined . . . Solomon Northrop."[9] Others found the Epps plantation in Louisiana: "Old Mr. Epps yet lives, and told us that a greater part of the book was truth, and that many old Negroes remembered Northrup," whom Epps called "smart."[1] Another soldier who visited the plantation located some blacks who "knew Platt well and have danced to the music of his fiddle often. Some . . . remember when he was taken out of the lot by the 'Northern gemman.'"[2]

Northup's narrative benefited from the antislavery movement, and first-hand stories of people who had lived under the American system of slavery became a rage, whether told in print or orally.

A Lecture Tour

The lecture circuit was a lucrative pursuit for former slaves. Speakers appeared before antislavery meetings, abolitionist conventions, and the general public at lecture halls. Soon after the publication of *Twelve Years*, Northup began an extended series of lectures in New York and New England. From the beginning, the book had received substantial coverage in the newspaper published by Frederick Douglass, and Douglass suggested, after hearing Henry Northup relate Northup's story to a teary-eyed crowd at Port Byron, New York, in July 1853, that he travel around the state and spread the word, and that "he should take Solomon with him."[3]

Whether Douglass's comment was the impetus or not, Northup *did* begin traveling to promote and sell his book in the second half of 1853. A surviving copy of the 1853 edition bears the inscription "Purchased on NYCRR [New York Central Railroad] Train of Solomon

9. *War Talks in Kansas* (Kansas City, Missouri: Franklin Hudson, 1906), 162.
1. Elias Porter Pellet, *History of the 114th Regiment, New York State Volunteers* (Norwich, New York: Telegraph & Chronicle Power Press, 1866), 77.
2. Joseph Logsdon, "Diary of a Slave: Recollection and Prophecy," in *Seven on Black: Reflections on the Negro Experience in America*, by William G. Shad and Roy C. Herrenkohl, eds. (Philadelphia: Lippincott, 1969), 43.
3. *FDP* (July 29, 1853).

Northrup himself 1853."[4] A newspaper reported that Northup had lost his pocketbook while in Syracuse in October,[5] probably when he was there for an appearance on October 1, 1853.[6] On that day, celebrations took place commemorating the Jerry Rescue, when anti-slavery advocates in Syracuse had successfully released a man who'd been arrested under the Fugitive Slave Law. Northup was introduced by Gerrit Smith, the famous abolitionist. The speaker who followed Northup was none other than Frederick Douglass. A newspaper account, unfortunately, gave no details of Northup's remarks.[7]

Though announcements of appearances made by Northup in 1854 were made in newspapers * * * , many accounts are brief (or even speculative): "In this lecture, we understand, he tells his own story, in his own way; and as he is a plain, uneducated man, it will probably be all the more interesting";[8] "We happen to be somewhat acquainted with 'Sol.' He is a man—every inch of him";[9] and "He will recount in his own simple and unvarnished way, the particulars of his kidnapping and twelve years' subsequent servitude in the South."[1]

A more substantial account of a lecture in Buffalo was reported by one of Douglass's correspondents: "Last night I had the pleasure of hearing Solomon Northup . . . His story is full of romantic interest and painful adventures, and gives as clear an insight to the practical workings and beauties of American Slavery. . . . Northup tells his story in plain and candid language, and intermingles it with flashes of genuine wit. It is a sure treat to hear him give some hazardous adventure, with so much *sans* [sic] *froid* that the audience is completely enraptured and the 'house brought down.'"[2]

A brief description of Northup's appearance at the courthouse in St. Albans, Vermont, similarly mentioned "his unaffected simplicity, directness and gentlemanly bearing" and, as some had said of his book, his straightforward presentation was more impressive "than many fervid appeals to which we have listened."[3]

It was speculated that Northup might go to England, probably to lecture, although it's unlikely that he did because at the time of these speculations he was in Syracuse organizing a theatrical production based on his book.[4] After the close of this dramatization,

4. Photocopy of inscription provided to author (Fiske) by Connecticut bookseller John D. Townsend.
5. *Auburn Weekly Journal* (October 5, 1853).
6. *Liberator* (October 14, 1853); *Wesleyan* (October 6, 1853); *Syracuse Evening Chronicle* (October 1, 1853).
7. *Wesleyan* (October 6, 1853).
8. *Syracuse Evening Chronicle* (January 30, 1854).
9. *Syracuse Daily Journal* (January 31, 1854).
1. *Syracuse Evening Chronicle* (February 2, 1854).
2. *FDP* (January 27, 1854). ["Sic" in original—Editors' note.]
3. *FDP* (March 3, 1854), attributed to the *Vermont Tribune*.
4. Field Horne, *Index to News of Saratoga Springs, New York 1819–1900*. (Privately printed, 1998.)

Northup resumed giving talks around the northeast, including ones at Montpelier, Vermont;[5] Concord, New Hampshire;[6] and in several Massachusetts cities.[7] Northup, along with a young fugitive slave called "Ida May," was presented to the Massachusetts Legislature on March 10, 1855.[8]

Henry C. Wright, the noted abolitionist, witnessed several appearances in Boston:

> [Though *Twelve Years a Slave* relates Solomon's story] it is far more potent to see the man, and hear him, in his clear, manly straight-forward way, speak of slavery as he experienced it, and as he saw it in others. Those who have read his Narrative can scarce fail to desire to see the man, thus kidnapped and tortured in body and soul, for twelve years, and to hear his story from his own lips.
>
> I heard him relate his experience in the Melonaon, on the evening of the 15th, and last evening, in a private social circle. To-morrow evening he is to lecture in the Bethel on Commercial Street. But he should have an opportunity to tell his experience in the country towns and villages. I understand that he intends to be at Worcester, at the Non-Resistance Convention. Cannot arrangements be made for him to relate what he has felt, seen and heard in the land of whips and chains, in the towns and villages of Massachusetts?[9]

Producing Two Plays

It is not surprising, given Northup's experiences as a musical performer, that he decided to tell his story using the stage. He produced two plays, one in the spring of 1854, the other in the fall of 1855. Again, he was following the precedent set by *Uncle Tom's Cabin*, which was adapted for theatrical production and was being performed in Troy at the time of Solomon's rescue. His first play opened in Syracuse: "Solomon Northup . . . is present at Syracuse. We learn that his history is to be dramatized and brought out on the stage, and that he is to take one of the characters."[1] Northup apparently played himself: "The history of Solomon Northup has been dramatized, and is now being enacted at Syracuse—Northup taking the principal character."[2] The play, presented at the National

5. *Green Mountain Freeman* (January 23, 1855).
6. *Syracuse Daily Standard* (March 31, 1855).
7. *FDP* (March 16, 1855); *Liberator* (March 23, 1855); *Liberator* (March 30, 1855).
8. *Boston Daily Atlas* (March 12, 1855); *FDP* (March 16, 1855).
9. *Liberator* (March 23, 1855).
1. *Lewis County [New York] Republican* (April 29, 1854).
2. *[Rome, New York] Sentinel* (May 1, 1854). Other papers also said Northup portrayed himself in the play: *Syracuse Daily Standard* (April 24, 1854); *Syracuse Daily Standard* (April 25, 1854); *FDP* (May 26, 1854).

Theater, was especially noticed by the local papers, and Northup spent several weeks in Syracuse, overseeing the play's development.[3]

The opening night was reported to have gone "tolerably well," but there were some problems. The presentation was very short (surprising, given the amount of dramatic material available from *Twelve Years*), and the playwright, a Mr. Kemble, apologized to the audience, promising additional dramatic pieces would follow the Northup play in future performances. Viewers unfamiliar with the book would likely have had trouble following the play, and "some of the characters were well performed, while others were poorly done."[4] The play was presented several times in late April and early May in 1854, and a farce was indeed added to follow it.[5]

The production also took to the road, at least briefly. "Solomon Northrup and his troupe have gone to Auburn, where they intend to perform the new drama of his history for a short season. Solomon is bound to make his fortune out of the new enterprise, if possible."[6]

This, however, was not to be. The production was ultimately a flop. Though acknowledging Northup's cleverness, one writer noted "we think theatrical management rather out of his line."[7] Responding to charges that they had not been sufficiently supportive of the production, local abolitionists said: "The enterprise was entered into by Solomon, without counseling them, and in fact, contrary to their advice . . ."[8] One editor wrote that "Solomon is an excellent fellow . . . We regret his adoption of this new line of business. . . . We hope Northup will not suffer pecuniarily by his operation."[9] In fact, * * * it may indeed have caused Northup financial stress and embarrassment.

Two years later, the production was recalled as having been unsuccessful "owing to adverse circumstances."[1] Nevertheless, the project is characteristic of Northup's willingness to use initiative and run risks.

There was another theatrical production based on Northup's book in the fall of 1855. More is known about this play's content than the first one. A poster advertising an October 4 presentation of "A Free Slave" at Worcester's Brinley Hall[2] shows that the cast included characters from *Twelve Years* (though Northup's character is played by a "C.H. Edwyn," and not Northup himself). The production consisted of five acts—apparently the earlier mistake of having too

3. *Syracuse Evening Chronicle* (April 21, 1854); *Syracuse Daily Standard* (July 19, 1856).
4. *Syracuse Daily Standard* (May 1, 1854).
5. *Syracuse Daily Standard* (May 2, 1854).
6. *Syracuse Daily Standard* (May 3, 1854).
7. *Syracuse Daily Standard* (May 3, 1854).
8. *Syracuse Daily Standard* (May 4, 1854).
9. *Syracuse Evening Chronicle* (April 28, 1854).
1. *Syracuse Daily Standard* (July 19, 1856).
2. Item 9169 from *American Broadsides* database, American Antiquarian Society collection.

brief a play was not repeated, as the poster notes "owing to the length of the piece no Farce will be presented."

The scenes listed on the poster provide some idea of how Northup's book was adapted for the stage. Some liberties were taken,[3] but the plot follows the story fairly well. The following shows the general content of the drama:

Act 1
Scene 1.—Saratoga Springs; the broken gamblers; Plot and Plan; the unsuspecting victim; the offer made and accepted; Solomon arranges for his departure.

Scene 2.—The Yankee taking Notes; Departure for the South.

Scene 3.—Custom House, New York; The Yankee still has his eye on Brown and Hamilton.

Scene 4.—Brown and Hamilton leave for Washington.

Act 2
Scene 1.—The City of Washington; Bass's opinion of the Capitol.

Scene 2.—The arrival of Solomon; THE WINE IS DRUGGED; Ichabod is rather elated; the Victim Sleeps; is robbed of his papers and money and Dragged to the Slave pen.

Scene 3.—Solomon finds himself in chains! I am betrayed and sold for a Slave! Cruel conduct of Birch; the Lash; Eliza and her child; a mother's wretchedness; Departure for Endless Slaver. TABLEAU.

Act 3
Scene 1.—New Orleans. Bass's arrival; the Yankee and Slave Dealer.

Scene 2.—Sale of Slaves; Solomon is sold for $1000 and sent to the plantation; Eliza begging that her child may be sold with her, but is refused; noble conduct of Ford; Freeman Murdered in the slave pen by Tibbets. TABLEAU

Scene 3.—The Plantation Workshop; Detestable and cruel Conduct of Tibbets; Dreadful Struggle of Solomon to save his life; 'Hang him to the first tree!' Interposition of Ford.

Scene 4.—Solomon resold; Old Pete Tanner; Planter Epps in his glory; a good drink of brandy.

Scene 5.—The way in which Tanner keeps his Slaves at home on Sunday.

Scene 6.—Negro Cabin; Abe and General Jackson; Patsey about; The Yankee and Epps; 'Wake up, Niggers;' Dance by Patsey; Entrance of Mrs. Epps. TABLEAU.

3. For example: the hero Bass appeared early, in Saratoga, when in reality he appeared only toward the end of Northup's years in Louisiana; Tibaut ("Tibbeats") murders Freeman in his slave pen; and Eliza dies on the Epps plantation.

Act 4

Scene 1.—Epps' Parlor; Jealousy of Mrs. Epps; Consoling of Solomon.

Scene 2.—COTTON FIELD; Slaves at work.

Scene 3.—Cabin; Breakdown by Patsey.

Scene 4.—Cotton Field; Epps; Solomon weighs the Cotton; Patsey is whipped.

Scene 5.—A real friend; exposition of facts; the Yankee on the right side; Solomon will soon be free; Interruption of Epps. 'If you strike, I fire.' TABLEAU.

Act 5

Scene 1.—Bass and Epps; Difference of opinion.

Scene 2.—Sol. and Bass; painful suspense.

Scene 3.—Arrival of friends from the North.

Scene 4.—Solomon identified; Sam and Patsey in trouble; Solomon taken home.

Scene 5.—The Yankee as happy as a clam at high water.

Scene 6.—Epps' Plantation; Death of Eliza! TABLEAU.

The play was presented on another occasion, most likely in Fitchburg, Massachusetts. An undated poster, printed by a press in Fitchburg, advertises its performance at the "Town Hall." Though undated, the performance probably took place around the same time as the one in Worcester, since the cast list is virtually identical. An extremely notable feature of the latter performance (and an indication of Northup's involvement) is that the poster promises "the veritable Solomon will be at the Door. He alone is worth 25 cts. a sight!"[4]

As the poster showed, the plot generally follows the book's outline. Eliza and Patsey are featured, although the former appears in widely separated (though dramatic) scenes. Patsey's story is given more extensive treatment, although much of this may have been musical performance. Bass's role is greatly expanded. He, not Henry Northup, is the "Yankee" supporting hero. The use of multiple rescuers may have showcased the community support of the rescue.

The scene titles show that the play was full of melodrama, with the use of tableaus and clearly delineated heroes and villains. There is an unvarnished appeal to regional pride and prejudice, with the Canadian Bass turned into a shrewd "Yankee" hero who overcomes the southern villains. But the play is not designed to be simply an entertaining melodrama, as the plays based on *Uncle Tom's Cabin* eventually became. Portraying slavery remains a central focus. This is

4. Item 23755 from *American Broadsides* database, American Antiquarian Society collections.

evident not just from the roles of villains with their lashes and chains, but from the scenes illustrating slave life that do not contribute directly to Northup's own drama.

The play was apparently not a success. The many episodes and story lines, often interrupted by other material, may have given it a fragmented quality. Also, play-going audiences may not have been ready to confront the topics of slavery and race in a performance designed, in part, to entertain. Moreover, Northup's story, both in *Twelve Years* and as presented by him in simple direct language on the lecture circuit, made powerful impressions because the factual narrations came across as authentic, and their compelling immediacy resonated with audiences. The playwrights may have failed to preserve this quality when they tried to dramatize the story and thereby force both interpretation and emotion on the playgoer.

The only evidence of this play's financial fortunes comes from newspaper advisories about the acting troupe leaving towns with unpaid bills. One paper warned printers about a "strolling band of theatrical performers under the charge of a black man calling himself Solomon Northrup," who had left Greenfield and Northampton, Massachusetts without settling their bills.[5] Another paper referenced the "Free Slave" production, warning merchants about the acting group, as "we learn that they have left several places at the north in debt to landlords and printers."[6] This second theatrical failure must have been a severe blow to Northup, and apparently he did not handle it well, because this same newspaper account stated "Solomon Northrup, ('the free slave') is said to have been quite profane and insulting, besides openly repudiating his debts. Solomon does the business, while someone else claims to own the property."

In December 1856, a Vermont newspaper could not recommend Northup's "moral exhibition" (likely some version of "The Free Slave," which the posters had billed the previous year as a "great moral and scenic representation"). While in St. Albans, Northup and some of the performers became intoxicated and fisticuffs had broken out.[7] These reports suggest that he continued to try to show the play, but had little success, instead generating negative personal publicity.

Speaking Engagements Decline—and End

Newspaper accounts of appearances by Northup taper off in 1856 and 1857. The story of his enslavement and rescue was becoming stale and the dramatizations were obviously attracting little positive attention. He may have had speaking engagements in other regions

5. *Barre [Massachusetts] Patriot* (November 17, 1855).
6. *Springfield [Massachusetts] Republican* (November 10, 1855).
7. *St. Albans Messenger* (December 11, 1856).

of the country, but accounts of these have not surfaced. If Northup ever went to England in search of fresh audiences, this may have been the time it happened, even though the one reference to that possibility, as mentioned, was two years earlier.

He *did* go to Canada, and the result was a disaster. In fact, the last newspaper notice of an appearance by him that the authors could locate related to a planned lecture in Streetsville, Ontario. Accounts vary somewhat, but one states that he was "prevented from lecturing . . . by a mob."[8] As Northup prepared to speak, "he was interrupted by cries of 'down with the bloody negro,' 'brain the blasted Sambo,' etc. The noise and confusion was so great and so universal on the part of the crowd that Northup was forced to leave the hall under an escort of friends."[9] It was also reported that "such a row was kicked up that he ran and locked himself into a room in fear of personal violence."[1] Northup was rescued by the local Quarter-Master.[2] Northup's reception may have been the result of racial tension following years of fugitive slaves moving to Canada.

This traumatic episode appears to be the end of Northup's public speaking career. It came at almost exactly the same time that the Saratoga County District Attorney dropped the charges against the kidnappers * * *. Northup was now 50 years old. It was time to refocus his life.

CALVIN SCHERMERHORN

Solomon Northup and Present-Day Slavery[†]

Solomon Northup's twelve-year nightmare odyssey through the American South seems to be an artifact of a bygone era. The Civil War and Thirteenth Amendment abolished slavery, and 150 years after ratification, the U.S. Congress updated a series of anti-slavery statutes with the "Justice for Victims of Trafficking Act of 2015." But Northup's ordeal bears striking resemblance to current prac-tices, and there is an eerie similarity between the cotton and sugar he was forced to make and the produce of today's captives: slavery's evils are hidden in global supply chains, its fruits leaving little trace of the brutality involved in their production. Then as now, captives

8. *Albany Evening Journal* (September 5, 1857).
9. Attributed to the *Streetsville Review*, via the *Louisville Journal*, in the *Detroit Daily Free Press* (August 26, 1857); and the *New Hampshire Patriot* (September 16, 1857).
1. *Charleston Mercury* (August 29, 1857); *Pittsfield Sun* (September 10, 1857).
2. *[Holmes County, Ohio] Republican* (August 27, 1857).
† A revised version of a post on *Historians Against Slavery* (June 2, 2015), www.historians againstslavery.org/main/2015/06/who-are-todays-solomon-northups/. Reproduced by permission of the author.

are made through the cunning of traffickers who use geographic distance as leverage, exploit vulnerabilities, and employ would-be slaves' goodwill as weapons against them.

In 1841, Northup witnessed the reverse alchemy of a golden opportunity turn into iron fetters. He was the thirty-three-year-old husband of Anne Hampton Northup and father of three children, Margaret, Elizabeth, and Alonzo. Northup was born free in New York and had both European and African ancestors. He had a flair for the violin and was adventurous, which fit with his entrepreneurial talents. Two strangers appeared in Saratoga Springs trolling for would-be captives, and Northup seemed a good mark. The pair said they were forming a traveling circus. They wanted a violin player and planned to go to New York City.

Northup brushed off warnings not to accompany them. The pay was good, and local work was scarce. The traffickers treated him well, luring him to Washington, D.C., during a period of national mourning. During the events surrounding the funeral of President William Henry Harrison, Northup went out for drinks with his employers but that night suffered severe aches and thirst, slipping in and out of consciousness. He was dragged across the National Mall and into the bowels of a slave trader's compound. There James H. Birch paid $650.

In a private Washington city jail, Northup awoke from a drug-induced delirium to a nightmare. He was in a "dungeon" in which Birch and one of his agents greeted him as their slave. They humiliated and tortured their captive, stripping his clothes off, shackling him to a floor, flogging him with a whip, and beating his naked body with a wooden paddle until the vile instrument broke. Violence, incarceration, and geographic isolation turned him from a free citizen into incarnate capital. Just steps from the U.S. Capitol, the captors lashed and humiliated Northup until he stopped insisting that he was free.

Those who captured Northup used the classic procedures of human trafficking. They enforced dependence with violence, gave the subject no alternative, and manipulated him into acting the role they crafted for him. They enforced complicity. And in about two weeks, Northup joined a small assemblage of men, women, and children, bound away from Washington, D.C., under cover of darkness, put on a Potomac River steamboat, and then transferred to railroad cars bound to Richmond. Virginia's capital city was becoming the region's largest slave market.

Kidnapping had long been part of North American slavery, but slave traders like Birch and his New Orleans partner Theophilus Freeman did not hesitate to traffic in freeborn African-descended Americans they could thrash into chattels. It was a way to cut purchasing costs. And like traffickers today, Birch and Freeman used violence to manage business risk.

Northup attempted to ally with fellow captives. They set about "learning the history of each other's wretchedness." He was hand-cuffed to a kidnap victim from Ohio named Robert, a "large yellow man, quite stout and fleshy, with a countenance expressive of the utmost melancholy." In a ship's slave manifest, he was identified as Robert Jones, perhaps an alias. Like Northup, Jones had left a spouse and young children in Cincinnati with the promise of employment in Virginia. Jones's family back in Ohio was left with the dread of not knowing to where he had disappeared. Northup recalled that Jones was "placed in confinement," in Fredericksburg, "and beaten until he had learned, as I had, the necessity and the policy of silence." Identifying the process as company policy was astute. Jones had been confined three weeks already. The two "became much attached." "We could sympathize with, and understand each other," Northup recalled.

Three weeks after being kidnapped Northup and some forty others were embarked on a sea passage to Louisiana aboard a tobacco ship, the *Orleans*. There was a hard commercial logic to the shipping company that owned it. Human trafficking was lucrative. Selling pas-sage to slave traders was good business. Hauling captives was woven into the fabric of coastal maritime commerce from Chesapeake ports. Freeman paid over $2,300 in shipping expenses on an 1839 passage in which the *Orleans* carried 135 involuntary passengers. If typical, the *Orleans*'s owners, Richard O. Haskins and Luther Libby, charged Freeman $20 per captive for adults and $10 for children. In New Orleans, Freeman gave a gratuity to the shipmaster for their safe arrival. He also paid the bill for barrels of drinking water and meal to feed the captives. The *Orleans* was nearly indistinguishable from the other oceangoing vessels that frequented the port.

And as with today's traffickers, who buy airline tickets or rent space in shipping containers, illegal trafficking and immoral slav-ing profited legitimate businesses. Birch and Freeman bought space aboard merchant vessels and railroad cars. Besides captors, customs officials and shipping agents were authors of a commercial tran-script in which captives were simply slaves. Trafficked victims were squeezed into regular categories of commerce. Their names often changed or were erased. Northup was listed as "Plat Hamilton" on the *Orleans*'s slave manifest. He would not hear the name Plat until reaching New Orleans. The other kidnapping victim, Robert, was not listed on the manifest in Richmond.

To the captives locked belowdecks as the *Orleans* sailed down the James River, the ship was a place of confinement rather than a node on a commercial network. The temperate behavior of the captain and crew disarmed Northup. To enforce discipline, shipmaster William Wickham used guile rather than the maritime prerogative of flogging insubordinates. The ship had a crew of six, besides a cook, a mate, and Wickham. Without tight security, nearly fifty captives could overwhelm that force. Instead of segregation and physical abuse, the master and mate elevated some captives above others, putting them to work while granting small privileges. If done right, they could get captives to guard or police other captives.

Yet Captain Wickham was willing to participate in slaving and kidnapping in the regular course of business. The ship anchored in Hampton Roads off Norfolk, and several more captives were embarked, including another kidnap victim, Arthur Curtis. Like slave ships plying the coastal slaving forts of West Africa, Wickham's vessel picked up trafficked Americans piecemeal, and the terror of such practices ran through nearly all African-descended neighborhoods and families. Shipboard, the captives were initially shackled and locked down at night belowdecks. Seasickness threatened to overwhelm those who had never left shore. During a "violent storm," the ship "rolled and plunged," Northup recalled. Some became ill, and "others [were] on their knees praying, while some were fast holding to each other, paralyzed with fear." Vomit made the hold "loathsome and disgusting." And Wickham's management strategy began to unravel when calm weather slowed the passage.

Off the Bahamas, the *Orleans* stalled and a plot developed. Kidnap victims Northup, Robert Jones, and Arthur Curtis talked of overthrowing the ship and sailing to freedom. None knew how to sail, but they planned to head to New York City, a thousand miles to the north, rather than the Bahamas, which were practically in sight. But the planners lost their nerve when Jones fell ill with smallpox and died four days later. All were "panic-stricken by the appearance of the small-pox." A crew member sewed Jones's lifeless body into his blanket along with a ballast stone. After a perfunctory prayer it disappeared into the blue Caribbean, far from loved ones in Cincinnati.

The plot died along with Robert Jones, but Northup befriended an English sailor who wrote a letter home informing his family what had become of him. The letter led to an abortive attempt to rescue Northup. Again, traffickers' tactics undermined an attempted rescue. Since Northup's captors had smuggled him under an alias there was little hope of locating him. The ship sailed upriver to New Orleans and upon arrival authorities freed Arthur Curtis. Word had reached the city that he was kidnapped.

But Northup's troubles were just beginning. Slave trader Theophilus Freeman appeared on the *Orleans* and seized Birch's "gang," including Northup—designated Plat Hamilton. Freeman disembarked him at the levee. Northup would be sold, beaten, tortured,

and humiliated over the next twelve years. Miraculously, Northup
returned home to a family who scarcely recognized him. *Twelve Years
a Slave* recounts an anguished story that fits inside our understanding of nineteenth-century African American history and the long
bitter legacy of race-based chattel slavery. But the process of enslavement resounds down the ages.

Lang Long was from Koh Sotin, Cambodia, about fifty miles up
the Mekong River from Phenom Penh. His family suffered from
severe poverty. Long's job as a janitor in a Buddhist temple near his
home paid poorly, and the family farm could not produce enough
rice to feed his siblings. In search of a construction job—and with it
family support—in 2011 he hopped on the back of a truck headed
west into neighboring Thailand. But after arriving at a seaport near
Samut Prakan, south of Bangkok, Long discovered that the recruiter
was a trafficker. And after being incarcerated for days under armed
guard, Long was sold for about $530 to a sea captain.

Long did not know it as he was forced up the gangplank of a
wooden fishing vessel with six other captives, but his feet would not
touch dry land again for three years. Such fishing vessels sailed for
months or years at a time, hauling in illegal catches with enslaved
crews, resupplied by motherships carrying fuel and food, and returning to port with fish. Thailand is the third-largest fish exporter in the
world. But most of the catch on Long's slave-staffed vessels and
trawlers like them ends up consumed by American pets as dog and
cat food or farm animals as feed.

Long's experience is not atypical. Alexis A. Aronowitz tells the
story of two sixteen-year-old boys who arrived in Bangkok from
their native Buriram Province. Before a day passed enslavers sized
the boys up as likely captives and drugged them. As his captors had
done to Northup, the boys' captors took the unconscious bodies
and put them on a fishing boat. When the boys awoke to the nightmare ordeal, they—like Northup—met two other kidnapped subjects. The master of the vessel was complicit in the kidnappings. If
he did not know the circumstances, he knew the process. And he
forced the children to work day and night doing the numerous dangerous tasks that were part of commercial fishing.

The sea voyage into slavery was arduous. The captives were worked
until they could not stand up; only then were they allowed to sleep.
They ate two meals a day. Drinking water was often boiled seawater.
Discipline was enforced with stories of other captives being murdered
or dying of disease, their bodies dumped overboard—a fate not unlike
that of Northup's fellow kidnap victim Robert. Shipmasters bound
captives' feet with rope. They were not paid for the fish and shrimp
they hauled in but instead were told they were working off the debt
corresponding to their purchase price.

After eight months of plying the fisheries of the Gulf of Thailand, the Andaman Sea, and beyond, the shipmaster freed the two captives. He gave them 3,000 baht (less than $100) and dropped them at a railroad station in Nakornsritamrat, far to the south of where they had been trafficked. That shipmaster was soft—and stupid—by industry standards. In contrast, Lang Long's ordeal stretched out like the landless horizon.

Out in the cold ocean, Long was a hot commodity. After he was initially put to sea, three short-staffed shipmasters scuffled over who would buy the captive in his late twenties who had never even seen the coast before his capture. That was the first of two sales among fishing trawlers operating sometimes hundreds or over a thousand miles off the coast, away from even the thinnest inspection regime.

Fights over Long's body initially centered on his potential rather than his experience. He worked slowly, subject to severe seasickness. He could not identify types of fish or untangle a net. But severe maritime discipline shocked him into learning. Long witnessed a skipper whip a fisherman to get him to work faster. When he failed to meet expectations, he was thrashed with a pole. Ship's officers withheld even the meager ration of food and made him work twenty-three-hour shifts when eighteen were standard. With drinking water in short supply, sailors were forced to pilfer filthy ice chips from fish barrels.

But as Long gained experience and worked to repay the trafficking debt he had supposedly incurred, his captors took more interest in keeping him enslaved. An experienced seaman was worth more than a fresh captive. Unable to swim, Long could not leap overboard to escape. Waves taller than the ship terrified him as they crashed over the deck. And even though the vessels on which he was enslaved never neared land, the shipmaster shackled him to the deck by the neck whenever other boats approached. As the months and then years passed and Long kept hauling in the illegal catch, he became too valuable a fisherman to free.

Like Northup's path back to Saratoga Springs, a line to freedom for Lang Long came unexpectedly in the person of a sympathetic interloper. Cambodian native Som Nang signed up to work a mothership, unprepared for the seascape of slavery he soon encountered. Nang came upon Long's vessel, which was fishing illegally in Indonesian waters. And Long was the sole Cambodian crew member among eight on the dilapidated wooden boat. Nang understood Long's desperate cry for help and was horrified at the sight of the three-foot chain locked to a rusty collar around Long's neck and linked to an anchor post. After returning to port, Nang alerted the Stella Maris Seafarers Center, a human rights organization that works to free trafficked mariners. Stella Maris raised 25,000 baht (about $750), which bought Long's freedom early in 2014.

Ian Urbina, who told Lang Long's story in the *New York Times*, reported that the former slave showed signs of post-traumatic stress disorder. He slept and cried during the days-long passage to port. Even Som Nang, who arranged for his rescue, refused to return to sea because of the pervasive violence and abuse. For his part, Long never wanted to eat fish again.

Just as those who mixed the sugar Solomon Northup made into their coffee or bought cloth woven from cotton he picked, those who eat slave-produced Thai seafood are not aware that their shrimp, mackerel, or tuna was hauled aboard, sorted, and processed initially by bound laborers. And just as the region in which Northup was enslaved was undergoing tremendous ecological change, so the fisheries trolled by trafficked fishermen are environmental disaster areas. Labor conditions and ecology complement each other: shipmasters drive slave fishing crews to hunt for fish that are declining in numbers and size, casting their nets farther and farther from the depleted zones that have collapsed from overfishing. Harder work catching fewer fish brings diminishing returns and consequent reliance on bound laborers gotten cheaply through kidnapping. Both human and sea life become cheapened in the pursuit of returns, and like fish, captives are being hunted from far-flung catchment areas spanning international borders.

Lang Long simply wanted to return home, but Northup turned his enslavement into an anti-trafficking campaign, publishing his autobiography and speaking against slavery thereafter. Northup's son Alonzo was just five when his father was abducted. Alonzo would eventually wear a U.S. Army uniform during the Civil War and participate in the 1864 Battle of Bloody Bridge in South Carolina. That legacy lives today in the Solomon Northup Foundation, founded by descendants, and in Northup's powerful witness to slavery and injustice. Like appeals to forgo sugar or cotton grown by slave labor, today's abolitionists ask citizens as consumers to consider the conditions under which their food, clothing, or electronics were produced. For it is certainly possible that the first human hands to touch the chunks of fish in gourmet cat food or the shrimp on a party cocktail platter were those of a slave.

2013 FILM ADAPTATION: CRITICISM, REVIEWS, INTERVIEW

HENRY LOUIS GATES, JR.

12 *Years a Slave:* Trek from Slave to Screen[†]

"Utter Darkness"

As a literary scholar and cultural historian who has spent a lifetime searching out African Americans' lost, forgotten and otherwise unheralded tales, I was honored to serve as a historical consultant on Steve McQueen's *12 Years a Slave,* most certainly one of the most vivid and authentic portrayals of slavery ever captured in a feature film. In its blend of tactile, sensory realism with superb modernistic cinematic techniques, this film is 180 degrees away from Quentin Tarantino's postmodern spaghetti Western–slave narrative, *Django Unchained,* occupying the opposite pole on what we might think of as "the scale of representation."

No story tells itself on its own; even "true" stories have to be recreated within the confines and various formal possibilities for expression offered by a given medium, and that includes both feature films and documentaries, as well. Both of these films offer compelling interpretations of the horrific experience of human bondage, even if their modes of storytelling are diametrically opposed, offering viewers—and especially teachers and students—a rare opportunity to consider *how* the ways that an artist chooses to tell a story—the forms, points of view and aesthetic stances she or he selects—affects our understanding of its subject matter.

One hundred and sixty years before Steve McQueen made any artistic choices, Solomon Northup, the narrator and protagonist of *12 Years a Slave,* was eager just to get his story out to the public—and have them believe that what had happened to him was authentic. Think of what it must have been like for Solomon during those first disorienting hours in the pitch black, when, in "the dungeon" of Williams' Slave Pen off Seventh Avenue in Washington, D.C., he had to reckon with the betrayal that had lured him out of a lifetime of freedom into a nightmare of bondage. "I found myself alone, in utter darkness, and in chains," Northup wrote, and "nothing broke the oppressive silence, save the clinking of my chains, whenever I chanced to move. I spoke aloud, but the sound of my own voice startled me."

Not only was Northup suddenly a stranger to himself, in an even stranger place, but with his money and the papers proving his status as a free black man stolen and a beating awaiting every

† *The Root,* Oct. 14, 2013. Reprinted by permission of *The Root.*

insistence on the truth, Northup was forced into a horrifying new role, that of the paradoxical "free slave," under the false name "Platt Hamilton," a supposed "runaway" from Georgia. That all this happened in the shadows of the U.S. Capitol—that in cuffs Northup was shuffled down the same Pennsylvania Avenue where just over a century later Dr. King would be heard delivering his "Dream" speech, a few decades before President Barack Obama and his wife Michelle would parade in hopes of fulfilling it—must have made Northup's imposed odyssey taste all the more bitter. "My sufferings," he recalled of the first whipping he received, "I can compare to nothing else than the burning agonies of hell!"

But unlike Dante's *Inferno,* the outpost to which Solomon Northup was forced to descend was no metaphorical space replete with various circles housing the damned, but the swamps, forests and cotton fields in the Deep South. "I never knew a slave to escape with his life from Bayou Bœuf," Northup wrote. After that, the driving force of his life—and story—could be summed up in one question: Would *he* be the exception?

Here are the facts.

Who Was Solomon Northup?

*   *   *

Solomon Northup spent his first 33 years as a free man in upstate New York. He was born in the Adirondack town of Schroon (later Minerva) July 10, 1807 (his memoir says 1808, but the evidence suggests otherwise). As a child, he learned to read and write while assisting his father Mintus, a former slave who eventually bought enough farm land in Fort Edward to qualify for the vote (a right that in many states, during the early days of the Republic, was reserved for landowners). Solomon's mother, Susannah, was a "quadroon," who may have been born free herself. Solomon's "ruling passion," he said, was "playing on the violin."

Married at 21, Northup and his wife Anne Hampton (the daughter of a free black man who was also part white and Native American) had three children: Elizabeth, Margaret and Alonzo. In 1834, they settled in Saratoga Springs, where Solomon toiled at various seasonal jobs, including rafting, woodcutting, railroad construction, canal maintenance and repairs, farming and, in resort season, staffing area hotels (for a time, he and his wife both lived and worked at the United States Hotel). His "ruling passion," the violin, also became a way of earning money, and his reputation grew.

In March 1841, Northup was lured from his home by two white men, using the aliases Merrill Brown and Abram Hamilton, who claimed to be members of a Washington, D.C.–based circus in need of musicians for their sightseeing tour. While in New York City, Brown and Hamilton convinced Northup to journey farther south with them, and arriving in Washington, D.C., on April 6, 1841, the trio lodged at Gadsby's Hotel. The next day, the two men got Northup so drunk (he implied they drugged him) that, in the middle of the night, he was roused from his room by several men urging him to follow them to a doctor. Instead, when Northup came to, he found himself "in chains," he said, at Williams's Slave Pen with his money and free papers nowhere to be found. Attempting to plead his case to the notorious slave trader James H. Birch (also spelled "Burch"), Northup was beaten and told he was really a runaway slave from Georgia. Birch paid more than $600 for his "slave." (Recollections varied: Birch later said $625. Others recalled it was $650.)

Shipped by Birch on the *Orleans* under the name "Plat Hamilton" (also spelled "Platt"), Northup arrived in New Orleans on May 24, 1841, and after a bout of smallpox, was sold by Birch's associate, Theophilus Freeman, for $900. Northup was to spend his 12 years in slavery (actually it was 11 years, 8 months, and 26 days) in Louisiana's Bayou Bœuf region. He had three principal owners: the paternal planter William Prince Ford (1841–1842), the belligerent carpenter John Tibaut (also spelled "Tibeats") (1842–1843), and the former overseer turned small cotton planter Edwin Epps (1843–1853).

Ford gave Northup the widest latitude, working at his mills. Twice Northup and Tibaut came to blows over work, the second time Northup coming so close to choking Tibaut to death (Tibaut had come at him with an ax) that Northup fled into the Great Cocodrie Swamp. Though prone to drink, Edwin Epps was brutally efficient with the lash whenever Northup was late getting to the fields, inexact in his work (Northup had many skills; picking cotton wasn't one of them), unwilling to whip the other slaves as Epps's driver, or too high on his own talents as a fiddler after Epps purchased him a violin to placate his wife, Mary Epps.

In 1852, Epps hired a Canadian carpenter named Samuel Bass to work on his house. An opponent of slavery, Bass agreed to help Northup by mailing three letters on his behalf to various contacts in New York. Upon receiving theirs, the Saratoga shopkeepers William Perry and Cephas Parker notified Solomon's wife and attorney Henry Bliss Northup, a relative of Solomon's father's former master. With bipartisan support, including a petition and six affidavits, Henry Northup successfully petitioned New York governor Washington Hunt to appoint him an agent of rescue. On Jan. 3, 1853, Henry Northup arrived at Epps's plantation with the sheriff of Avoyelles Parish, La. There was no need for questioning. A local attorney, John

Pamplin Waddill, had connected Henry Northup to Bass, and Bass had led him to the slave "Platt." The proof was in their embrace.

Traveling home, Henry and Solomon Northup stopped in Washington, D.C., on Jan. 17, 1853, to have the slave trader James Birch arrested on kidnapping charges, but because Solomon had no right to testify against a white man, Birch went free. Solomon Northup was reunited with his family in Glens Falls, N.Y., on Jan. 21, 1853.

Over the next three months, he and his white editor, David Wilson, an attorney from Whitehall, N.Y., wrote Northup's memoir, *Twelve Years a Slave*. It was published July 15, 1853, and sold 17,000 copies in the first four months (almost 30,000 by January 1855). "While abolitionist journals had previously warned of slavery's dangers to free African-American citizens and published brief accounts of kidnappings, Northup's narrative was the first to document such a case in book-length detail," Brad S. Born writes in *The Concise Oxford Companion to African American Literature*. With its emphasis on authenticity, *Twelve Years a Slave* gave contemporary readers an up-close account of slavery in the South, including the violent tactics owners and overseers used to force slaves to work, and the sexual advances and jealous cruelties slave women faced from their masters and masters' wives.

Since then, it has been "authentic[ated]" by "[a] number of scholars [who] have investigated judicial proceedings, manuscript census returns, diaries and letters of whites, local records, newspapers and city directories," wrote the ultimate authority on the authenticity of the slave narratives, the late Yale historian John W. Blassingame, in his definitive 1975 essay "Using the Testimony of Ex-Slaves: Approaches and Problems," in the *Journal of Southern History*.

In 1854, Northup's book led to the arrest of his original kidnappers, Brown and Hamilton. Their *real* names, respectively, were Alexander Merrill and James Russell, both New Yorkers. Though Solomon was able to testify at their trial in Saratoga County, the case dragged on for three years and was eventually dropped by the prosecution in 1857, the same year the U.S. Supreme Court handed down its decision in *Dred Scott v. Sanford*, which, in part, denied that black people were citizens of the United States (and thus ruled that they could not sue in federal court).

A free man returned from slavery, Solomon Northup remained active in the abolitionist movement; lectured throughout the Northeast; staged, and performed in, two plays based on his story (the second, in 1855, was titled "A Free Slave"); and was known to aid fugitive slaves on the Underground Railroad. To this day, the date, location, and circumstances of his death remain a mystery. Northup's last public appearance was in August 1857 in Streetsville, Ontario,

Canada. The last recollected contact with him was a visit to the Reverend John L. Smith, a Methodist minister and fellow Underground Railroad conductor, in Vermont sometime after the Emancipation Proclamation, likely in 1863.

An "American" Story

Since D. W. Griffith premiered his scandalous whitewashing— really, one of the grossest historical distortions—of the history of slavery and Reconstruction in his 1915 silent film *The Birth of a Nation,* there have been all too few films that have captured, or even attempted to convey, the truth about American slavery in all of its complexity. Of those that have taken slavery as their subject matter, few are worthy of recognition. Yet, the well-crafted personal testimonies of African Americans who spent time as slaves are both gripping narratives (many, like Solomon Northup's and Frederick Douglass's, were instant best-sellers), and are subject matter central to the fullest understanding of *American* history, told from the points of view of victims of one of our country's most heinous institutions.

And those stories documenting "America's original sin" cannot be told and retold enough. Steve McQueen, a black Briton, is to be praised for turning to one of our canonical slave narratives (101 were published between 1760 and the end of the Civil War) and bringing it so vividly, sensitively, and brilliantly to the screen.

What makes *12 Years a Slave,* the film, especially worthy of attention is what audiences in Northup's own time appreciated about his tale: its sober presentation of American slavery as it really was, interwoven with the universal themes of identity, betrayal, brutality, and the need to keep faith to survive confrontations with evil. Most of all, Northup reminds us of the fragile nature of freedom in any human society and the harsh reality that whatever legal boundaries existed between so-called free states and slaves states in 1841, no black man, woman, or child was permanently safe.

Twelve Years a Slave has a trajectory unlike the other antebellum slave narratives, which usually chart a protagonist's path from slavery to freedom. Its drive is in reverse, from freedom *to* slavery, in both a single human life and as a larger allegory for slavery itself. In this way, it defies the more common (and reassuring) American story of upward mobility, of attaining ever greater badges of liberation with "luck and pluck," from "rags to riches." Instead, Northup's trajectory is down—down from New York to Louisiana—and thus an inversion of most of America's popular literature, which, to my amazement, makes it all the more uncanny that the name of the place where Northup was kidnapped was Gadsby's Hotel (I know: When I read it,

I thought *Gatsby*, too). In his prefiguring of the *counter*-narrative, the isolation in darkness that Ralph Ellison later made famous in his unparalleled novel, *Invisible Man* (1952), *Twelve Years a Slave* gives us the soul of African-American literature and culture, the "sound of life" in "oppressive silence."

"A Man—Every Inch of Him"

In many classic tales, the protagonist functions as our guide, the reader's eyes, ears, nose, hands, and tongue, the one through whom we think and feel. In Solomon Northup, unlike even the greatest African-American writer and speaker of his day, ex-slave Frederick Douglass, the audience has a guide who is as surprised, shocked, and horrified by slavery as we might have been, because we begin from the same place: freedom. At times, Northup's story seems almost biblical, structured as it is as a descent-and-resurrection narrative of a protagonist who, like Christ, was 33 at the time of his abduction. But unlike a God humbling Himself in the form of man, however, Northup was a man forced into the life of a slave, a slave chained in the hell of slavery for more than a decade.

What ensues in his book—and in Steve McQueen's film—is frightening, gripping, and inspiring, because, as a reviewer of Northup's own theatrical staging of his narrative in Syracuse, N.Y., put it in the *Syracuse Daily Journal* on Jan. 31, 1854, "He is a man— every inch of him." Yet because of the color of Northup's skin, every inch of his manhood was vulnerable to being falsified, stolen, emasculated, and denied, and there was virtually nothing he could do about it. In fact, Northup quickly learned that protesting his enslavement represented an even greater threat to his survival, because, to his traders and his owners, he was worth quite a lot of money as a slave, money that would simply disappear if he could confirm his status as free man.

North and South, Free State and Slave

At the same time, it is important not to overdraw the boundaries between North and South, free state and slave, before the Civil War. As Ira Berlin writes in his book *Slaves Without Masters* (1974), at no time before the end of the Civil War did the number of free black people in the North *outnumber* those living in the South, a fact that most of us find astonishing and quite counterintuitive today. And while there were important differences between the freedoms Solomon Northup could exercise as a free man in New York versus his free counterparts, say, in South Carolina or Louisiana, there was persistent, widespread antiblack discrimination in the North. In many states, restrictions on voting and segregation regimes anticipated the de jure "Jim Crow" segregation era that commenced in the 1890s, which rendered true freedom a myth for African Americans until the civil rights movement of the 1950s and '60s.

Also surprising, Ira Berlin reminded me in an email exchange, "free blacks in the South," while denied "political and civil rights," were "much more prosperous" (they "openly practiced skilled trades" and were "often propertied") than their northern counterparts, who, despite their "great civic and political tradition," were more often "impoverished."

Nevertheless, the farther that North and South pulled apart in the antebellum years, the more tempting it became for slave catchers to venture north, across the Mason-Dixon Line, to steal free black people under the pretense of retrieving "fugitive slaves" (the latter practice authorized by the Fugitive Slave Act of 1850). The bottom line for most of these thieves was the proverbial bottom line: Trading in slaves was an extremely lucrative business, especially after importing them from abroad was banned by Congress (under the Constitution) in 1807, the year of Solomon Northup's birth.

Most of this kidnapping activity understandably occurred along the Mason-Dixon Line, not where Northup resided in Saratoga Springs, in upstate New York. But the farther south he traveled with Brown and Merrill, the riskier the adventure became—risks about which Northup himself had been warned before his kidnapping, he later admitted. Given the concealed nature of this type of crime, there are no official estimates of the number of free blacks kidnapped into slavery in the United States (abolitionists put it in the thousands a year, while Harriet Beecher Stowe, the author of *Uncle Tom's Cabin*, to whom Northup dedicated his book, put it in the "hundreds . . . all the time"), but it was not uncommon, and it continued through the Civil War, Paul Finkelman and Richard Newman write in the *Encyclopedia of African American History, 1619–1895: From the Colonial Period to the Age of Frederick Douglass*.

Signification—and Its Significance

What makes Steve McQueen's and screenwriter John Ridley's retelling of Northup's *Twelve Years* so powerful is that it comes closer than any other representation to the true intent of Northup's original book and the lecture tours he went on throughout New York and New England in the short years that followed. In reading Northup today, one immediately senses how determined he was to prove the veracity of his tale (to this end, he even included details on how sugar mills worked). Had this approach fit the theatrical conventions of the day, Northup might have retired a rich man. Because it did not, the attempts he made in translating his tale to the stage were, well, less than stellar, even with Northup in the starring role.

In this way, Chiwetel Ejiofor, playing Solomon Northup in Steve McQueen's film, can do—and does—a better job. Instead of melodrama, we, the audience, are left with the haunting images of the eternity of suffering implicit in perpetual, hereditary bondage, which McQueen's cinematographer, Sean Bobbitt, unflinchingly captures. Then there are the astonishingly vivid and realistic, up-close performances of the film's central characters: Michael Fassbender's remarkably complex portrayal of the conflicted, sadistic slave master Edwin Epps; Lupita Nyong'o's recreation of the slave Patsey, the innocent, yet multidimensional object of Epps's conflicted desire, guilt, self-hatred, and sadism; Paul Dano's John Tibeats, the jealous and insecure carpenter who is quick to blows to maintain his status; Brad Pitt's heroic Canadian, Samuel Bass, who intervenes at last to contact Solomon's friends back home in the North, and who subsequently aids in the rescue; and the great Chiwetel Ejiofor, a revelation on screen whose personification of Solomon already has many critics predicting an Academy Award nomination.

Some will ask, Is everything in the film version of *Twelve Years a Slave* accurate? My response is yes *and* no, for the truth is Solomon Northup himself changed some of the facts, including his birth and marriage dates, the spellings of certain names and, in an early play version, he even made the character of Samuel Bass more of a "Yankee" than a Canadian. This points to a deeper truth about African-American culture, and one I have written about throughout my career: that signifying or black signification, by its very nature, is an act of repetition and revision, of invocation and improvisation, and so to me, the far more relevant question to ask of any representation of *Twelve Years a Slave* is not whether it is strictly factual but whether it is true.

To this I say yes, without question, and, in viewing it, we each must test our own commitment to freedom, just as Northup's audiences were tested (though with much higher stakes). As the film rolls on, we are the ones willing him first to survival and then to freedom. We are the ones fearing for his life. We are the ones confined as he was confined. In our hopes, we are the ones emulating the petitioners and affidavit-signers who testified to his status as a free man, including his wife, Anne. And in following his story to the end, we are the ones sitting in the shadows determined to reclaim what has been lost, to the extent that this is possible, having been robbed of 12 years of one's life.

"Completely Enraptured"

Did anyone challenge the authenticity of Northup's book when it was published? Quite the contrary. In fact, the most "representative" black man of the nineteenth century, Frederick Douglass, wrote that "We think it will be difficult for any one who takes up the book in a candid and impartial spirit to lay it down until finished . . ." (*Frederick Douglass' Paper*, July 29, 1863). Of Northup's story onstage, *Frederick Douglass' Paper* also had this to say nine years earlier: "His story is full of romantic interest and painful adventures, and gives [a] clear insight to the practical workings and *beauties* of American Slavery . . . It is a sure treat to hear him give some hazardous adventure, with so much *sans* [sic] *froid* that the audience is completely enraptured and the 'house brought down.'"

I'll tell you one thing: When the house lights went back up in the theater where I saw *12 Years a Slave* for the first time, I, too, like Frederick Douglass, felt "completely enraptured," and full of admiration for the spectacularly moving result of the collaboration between the film's director, Steve McQueen, a black man from Great Britain, and his screenwriter, John Ridley, an African American.

The last amazing fact I'll share without giving the entire film away: You could sit in a dark theater and watch Steve McQueen's *12 Years a Slave*, with its 133-minute running time, close to 50,000 times in the amount of time Solomon Northup actually spent as a slave. The difference between your time in the dark and his: You are free to leave.

Further Reading

* * *

The best current biography (and the *indispensable* source to me in writing this column) is *Solomon Northup: The Complete Story of the Author of* Twelve Years a Slave, by David A. Fiske, Clifford W. Brown, Jr., and Rachel Seligman. I personally want to thank the authors for sharing a copy of their manuscript with me in advance and for working so hard to set as much of the record straight as can be set straight. The facts, figures, quotes, names, and dates you've uncovered are invaluable—the living descendants you've connected to their family's history, precious.

MANOHLA DARGIS

The Blood and Tears, Not the Magnolias[†]

"12 Years a Slave" isn't the first movie about slavery in the United States—but it may be the one that finally makes it impossible for American cinema to continue to sell the ugly lies it's been hawking for more than a century. Written by John Ridley and directed by Steve McQueen, it tells the true story of Solomon Northup, an African-American freeman who, in 1841, was snatched off the streets of Washington, and sold. It's at once a familiar, utterly strange and deeply American story in which the period trappings long beloved by Hollywood—the paternalistic gentry with their pretty plantations, their genteel manners and all the fiddle-dee-dee rest—are the backdrop for an outrage.

The story opens with Solomon (Chiwetel Ejiofor) already enslaved and cutting sugar cane on a plantation. A series of flashbacks shifts the story to an earlier time, when Solomon, living in New York with his wife and children, accepts a job from a pair of white men to play violin in a circus. Soon the three are enjoying a civilized night out in Washington, sealing their camaraderie with heaping plates of food, flowing wine and the unstated conviction—if only on Solomon's part—of a shared humanity, a fiction that evaporates when he wakes the next morning shackled and discovers that he's been sold. Thereafter, he is passed from master to master.

It's a desperate path and a story that seizes you almost immediately with a visceral force. But Mr. McQueen keeps everything moving so fluidly and efficiently that you're too busy worrying about Solomon, following him as he travels from auction house to plantation, to linger long in the emotions and ideas that the movie churns up. Part of this is pragmatic—Mr. McQueen wants to keep you in your seat, not force you out of the theater, sobbing—but there's something else at work here. This is, he insists, a story about Solomon, who may represent an entire subjugated people and, by extension, the peculiar institution, as well as the American past and present. Yet this is also, emphatically, the story of one individual.

Unlike most of the enslaved people whose fate he shared for a dozen years, the real Northup was born into freedom. (His memoir's telegraphing subtitle is "Narrative of Solomon Northup, a Citizen of New-York, Kidnapped in Washington City in 1841, and Rescued in 1853, From a Cotton Plantation Near the Red River, in Louisiana.")

---

† From the *New York Times*, Oct. 17, 2013. © 2013 The New York Times. All rights reserved. Used by permission and protected by the Copyright Laws of the United States. The printing, copying, redistribution, or retransmission of this Content without express written permission is prohibited.

That made him an exceptional historical witness, because even while he was inside slavery—physically, psychologically, emotionally—part of him remained intellectually and culturally at a remove, which gives his book a powerful double perspective. In the North, he experienced some of the privileges of whiteness, and while he couldn't vote, he could enjoy an outing with his family. Even so, he was still a black man in antebellum America.

Mr. McQueen is a British visual artist who made a rough transition to movie directing with his first two features, "Hunger" and "Shame," both of which were embalmed in self-promoting visuals. "Hunger" is the sort of art film that makes a show of just how perfectly its protagonist, the Irish dissident Bobby Sands (Michael Fassbender), smears his excrement on a prison wall. "Shame," about a sex addict (Mr. Fassbender again), was little more than glossy surfaces, canned misery and preening directorial virtuosity. For "12 Years a Slave," by contrast, Mr. McQueen has largely dispensed with the conventions of art cinema to make something close to a classical narrative; in this movie, the emphasis isn't on visual style but on Solomon and his unmistakable desire for freedom.

There's nothing ambivalent about Solomon. Mr. Ejiofor has a round, softly inviting face, and he initially plays the character with the stunned bewilderment of a man who, even chained, can't believe what is happening to him. Not long after he's kidnapped, Solomon sits huddled with two other prisoners on a slaver's boat headed south. One man insists that they should fight their crew. A second disagrees, saying, "Survival's not about certain death, it's about keeping your head down." Seated between them, Solomon shakes his head no. Days earlier he was home. "Now," he says, "you tell me all is lost?" For him, mere survival cannot be enough. "I want to live."

This is Solomon's own declaration of independence, and an assertion of his humanity that sustains him. It's also a seamlessly structured scene that turns a discussion about the choices facing enslaved people—fight, submit, live—into cinema. In large part, "12 Years a Slave" is an argument about American slavery that, in image after image, both reveals it as a system (signified in one scene by the sights and ominous, mechanical sounds of a boat water wheel) and demolishes its canards, myths and cherished symbols. There are no lovable masters here or cheerful slaves. There are also no messages, wagging fingers or final-act summations or sermons. Mr. McQueen's method is more effective and subversive because of its primarily old-fashioned, Hollywood-style engagement.

It's a brilliant strategy that recognizes the seductions of movies that draw you wholly into their narratives and that finds Mr. McQueen appropriating the very film language that has been historically used to perpetuate reassuring (to some) fabrications about

American history. One of the shocks of "12 Years a Slave" is that it reminds you how infrequently stories about slavery have been told on the big screen, which is why it's easy to name exceptions, like Richard Fleischer's demented, at times dazzling 1975 film, "Mandingo." The greater jolt, though, is that "12 Years a Slave" isn't about another Scarlett O'Hara, but about a man who could be one of those anonymous, bent-over black bodies hoeing fields in the opening credits of "Gone With the Wind," a very different "story of the Old South."

At one point in Northup's memoir, which was published a year after "Uncle Tom's Cabin" and eight years before the start of the Civil War, he interrupts an account of his own near-lynching to comment on the man largely to blame for the noose around his neck. "But whatever motive may have governed the cowardly and malignant tyrant," he writes, "it is of no importance." It doesn't matter why Northup was strung up in a tree like a dead deer in the summer sun, bathed in sweat, with little water to drink. What matters is what has often been missing among the economic, social and cultural explanations of American slavery and in many of its representations: human suffering. "My wrists and ankles, and the cords of my legs and arms began to swell, burying the rope that bound them into the swollen flesh."

Part of the significance of Northup's memoir is its description of everyday life. Mr. McQueen recreates, with texture and sweep, scenes of slavery's extreme privations and cruelties, but also its work rhythms and routines, sunup to sundown, along with the unsettling intimacies it produced among the owners and the owned. In Louisiana, Solomon is sold by a brutish trader (Paul Giamatti) to an outwardly decent plantation owner, William Ford (Benedict Cumberbatch), who, in turn, sells him to a madman and drunk, Edwin Epps (Mr. Fassbender). In his memoir, Northup refers to Ford charitably, doubtless for the benefit of the white readers who were the target of his abolitionist appeal. Freed from that burden, the filmmakers can instead show the hypocrisies of such paternalism.

It's on Epps's plantation that "12 Years a Slave" deepens, and then hardens. It's also where the existential reality of what it meant to be enslaved, hour after hour, decade after decade, generation after generation, is laid bare, at times on the flayed backs of Epps's human property, including that of his brutalized favorite, Patsey (Lupita Nyong'o). Mr. Fassbender, skittish and weirdly spiderlike, grabs your attention with curdled intensity. He's so arresting that at first it seems as if the performance will soon slip out of Mr. McQueen's control, and that the character will become just another irresistibly watchable, flamboyant heavy. Movie villainy is so easy, partly because it allows actors to showboat, but also because a lot of filmmakers can't resist siding with power.

Mr. McQueen's sympathies are as unqualified as his control. There is much to admire about "12 Years a Slave," including the clear-eyed, unsentimental quality of its images—this is a place where trees hang with beautiful moss and black bodies—and how Mr. Eji-ofor's restrained, open, translucent performance works as a ballast, something to cling onto, especially during the frenzies of violence. These are rightly hard to watch and bring to mind the startling moment in "Maus," Art Spiegelman's cartoon opus about the Holocaust, in which he asks his "shrink" to explain what it felt like to be in Auschwitz. "Boo! It felt like **that**. But ALWAYS!" The genius of "12 Years a Slave" is its insistence on banal evil, and on terror, that seeped into souls, bound bodies and reaped an enduring, terrible price.

* * *

DAVID DENBY

From Fighting to Survive[†]

The most striking image in "12 Years a Slave"—a film of many powerful moments and sequences—is of Solomon Northup (Chiwetel Ejiofor), a freeborn African-American kidnapped into slavery, hanging from a tree with a noose around his neck and one foot touching the muddy ground. Behind him, other slaves go about their labors—it's a normal day on a Louisiana plantation in the eighteen-forties. Solomon was almost hanged for defending himself against an overseer; now he's left to dangle, halfway between stability and annihilation. That's essentially his situation for a dozen long years. The movie is based on a true story, which Northup told in a book of the same title, published in 1853. Born in the Adirondack Mountains in 1807, he becomes a violinist, and lives a gracious life (which we see) with his wife and children in Saratoga Springs, New York. Then a couple of top-hatted circus gents offer him a job playing on tour, and, one night in Washington, D.C., they get him drunk. When he wakes up in the morning, he's in chains, in a foul hole. As he's taken out of the city by slavers, the director, Steve McQueen, raises the

† From "Fighting to Survive: *12 Years a Slave* and *All Is Lost*," *The New Yorker* (Oct. 21, 2013): 108–09. Reprinted by permission of the publisher, Condé Nast.

camera to reveal the Capitol in the distance. After a journey by ship, Solomon winds up on plantations in Louisiana, where he's traded, loaned out, and, at one point, used as service for debt. Throughout, he has the enraged consciousness of a free man. Yet he can't reveal much of his mind or his temperament without incurring the wrath of men and women whose self-esteem is based on the belief that he's an animal. What remains awake in his soul of a better life puts the moral condition of slavery in the harshest possible light.

"12 Years a Slave" is easily the greatest feature film ever made about American slavery. It shows up the plantation scenes of "Gone with the Wind" for the sentimental kitsch that they are, and, intentionally or not, it's an artist's rebuke to Quentin Tarantino's high-pitched, luridly extravagant "Django Unchained." For McQueen, who comes out of the London gallery-and-museum world of short films and videos, the movie is an enormous step forward. "Hunger" (2008), his first feature, was a kind of sacerdotal monument to Bobby Sands and other I.R.A. prisoners who staged a hunger strike. The movie, which starred Michael Fassbender, was marked by a fetishistic absorption in beatings, self-denial, the disintegration of the body. His next feature, "Shame" (2011), also starring Fassbender, was a sexually explicit folly about the utter hell of being a single, straight, handsome, well-employed young white male in New York. Both movies were staged as austere rituals. But now McQueen has opened himself up to society, history, and narrative. There are expertly composed short scenes set in Saratoga and at various slave-trading posts on the journey to Louisiana. McQueen and his screenwriter, John Ridley, might have done more with the minor characters that Northup encounters—Paul Giamatti as a fussy slave broker, Alfre Woodard as a cynical plantation mistress—but they move on fast.

Northup's kindly but hapless first owner, William Ford (Benedict Cumberbatch), protects him for a while, but is forced to pass him to the sadistic Edwin Epps (Fassbender). At Epps's plantation, crested by a large house with columns, Solomon gets caught in an anguished sexual tangle involving Epps; his beautiful field slave Patsey (Lupita Nyong'o); and his calculating wife, Mary (Sarah Paulson). The filmmakers drive the scenes toward a frenzy of humiliation, loathing, and savage beatings. McQueen spares us nothing of the horror of human dignity betrayed by base everyday cruelty. If there's a weakness in these scenes, it's a reliance on the mesmerizing Fassbender. Epps is so far gone into psychosis that there's nothing Fassbender can do but repeat his outbursts with greater hysteria. For a while, the movie becomes a redundant moral and physical struggle between a noble, forbearing African-American and a white madman.

Yet there are scenes and shots staged and photographed with such sober beauty that I will never forget them: in Washington, the men and women about to be shipped south, standing naked in a yard and washing themselves; the dripping woods and the languor of Louisiana in summer; Chiwetel Ejiofor's face—square jaw, furrowed brow, eyes appalled by a situation in which Solomon is forbidden to demonstrate exactly what, in his own eyes, makes him a man. Northup is a gentleman of mild disposition, easy to like; anyone who has ever feared losing everything will identify with him. But the movie leaves us grieving for the thousands who never knew freedom, who were never able to tell their stories for future generations.

* * *

VALERIE SMITH

Black Life in the Balance: 12 Years a Slave[†]

In one of the most arresting sequences in 12 Years a Slave, Solomon Northup's (Chiwetel Ejiofor) life hangs by a thread. A malicious white journeyman carpenter named John Tibeats (played by Paul Dano) criticizes the quality of Northup's work on an outbuilding on his master's plantation. Northup initially tries to defend the quality of his work; then realizing that he cannot reason with a man who is determined to assert his authority, he agrees to hang the clapboards again according to Tibeats's specifications.

Tibeats later returns to check on Northup, criticizes the work again, and flies into a rage when Northup defends his work and tries to explain that he is only following Tibeats's earlier orders. When he attempts to whip Northup (ostensibly because of the quality of his work but really for daring to answer back), Northup loses his self-restraint. Unable to feign subservience any longer, he asserts his own superior physical strength, mercilessly whipping the white man. Any vindication Northup may feel is short-lived, however, for the humiliated carpenter returns with his two henchmen, who together restrain Northup, bind his hands, and prepare to lynch him—making a public example of him by hanging him in a central location between the slave quarters and the main house. Chapin (J. D. Evermore), the overseer from his master's plantation, prevents the lynching, but leaves Northup hanging for hours until his master, Ford (Benedict Cumberbatch), orders that he be cut down. Until Ford's

† From American Literary History 26.2 (Summer 2014): 362–66. © Valerie Smith 2014. Reprinted by permission of Oxford University Press.

intervention, Northup is literally suspended in the balance between life and death. In this visually arresting scene—an excruciatingly long set piece—we witness Northup's fellow slaves go about their duties; only one is willing to risk her own safety and offer him any comfort. Only by maintaining the slightest contact between his toes and the ground does Northup keep himself from suffocating.

Whenever I watch this scene, I am struck by several elements—themes and techniques—that resonate throughout the film. First, it is one of a number of scenes that enacts the dramatic differences between life as free and life as enslaved. The very qualities that Northup valued in himself as a freedman—his intelligence and resourcefulness—imperil him as a slave. As a freedman, he prides himself on his deportment, his talents, his possessions, and his ability to provide his family with the accoutrements of middle-class life. Once he is enslaved, however, his name and his claim to all of these attributes are snatched from him; this scene is one in a series that shows the process by which he is forced to adapt his behavior to his changed citizenship status in order to stay alive.

Second, the scene captures the extent to which the institution of slavery threatened the bonds of community that enrich human life. As he dangles from the tree limb in the foreground, Northup's fellow slaves go about their daily tasks as usual behind and around him. The only person who breaks her routine wordlessly puts a cup of water to his lips. Northup's quasi-lynching is meant not only to punish and humiliate him, but also to police his fellow slaves by reminding them of the consequences of self-assertion; in no small way, their survival depended upon their ability to become inured to each other's suffering.

Moreover, the scene is emblematic of the visual and sonic aesthetics of the film. The unbearably long take requires viewers to watch the scene of Northup's torment and to be aware of our status as spectators. Ironically, we are also drawn into the scene by its very beauty—the symmetrically arranged cabins, the trees dripping with moss, the sounds of cicadas and of children playing in the background all seduce us into looking even as we want to look away. Through his use of these elements, Steve McQueen asks us to look long beyond the point at which we would prefer to avert our eyes and to be distracted by the next plot twist. The length of the take underscores the length of time Northup was made to hang from the tree. It may make us uncomfortable, but our discomfort pales in comparison to "the paralyzing agony Solomon is going through," as Bilge Ebiri observes.[1]

---

1. For a thoughtful discussion of the ethics of looking in this scene, and in McQueen's films more generally, see Lowry Pressly, "*12 Years a Slave*: On Humane Suffering," *LA Review of Books* 9 Nov. 2013, web.

This scene registers for me on all of these levels, but most of all, when I watch it my attention is drawn to Northup's feet twitching in a frantic dance to maintain tenuous contact with the ground. His feet, a symbol of his desperate condition, provide us with a fitting image of the fragility of black life in the antebellum period. As the opening scenes set in 1841 demonstrate, a putative free black man in an ostensibly free state was never as secure as he believed himself to be. At a time when a white person could claim ownership of a free black person, and a black person required documentation or the word of a white person to confirm her or his status as a free person, the category of a free black person was a site of contestation.

I suspect that Northup's *12 Years a Slave* has achieved success with a global viewing audience precisely because it is a story about the tenuous nature of black freedom. The lives of enslaved persons in the antebellum period have so little in common with the way we live in the twenty-first century that a realistic film based on a slave narrative might have struggled to find its audience. But despite the obvious differences between the world we inhabit and the world of Northup, responses of contemporary viewers to the film suggest that they see something in Northup that they recognize and with which they identify. The confidence with which Northup inhabits his life as a free man is akin to the confidence with which twenty-first century black people in the US and across the African diaspora—at least those with some measure of financial stability—are able to inhabit and move within identities, communities, nations, professions, and indeed in their own bodies.

When the story opens, Northup is a propertied freedman, the son of a free parents, who comfortably occupies his middle-class status. He, his sophisticated wife, Anne, and his appealing, well-mannered son and daughter lead a secure existence in their well-appointed home in Saratoga, NY, a city associated even in the nineteenth century with a culture of leisure and refinement due to its mineral springs and imposing hotels. A worldly man, Solomon makes his living as a carpenter and a violinist; his wife has built a successful business as a caterer both locally and throughout the Northeast. As portrayed by Ejiofor, Northup takes great pride in and is defined by his talents, his family, his possessions, and even his attire. As he strolls the streets of Saratoga whether alone or with his family, he greets others and is in turn greeted with respect. These scenes contradict our expectations of the way African Americans were treated during the antebellum and Jim Crow eras. We might expect that blacks would avert their gaze when encountering whites or that white store-owners would transact business with them begrudgingly. (These types of humiliating interactions regularly appear in cinematic representations of these periods and provide a shorthand for the governing racial protocols of the time.) Indeed, the enslaved man who sees the Northup family in Mr. Parker's store is clearly in awe of this freedman who is at ease with the shopkeeper and with the merchandise around him. The scenes set in Saratoga create a false sense of the security of Northup's position, however; at the end of the film, this same shopkeeper reappears as Northup's white guarantor. He may treat Northup as his equal, but in the eyes of the law, only his word as a white man and the documents he carries possess the power to liberate Northup from his captors.

Just as Northup's circumstances as a free man are legible to a contemporary viewer, so too are his responses to the sudden change in his circumstances. Were we in his shoes, we imagine that we would share his sense of outrage, incredulity, and resourcefulness when he first realizes that he has been sold into slavery. His frequent statement of his name, his demand for his clothing, his assertion of his identity as a free person all testify to his faith in the protections his citizenship status afford. Once transported to Louisiana, he draws on prior knowledge and experience to develop a plan for moving lumber down the river on Ford's plantation. While this innovation marks him as special in his master's eyes, it humiliates and enrages Tibeats. In the end, it cannot protect him from being sold into even more brutal circumstances when Ford needs money to settle his debts.

At the risk of drawing too facile a comparison, I want to suggest that the film resonates with contemporary viewers because of what it has to say about the fragility of black freedom. In 2008, even many critics of neoliberalism could not help but hope that the election of an African-American president might signal a sea change in the national political landscape, hence the rush in certain quarters to herald the advent of the era of supposed postracialism. But the range and frequency of assaults on black life in the early decades of the twenty-first century undermine national narratives of racial progress from slavery to Emancipation, the civil rights revolution, and the so-called Age of Obama.

One need only look at the polarization of political and civil discourse and racial disparities in markers of well-being, among them wealth, employment, education, health, and mortality rates, to recognize that that optimism was misguided and to be reminded that the evolution of national racial politics is far from linear and progressive. When we consider all the ways in which fears of a change in the racial landscape of the nation have led to an assault on black lives, we can see why *12 Years* would have meaning for contemporary viewers.

12 *Years a Slave* offers a nuanced view of the racial, gender, class, and power dynamics that underwrote and enabled the system of slavery. Both through the narrative of a northern black man captured into slavery, and in the casting of actors from across the diaspora, the film reminds viewers of the national and global reach of the institution. Northup's twitching foot reminds us of the proximity of freedom to enslavement and of the fragility of black life, both then and now. As numerous reviewers and critics have noted, Northup's sudden descent from freedom into captivity recalls the numbers of African Americans wrongfully convicted and incarcerated due to the racialized policies and profit motives that sustain a criminal justice system fueled by sentencing requirements, three-strikes laws, drug laws spawned by the failed policies of the war on drugs, stop-and-frisk laws, and so on.[2] Racial disparities in the criminal justice system threaten both those who are incarcerated—limiting their voting rights and denying equal access to employment, housing, public benefits, and education—and the communities they leave behind on the outside. Northup's twitching foot calls to mind as well Trayvon Martin, Renisha McBride, Jonathan Ferrell, and the hosts of other African Americans, largely invisible in the media, gunned down each year and whose shooters (whether law enforcement officers or civilians) go unpunished. How fragile indeed is black life in the Age of Obama.

Work Cited

Ebiri, Bilge. "Horrendous Acts in a Beautiful Way: Behind the Scenes of 12 *Years a Slave*." *Vulture.* New York Media, 13 Nov. 2013. Web.

2. Some of the best-known and most influential scholarship on the racialized prison industrial complex in the US includes Angela Y. Davis, *Are Prisons Obsolete?* (2003); Ruth Wilson Gilmore, *Golden Gulag: Prisons, Surplus, Crisis, and Opposition in Globalizing California* (2007); and Michelle Alexander, *The New Jim Crow: Mass Incarceration in the Age of Colorblindness* (2010). See also Dennis Childs, "Slaves of the State: Cultures and Politics of Black Incarceration from the Chain Gang to the Penitentiary" (forthcoming 2014).

JOHN STAUFFER

12 Years between Life and Death[†]

The most memorable image in *12 Years a Slave* is of Solomon Northup (Chiwetel Ejiofor) hanging from a tree with a noose around his neck, his arms and legs tightly bound, and his toes barely reaching the muddy ground. It is also the longest shot in the film, lingering for about three minutes. In the background slaves do chores, children play, the overseer Mr. Chapin (J. D. Evermore) paces on the piazza, and Mistress Ford (Liza Bennett) watches from her balcony. Chapin, having saved Northup from being lynched by the carpenter John Tibeats (Paul Dano), now allows him to endure this torture all day, until Master Ford cuts him down. Only the slave Rachel (Nicole Collins) intervenes. She enters the foreground of the scene, as if to underscore the unusual nature of her act, and gives Northup water from a drinking gourd. Given the strain on Northup's neck, it seems surprising that he survives the ordeal.

The scene provides the central metaphor of the film. During his 12 years as a slave, Northup dangles between life and death, or "social death," as the sociologist Orlando Patterson called it.[1] The term captures the extreme power imbalance between master and slave resulting from violence coupled with psychological coercion.

The scene and the film highlight a defining feature of slavery that previous feature films about the institution have either downplayed or ignored. "Social death" recognizes slavery as a state of war; and a slave society such as the antebellum South is a "closed society" or totalitarian state.[2] These are also central themes in Northup's own narrative, *Twelve Years a Slave* (1853), on which the film is closely based, and the writings and speeches of most black and white abolitionists, notably Frederick Douglass, who explicitly called slavery "a *state of war*" (153).

In seeking to dehumanize people, chattel slavery corrupts everyone within the system, from heroic slaves to humane masters. Chapin saves Northup's life but tortures him. Ford protects (and

---

† From *American Literary History* 26.2 (Summer 2014): 317–25. © John Stauffer 2014. Reprinted by permission of Oxford University Press.

1. Vincent Brown offers an important corrective to Patterson's concept of "social death," showing how scholars, by treating it as "a theoretical abstraction," have misused it. It is as though *12 Years a Slave* incorporates both Patterson's book and Brown's article in its depiction of slavery. See "Social Death and Political Life in the Study of Slavery," *American Historical Review* 114 (2009): 1231–49.

2. James Silvers's (*Mississippi: The Closed Society* [1964]) characterization of the deep South as a closed society resembles a totalitarian state. Although he focuses on Mississippi in the postbellum years, he traces the origins of the South's closed society to the antebellum years.

respects) him but sells him to the psychotic master Edwin Epps (Michael Fassbender). Mistress Shaw (Alfre Woodard) marries her former master and enjoys having slaves work for her: "Once I served; now I have others to serve me."[3] Northup tries to protect Patsey (Lupita Nyong'o), but he also whips her and commits adultery with her. And during his near lynching, only one slave—a minor character—comes to his aid.

The quest to survive trumps morality. Here the film brilliantly dramatizes the psychology of slavery, which critics have so far failed to grasp.[4] Survival is the slaves' basic aim, much as it has been for POWs, even as they dream of freedom. It is a naturalist world, in which people have become "plaything[s]" of social forces (Burt 177).[5] Free will has given way to coercion, and choice has been replaced by chance, making it extremely difficult, if not suicidal, for people to act on moral principle.

Within this naturalist world, expressionistic imagery offers access into the subjectivity of the characters, especially Northup. The steamboat ride to Louisiana often appears surreal. In one shot, the paddlewheel zooms toward us, filling the screen, suggesting the closed society into which it heads. Northup's memory while on board the steamer, of entering the general store back home and noticing a slave stare at him until his master retrieves him, appears on screen as a flashback. In Louisiana there are surreal sunsets of trees reflecting off blood-red water. And there are long, close-up camera shots of Northup's face, as if to invite us into his consciousness. The director Steve McQueen explained the relationship between environment and character in an interview with Henry Louis Gates, Jr.: "The story is about the environment, and how individuals have to make sense of it, how we locate the self in events" ("Part 3"). McQueen locates the self in events through his expressionistic imagery.

Much of the imagery was inspired by Francisco Goya, a progenitor of the "modern temper in art," according to the art historian Fred Licht. In an interview with Luke Goodsell, McQueen explained Goya's influence on him: he "painted the most horrendous pictures of violence and torture and so forth, and they're amazing, exquisite paintings. . . . What he's saying is, 'Look—look at this.'" The lesson from Goya is that if the perspective is wrong, "you draw more attention to what's wrong with the image rather than looking at the image." The depictions of violence and suffering in the film do not generate a

3. This and all other quotes from the film are from my transcriptions while watching it.
4. In his short, excellent review of *12 Years a Slave* in the *New Yorker*, David Denby hints at the psychology of survivalism but does not develop it (see "Fighting to Survive: '12 Years a Slave' and 'All Is Lost,'" 21 Oct. 2013, web).
5. I quote from John Burt's brilliant analysis of "the world Lincoln feared in the 'House Divided' speech" in order to suggest that literary naturalism can be applied to narratives other than novels (177).

voyeuristic "pornography of pain" that is "obscenely titillating," which is how Karen Halttunen described abolitionist descriptions of slavery (304). Nor do they exploit and objectify black bodies, as Marcus Wood (*Blind Memory: Visual Representations of Slavery in England and America, 1780–1865* [2000]) said of visual representations of slavery. And they do not come across as "weirdly antiseptic, history made safe through art," as Stephanie Zacharek wrote in her review of *12 Years a Slave*. Rather, they enable viewers to empathize with the plight of slaves, offering access into their emotional and psychological states.[6] The film succeeds at forcing viewers to "look—look at this" in order to understand slavery, as reflected by the extraordinary reviews and audience response. Both times I saw the film, in San Juan, Puerto Rico, and Arlington, Massachusetts, the sounds of sniffling were audible, especially at the end as credits rolled.

12 Years a Slave highlights the theme of survivalism in several ways. Immediately after Northup becomes a slave, after having enjoyed a successful—indeed "distinguished"—middle-class life in Saratoga Springs, New York, he repudiates the ethos of survivalism. While on board the steamer heading to New Orleans, Northup and some fellow slaves debate whether or not to rebel. "I say we fight," says Robert (Michael K. Williams). Northup agrees, telling the other slaves that he is a free man who has been illegally kidnapped and enslaved. But another slave characterizes rebellion as suicidal: "Do and say as little as possible. Tell no one who you are. Survival's about keeping your head down." Northup protests this ethos of survivalism: "You're telling me that's how to survive? I don't want to survive; I want to *live*." But after acclimating to slavery, he explains to Eliza (Adepero Oduye), whose children have been sold away from her, how he manages the horror of slavery and the loss of his family: "I *survive*."

But the film subtly complicates this ethos of survivalism. At times slaves perceive living in slavery as worse than death, and it is at these moments when they rebel. After Robert's corpse is thrown overboard, another slave (who had also advocated rebellion) says: "He's better off than us." When Northup stands up to Tibeats and whips him, anger has replaced fear, dignity has trumped humiliation. It is a visual counterpart to the book, in which Northup says: "My fear changed to anger, and before he reached me I had made up my mind fully not to be whipped, let the result be life or death" (80). Viewers understand that in fighting Tibeats, Northup risks his life.

Accepting death as the cost of rebellion is a common theme in the literature on slavery. When Frederick Douglass decides to stand

6. On the importance of empathy for humanitarian reform, especially in relation to slavery, see Joseph Yannielli's prizewinning article, "George Thompson among the Africans: Empathy, Authority, and Insanity in the Age of Abolition," *Journal of American History* 96 (2010): 979–1000.

up to the slave breaker Edward Covey, he declares, "I had reached the point, at which I was *not afraid to die*. This spirit made me a freeman in *fact*, while I remained a slave in *form*" (*My Bondage* 140). The spirit of freedom trumped the bodily quest to survive. The film accurately portrays the psychology of historical slave rebellions. As David Brion Davis has concluded, they "were suicidal" (220).

In the film, suicide is also a form of rebellion. Patsey, who suffers more than any other slave in the story, asks Northup one night to drown her in the swamp. Surprised by her request, he refuses: "How you fall into such despair?" He is surprised because by temperament she is energetic and full of life, making masterful dolls out of corn-husks and picking five times as much cotton as other slaves. Her death-wish stems from her plight as an attractive young slave woman, inducing rape by her master—"God gave her to me," Epps declares—and the odium of Mistress Epps (Sarah Paulson). "The enslaved victim of lust and hate, Patsey had no comfort of her life," Northup summarizes in his book (143).

Patsey's death-wish is a slight departure from the book in order to dramatize the psychology of slavery. In the book it is Mistress Epps who "tempted [Northup] with bribes to put [Patsey] secretly to death, and bury her body in some lonely place in the margin of the swamp" (143). Patsey's death-wish comes near the end of Northup's narrative, after her horrible whipping. Northup concludes that Patsey had lost the will to live: "A blessed thing it would have been for her . . . had she never lifted her head in life again. Indeed, from that time forward she was not what she had been. . . . If ever there was a broken heart—one crushed and blighted by the rude grasp of suffering and misfortune—it was Patsey's" (199). A page later he explains her death-wish in relation to freedom: "Patsey's life, especially after her whipping, was one long dream of liberty. Far away, to her fancy an immeasurable distance, she knew there was a land of freedom. . . . In her imagination it was an enchanted region, the Paradise of the earth" (200–201). Her dream of freedom, a form of rebellion, is also a death-wish. In altering details from the book, the film has not so much "removed [its] bright sides," as Stanley Fish argued; rather, it has compressed the plot in order to heighten the emotional and psychological drama.

In some respects, the film captures the psychology of slavery even better than the book. This is because it borrows images from the book and interprets them in compelling ways. For example, it is unclear in the book how to visualize the scene in which Northup is almost hanged. Northup describes Tibeats's tying his wrists and ankles "with his utmost strength," and his two companions' slipping "a cord within my elbows, running it across my back, and tying it firmly" (82). Then Tibeats "made an awkward noose, and placed it about my neck" (82). As the three men drag Northup "towards the tree," the overseer Chapin appears "with a pistol in each hand" (83). Tibeats and his companions leave, and Northup continues "standing where I was, still bound, with the rope around my neck" (85). It is in this position that Northup remains all day: "I was yet bound, the rope still dangling from my neck, and standing in the same tracks where Tibeats and his comrades left me. I could not move an inch, so firmly had I been bound" (86). But *what*, exactly, is his position? Is the rope that dangles from Northup's neck also wrapped around a tree? Apparently not, for Northup implies that he could have fallen to the ground: "The ground was so parched and boiling hot I was aware it would but add to the discomfort of my situation" (86), he says, as if to explain why he remains standing. But two sentences later he notes that the sun "produced not half the suffering I experienced from my aching limbs. My wrists and ankles, and the cords of my legs and arms began to swell, burying the rope that bound them into the swollen flesh" (86). He clearly suffers, but the book obscures the image of his suffering, whereas the film clarifies it, turning it into a central metaphor of the slave experience.

Apparently, McQueen looked for sources that would highlight the psychology of slavery. He sought not a traditional slave narrative, in which the protagonist is born into slavery, but a free man who becomes a slave, in order to contrast the condition of freedom with that of slavery. "I had an idea of a free man—a free African American who gets kidnapped into slavery," he told Gates ("Part 1"). But he "got stuck" in his search for a source, until his wife pointed him to Northup's narrative.

12 Years a Slave has been compared with other films about slavery, from *Django Unchained* (2012) and *Jezebel* (1938) to *Schindler's List* (1993). But arguably a better comparison is *The Deer Hunter* (1978). In both *Deer Hunter* and *12 Years a Slave*, the protagonists descend into slavery and then return from it, a racial divide distinguishes slaves from slave-owners, and our sympathies are with the slaves. In *Deer Hunter*, three protagonists—Mike Vronsky (Robert De Niro), Steven Pushkov (John Savage), and Nick Chevotarevich (Christopher Walken)—descend from their respectable, working-class lives in Clairton, Pennsylvania, into the hell of Vietnam, where they immediately become POWs. Much like *12 Years a Slave*, there is a three-part structure with a double reversal, what Aristotle called a "complex plot," to contrast freedom and slavery.[7] And like

---

7. Filmmakers have been influenced by Aristotle's *Poetics*. Gary Ross, the writer and director of *Seabiscuit* and *Hunger Games*, emphasized the importance of Aristotle in his lecture on screenwriting at the Academy of Motion Picture Arts and Sciences on 10 September 2004. As he put it:

12 Years a Slave, there is an abrupt shift from freedom in part one to bondage in part two. In *Deer Hunter*, the camera cuts abruptly from a pub in Pittsburgh, in which Mike, Steve, and Nick listen to Chopin's Nocturne 15 in G minor, to a Vietnamese village under attack. In *12 Years a Slave*, there is a similar sharp break after Northup eats dinner with his kidnappers at a fashionable restaurant, and then suddenly wakes up in a dark slave pen. Unlike *12 Years a Slave*, the central metaphor in *Deer Hunter*, Russian roulette, is a historical lie—"there was not a single recorded case of Russian roulette" in Vietnam, according to Peter Arnett, who covered the war (qtd. in Biskind).[8] But at the same time, it reveals a psychological truth that captures the "deliberately random violence" of war, especially among POWs, as Roger Ebert noted.

The *Deer Hunter*, much like *12 Years a Slave*, ends with the dilemma of returning home and living once again in freedom after having suffered the agony of slavery. In *Deer Hunter*, Nick returns home in a casket, having killed himself playing Russian roulette professionally; he and Mike had previously been forced to play it as POWs, and he had not recovered from the experience. Steve is legless and wants to stay in the VA hospital. Only Mike returns in one piece, as it were, trying to confront the problem of living again in freedom. Laura Hillenbrand's summary of the plight of returning POWs from the Pacific in World War II, from her biography of Louis Zamperini, speaks to the return home in *Deer Hunter*: "nothing was ever going to be the same" (346). (Her biography of Zamperini will no doubt become a movie.) For returning POWs, "their dignity had been obliterated, replaced with a pervasive sense of shame and worthlessness" (349). After being released, they needed to restore their dignity without succumbing to resentment, an emotion that "nails every one of us onto the cross of his ruined past," according to the Holocaust survivor Jean Améry (68). Zamperini liberated himself from his resentment only after being converted by the evangelist Billy Graham, four years after coming home.

[T]he best book I ever read about screenwriting was Aristotle's *Poetics*. I don't mean that to sound show-offy—it's an unbelievably practical primer on story structure. Aristotle said there were two kinds of plots: simple and complex. A *simple plot* is one where the question asked at the outset is answered at the end: "Can they steal the Gold? Yes they can." But a story like that can only *ever* be about stealing gold. Then he said there was a richer kind of story, one that he called a *complex plot*, in which the theme of the piece is complex enough to reveal a deeper question in the middle. And that deeper question will inevitably demand a richer more satisfying answer. And that richer answer becomes a more satisfying resolution. And that inevitability *is* structure. That *is* clarity. And it all comes from challenging yourself with the right kind of questions at the outset. Then suddenly it's not a movie about stealing gold; it's about greed and desperation and illusion and self-deception . . . and it turns into *The Treasure of the Sierra Madre*.

8. Peter Arnett's quote is from Peter Biskind, "The Vietnam Oscars."

The final scene in *Deer Hunter* is richly ambiguous. The film ends after Nick's funeral, with Mike, Steve, and their friends singing "God Bless America." The anthem connects the protagonists to their nation, raising questions about the legacy of the Vietnam War. But the specific meaning of this final scene is unclear. In it is tragedy, sadness, and hope. Was the song "a critique of patriotism or a paean to it?" the critic Peter Biskind wondered.

Similarly, *12 Years a Slave* ends with Northup's return to freedom, and it raises questions about the legacy of slavery. Northup arrives at the front door of his house, looking dazed, as if he is afraid to enter. The scene recalls Mike's return from Vietnam in *The Deer Hunter*; he cannot face his friends, cannot bear to attend his homecoming celebration, and instead spends the night alone in a hotel. Northup cautiously enters his home, and then betrays a sense of shame: "I apologize for my appearance, but I've had a difficult time these past several years." He seems not to be able to distinguish his daughter, Margaret (Devyn Tyler), from his wife, Anne (Kelsey Scott), for he asks, "Margaret, where are you?" He apologizes again, saying "forgive me." His wife responds, "There is nothing to forgive." There is nothing for Anne to forgive of him. Yet the theme of forgiveness looms large. In one sense, Solomon will need to learn how to forgive his tormenters in order to overcome resentment and release himself from his past sufferings.[9]

But in another sense, since the film ends with Northup having just returned home, it places the burden of the past on us, urging us as viewers to confront the legacy of slavery in a free society. This legacy has already been foreshadowed in the film's central metaphor. Northup's hanging from a noose, dangling between life and death, "had to represent all the hundreds of thousands of people who were lynched" in the postbellum era, McQueen told Gates ("Part 3").

Northup's last two lines—an apology and a plea for forgiveness—offer a way to confront the legacy of slavery. When he apologizes, he is also asking the US to apologize for slavery and its slave society. "When has a US president ever apologized?" McQueen told Gates. "How do we go forward? It's time for the US, it's time for the British, it's time for the Dutch, the French, the Portuguese, et cetera, to apologize" ("Part 2"). Only then can the legacies of slavery be confronted. With an apology, there can then be forgiveness, and the beginning of healing.

---

9. See Charles L. Griswold's brilliant book *Forgiveness: A Philosophical Exploration* (2007), which focuses on the role of forgiveness in secular, interhuman connections, from individuals to nation-states.

Works Cited

Améry, Jean. *At the Mind's Limits: Contemplations by a Survivor of Auschwitz and Its Realities.* Bloomington: Indiana UP, 1998.

Biskind, Peter. "The Vietnam Oscars." *Vanity Fair.* Conde Nast, Mar. 2008. Web.

Burt, John. *Lincoln's Tragic Pragmatism: Lincoln, Douglas, and Moral Conflict.* Cambridge: Harvard UP, 2013.

Davis, David Brion. *Inhuman Bondage: The Rise and Fall of Slavery in the New World.* New York: Oxford UP, 2006.

Douglass, Frederick. "Slavery, the Slumbering Volcano." 1849. *The Frederick Douglass Papers.* Ser. 1, Vol. 2. Ed. John W. Blassingame. New Haven: Yale UP, 1982. 148–58.

———. *My Bondage and My Freedom.* 1855. Ed. John Stauffer. New York: Modern Lib., 2003.

Ebert, Roger. "The Deer Hunter." *Chicago Sun-Times* 9 Mar. 1979. Web.

Fish, Stanley. "No Way Out: *12 Years a Slave.*" *New York Times* 25 Nov. 2013. Web.

Halttunen, Karen. "Humanitarianism and the Pornography of Pain in Anglo-American Culture." *American Historical Review* 100 (1995): 303–34.

Hillenbrand, Laura. *Unbroken: A World War II Story of Survival, Resilience, and Redemption.* New York: Random House, 2010.

Licht, Fred. *Goya, The Origins of the Modern Temper in Art.* New York: Harper & Row, 1983.

McQueen, Steve. Interview with Luke Goodsell. *Rotten Tomatoes.* Flixster, 17 Oct. 2013. Web.

———. "Steve McQueen and Henry Louis Gates, Jr. Talk *12 Years a Slave*, Part 1." *Root.* The Slate Group, 24 Dec. 2013. Web.

———. "Steve McQueen and Henry Louis Gates, Jr. Talk *12 Years a Slave*, Part 2." *Root.* The Slate Group, 25 Dec. 2013. Web.

———. "Steve McQueen and Henry Louis Gates, Jr. Talk *12 Years a Slave*, Part 3." *Root.* The Slate Group, 26 Dec. 2013. Web.

Northup, Solomon. *Twelve Years a Slave.* 1853. Ed. Sue Eakin and Joseph Logsdon. Baton Rouge: Louisiana State UP, 1968.

Zacharek, Stephanie. "*12 Years a Slave* Prizes Radiance Over Life." *Village Voice.* Village Voice, 16 Oct. 2013. Web.

SALAMISHAH TILLET

"I Got No Comfort in This Life": The Increasing Importance of Patsey in 12 Years a Slave[†]

* * *

In interview after interview, British director Steve McQueen has con-fessed that he broke down only once during the filming of *12 Years a Slave*. It was during the scene in which the enslaved woman, Patsey (played by Lupita Nyong'o), is being tended to by other slaves after both her friend, Solomon Northup (Chiwetel Ejiofor), and her master, Edwin Epps (Michael Fassbender), have whipped her. McQueen recalls, "She lifts her head up and she sees Chiwetel . . . and she weeps and cries. And there's acknowledgement, I suppose, that I asked you to kill me and now this." He goes on, "And we cut to Chiwe-tel acknowledging her gaze, and then Chiwetel cries. This tear just drops from his face out of nowhere. I said, 'Cut! I have to go for a walk.' [. . .] I had to go for a walk" ("Where It Hurts").

McQueen's comments are noteworthy for several reasons. First, he moves us past the horror of the beating itself—a scene that some critics have described as excessive and, as Henry Louis Gates, Jr. suggests, a "potential too-much-ness" ("Steve McQueen"). Both its length, a 10-minute sequence taken in one shot, and its height-ened sensory experiences, causes its cinematic excess. In contrast to the sensory deprivation that haunts most of the film, the whip-ping is a spectacle of gruesome beauty: the steadied handheld cam-era closes up on Solomon's face and then slowly follows the whip's arc from his grief-stricken eyes to Patsey's tortured back; the wel-coming hues of the Louisiana plantation and the brazen whiteness of the Big House collide with Patsey's tattered clothes and bloodied back. Only laughing birds, the stinging lash, and a desperate human wail puncture a strange and overwhelming silence. When asked about her experience filming that scene, actress Nyong'o said, "that day was as real as it could have possibly been for me, because in pre-paring for it, all I could do was be present."

Despite its gravity, the whipping scene itself is hardly unex-pected. American audiences have long come to anticipate such a savage whipping in a film on slavery, especially when it is based on a true story. McQueen's task then was to de-familiarize his audience with the most oft-repeated scene of slavery to evoke empathy for his characters and repulsion at their predicament. He does this by

† From *American Literary History* 26.2 (Summer 2014): 354–61. © Salamishah Tillet 2014. Reprinted by permission of Oxford University Press.

shifting our gaze, and thus our identification, from that of Northup, to Patsey's, to Epps's, and back to hers. And it is in that visual
exchange that the young actress Nyong'o not only overwhelms vet-
erans Ejiofor and McQueen to the point of tears but also skillfully
maintains Patsey's subjectivity against America's larger history of
anesthetizing black pain. By turning to Patsey here, I build on previous generations of black feminist scholars, particularly Saidiya
Hartman and Deborah McDowell's eloquent reading of Frederick
Douglass's voyeuristic depiction of the whipping of his Aunt Hester
by their slave master in the opening chapter of his 1845 *Narrative*.[1]
Rather than considering Patsey to be the sole victim of Epps's lash
or even the object of Northup's detached prose, her centrality in
McQueen's *12 Years a Slave* asks us to reconsider the implications
of seeing *woman* and *slave* as mutually constitutive terms.

Her growing significance in his film also extends *and* departs
from earlier versions of Northup's story: his own slave narrative,
*Twelve Years a Slave: Narrative of Solomon Northup, a Citizen of
New-York, Kidnapped in Washington City in 1841, and Rescued in
1853, from a Cotton Plantation Near the Red River, in Louisiana*
(1853), and Gordon Parks, Sr.'s 1984 television version, *Solomon
Northup's Odyssey*. A formidable figure in Northup's original narrative, Patsey is one of the many black women, free and enslaved,
featured. Her beating, nevertheless, has ultimate significance
because Northup uses it to make his biggest case against slavery:
even those whose entire lives are spent under its lash still yearn for
and deserve to be free. "Patsey's life," Northup laments, "especially
after her whipping, was one long dream of liberty. Far away, to her
fancy an immeasurable distance, she knew there was a land of freedom. A thousand times she had heard that somewhere in the distant North there were no slaves—no masters" (174). Ironically, after
this scene, Patsey is effectively silenced for the rest of the story—
an absence that reveals that her primary function was to substantiate Northup's abolitionist agenda and appeal to the sympathy of
white northerners who had yet to convert to his cause.

If Northup abruptly distances Patsey to sustain his narrative
authority, Parks completely erases her from his 1984 adaptation,
Solomon Northup's Odyssey. Whereas other women, such as Anne
(Northup's wife) and Eliza (the mother who loses both her children
and eventually her mind to slavery) appear in much greater depth and
despair in both Northup's original and Parks's televisual version
than they do in McQueen's film, a fictional character named Jenny
(played by subtle Rhetta Greene) stands in for Patsey in *Odyssey*.

---

1. See "In the First Place: Making Frederick Douglass & the African-American Narrative
Tradition," William Andrews, ed., *Critical Essays on Frederick Douglass* (1991).

We meet her as a young woman on a slave boat to Louisiana with the kidnapped Solomon (played by the dashing Avery Brooks). As the storyline progresses, she initially is Solomon's lover at the Ford plantation and eventually becomes the object of her master's lust and mistress's loathing at the Epps's estate. The messiness of this new quadrangle with Jenny, Master and Mistress Epps, and Solomon comes to a head in Parks's version of the whipping scene. When Mistress Epps learns of their past affair and forces Solomon to whip Jenny, he responds by going into a woodshed, out of her sight, and pretends to beat Jenny. In that moment, Solomon emerges as Jenny's protector, a role previously denied to him as an enslaved black man on Epps's plantation, but one that he relished as a free man with his wife. In that same scene, Jenny moves between play-screaming and hysterically laughing at their outwitting of Mistress Epps.

But, unlike Solomon's heroism, Jenny emerges as a much more ambivalent character in Parks's adaptation. She is depicted as a character whose simultaneous longing for Solomon and vexed appreciation of Epps's gifts and sexual attention distress Solomon and ultimately put him at great risk. When she proudly tells Epps of Solomon and her deception of Mistress Epps, the enraged slave-master violently attacks Solomon. After it aired, Parks admitted that he made aesthetic and political choices "to minimize the violence in it, if I could, and still tell the truth" ("TV Film"). Thus Parks chose to ignore Northup's near-hanging, a scene that McQueen describes as embodying "the physical and psychological aspects of slavery in one frame" (qtd. in Gettell)[2] because he wanted to make the film "bearable for people to look at" (Parks, "TV Film"). He also experienced outside pressure to censor the film from those same historians who were on set as advisors. "They were always there, breathing over your shoulder," Parks revealed, "I was asked in certain areas to keep it toned down. I would say, 'But these things happened.'" Whether the decision to replace Patsey with Jenny was Parks's, the historians' on the set, or both, her absence is troubling. Though somewhat sympathetic to her fate, *Odyssey* risks reproducing the revisionist histories of slavery of the 1970s by those same historians who advised the film, like John Blassingame's *Slave Community* (1972) and Eugene Genovese's *Roll, Jordan Roll: The World the Slaves Made* (1974), which privileged African-American male subjectivity but barely mentioned the lives and experiences of enslaved women, while at the same

2. At the Envelope Screening Series, Steve McQueen and his cinematographer, Sean Bob-bitt, discussed how they approached shooting this pivotal scene. McQueen said he wanted audiences "not just to see the sort of physical aspects of slavery but the mental aspects of slavery. If one of those slaves did actually try to help Solomon, they'd be strung up next to him," McQueen said. "So to have the two parallel things at the same time—the physical and the psychological aspects of slavery in one frame—that's exactly what I wanted to do."

time, reinforcing the patriarchal logic of certain male-authored nineteenth-century slave narratives and post–civil rights black nationalists texts, such as Eldridge Cleaver's *Soul on Ice* (1968), that suggested the real tragedy of the sexual exploitation of enslaved women by slavemasters was the "affront to the men with whom the women are associated" (Foster 67). Ultimately, Patsey's absence and Jenny's ambiguity enable Solomon to emerge as a thoroughly uncompromised hero at the expense of enslaved black women.

In contrast, the importance of Patsey to McQueen's vision in *12 Years a Slave* should not be underestimated, for it is upon her that all his "representations of slave women" hang (Stevenson). Unlike his ready casting of British actor Chiwetel Ejiofor and German actor Michael Fassbender, with whom he was well acquainted (Fassbender even starred in McQueen's earlier two films), actress Lupita Nyong'o was unknown. In fact, McQueen compared the search for Patsey to the notorious problem of casting *Gone with the Wind*'s Scarlett O'Hara. After seeing more than 1,000 auditions for Patsey, McQueen told *New York Magazine*'s Dan Lee that when he received Nyong'o's audition video over e-mail, he called his wife over to confirm what he was seeing, and two weeks later Nyong'o was on set in New Orleans. After they first rehearsed the scene that leads to Patsey's whipping, McQueen told her, "Thank you for being born."

Yet his emphasis on Patsey shows how his vision converses with and incorporates an essential trope within post–civil rights African-American cultural production: the centrality of the black female body in African-American remembering of slavery. Since the late 1960s, African-American artists, writers, and intellectuals have produced a large corpus of works that take American chattel slavery as their central theme. Animating these contemporary representations of slavery is *civic estrangement*, my term for post–civil rights African Americans' paradoxical experience of simultaneously being citizens and noncitizens. *Civic estrangement* describes an affective and ascriptive state of black nonbelonging because African Americans have been marginalized or underrepresented in the civic myths, monuments, narratives, icons, creeds, and images of the past that constitute, reproduce, and promote an American national identity. While the centering of enslaved black women in post–civil rights representations of slavery is not guaranteed (as *Odyssey* attests), the emphasis on enslaved women's bodies, experiences, and histories has emerged as a defining feature across media and methodologies. The result: a direct contrast to those founding fictions of whiteness, blackness, and femininity that have historically posited enslaved women, to quote Hortense Spillers, as "vestibular to culture" and outside the rights and rites of US citizens (158). In such radical re-imaginings of our slave past and our shared futures, enslaved black women, such as Sally Hemings, often emerge as new symbols of an inclusive citizenship and racial democracy.

Through Patsey, McQueen does not fully embrace this centralizing black women's subjectivity, but he does echo some of its features and concerns. It is Solomon's, not Patsey's, point of view that shapes most of the narrative. However, her significance and potential countervalence emerge in the three critical revisions of Northup's narrative by McQueen and screenwriter John Ridley: Patsey's suicidal plea to Solomon; the glance exchanged between them after she is brutally whipped; and the second-to-last scene, when Solomon must literally turn away from Patsey in order to gain his freedom. I focus on these three scenes because they, for the first time in the film, not only pull our sympathetic gaze away from Solomon but also enable Patsey to assert her subjectivity and authorial control within Solomon's tale. Though fleeting and ultimately incomplete, Patsey's voice takes over the narrative, and ultimately our post–civil rights memory of slavery.

In Northup's narrative, he reveals that Mistress Epps "more than once, when Epps had refused to sell [Patsey], . . . tempted me with bribes to put her secretly to death, and bury her body in some lonely place in the margin of the swamp" (124). In the film version, it is Patsey who begs Solomon to put her to death; this scene is substantially more harrowing and Patsey is more heart-broken. Structurally, Solomon and Patsey's conversation happens after we have already witnessed so much gender-based violence: Mistress Epps's disfigurement of Patsey's face and Epps's choke-holding rape of her. In response to these repeated attacks, a distraught Patsey turns to Solomon, not for protection, but for mercy when she begs him to kill her. Rather than Solomon's refusal to help Patsey here, I am more interested in the portrayal and potential interpretations of his incredulity. "How does such despair even come to you?" he asks, to which a crestfallen Patsey replies, "How can you not see it? I got no comfort in this life; caught up between Massa's lust 'n Mistress's hate. If I cain't buy mercy from yah, I'll beg it." Up until this point, the film has aligned the audience's and Solomon's points of view: we learn the horrors and hell of slavery, bit by bit, as Solomon travels further south and falls deeper into its clutches. And with the notable exception of his argument with Eliza, who warns him against Master Ford's intentions, he is our most trusted interpreter of what it means to survive in and perhaps outlive slavery. That is, until Patsey directly challenges his reading and reveals his inability to "see" how the experiences of his fellow slaves, particularly enslaved women, might be so abject that death, by suicide or murder, might be a viable alternative.

In the shift of narrative authority—from Solomon's gaze to Patsey's—that I cited earlier, McQueen has Patsey hold Solomon accountable both for his own unwilling participation and for Epps's fanatic whipping of her nearly to death. As her slave friend, Phebe, tries nursing her lacerations, Patsey opens her eyes and (without uttering a word) stares at Solomon, and then closes them. Solomon's tearful response (an improvised, seemingly involuntary reflex on Ejiofor's part) appears to be one of remorse and recognition. In that moment, McQueen enables us to see slavery through Patsey's lens, and in her world, Solomon befriends and betrays her. This portrayal undermines Northup's own self-depiction as a detached observer in his slave narrative and Parks's reconstruction of him as an unblemished hero in *Odyssey*. In a *New York Times* conversation with Nelson George, Kara Walker observes, "I didn't find him particularly heroic, in that Frederick Douglass sense. He's a little bit more compromised by more than just slavery. There's this past, what he does or doesn't do for Patsey. All of that makes him a much more complicated figure in a way."

In the end, McQueen does not only hang all his representations of slave women on Patsey, but also Solomon's narrative authority as well. This partly explains why he concludes the film with two competing images: Solomon's final departure from Patsey and the Epps plantation and his return to his family in New York. Refusing the Hollywood conventions of a nice and neat prodigal return, McQueen gives us only a glimpse of Solomon in domestic safety. Instead, he lingers on the preceding scene, in which Patsey cries out to Solomon as he leaves the plantation for the last time. Her plea is for Solomon not to abandon her again but rather to give her the freedom that she so desperately longs for and that he is now guaranteed. In their interview, McQueen told Gates that he did not focus on Solomon's reunion with his family "because the story goes on. And the thought I wanted them to leave with was what happened to Patsey and all the other millions of slaves."

As Patsey emerges as the representative of not just all black slave women, but all enslaved African Americans, McQueen begins to undo the limiting and hypermasculine categories of the "Heroic Slave" as famously invented by Frederick Douglass and the "exceptional slave" as imagined in Quentin Tarantino's *Django Unchained*.[3] And while McQueen does not offer us a full chorus, like the "singing women" (301) who literally save Sethe from the haunt of slavery in both the novel and film versions of Toni Morrison's *Beloved* (1987), he give us an ensemble of African-American women's experiences during both freedom and slavery that *start* to complicate this

---

3. See my "Hollywood Finally Catches Up with History," *Root* 15 Oct. 2013, web; "Quentin Tarantino Creates an Exceptional Slave," *CNN* 25 Dec. 2012, web; *Sites of Slavery: Citizenship and Racial Democracy in the Post-Civil Rights Imagination* (2012).

American story and fill in those silences and omissions of the old
and new historiographies of slavery.

Works Cited

Foster, Frances. "'In Respect to Females . . .': Differences in the
Portrayals of Women by Male and Female Narrators." *Black
American Literature Forum* 15.2 (1981): 66–70.
Gettell, Oliver. "'12 Years a Slave': Steve McQueen on Shooting a
Pivotal Scene." *Los Angeles Times* 17 Oct. 2013. Web.
Hartman, Saidiya V. *Scenes of Subjection: Terror, Slavery, and Self-
Making in Nineteenth-Century America.* New York: Oxford UP,
1997.
McQueen, Steve, dir. *12 Years a Slave.* Regency Enterprises, 2013.
Film.
———. "Where It Hurts: Steve McQueen on Why '12 Years a Slave'
Isn't Just about Slavery." Interview by Dan P. Lee. *New York Maga-
zine* 16 Dec. 2013: 46.
———. "Steve McQueen and Henry Louis Gates, Jr. Talk *12 Years a
Slave,* Part 3." *Root.* The Slate Group, 26 Dec. 2013. Web.
Morrison, Toni. *Beloved: A Novel.* New York: Knopf, 1987.
Northup, Solomon. *Twelve Years a Slave.* New York, NY: Penguin
Books, 2013.
Nyong'o, Lupita. "Lupita Nyong'o on *12 Years a Slave*: Getting into
Character, and 'Impostor's Syndrome.'" Interview by Jada Yuan.
Vulture. New York Media, 2 Oct. 2013. Web.
Parks, Gordon, dir. Avery Brooks, perf. *Solomon Northup's Odyssey.*
1984. Thousand Oaks, Calif.: Monterey Video, 2004. DVD.
———. "TV Film by Parks Looks at Slavery." Interview by Leslie
Bennett. *New York Times* 11 Feb. 1985. Web.
Spillers, Hortense. "Interstices: A Small Drama of Words." *Black,
White, and in Color: Essays on American Literature and Culture.*
Chicago: U of Chicago P, 2003.
Stevenson, Brenda. "The Surprisingly Central Role of Slave
Women in *12 Years a Slave.*" *History News Network* 18 Oct. 2013.
Web.
Toplin, Robert Brent. "Making a Slavery Docudrama." *OAH Maga-
zine of History* 1.2 (1985): 17–19.
Walker, Kara. "An Essentially American Narrative: A Discussion of
Steve McQueen's Film '12 Years a Slave.'" Interview by Nelson
George, ed. *New York Times* 11 Oct. 2013: AR18.

THE ROOT

Steve McQueen and Henry Louis Gates, Jr. Talk
12 Years a Slave[†]

Part 1: The director of the gripping slavery narrative tells
The Root how President Obama's influence was instrumental
in its very creation.

When the creators of a drama that would bring Solomon Northup's
12 Years a Slave to the big screen needed a historical consultant,
Henry Louis Gates, Jr., who edited a recent edition of the memoir,
was a natural choice.

Gates, a Harvard scholar, producer of PBS's *The African Americans: Many Rivers to Cross,* and editor-in-chief of *The Root,* read the
script and offered notes on the accuracy of the film's unflinching
depiction of the story of a man who was sold into slavery in 1841
and forced to work on a Louisiana plantation.

Directed by Steve McQueen, with an adapted screenplay by John
Ridley, the movie premiered in the U.S. in August at the Telluride
Film Festival. Since opening in limited release in October and wide
release in November, it has enjoyed box office success and become
a consensus front-runner in the race for best picture at the Academy Awards.

Now Gates turns from consultant to interviewer, probing
McQueen about his intentions, as well as his experiences and lessons learned, in making the gripping film.

In part 1 of the conversation, the two discuss Pan-African diversity among cast members and the unexpected role that President
Barack Obama played in exposing the nation to Northup's story.

Henry Louis Gates, Jr.: How did you discover the Solomon Northup
story?

Steve McQueen: What happened was that, from the beginning, I
wanted to tell a story about slavery. I just felt there was a hole in the
canon of cinema. Also, I sometimes feel that slavery has disappeared
from the discussion, that it's not looked at in a way that it is deemed
important. I wanted to take a look again, and I had an idea of a free
man—a free African American who gets kidnapped into slavery,
and that's where I got stuck. After that, I met John Ridley and had a
conversation with him about this original idea, but things weren't
going so well . . . That's when my wife said to me, "Why don't you
look into firsthand accounts of slavery?"

† From *The Root,* Dec. 24–26, 2013. Reprinted by permission of *The Root.*

HLG: So we have your wife to thank?

SM: Yes. With *Twelve Years a Slave,* every page was a revelation. When I first read it, I felt so angry and upset with myself. Why didn't I know this book? Then I realized no one I knew knew this book. I had to make this into a film. So it became my passion.

HLG: So you started with the concept, and there was old Solomon Northup 150 years ago, and he fit the bill?

SM: Absolutely.

HLG: Describe your journey of getting the film made. We almost never have slave narratives turned into films.

SM: The production company Plan B was interested in working with me after they saw *Hunger,* my first film. I came up with the idea of slavery; they never blinked. They never stuttered; they just backed me. In a way it was simple. But at the same time, one cannot underestimate the influence that President Barack Obama has had on all these recent films on African-American life.

HLG: Explain that . . .

SM: Well, previously, people wanted to make these stories, but maybe now they thought they had the authority to. Also, now studios realized that they could make some money telling these stories. The fact that he's the president can never be underestimated when it comes to the influence he's had on culture, and particularly in film.

HLG: That's something—President Obama's implicit influence on the creation of culture. That's not always noted.

SM: Oh, it's huge. I guarantee you—well, I really strongly believe—that these films wouldn't have been made if Obama wasn't president.

HLG: How did you interest [producer] Brad Pitt in the project?

SM: Brad was in London and I was at the same time, and I went to see him. I told him what I wanted to do, and he was just down. You cannot have a better producer. He's a cinephile, a great actor, a great producer. He was instrumental.

HLG: I was struck by the Pan-African diversity of the cast—African, African American, British. Was this something you consciously thought to do when casting the film, or did it just come about?

SM: It just came about. I'm happy for it, but these were the best persons for the job, and that was it. It was a beautiful sort of group. We had African-American, we had Irish, German . . . we had the mix. It was beautiful.

HLG: I don't think there's ever been a more diverse cast, and I applaud you for it. What was the most difficult day of shooting?

SM: Every day was emotionally draining. The concentration was so high. You could hear the buzzing in your ears because the concentration was so great. When we got home at night, we were exhausted. So keeping concentration was the hardest thing. But what helped us was the crew, from hair and makeup [to] catering, camera, sound, electricians, grips.

It was our film. We were making our film. People were free to experiment, to speak, to find things in their performances. [When that happens] it becomes a real kind of honor to be there making the film.

Part 2: The director of the gripping narrative tells The Root *that slavery is "the elephant in the room," and says it's time for official apologies.*

* * *

In part 2 of their conversation, [Gates and McQueen] discuss the lasting effects of slavery and McQueen's belief that it's time for official apologies from leaders around the world.

Henry Louis Gates, Jr.: What surprised you most in translating Solomon Northup's story as he narrated and wrote it from the page to the screen?

Steve McQueen: Seeing the images. All I wanted to do was see those images. That has always been the power for me. Seeing those images. When I read the book, I wanted to see those images. Slavery is like the elephant in the room, and what you do is sprinkle flour over it and make it visible. We have to confront this topic in a real way. No one's blind anymore. No excuses. That's the power of cinema.

HLG: Why do you think the West is blind to the elephant in the room? Is it only the West or is it everywhere?

SM: It's the embarrassment of slavery and what went down. There's never been anything like the Truth and Reconciliation Commission. And the effects of slavery are all around us. You can be blind, but you can't be stupid. Look around us. In education. In prison populations. Et cetera, et cetera, et cetera. That's the evidence of what happened.

One can say, "It was 100-odd years ago, get over it!" OK, let's get over it. But things have to be put in place for us to get over it. We're talking about 400 years of slavery and mental torture. So guilt isn't productive. I'm not interested in guilt. But something like the Truth and Reconciliation Commission in South Africa. It wasn't perfect, but at least there was some kind of acceptance. Of course the people who did it aren't here anymore, so there's no use talking about guilt. And you even had Africans selling Africans. I know some presidents who have apologized for that . . .

HLG: Yes, the president of Benin actually got on his knees at the altar at a church in the U.S. and asked for forgiveness.

SM: Yes, and a president of Ghana has apologized as well. When has a U.S. president ever apologized? How do we go forward? It's time for the U.S., it's time for the British, it's time for the Dutch, the French, the Portuguese, et cetera, to apologize.

HLG: Yes, and perhaps the airing of *12 Years a Slave* will be the first step. What about your opinion of African Americans? Do you feel making this film helped you understand them better?

SM: I've always had a connection with African-American culture. I remember looking at Michael Jordan, black sportsmen, and saying, "Wow, people are equal over there." I remember coming to America in 1977 to visit my family. I've always had that connection with America.

But the thing that shocked me about America for black Americans is education. I was so lucky in that way, being brought up in the U.K. But only for this reason: We had free education, so everyone to some extent—obviously it's not perfect—at least had a shot.

What I love about black people is that there's a certain connection immediately . . . it's natural. There's a connection without even trying . . . there is something that is intrinsically common. No water, no continent, no country can separate that.

HLG: You know, we're all black. We're all products of our specific time, place, circumstances, and cultures. Do African-American filmmakers have certain blind spots, inhibitions, and perceptual habits that a black British filmmaker has?

SM: I don't think so, no. I hope not. I wouldn't dare say that.

HLG: Do you think being English was an advantage or disadvantage in making the film?

SM: I must say no. I don't think it adds an advantage. My education was my advantage. I was allowed to go to university and study for free. I didn't pay. The only difference between me and an African-American filmmaker was that at a certain stage of my life, I had free education. Free, free, free! I had possibilities where I think a lot of African Americans had limitations.

HLG: Do you think you had more distance on the subject? It's so hard for us on this side of the Atlantic to think about slavery without wanting to scream, to point fingers, to feel guilty about what our ancestors went through. But do you think being British gives you that aesthetic distance that all art demands?

SM: No, it's not who you are. It's like James Brown said, I think: It's not who you are, it's where you're at. And my parents are from the West Indies, where slavery was particularly brutal.

Part 3: The director of the gripping narrative tells The Root *that slavery was 100 times worse than the film conveyed, and responds to a* Schindler's List *comparison.*

✳   ✳   ✳

In part 3 of their conversation, [Gates and McQueen] discuss why the hardest scenes to watch were important, and McQueen's reaction to a *Schindler's List* comparison.

Henry Louis Gates, Jr.: Do you think that this year's remarkable slate of films—*Fruitvale, 12 Years a Slave, Many Rivers to Cross*—are an aberration, or do they signal the start of a new chapter in black cinema and documentary?

Steve McQueen: I hope so, because there are thousands of stories to tell. No one knew who Solomon Northup was, and that story should be engraved in everyone's head. How come there's not a feature film about the Underground Railroad? They're just amazing stories, as well as them being from the African-American experience. At the end of the day we are in the entertainment business, and these are amazing stories, period.

HLG: And they remain to be tapped?

SM: Yes, and of course Hollywood always wants to make money. But as long as they're great stories and well told, brilliant.

HLG: I'd like to talk about your transition from making art films to feature films. Is there a tension between the narrative and the aesthetic?

SM: For me, art is like poetry and filmmaking is like the novel. I'm using the same words to say the same thing but saying them differently. With artworks, it's more abstract, more fractured.

HLG: The body has always been central to your work, from naked wrestlers to exposed sex addicts in *Shame* to the flogged black body in *12 Years*. What was your vision? Talk about the use of the body in your work.

SM: I think people overexaggerate that, but at the same time, I totally understand why. All we have is our bodies. That's our vessel. But what I'm interested in is not necessarily that but the subjects that are around it. *Shame* is about sexual addiction and how the Internet fuels that addiction. Same thing with slavery. The story is about the environment, and how individuals have to make sense of it, how we locate the self in events. The body is used, but it's a byproduct of the bigger question.

HLG: Now I'd like to know how you depicted the extreme and relentless scenes of cruelty. The potential too-much-ness of, for example, the lynching scene, and when Solomon beats Patsey. What political purpose does it serve?

SM: That picture of Solomon hanging there was, for me—it had to represent all the hundreds of thousands of people who were lynched. I had to do that because in some way it was representing those people who never had a name and who never had a grave. People talk about what happened, but when you visualize it, when you see it . . . I was very careful about how I brought that to the narrative.

There's a subtlety that leads up to the crescendo of Patsey being whipped by Solomon. I had to do it because I couldn't look at myself in the mirror as an artist and not do it that way . . . I'm making a picture of what took place in those times, and if I didn't do it justice, I wouldn't be able to look at myself.

HLG: Talk about the tension between portraying the South as beautiful and conveying the horrors of slavery.

SM: People have said to me "It's so beautiful," and that's because it *is* so beautiful. Horrific things happen in beautiful places. I can't put a filter on life. Life is perverse. Just the other day I was taking my son to school on my bike, and two police cars and an ambulance zoomed past us. After dropping him off, I went to the café where I have my coffee every morning. They told me before I got there [that] a 7-year-old child was run over by a garbage truck . . . the father was there.

Life is perverse. It was a beautiful day. You had these beautiful plantations, but horrific things happen in the most beautiful places.

HLG: That's a beautiful way to put it. And that's a surprise to the audience. The scene with Solomon dangling from the tree and the scene where he was forced to beat Patsey were draining and disturbing to watch. What were the most draining and disturbing scenes for you and the cast?

SM: The rape scene [when Epps rapes Patsey] was very difficult . . . and again, like I said before, it was one of those things you had to do, and everyone trusted each other. Trust is the most important thing.

HLG: Do you think the beating scene was more powerful because a black man would be forced to beat a black woman?

SM: Yes, and most of the beatings were done by black people. It was all part of it . . . part of the psychological torture.

HLG: So, you don't think the Patsey scene was too much? Some critics have said it's too brutal to be seen.

SM: Either I was making a movie about slavery or I wasn't, and I decided I wanted to make a movie about slavery.

HLG: And thank God you did. Let's talk about the portrayal of Epps. Was it important to illustrate the complexity of white folks, masters?

SM: Yeah, the situation is that there were two victims: the perpe-trator and the victim. One has to look, to some extent—don't get me wrong, it's difficult—at those people. They had a choice, while the slaves didn't.
    You think about Nelson Mandela recently passing away. He wanted to understand what was going on with whites as well as black people. Epps—yes, he's horrible, disgusting, but—why is he in love with a slave? Of course, Patsey does not return that love at all. But it's one of those things where he takes out his love for her by try-ing to destroy her.

HLG: Did you study earlier depictions in film of slavery?

SM: No. I just went into historical accounts. Did some research. Spoke to you. It was a case of sort of immersing myself in the his-tory and that world.

HLG: *12 Years* has been called the anti-*Django*. Do you think of it that way?

SM: No. I'm a huge admirer of [Quentin] Tarantino; it's just differ-ent. One is action, adventure, comedy and one is drama. What's important is that people are talking about and looking at that sub-ject. I met Tarantino and [we talked about how] there can be more than one film about slavery, just like there's more than one gangster movie or Western. In *Django,* for me, the Samuel L. Jackson char-acter is such a complex character, and I was really hoping that Sam-uel L. Jackson would be sort of recognized in a way.

HLG: I agree. I had dinner with him recently and I told him the same thing . . . Do you think the audience more easily identifies with Solomon because of his earlier middle-class existence—free man captured, tricked and enslaved—than it would have had the story been of a man or woman born into slavery?

SM: Absolutely. And that's what I was interested in. It was a man who was an American who was hardworking, was a musician and was fairly well-to-do. It is also a parallel to today. We can't take our liberties and our freedoms for granted, because at any time it could be taken away. Look at Trayvon Martin, killed . . .

HLG: Arbitrarily.

SM: Yep.

HLG: Let's return for a second to the scene with Solomon dangling from the tree. Only one slave is brave enough to give him a draft of water. It's a haunting scene. Do you see that as a metaphor for the African-American condition? Because in some ways we still have so many Americans strung up. Was that what was on your mind?

SM: I think what was more on my mind was what most of us do. It's what we do. We don't want to get involved. We walk by . . . it's what we do. The whole movie in a way is a call to arms. There's so much that we can do and should do.

HLG: So it was a call to arms, and I think audiences took away that message. I screened *12 Years* a few times, once on Martha's Vineyard, and my friend and colleague Alan Dershowitz was in the audience. He was so moved, and he said, "This is the African-American *Schindler's List*." Do you agree?

SM: It's a compliment. All I can say is, I'm flattered if that's the case.

HLG: What's the most surprising reaction to the film?

SM: People say to me, "I never knew it was that bad!" I say it was worse. It was 100 times worse.

HLG: One hundred times worse, at least, without a doubt. I tell people that when they say they can't see Patsey beaten. Can we expect a director's cut?

SM: No, this is the cut I wanted. This is it.

HLG: One of our readers at *The Root* asked—the reconciliation scene was very powerful and provided much-needed relief for the audience. But for one reader it seemed short. Why not linger more on Solomon's reunion with his family?

SM: Because the story goes on. And the thought I wanted them to leave with was what happened to Patsey and all the other millions of slaves.

HLG: That last look Patsey gives to Solomon is so sad. Just tore me up . . . Steve McQueen, what did you learn about yourself during the filming of *12 Years*?

SM: That I thought I was strong. But I realized I was fragile.

HLG: How so?

SM: Because going into this journey, I thought I would be protected from the pain through the process of making [the film]. But that could only hold for so long, until my armor was pierced.

HLG: Were there moments when you cried?

SM: There was one situation, when Solomon and Patsey are in the room after the beating, and Patsey looks at Solomon and his reaction is, a tear drops from his eye. I saw what happened and I said, "Cut," and I had to go for a little walk. That was the only time my defenses were penetrated as such.

I had my blinkers on. I was focused. The only interesting thing about all this stuff is evidence. The only thing that is interesting is the film. The book. The piece of literature you're writing. It's all about the evidence. So I had to put all my emotions and all of that to one side. I don't even think about it. But at the end of the day I'm fragile. Because I'm human. That's it.

HLG: And I think that that's the take-away for members of your audience. The human condition means we're vulnerable and fragile and we need each other.

SM: Absolutely. In the Declaration of Independence [is] the right to pursue happiness. If that's not one of the most beautiful things in the world as a document for a country, I don't know what is. It should be true for everyone.

HLG: Thank you, Steve McQueen.

Solomon Northup: A Chronology[†]

July 10, 1807	Solomon Northup is born free to Mintus and Susannah Northup in the Adirondack town of Schroon, New York.
December 25, 1828	Northup marries Anne Hampton. The couple has three children: Elizabeth, Margaret, and Alonzo.
March 1834	Northup and his family settle in Saratoga Springs, New York, where he toils at various seasonal jobs while fulfilling his "ruling passion" of playing the violin.
March 1841	Two white men, using the aliases Merrill Brown and Abram Hamilton, lure Northup from his home by claiming to be members of a Washington, D.C.–based circus in need of musicians like him for their tour. While in New York City, Brown and Hamilton convince Northup to journey with them farther south. Before departing, and at their suggestion, Northup secures his free papers at the city's Custom House.
April 6, 1841	Northup arrives with Brown and Hamilton in Washington, D.C., and the trio lodges at Gadsby's Hotel. The next day, Brown and Hamilton get Northup so drunk (he implies they drug him) that, in the middle of the night, he is roused from his room by several men urging him to follow them to a doctor. Yet when Northup comes to, he finds himself locked up inside Williams's

† This chronology is based on Solomon Northup's memoir and the other sources in this Norton Critical Edition. We are especially indebted to Northup's current and most devoted biographer, David Fiske, coauthor with Clifford W. Brown, Jr. and Rachel Seligman of 2013's *Solomon Northup: The Complete Story of the Author of* Twelve Years a Slave (Praeger). In their book, Fiske et al. have done impeccable research in comparing Northup's memoir against the historical paper trail and enhancing it with context that fascinates and enlightens. We commend them for working so tirelessly to set the record straight and encourage the readers of this critical edition of *Twelve Years a Slave* to consult their work and keep track of their findings at www.solomonnorthup.com.

Slave Pen under the lash of the notorious slave trader James H. Birch (or "Burch"). Northup's money and free papers are nowhere to be found, and he is beaten viciously and told he is not who he says he is—that he is *actually* a runaway slave from Georgia. Birch paid more than $600 for his "slave." (Recollections varied: Birch later said $625. Others recalled it was $650.)

May 24, 1841   Under the imposed slave name "Plat Hamilton" (or "Platt"), Northup arrives in New Orleans, Louisiana, on the ship *Orleans* and, after suffering a bout of smallpox, is sold by Birch's associate, Theophilus Freeman, for $900.

June 23, 1841   The planter who buys Northup is William Prince Ford, who takes "Plat" and the other slaves he has purchased to the steamer *Rodolph* for the three-day trip to Ford's plantation in Louisiana's "Great Pine Woods."

1842   Northup's second owner is the belligerent carpenter John Tibaut ("Tibeats" in the book). Ford keeps a partial ownership stake in Northup, though, through a chattel mortgage, since he is worth more than what Tibaut is able to pay. Before long, Northup and Tibaut come to blows. The second time it happens, Northup comes so close to choking his master to death, after Tibaut wields an ax at him, that Northup flees into the Great Cocodrie Swamp.

April 9, 1843   Instead of returning to Ford's plantation, Northup learns he has been sold for $1,500 to the former overseer turned small cotton planter Edwin Epps. Prone to drink, Epps is a jealous and brutally efficient master who exhorts Northup to drive the other slaves while cracking down on him when he perceives Northup as being too high on his talents as a fiddler. It is on Epps's plantation in the Bayou Bœuf region of Louisiana that Northup encounters the slave Patsey.

June 1852   Samuel Bass, a sympathetic Canadian carpenter Epps hires to work on his house, agrees to help Northup by mailing three letters on his behalf to various contacts in New York. Upon receiving theirs, a pair of Saratoga shopkeepers notify Solomon's wife Anne and attorney Henry Bliss Northup, a relative of Solomon's father's former master. With bipartisan support, including a petition and six affidavits, Henry Northup successfully petitions New York governor Washington Hunt to appoint him an agent of rescue.

January 3, 1853   Henry Northup arrives at Epps's plantation to recover Solomon Northup with support from the sheriff of Avoyelles Parish, Louisiana. Northup's 12 years of enslavement (actually 11 years, 8 months, and 26 days) are over.

January 17, 1853   On their return trip to New York, Henry and Solomon Northup see to it that the slave trader James Birch is arrested on kidnapping charges in Washington, D.C. Because Solomon has no right to testify against a white man, however, Birch goes free.

January 20, 1853   News of Northup's odyssey makes the cover of the *New York Daily Times* (a forerunner of the *New York Times*) under the headline "The Kidnapping Case: Narrative of the Seizure and Recovery of Solomon Northrup [*sic*]. Interesting Disclosures."

January 21, 1853   Northup is reunited with his family in Glens Falls, New York.

May 16, 1853   Northup buys real estate in Glens Falls, New York.

July 15, 1853   Following a three-month collaboration between Northup and his white editor, David Wilson, an attorney from Whitehall, New York, Northup's memoir, *Twelve Years a Slave*, is released by publishers in Auburn and Buffalo, New York, as well as in London. It sells 17,000 copies in the first four months and propels Northup onto the antislavery lecture circuit. The following year, an updated edition of *Twelve Years a Slave* features a quotation about Northup from Harriet Beecher Stowe, author of *Uncle Tom's Cabin* and *A Key to Uncle Tom's Cabin*, to whom Northup dedicates his memoir. By January 1855, *Twelve Years a Slave* has sold almost 30,000 copies.

April 1854   Northup stages, and performs in, two plays based on his story: the first premieres in Syracuse, New York, in April 1854. Commercial

	success eludes him, however, and soon Northup finds himself in financial straits.
July 1854	As Northup's book is absorbed by the reading public, it leads to the arrest of his original kidnappers, Brown and Hamilton. Their *real* names are Alexander Merrill and Joseph Russell, both of New York. At a hearing to establish probable cause against the accused in Ballston Spa, New York, on July 11, Northup is able to testify.
September 1, 1854	A grand jury convened in Ballston Spa, New York, returns a four-count indictment against Merrill and Russell. After the accused request a postponement in October, the trial is put over until the following winter.
January 30, 1855	Northup's Glens Falls, New York, property is sold at a foreclosure auction.
February 8, 1855	The trial against Merrill and Russell commences in Ballston Spa, New York, in the Circuit Court of Oyer and Terminer, but when the defendants question the legality of the indictment against them, the court agrees to dismiss three out of four counts, preserving the one that charges the defendants with "inveigling" Northup with the intent to sell him into slavery. Not long after, bail is set at $800, permitting Merrill and Russell to leave jail. The district attorney takes the case to a higher court.
May 3, 1855	The property in Glens Falls, New York, is purchased solely in the name of Anne Northup, Solomon's wife.
July 1855	The New York Supreme Court upholds the lower court's ruling in *The People v. Alexander Merrill and Joseph Russell.*
Fall 1855	Northup stages the second of his plays, titled "A Free Slave," in five acts, with performances in New England.
June 1856	The Court of Appeals, New York's highest court, issues a legally intricate opinion reversing the state Supreme Court in *The People v. Merrill and Russell,* finding that the lower court erred in issuing a ruling that dismissed three out of four charges before the actual trial was held. As a result, the matter is sent back to the Circuit

Court of Oyer and Terminer so that Merrill and Russell can be tried.

May 1857
The new district attorney in Saratoga County, John O. Mott, using his prosecutorial discretion, elects to drop the charges against Northup's kidnappers, Merrill and Russell, instead of bringing them to trial. When the May term of the Circuit Court of Oyer and Terminer opens, the *Ballston Journal* reports on May 26, "business . . . disposed of" includes "The People agst Henry [Alexander] Merrill and Joseph Russell, under an indictment for kidnapping Solmon [*sic*] Northup. Case discharged." With that, Northup's effort to bring his kidnappers to justice ends.

August 1857
Northup travels to Streetsville, Ontario, Canada, but when he arrives, racial tensions force the cancellation of his planned lecture. It is Northup's last known public appearance.

c. 1863
The last recollected contact with Solomon Northup occurs during his visit to the Reverend John L. Smith, a Methodist minister and fellow Underground Railroad conductor, in Vermont sometime after the Emancipation Proclamation.

1900
With Northup's memoir out of copyright, at least three editions appear in print between 1881 and the turn of the century.

1901–67
Despite the fact that *Twelve Years a Slave* falls out of print in the first half of the twentieth century, knowledge of Northup's story (even when his name is spelled incorrectly) is carried forward by generations of scholars, writers, and bibliographers, from the Harvard historian Albert Bushnell Hart to the black poet and literary critic Sterling Brown to the NYU doctoral student, and later esteemed African American professor at Brooklyn College, Marion Wilson Starling.

1968
The year that marks the assassination of civil rights leader Rev. Dr. Martin Luther King, Jr. also witnesses the return of *Twelve Years a Slave* to print in a new edition with a well-researched introduction by co-editors Sue Eakin and Joseph

	Logsdon. The publisher is Louisiana State University Press, located in the same state where Northup was enslaved over a century before. With the renewed focus on Northup ushered in by Eakin and Logsdon, *Twelve Years a Slave* remains in print, with various other editions released, from 1968 until the present.
1999	Saratoga Springs, New York, dedicates a historical marker to Northup near the street corner where he was kidnapped in 1841: Broadway and Congress. Descendants of Northup take part in the event, which includes an exhibit on Northup's life at the local visitor center.
2002	Saratoga Springs gives official recognition to "Solomon Northup Day," begun a few years earlier by Renee Moore, a black resident of the city.
July 19, 2003	The U.S. Postal Service honors Solomon Northup Day with a cancellation stamp at its Saratoga Springs station.
October 8, 2013	*12 Years a Slave,* a film adaptation directed by Steve McQueen, who is black and British, and a production team that includes the actor Brad Pitt, premieres in U.S. theaters, with distribution by Fox Searchlight Pictures.
March 2, 2014	At the 86th annual Academy Awards in Los Angeles, *12 Years a Slave* wins Best Picture, the first time a film directed by a black auteur (McQueen) receives the Academy's top prize. On the same night, Lupita Nyong'o takes home the Best Supporting Actress Award for her performance as Patsey, while screenwriter John Ridley earns Oscar gold for Best Adapted Screenplay. *12 Years a Slave* receives nine nominations overall and numerous other prizes during the year's awards season.
March 4, 2014	The *New York Times* issues a correction fixing the spelling of Solomon Northup's name, which appeared variously as "Northrup" and "Northrop" in the paper's January 20, 1853 story.

Selected Bibliography

• Indicates works included, excerpted, or adapted in this volume.

EDITIONS OF *TWELVE YEARS A SLAVE**

Northup, Solomon. *Twelve Years a Slave: Narrative of Solomon Northup, a Citizen of New-York, Kidnapped in Washington City in 1841, and Rescued in 1853, from a Cotton Plantation near the Red River, in Louisiana.* Auburn, NY: Derby and Miller; Buffalo, NY: Derby, Orton and Mulligan; London: Sampson Low, Son & Company, 1853.

———. *Twelve Years a Slave: Narrative of Solomon Northup, a Citizen of New-York, Kidnapped in Washington City in 1841, and Rescued in 1853, from a Cotton Plantation near the Red River, in Louisiana.* Auburn and Buffalo, NY: Miller, Orton and Mulligan; London: Sampson Low, Son & Company, 1854.

———. *Twelve Years a Slave: Narrative of Solomon Northup, a Citizen of New-York, Kidnapped in Washington City in 1841, and Rescued in 1853, from a Cotton Plantation near the Red River, in Louisiana.* New York: C. M. Saxton, 1859.

———. *Twelve Years a Slave: The Thrilling Story of a Free Colored Man, Kidnapped in Washington in 1841, Sold into Slavery, and after a Twelve Years' Bondage, Reclaimed by State Authority from a Cotton Plantation in Louisiana.* Philadelphia: J. E. Potter and Company, 18[?].

———. *A Freeman in Bondage: Or, Twelve Years a Slave: A True Tale of Slavery Days.* Philadelphia: Columbian Pub. Co., 1890.

———. *Twelve Years a Slave: The Thrilling Story of a Free Colored Man, Kidnapped in Washington in 1841, Sold into Slavery, and after a Twelve Years' Bondage, Reclaimed by State Authority from a Cotton Plantation in Louisiana.* Dallas, TX: Talty & Wiley, 1890.

———. *Twelve Years a Slave: The Thrilling Story of a Free Colored Man, Kidnapped in Washington in 1841, Sold into Slavery, and after a Twelve Years' Bondage, Reclaimed by State Authority from a Cotton Plantation in Louisiana.* New York: International Book Company, 1900.

———. *Twelve Years a Slave.* Edited with an introduction by Sue Eakin and Joseph Logsdon. Baton Rouge: Louisiana State University Press, 1968.

———. *Twelve Years a Slave.* Edited with an introduction by Philip S. Foner. New York: Dover, 1970.

* The book has also been translated into various languages, including Chinese, French, Hebrew, Italian, Russian, and Spanish.

————. *Twelve Years a Slave: Narrative of Solomon Northup, a Citizen of New-York, Kidnapped in Washington City in 1841, and Rescued in 1853.* Documenting the American South. University Library, The University of North Carolina at Chapel Hill, 1997. http://docsouth.unc .edu/fpn/northup/northup.html.

————. *Twelve Years a Slave.* Introduction by Ira Berlin; general editor, Henry Louis Gates, Jr. New York: Penguin Books, 2012.

————. *12 Years a Slave: A True Story of Betrayal, Kidnap and Slavery.* London: Hesperus Press, 2013.

————. *Solomon Northup's* Twelve Years a Slave. Research-editor, Sue L. Eakin. Enhanced Final Edition. Eakin Films & Publishing, 2013.

————. *Twelve Years a Slave.* Audio edition narrated by Louis Gossett, Jr. Eakin Films & Publishing, 2013.

————. *Twelve Years a Slave.* Foreword by Steve McQueen; introduction by Ira Berlin; afterword by Henry Louis Gates, Jr., general editor. New York: Penguin Books, 2013.

ADAPTATIONS

Bleby, Henry. *Scenes from Transatlantic Life.* London: Wesleyan Mission House, 1879.

Solomon Northup's Odyssey (motion picture). American Playhouse: Season 4, Episode 3; directed by Gordon Parks; teleplay by Lou Potter and Samm-Art Williams. American Playhouse, Monterey Media, and Public Broadcasting Service, 1984.

Eakin, Sue. *Solomon Northup's* Twelve Years a Slave: *1841–1853.* Rewritten for young readers. Gretna, LA: Pelican, 1998.

12 Years a Slave (motion picture). Fox Searchlight Pictures; directed by Steve McQueen; screenplay by John Ridley; produced by Brad Pitt, Dede Gardner, Jeremy Kleiner; produced by Bill Pohlad, Steve McQueen, Arnon Milchan, Anthony Katagas; executive producers, Tessa Ross, John Ridley; Regency Enterprises and River Road Entertainment present a River Road, Plan B, and New Regency production; in association with Film4; a film by Steve McQueen, 2013.

ARTICLES AND BOOKS

• Andrews, William L. *To Tell a Free Story: The First Century of Afro-American Autobiography, 1760–1865.* Champaign: University of Illinois Press, 1988.

• Aptheker, Herbert. "The Negro in the Abolitionist Movement." *Science & Society* (1941): 148–72.

Berlin, Ira. "Introduction, Solomon Northup: A Life and a Message," in Solomon Northup, *Twelve Years a Slave.* New York: Penguin, 2012.

Blassingame, John W. "Black Autobiographies as History and Literature." *The Black Scholar* 5.4 (1973): 2–9.

————. "Using the Testimony of Ex-Slaves: Approaches and Problems." *The Journal of Southern History* 41.4 (1975): 473–92.

————. *The Slave Community: Plantation Life in the Antebellum South.* New York: Oxford University Press, 1979.

Born, Brad S. "Northup, Solomon." *The Concise Oxford Companion to African American Literature*. Ed. William L. Andrews, Frances Smith Foster, and Trudier Harris. New York: Oxford University Press, 2008.

• Brown, Sterling Allen, Arthur Paul Davis, and Ulysses Lee, eds. *The Negro Caravan: Writings by American Negroes*. Vol. 2. New York: Citadel Press, 1941 (rpt. New York: Arno Press, 1969).

Cobb, Jasmine Nichole. "Directed by Himself: Steve McQueen's *12 Years a Slave*." *American Literary History* 26.2 (Summer 2014): 339–46.

Cox, John D. "Moving Slaves: Frederick Douglass, Solomon Northup, and the Politics of Travel in Antebellum America," in *Traveling South: Travel Narratives and the Construction of American Identity*. Athens: University of Georgia Press, 2005.

• Dargis, Manohla. "The Blood and Tears, Not the Magnolias," *The New York Times*. October 17, 2013. C1.

Davis, Charles T., and Henry Louis Gates, Jr., eds. *The Slave's Narrative*. New York: Oxford University Press, 1985.

• Denby, David. "Fighting to Survive: *12 Years a Slave* and *All Is Lost*," *The New Yorker*. October 21, 2013. 108–09.

• Derby, James Cephas. *Fifty Years Among Authors, Books and Publishers*. New York: G. W. Carleton & Company, 1884.

Du Bois, W. E. B. *A Select Bibliography of the Negro American: A Compilation Made Under the Direction of Atlanta University; Together with the Proceedings of the Tenth Conference for the Study of the Negro Problems, Held at Atlanta University, on May 30, 1905*. Atlanta, GA: Atlanta University Press, 1905.

Eakin, Sue L., and Joseph Logsdon. "Introduction." *Twelve years a Slave*. Baton Rouge: Louisiana State University Press, 1968.

Eakin, Sue. *Solomon Northup's* Twelve Years a Slave *and Plantation Life in the Antebellum South*. Lafayette: Center for Louisiana Studies, University of Louisiana at Lafayette, 2007.

• Elkins, Stanley. *Slavery: A Problem in American Intellectual and Institutional Life*. Chicago: University of Chicago Press, 1959.

• Ernest, John. *Liberation Historiography: African American Writers and the Challenge of History, 1794–1861*. Chapel Hill: University of North Carolina Press, 2004.

———. *The Oxford Handbook of the African American Slave Narrative*. New York: Oxford University Press, 2014.

• Fiske, David, Clifford W. Brown, Jr., and Rachel Seligman. *Solomon Northup: The Complete Story of the Author of* Twelve Years a Slave. Santa Barbara, CA: Praeger, 2013.

Fiske, David. "Authenticity and Authorship: Solomon Northup's *Twelve Years a Slave*." New York History Blog, November 2013.

———. *Solomon Northup's Kindred: The Kidnapping of Free Citizens before the Civil War*. Santa Barbara, CA: Praeger, 2016.

Foner, Philip. "Introduction to *Twelve Years a Slave*, by Solomon Northup." New York: Dover, 1970.

• Gates, Henry Louis, Jr. "'12 Years a Slave': Trek From Slave to Screen." *The Root*. October 14, 2013.

Gates, Henry Louis, Jr., Valerie Smith, et al., eds. *The Norton Anthology of African American Literature*. 3rd ed. 2 vols. New York: W. W. Norton & Company, 2014.

• Gates, Henry Louis, Jr., and Steve McQueen. "Steve McQueen and Henry Louis Gates, Jr. Talk *12 Years a Slave*, Parts 1–3." *The Root*. December 24–26, 2013.

Goode, James. *Capitol Losses*. Washington, D.C.: Smithsonian, 1979.

• Hart, Albert Bushnell. *Slavery and Abolition, 1831–1841*. New York: Harper & Brothers, 1906.

Hartnett, Stephen John. *Democratic Dissent and the Cultural Fictions of Antebellum America*. Carbondale: University of Illinois Press, 2002.

Kachun, Mitch. "Solomon Northup's *12 Years a Slave*, Slave Narratives, and the American Public." Oxford University Press Blog. October 2013.

Kim, Heidi. "How *Twelve Years a Slave* Was Made, 150 Years Before '12 Years a Slave.'" *Los Angeles Review of Books*. February 17, 2014.

Li, Stephanie. "*12 Years a Slave* as a Neo-Slave Narrative." *American Literary History* 26.2 (Summer 2014): 326–31.

• Loggins, Vernon. *The Negro Author: His Development in America*. New York: Columbia University Press, 1931.

• Loughran, Trish. *The Republic in Print: Print Culture in the Age of U.S. Nation Building, 1770–1870*. New York: Columbia University Press, 2009.

• McDougall, Marion Gleason. *Fugitive Slaves, 1619–1865*. No. 3. Boston: Ginn & Co., 1891.

Mitchell, Mary Niall. "In the Margins of *Twelve Years a Slave*." *Harper's Magazine* blog. February 27, 2014.

————. "All Things Were Working Together for My Deliverance." *Common-place.org*. February 2014.

• Nelson, John Herbert. *The Negro Character in American Literature*. Lawrence, KS: Department of Journalism Press, 1926.

Newman, Richard, and Paul Finkelman. "Kidnapping." *Encyclopedia of African American History, 1619–1895: From the Colonial Period to the Age of Frederick Douglass*. Ed. Paul Finkelman. New York: Oxford University Press, 2008.

Olney, James. "'I Was Born': Slave Narratives, Their Status as Autobiography and as Literature." *Callaloo* 20 (1984): 46–73.

• Osofsky, Gilbert, ed. *Puttin' On Ole Massa: The Slave Narratives of Henry Bibb, William Wells Brown, and Solomon Northup*. New York: HarperCollins, 1969.

Oubre, Claude F., and Keith P. Fontenot. "Liber Vel Non: Selected Freedom Cases in Antebellum St. Landry Parish," *Louisiana History: The Journal of the Louisiana Historical Association*. 39.3 (Summer 1998): 319–45.

• Phillips, Ulrich B. *Life and Labor in the Old South* (1929). Columbia: University of South Carolina Press, 2007.

• Quarles, Benjamin. *Black Abolitionists*. Boston: Da Capo Press, 1969.

Seward, William Henry, and Frederick William Seward. *1846–1861*. Vol. 2. New York: D. Appleton, 1891.

Schermerhorn, Calvin. *The Business of Slavery and the Rise of American Capitalism, 1815–1860*. New Haven: Yale University Press, 2015.

• ————. "Who Are Today's Solomon Northups?" Historians against Slavery Blog. June 2, 2015.

Smith, David Lionel. "Northup, Solomon." *African American National Biography*. Ed. Henry Louis Gates, Jr. and Evelyn Brooks Higginbotham. New York: Oxford University Press, 2008.

Smith, Sidonie. *Where I'm Bound: Patterns of Slavery and Freedom in Black American Autobiography*. New York: Praeger, 1974.

• Smith, Valerie. "Black Life in the Balance: *12 Years a Slave*." *American Literary History* 26.2 (Summer 2014): 362–66.

• Stampp, Kenneth. *The Peculiar Institution: Slavery in the Ante-Bellum South*. New York: Alfred A. Knopf, 1956.

• Starling, Marion Wilson. *The Slave Narrative: Its Place in American History*. 2nd ed. Washington, D.C.: Howard University Press, 1988. (Originally published as a Ph.D. dissertation at New York University in 1946.)

• Stauffer, John. "12 Years between Life and Death." *American Literary History* 26.2 (Summer 2014): 317–25.

• Stepto, Robert B. "'I Rose and Found My Voice': Narration, Authentication, and Authorial Control in Four Slave Narratives," in *From Behind the Veil: A Study of Afro-American Narrative*. Champaign: University of Illinois Press, 1991. 3–31.

Stevenson, Brenda. "The Surprisingly Central Role of Slave Women in '12 Years a Slave.'" History News Network. October 18, 2013.

• Tillet, Salamishah. "'I Got No Comfort in This Life': The Increasing Importance of Patsey in *12 Years a Slave*." *American Literary History* 26.2 (Summer 2014): 354–61.

Waters, Carver Wendell. *Voice in the Slave Narratives of Olaudah Equiano, Frederick Douglass, and Solomon Northrup*. Lewiston, NY: Edwin Mellen Press, 2003.

Wesley, Dorothy Porter. *The Negro in the United States: A Selected Bibliography*. Washington, D.C.: Library of Congress, 1970.

Williams, Andrea N. "Sex, Marriage, and 12 Years a (Single) Slave." *American Literary History* 26.2 (Summer 2014): 347–53.

• Williams, Daniel Barclay. *Freedom and Progress: And Other Choice Addresses on Practical, Scientific, Educational, Philosophic, Historic and Religious Subjects*. 4th ed. Petersburg, VA: Daniel B. Williams, 1890.

• Williams, George Washington. *History of the Negro Race in America from 1619 to 1880: Negroes as slaves, as soldiers, and as citizens: together with a preliminary consideration of the unity of the human family, an historical sketch of Africa, and an account of the Negro governments of Sierre Leone and Liberia*. 2 vols. New York: Putnam, 1883.

• Wilson, Carol. "'From Their Free Homes into Bondage': The Abduction of Free Blacks Into Slavery," in *Freedom at Risk: The Kidnapping of Free Blacks in America, 1780–1865*. Lexington: University Press of Kentucky, 1994.

• Worley, Sam. "Solomon Northup and the Sly Philosophy of the Slave Pen." *Callaloo* 20.1 (1997): 243–59.

WEBSITES

www.docsouth.unc.edu. Documenting the American South. University Library, The University of North Carolina at Chapel Hill. An online archive containing electronic versions of North American slave narratives, as well as supporting materials and scholarly resources.

www.foxsearchlight.com/12yearsaslave. Film website maintained by the U.S. distributor of *12 Years a Slave,* Fox Searchlight Pictures. The site includes resources for teachers.

www.oxfordaasc.com. The Oxford African American Studies Center. Henry Louis Gates, Jr., editor-in-chief. A comprehensive, online collection of scholarship, featuring the following core reference works: *Africana; Encyclopedia of African American History, 1619–1895; Encyclopedia of African American History, 1896 to the Present; Black Women in America,* 2nd ed.; *African American National Biography; Dictionary of African Biography;* and *The Oxford Encyclopedia of African Thought.*

www.solomonnorthup.com. A website maintained by Northup biographer and researcher David Fiske.

www.twelveyearsaslave.org. A website dedicated to preserving *Twelve Years a Slave* and to the work of the late author and editor Sue Eakin.